W. Terry Whalin

D0580395

Alpha
Teach Yourself
The Bible

ALPHA

A Pearson Education Company

in 24 hours

Alpha Teach Yourself the Bible in 24 Hours

Trademarks

SENIOR ACQUISITIONS EDITOR
Renee Wilmeth

DEVELOPMENT EDITOR
Joan D. Paterson

SENIOR PRODUCTION EDITOR
Christy Wagner

COPY EDITOR
Michael Dietsch

INDEXER
Tonya Heard

PRODUCTION
John Etchison
Rebecca Harmon

COVER DESIGNER
Alan Clements

BOOK DESIGNER
Gary Adair

MANAGING EDITOR
Jennifer Chisholm

PRODUCT MANAGER
Phil Kitchel

PUBLISHER
Marie Butler-Knight

To my parents, Wallace E. Whalin and Rose E. Whalin, who loved our family so much that we've always been involved in the local church. As a child my hours in Sunday school and church didn't mean much, but in college, I found a personal relationship with Jesus Christ. Then the dedication and consistency of my parents' love for the church and Jesus Christ paid off. Mom, stay strong, you are doing great and without you I would be nothing, and Dad, I've missed your physical presence as you've watched from heaven during the last few months.

Overview

Contents

Appendixes

Introduction

Almost every home has a Bible. It's one of those black books that you have tucked in a drawer of your nightstand or possibly on the bookshelf in a family room. About the only time you ever pull it down to look at it is when there is a significant family event like a wedding, a birth, or a death. Then you open the Bible and keep a family record. Or maybe you carry your Bible to church occasionally but you have little idea of what's between the covers.

Get ready, because you are about to embark on an adventure. Blow the dust off the cover of that book and see the Bible as God's love letter to mankind. As you teach yourself the Bible in the next 24 one-hour sessions, you will be amazed at the discoveries. I'll let you in on a secret from the beginning: The Bible is a book that can withstand a lifetime of study. Like a classic novel that you love to read, the Bible will become a book you will increasingly want to read over and over. One of the beautiful aspects of the Bible is that everyone always has more to learn from the stories and the practical teachings. More than head knowledge, the Bible is a book to be read with an open heart.

I have no idea where you are in life's journey at the moment, but I'm excited about what's going to happen in your life as you learn about the Bible from Genesis to Revelation. This experience will be life-changing and different for every reader. I write to you with expectancy about what these 24 hours are going to do for you—in any situation.

What You'll Find in This Book

Part I, "Introduction to the Bible," will help you learn some basics about the Bible. You'll learn about the authors, the organization, why Bibles come in a variety of translations, and some of the tools or helps to Bible study. You will also learn about the birth of the world and the birth of the nation of Israel.

Part II, "The Kings and the Prophets," reveals how the nation of Israel moved from a theocracy (where God was its leader) to a kingdom (with a king as its leader) and the various major and minor prophets, whom God sent to continue to provide spiritual guidance for the Jewish people.

Part III, "The Old Testament Wisdom Books," will explore the Jewish hymnal (the Psalms) as well as Job, Proverbs, Ecclesiastes, and the Song of Solomon.

Part IV, "Meet Jesus Christ," shifts from the Old Testament, or Old Covenant, into the New Testament or New Covenant. In these hours, you will learn more about the birth, miracles, parables, death, and resurrection of Jesus Christ from first-hand accounts told in the four Gospels. In these hours, you will explore the answers to the question: Who is Jesus Christ?

Part V, "The Church Is Born and Letters from the Apostle Paul," includes the beginning of the church and how the church spread throughout the known world. Also in this section, you will meet the Apostle to the Gentiles, Paul, and learn about his extensive writings to the new churches, which form the majority of the New Testament epistles. You will learn about teachings from Apostles other than Paul and finally get a glimpse of the future in the final book in the New Testament: the Book of Revelation.

EXTRAS

At the end of each hour, you will find an Hour's Up! section. The Bible is more than a series of good stories or practical advice; it's a book that provides people with personal applications for everyday life. The series of 10 questions at the end of each hour will help you focus on the personal nature of the content of the hour.

We know you don't have a lot of extra time. Your life is crammed with work or family or something you want to do for yourself. We've created this book for you to make learning about the Bible easy and fun.

Last, but not least, there are a series of sidebars scattered throughout the book, which will give you additional information such as:

CULTURAL FACT

These sidebars will help you see that the Bible is not a fairy tale but that the stories and events are rooted in cultural history.

HISTORICAL FACT

The events of the Bible are based on historical facts. Some of these facts are highlighted in these sidebars scattered throughout the text.

JUST A MINUTE

 These sidebars provide tips and biblical insight and advice.

BIBLICAL FACT

Often the facts of the Bible are validated and affirmed through archaeology. These sidebars strengthen the concerns of some people about the accuracy of the Bible and the affirmation from biblical facts.

PEOPLE TO KNOW

Certain people are emphasized in these sidebars that will provide you additional insight about these interesting individuals.

About the Author

W. Terry Whalin knows and understands the editor and writer side of the editorial desk. He worked as an editor for *Decision* and *In Other Words* magazines. For eight years, Terry lived in Colorado Springs and launched a full-time career of freelance writing and editing. His magazine articles have appeared in more than 50 Christian and general market publications, plus he's written more than 55 books. For almost two years, Terry was a feature writer at Christianity.com. Currently Terry is the acquisitions editor at Cook Communications Ministries.

Terry earned a B.A. in journalism/political science from Indiana University, an M.A. in linguistics from the University of Texas at Arlington, and a Certificate in Bible from Multnomah School of the Bible. Whalin is a member of the American Society of Authors and Journalists (ASJA), the Evangelical Press Association (formerly a board member), and the Author's Guild.

Terry writes on a wide spectrum of subjects and topics for the magazine and book marketplace—from children to teen to adult. Two of his numerous biographies are *Billy Graham* (Bethany House) and *Chuck Colson* (Zondervan). Also he has co-authored books like *The World at Your Door* by Tom Phillips and Bob Norsworthy (Bethany House); *Let the Walls Fall Down* by Bishop Phillip H. Porter, chairman for Promise Keepers (Creation House); and *First Place, the Bible-Based Weight-Loss Plan Used Successfully by Over a Half Million People,* by Carole Lewis with W. Terry Whalin (Regal Books). Terry and his wife, Christine, live in Colorado Springs, Colorado. His personal website is located at www.terrywhalin.com.

Acknowledgments

My editors: Renee Wilmeth (Senior Acquisitions Editor), Joan Paterson (Developmental Editor), Nancy Caine (Technical Editor), and Christy Wagner (Senior Production Editor). It's always valuable to work with professional editors who improve every page of the book. Also with gratitude, I acknowledge my agent, Scott Waxman. Without you, Scott, I wouldn't have known about this tremendous project. Thank you.

To a small group of writer friends (you know who you are), who have stayed behind the scenes yet consistently written notes of encouragement, cheering each completed chapter, and bathing the entire writing process with prayer and praise.

Finally, I want to acknowledge my wife, Christine, who with the patience of Job has endured many evenings and weekends without companionship as I worked diligently on the details of this book. I promise not to jump into another book project—for at least a week, well, maybe a month or two. You are the best, Christine.

PART I

Introduction to the Bible

HOUR 1

Bible Basics

CHAPTER SUMMARY

LESSON PLAN:

In this hour, you will learn about …

- Who wrote the Bible.
- How the Bible is organized.
- Why there are so many translations and which you should use.
- Some of the helps to Bible study.

One book will likely never appear on *The New York Times* bestseller list. To reach this list, a book usually sells about 100,000 copies and if a book is on the list for a particularly long time, it may sell a million copies. On some rare occasions a book will sell in multiple millions. When a book reaches this level, everyone is talking about it.

From the beginning of the first century, scribes have been copying the Bible by hand. Billions of copies of the Bible have been distributed and it continues to be the all-time best-selling book, yet it never appears on a best-seller list. The massive distribution of this book alone should raise the average person's curiosity about what's inside the pages of this book.

NOT AS HARD AS IT LOOKS AT FIRST

When a person picks up a Bible, it can appear like a complex book that would be difficult for anyone to understand. The 66 different books were written by 45 writers over a period of 15,000 years, and then packed into a single volume of almost 2,000 pages. In a typical printed Bible, the longest book (Psalms) takes up more than 100 pages; the shortest book (2 John) less than a page. Some writers were rich, whereas others were poor. Among the writers were kings, poets, prophets, musicians, philosophers, farmers, teachers, a priest, a statesman, a sheepherder, a tax collector, a physician, and a couple of fishermen.

How was the Old Testament passed down? The Old Testament was written between 1440 B.C. and approximately 400 B.C. The priests of the temple in the Hebrew communities maintained the Law of Moses. Later books continued to be deposited with these leaders until the destruction of the Jewish temple and then found their way into the teaching communities that the prophet Ezra started and continued in the synagogues. Trained scribes copied the biblical texts by hand until the modern printing press came into use. The copies of the Masoretes of the ninth century A.D. (traditional Hebrew texts preserved in rabbinic circles) are very close to the recently discovered Dead Sea Scrolls, which originated a thousand years earlier.

For some people, the prospect of studying the Bible from Genesis to Revelation can be a challenge. Yet it's worth the challenge because the Bible is not a textbook or a book of abstract theology to be understood only by a few scholars. The Bible is a book about real people and about the God who is real. Theologians and scholars have debated endlessly about the question of how a book written by so many people could possibly be the inspired word of God. But to enter this argument is like sitting down at dinner and arguing about the recipe instead of tasting the good food, enjoying it, and gaining nourishment from it. Like the saying, "the proof of the pudding is in the eating," the proof of the Bible is in the reading—with an open mind and heart. If a person reads the Bible with this attitude, then the Bible will be proven to be divinely inspired.

The Bible is *the* source of information about God, the Creator of the Universe. No other single book gives more information about God than the Scriptures. Beginning with the dust of creation and ending with Revelation's promise of a New Jerusalem in heaven, the Bible details God's continual desire for fellowship and love from mankind.

WHO WROTE THE BIBLE?

Many people contributed to the writing of the Bible. For example, the Book of Psalms collects the works of several authors, of whom David, the "sweet singer of Israel," is the best known. But Moses, Asaph, and others also wrote psalms.

The accounts preserved in the Old Testament date from the earliest times and were both written down and transmitted orally. As time passed they were collected together and received by the Hebrews as coming to them by God's mandate. The prophets transmit God's message to humans, while many of the psalms articulate cries of people to God. Yet these psalms are also preserved in the Bible as part of God's message to humankind. The Old Testament was originally written in Hebrew, but at the time of Christ, the Jewish people were using the Septuagint, a Greek translation of the Hebrew.

JUST A MINUTE

How were the New Testament writings passed down? Local Christian communities copied the New Testament books and passed them from one to another for decades before they compiled an entire collection. Because the early letters were written on papyrus, they wore out rapidly and required regular copying. In the early fourth century A.D., 50 copies of the entire Old and New Testament Greek Scriptures were made at the order of the first Christian emperor, Constantine. It is likely that the Vaticanus and Sinaiticus codices, two of the longest early manuscripts to survive, originated from this order.

The New Testament stories and teachings were widely circulated among the early Christian churches. The letters of Paul to the Christians in several cities were likely the earliest writings now found in the New Testament. But many other letters and epistles were circulated as well. Gradually it became clear to the early churches which writings were truly inspired and which were simply edifying messages from pious authors.

Some of these books that were circulating were decidedly different in their teaching. By the end of the second century, the Church fathers were forced to resolve the issue of which writings were inspired by God and which were not. Through Church councils which met periodically over the next hundred years, they determined which writings were "canonical" or biblically worthy. They considered and answered such questions as: Did the earliest disciples and apostles consider this writing fully from God? Did this writing contain sound theology and accurate facts?

BIBLICAL FACT

What is the canon of Scripture? The word *canon* identifies the writings of the prophets, the apostles, and their companions, which are inspired by God and authoritative for truth pertaining to doctrine and life. It means "rule" or "standard." A book is not inspired because it is declared to be canonical but is canonical because it is considered inspired. Therefore, the Church discovered the canonicity of the Old and New Testament books; it did not determine or cause their canonicity.

By the middle of the fourth century, all these questions had been settled. Church fathers agreed on the particular books and the canon was closed.

WHY ARE THERE NUMEROUS TRANSLATIONS OF THE BIBLE?

As missionaries took the Gospel to other places in the world, the Scriptures were translated. The Vulgate, a Latin version of the Bible, was brought to England from Rome. In the fourteenth century, John Wycliffe, an Oxford scholar, translated the whole Bible from Latin into English. Because he questioned Roman Catholic practices and advocated reform in the Church against the Pope, he lost his teaching job at Oxford and was mercilessly persecuted. Long after his death, the Roman Catholic Church exhumed his body, burned his bones, and proclaimed him a heretic.

In 1525, another Oxford scholar, William Tyndale, who spoke seven different languages, began to translate using Hebrew and Greek instead of Latin. Church authorities harassed him and he was arrested in 1536 and burned at the stake. Others secretly completed his translation project. Consulting Tyndale's work, John Rogers attempted another version; in time it was called the Great Bible. In 1568, the Church of England published its revision of the Great Bible called the Bishop's Bible. It was widely read until 1611, when King James commanded his learned men to develop a new version, using the Bishop's Bible as the foundation.

Eventually they produced the Authorized Version, or King James Version, of the Bible. It became the primary Bible for the English-speaking people for more than 300 years. From 1881 to 1884, a group of American and English scholars assembled to translate the Revised Version of the Bible using manuscripts that had been unavailable to the King James translators. From 1900 to 1901, the American Standard Version was translated. In 1978, the New International Version of the Bible was completed. Today there are many different translations of the Bible.

It is remarkable that all 40 of these authors, spread out over 1,600 years, have such a unified message in spite of their great diversity in language, culture, and time. The reason for this unity is the authors were actually secondary authors. There is actually only one primary author, the one who inspired all the human authors, the eternal God.

Christians believe that the Bible came to us from God himself, who used all these human authors to give us his message, through the presence and inspiration of his Spirit. He did not simply give dictation to these authors, because we observe their unique personalities and varying styles of writing shining through. But God's message, God's authorship, is always there, providing in the end through all the years, exactly what he wanted us to have. In this way the Bible is our own ageless treasure.

ORGANIZATION OF THE BIBLE

At first glance, the Bible appears to consist of shorter and longer writings without any apparent organization, except for the main division of two parts—the Old Testament and the New Testament. The Old Testament takes up about three fourths of the Bible and the New Testament about one fourth. The Book of Psalms (the longest book) is approximately in the middle of the Bible.

JUST A MINUTE

Are there many Old Testament manuscripts? Fragments of Hebrew Scriptures number in the tens of thousands, the majority dating between the third century B.C. and the fourteenth century A.D. The greatest validation of the Hebrew Old Testament is the manuscripts found in the Dead Sea Scrolls, which date mostly from the third century B.C. to the first century A.D. The Dead Sea Scrolls were discovered between 1947 and 1956 at seven sites along the northwest shore of the Dead Sea.

TWO TESTAMENTS

The Old Testament was written before the time of Christ. It was written in Hebrew, the language of the Jewish people, and the Old Testament continues to be the Bible for the Jewish people. In the very early days of the Church, during the first decades after Jesus' death and resurrection, the Hebrew Bible was the only Bible Christians had available. Only later, after the New Testament came into existence, did people begin to call the Hebrew Bible the *Old Testament*. The word *testament* means "covenant," which is a solemn agreement or contract that establishes a formal relationship with mutual obligations. The Hebrew Bible speaks of the covenant God made with Abraham, the patriarch of the Jewish people. The New Testament is about the covenant that God made with all people through Jesus Christ.

The Old Testament looks forward to the coming of Jesus, the Messiah (or Christ). The New Testament tells the story of Jesus and contains the writings of his early followers.

THE OLD TESTAMENT BOOKS

Each testament contains three groups of books. The Old Testament contains historical books, poetic books, and prophetic books. The New Testament contains historical books, letters (or epistles), and one prophetic book (Revelation). Let's examine some further detail about each testament.

THE HISTORICAL BOOKS

The Old Testament contains 17 historical books, arranged in chronological order. The Jewish people call the first five historical books the *Torah* (Hebrew for "law," since these books contain the laws God gave to Moses). These five books are also called the *Pentateuch* (Greek for "five books").

THE POETIC BOOKS

Between the historical books and the prophetic books of the Old Testament are five poetic books. These books contain some of the most beautiful poetry ever written. The Book of Psalms, which expresses the full range of human emotions from depression to jubilant trust in God, has especially been a source of comfort and inspiration to Jews and Christians for three millennia.

THE PROPHETIC BOOKS

The Old Testament contains 17 prophetic books. The first five of these books are called the Major Prophets because they are much longer than the other 12, which are called the Minor Prophets. Lamentations is a short book, which is included with the Major Prophets because Jeremiah wrote it; he also wrote the second book of the Major Prophets, Jeremiah.

JUST A MINUTE

What is a *gospel?* The four Gospels represent a different kind of literature than other ancient and modern writings. They are not biographies of Christ, seeking to develop a full understanding of Jesus' life, his friendships, his family, or his mental and psychological dimensions. Also, they are not histories of heroic deeds or collections of his famous sayings (although some of these kinds of materials are found in the Gospel accounts). The four Gospels appear to be a new genre for which other categories are inadequate. These books record the life, works, and words of Jesus regarding the redemptive work of God in Jesus Christ. They are the good news from God that is manifest in the life, ministry, death, burial, resurrection, and ascension of Christ.

THE NEW TESTAMENT BOOKS

One of the major Bible divisions is the Old Testament and the New Testament. The New Testament writings bring a new focus to the entire Bible. Let's look at the New Testament books: historical books, letters or epistles, and one prophetic book.

THE HISTORICAL BOOKS

Between the end of the Old Testament and the beginning of the New Testament is a period of 400 years known as the silent years. The New Testament begins with five historical books: the four Gospels, which describe the life of Christ, and the book of Acts, which tells the story of the early church, mostly through the work of the Apostle Paul.

THE LETTERS OR EPISTLES

The New Testament contains 21 letters or epistles. The Apostle Paul wrote the first 13 of these epistles and they are arranged by length from the longest (Romans) to the shortest (Philemon). Other epistles were written by the Apostle John (three letters), Peter (two letters), and James and Jude (one letter each); scholars disagree who wrote the letter to the Hebrews. All of these letters were written during the early decades of the Church.

THE PROPHETIC BOOK

The New Testament has only one prophetic book: Revelation. The Greek word for revelation is *apokalupsis,* meaning an unveiling or uncovering. For this reason, the book of Revelation is also called the Apocalypse.

COMPARING TRANSLATIONS OF THE BIBLE

Would you believe that there are literally hundreds of different translations of the Bible into English? For many people this huge variety is totally confusing and they just don't know which Bible to choose. How did we get into this situation anyway? Sometimes the Bibles are for a particular audience such as the Women's Devotional Bible or the African American Study Bible. Other Bibles are for a particular emphasis such as the Fruit of the Spirit Bible or the Prophecy Bible or the Encouragement Bible. The range and number of various Bibles are astounding and continue to grow each year.

At the heart of the problem are two views as to what a translation should be. On one side are those who feel a translation should stick just as closely as possible to every word of the original Hebrew and Greek. They want the translation to be a literal transfer, word for word, of the original words into English. They feel this will provide the greatest accuracy possible, and, after all, this is the aim, isn't it?

Unfortunately, that approach encounters real problems. Some words simply don't have an exact equivalent in English. The word order and the entire sentence structure just don't match from one language to another. So these word-for-word translations are wooden and unnatural. They may be used for close study, but they often fail in terms of comprehension and readability.

JUST A MINUTE

Are there many original New Testament manuscripts? There is abundant manuscript evidence for the New Testament. More than 5,000 copies, many of which cover the entire New Testament, are largely intact. Also, there are several older translations of the New Testament in languages like Syriac, Coptic, and Latin that survive in thousands of manuscripts. No work of antiquity even approaches the New Testament for authenticity.

On the other side of the translation issue are those who believe a translation should transfer the message, that is, the exact thought and emotion of the original text. To do this, it should use as many words as are necessary to reproduce the idea precisely in English. Accuracy is not obtained, they contend, by a word-for-word translation, but is done when you convey the concept, the message, of the original, so that the reader understands it. In the end, they say, a thought-for-thought translation is actually more accurate and more understandable than a word-for-word translation. They invite us to compare Job 36:33 in a literal translation (the venerable King James Version) and a thought-for-thought translation (the New International Version):

KJV	NIV
The noise thereof showeth concerning it, the cattle also concerning the vapor.	His thunder announces the coming storm; even the cattle make known its approach.

Of course, since the KJV dates from 1611, it contains some archaic language, but the message of the KJV in this verse is also very difficult to decipher. In the NIV, in this case, the thought comes through with more clarity.

Translations also differ as to the reading level of the reader. They vary from a third-grade to a twelfth-grade reading level. The lower reading level translations have shorter sentences, draw from a smaller English word pool, and avoid all uncommon words. Some employ a vocabulary limited to 1,000 words.

JUST A MINUTE

The first true English Bible is Wycliffe's (or Wyclif's) translation, published in 1382. He based his translation on the Vulgate (the authorized Latin version of the Bible). The earliest copies of Wycliffe's Bible existed only in manuscript form, because Johannes Gutenberg did not invent the printing press until 70 years later. This means that not many copies were in circulation, but traveling preachers used these copies and reached many people throughout England. The Roman Catholic Church condemned Wycliffe's work. He was excommunicated, and many copies of his Bible were burned. About 150 original copies survive, but only 1 of those is complete.

Let's review several of the best-known translations. We cited two translations in the passage just quoted, and they are the two most widely used of all English translations.

The King James Version is loved for the majesty of its language and for the way God has used it in ministering to millions through the centuries. Some Christians believe that no other translation can possibly replace it.

The New International Version is today the most widely distributed and utilized translation in the world. It is a thought-for-thought translation, but employs a moderately traditional tone that makes it appropriate for both public worship and personal reading.

A recent translation that is gaining widespread acceptance and uses contemporary terminology is the New Living Translation. It is both accurate and very readable.

Another widely used translation is the New American Standard Bible, which is a more literal rendition.

The New Revised Standard Version, is a contemporary thought-for-thought translation.

Many Roman Catholic readers prefer the New Jerusalem Bible.

WHAT KIND OF READER ARE YOU?

As you can see, there are many audiences and many different kinds of readers. You should decide what kind of reader you are and estimate your reading level. Are you seeking a literal translation or one that provides a thought-for-thought presentation? Do you prefer the historic dignity of the King James Version, the widely accepted and respected New International Version, or the very readable and contemporary New Living Translation? Consult a knowledgeable Christian and then immerse yourself in God's Word!

Each translation has the power to transform your life. Though the cadence and the terminology may differ, the voice of God can speak to you through each one. Then the question remains: How will you respond to God's voice as he speaks to you from the pages of this life-changing book?

Before you buy a study Bible, take a few minutes and compare them with these questions:

- Do the notes that explain the text address things I want to know?
- How clear, detailed, and helpful are the introductions and outlines to each book of the Bible?
- How many cross-references to other Scriptures are there? Are they easy to read?
- How extensive is the dictionary? Are the definitions clear and helpful?
- What kind of information is in the index? Are the topics in the topical Scripture index helpful for today's reader?
- How long is the concordance? Does it list words I would want to look up?
- How many maps are there and of what quality?
- Do I prefer a "red-letter edition" (with the words of Jesus printed in red)?

SELECTING A BIBLE THAT'S RIGHT FOR YOU

In light of the variety of translations, it's important to select the right one for you. Bibles vary in price and quality. Normally, additional Bible features and helps will increase the cost of the Bible as well as the type of cover (hardcover or leather). This section explains some of the factors to consider when selecting a Bible.

TRANSLATION OR PARAPHRASE

If accuracy and authenticity is important to you, then make sure you have a translation rather than a paraphrase. Some of the most common translations are the King James Version (KJV), the New King James Version (NKJV), the New Revised Standard Version (NRSV), the New American Standard Version (NAS), the New International Version (NIV), and the New Living Translation (NLT).

Translations are concerned with accuracy and precise interpretation of the original texts and some of the current ones are extremely readable. If you are looking for a "readable" Bible, consider a paraphrase such as The Living Bible (TLB). A paraphrase isn't quite as true to the original and uses some slang terms and a more familiar writing style. Because of these distinctions, a paraphrase brings a different perspective to the text and offers a refreshing change of pace.

FAMILIAR OR CONTEMPORARY

What Bible did you hear in church as you were growing up? Some people frequently heard the King James Version and they may be able to recall some passages from memory. If they return to reading the Bible and use a contemporary translation, the familiar passages may not sound right.

If you want to pick up where you left off with the Bible, the King James Version possibly might be the only translation that will provide this type of familiarity. More recent translations use contemporary language and are easier to study, but for some people who have always used the KJV, it's the only translation that will "feel right."

BASIC BIBLE OR STUDY BIBLE

What is your goal in reading the Bible? If it's simply to read the text, then you can get a basic Bible, which will not have any of the additional study helps. A basic Bible will have the text from Genesis to Revelation. If you are curious and ask a lot of questions as you read the Bible, then you will probably want a study Bible. Study Bibles are available in a variety of contemporary translations and include a number of Bible helps such as a concordance, Bible dictionary, atlas, and study notes. The drawback to a study Bible is that it is more expensive and heavier to carry around because of the space the notes and other helps take in the text. Many study Bibles are targeted to a particular demographic audience such as men, women, students, couples, and so on; other study Bibles focus on a topic such as prophecy, spiritual formation, fruits of the spirit, and many other topics.

OTHER FACTORS TO CONSIDER

Do you travel a great deal? If so, you might want to consider a smaller travel Bible, which doesn't take up a lot of space. Some of these travel Bibles have a fold-around snap to protect the Bible.

If your eyesight is poor, consider a large-print Bible. Even standard Bibles have several different type options, so be sure to check out the printing size before you purchase your Bible.

Do you want paperback or hardcover? The paperback versions are considerably cheaper. Yet with moderate use these paperbacks tend to tear and become easily destroyed. For a little extra expense, a hardcover or leather-bound Bible is ideal for a continued commitment to study the Bible or regular Bible reading.

A final consideration is the size of the margins for the Bible. Some people treat their Bible as a sacred book they can't write in. Others have decided that to internalize biblical truth, they need to mark and highlight portions of their Bible. Some Bibles have extra wide margins for people to write in their Bible and make notes from sermons or other insights.

WHERE TO BUY YOUR BIBLE

Possibly you've read through this last section about the various possibilities for Bibles and decided to stick with your King James Version, which you've had most of your life. If you investigate, you will be surprised at the various possibilities in terms of a Bible. Your best place to search for a Bible is not a chain bookstore. If you don't find what you want, don't be hesitant to ask for help and the ability to order something that isn't at the store.

The best place for Bible selection is your local Christian bookstore. The store personnel are usually trained to answer Bible purchase questions, show you the various types of Bibles, and then help you make a choice that will be appropriate for your needs. After you determine which Bible, always shop around for a good price. Mail order and Internet bookstores often provide good discounts on a particular Bible—after you know what you want to purchase.

JUST A MINUTE

Do you need Bible reference books? (See Appendix C for a list.) The more tools or Bible reference books you try to use, your time for Bible study will increase. However, the Bible is not exactly like a good novel, where you are eager to get to the last page and finish it. If you use one or more of the Bible reference tools, your comprehension level will be significantly higher. If your goal is to get through the Bible, don't fool with the tools. But if you'd rather get into the Bible, and increase your understanding, these tools can help.

HELPS TO BIBLE STUDY

The Bible is a big book—in reality, a library of books—from a distant past. Each person needs help to try and understand it. Even so, it is surprising how largely the Bible is self-interpretative when we know what is in it. The main teachings of the Bible are so plain that a child can understand the heart of the Bible. Read the Bible with an open heart and mind. Here are some guidelines that will help you with the rest of this book:

- **Memorize the names of the Bible books.** Appendix A lists the books of the Bible. A first step will be to learn the names of the 66 books and where they are located.

- **Accept the Bible just as it is.** Don't worry about theories of the critics. Ingenious efforts of modern criticism to undermine the historical reliability of the Bible will pass; the Bible itself will stand as the light of the human race to the end of time. Pin your faith to the Bible. It's God's Word and will never let you down. Trust its teachings.

- **Read the Bible with an open mind.** Don't try to straightjacket all its passages into the mold of a few particular teachings. And don't read into the passages ideas that are not there. But try to search out fairly and honestly the main teachings and lessons in each passage. Then you will believe what you ought to believe; the Bible is abundantly able to take care of itself if given a chance.

- **Read the Bible thoughtfully.** In Bible reading, we need to watch ourselves very closely or our thoughts will wander and our reading will become routine and meaningless. We must determine to keep our minds focused on what we are reading, do our best to understand what we can, not worry too much about what we don't understand, and be on the lookout for lessons for ourselves.

JUST A MINUTE

How can you meditate or think about the Bible as you read it? One of the best ways is to ask questions, and here are a few to get you started:

- What is the main subject of the passage?
- To whom is the passage addressed?
- Who is speaking?
- About what or whom is the person speaking?
- What is the key verse?
- What does this passage teach me about God?

- **Keep a pencil at hand.** It is a good thing, as we read the Bible, to mark passages we like and to go now and then through the pages and reread passages we have marked. In time, a well-marked Bible will become very significant in your life.

- **Create a pattern of systematic and habitual reading.** Occasional or sporadic reading doesn't mean much. Unless you have a system to follow and hold to it with determination, the chances are that you will not read the Bible very much. Your inner life, like your body, needs daily nourishment.

- **Select a certain time each day for reading.** Without a specific plan for reading or studying the Bible, then you are likely to neglect or forget it. First thing in the morning is good if your work routine allows it. Or in the evening at the close of the day's work, you might find yourself freer from the constraints of life. Perhaps in the morning and the evening would be a possibility. For others, a period in the middle of the day may be more suitable.

  The particular time doesn't matter. The important aspect is to select a time, stick with it, and not grow discouraged when the routine is broken by things beyond your control.

- **Use a Bible-reading plan.** A Bible-reading plan is included in Appendix D. This plan will help you read the Bible consistently.

The key to successful reading of the Bible is an open heart and an open mind. In the following hours, you will examine the principle themes of the entire book from Genesis to Revelation. An old Chinese proverb says, "The journey of a lifetime begins with a single step." Let's get going.

HOUR'S UP!

The Bible is a best-selling book, but more than another book on the shelf, it contains words that can change your life. The following questions will help you personalize the contents of this first hour.

1. List several reasons why you want to learn more about the Bible.

2. Many men and women have studied the Bible over the years and written volumes of commentaries. Yet there is still more spiritual insight to gain from the pages. Now rejoice in this fact and list what you imagine happening from your time in the Bible.

3. Although the English Bible isn't in the original language, it retains the thoughts and inspiration of the original writers. Take a few minutes and celebrate how the Lord has preserved the Bible over the centuries, and pause in gratitude.

4. The word *testament* means covenant or solemn agreement. What agreement or covenant are you making to begin this journey through the Scriptures from Genesis to Revelation? Write down a few of your hopes and dreams as you go through this experience.

5. The Poetic books are some of the most inspirational ever written. Turn to Psalm 19, read it, and consider how you can begin to take continual delight in the Law of the Lord.

6. Translations are often like people—each of us prefers a different kind of translation. Which translation of the Bible will you use? Make sure you give yourself permission to use several different ones if you would like to do so.

7. Which is more important to you with a Bible translation—familiarity or contemporary? Some of your choices in a translation may be influenced by your church, your friends, your pastor, and your personal reading tastes.

8. How can you read the Bible with an open mind, removing your preconceived notions about what it contains? Pause each time before reading and ask the Lord to open your heart and mind as you read.

9. How are you keeping focused on the Bible as you read? If your mind begins to wander, feel free to stand as you read or kneel or get into a different and more proactive reading position.

10. How will you read the Bible systematically and regularly? What plan have you selected to be consistent, and when during the day will you read? Make a goal; then if you can't achieve it, modify it until you find something that works for your life and lifestyle.

HOUR 2

Creation and God's Promise to Man

LESSON PLAN:

In this hour, you will learn about …

- How God created the world and man.
- Why man and woman were kicked out of the Garden of Eden.
- God's promise to Abraham and God's faithfulness to honor the patriarchal blessing.

Imagine runners lining up at a track meet. They crouch down in the starting blocks and prop up on their fingertips. The official raises a small pistol into the air and says the words, "Runners to your mark … set …," and then he squeezes the trigger and the athletes sprint down the track. Each race has a starting point. It was the same way with creation.

"In the beginning God created the heavens and the earth." (Genesis 1:1)

This verse is one of the most controversial sentences in the entire Bible. At first, there was nothing; then God suddenly made a move. From nothing, God created the heavens and the earth. The world began—just like the gun starts the race, God started the world.

The word *genesis* means "a starting point in time, a beginning." The Bible instantly underscores the worldview that life has a starting point from God. This hour marks the beginning of the Bible and learning the key events of the Bible.

JUST A MINUTE

Who wrote Genesis? Ancient Hebrew and Christian traditions say that Moses, guided by God, wrote Genesis from ancient documents, which were already in existence during his day. The book of Genesis ends about 300 years before Moses. The stories and information in Genesis could only have been written through direct revelation from God or through historical records that had been handed down from Moses' forefathers.

SUMMARY OF THE BOOK OF GENESIS

Genesis contains two parts. The first portion of the book (chapters 1 through 11) serves as a prologue to the second part (chapters 12 through 50), which is the main event: God's sovereign work in Abraham's family to accomplish his good will for all nations. The prologue (chapters 1 through 11) provides keys that unlock the rest of the book and the rest of the Bible as well. The four key concepts, which are presented in Genesis 1 through 11, are crucial for understanding the rest of the Bible.

- First, the God who entered the lives of Abram and Sarai is the same God who created the entire universe. He is the only true and living God, Yahweh, the Creator and Savior of the world.

- Second, all people have rebelled against God, their benevolent Creator, and his good will for them. Humanity has inherited a state of sinfulness from Adam and Eve's rebellion in the Garden of Eden.

- Third, God judges and will judge the actions of all people. By sending the Flood, God made it clear to Noah and to everyone that human wickedness is entirely unacceptable. God cannot let evil reign free in his creation.

- Fourth, sin continues to plague all of humanity even after the Flood. Although the Flood did not wash away sin, God, as the second half of Genesis (chapters 12 through 50) reveals, has a plan to save humanity from its own evil deeds.

HISTORICAL FACT

The Garden of Eden was on the Euphrates and Tigris rivers, at their junction with the Pishon and Gihon. (Genesis 2:10–14) The Pishon and Gihon have not been identified. The Euphrates and Tigris originate in the Caucasus mountain region of southwest Asia, flow eastward, and empty into the Persian Gulf. Two possible locations have been suggested, one near the headwaters of the Tigris and Euphrates, the other near the mouth of the Euphrates in ancient Babylon. God didn't want anyone to ever enter the Garden of Eden after he banished Adam and Eve. "The Lord God stationed mighty angelic beings to the east of Eden. And a flaming sword flashed back and forth, guarding the way to the tree of life." (Genesis 3:24, New Living Translation)

The first portion of Genesis provides the setting for the story of Abram and Sarai. (chapters 12 through 50) Their world is populated by a broad spectrum of "people groups," each with its own language, customs, values, and beliefs, and all have adopted their own imaginary gods.

The main story in Genesis—God's plan to bless all nations through Abraham's descendants—begins in chapter 12. It starts with God's call to Abram and Sarai (Abraham and Sarah) to become the parents of a new people, a new nation. This new nation would become God's tool for blessing all peoples. Even though Abram and Sarai are an elderly couple with the means to travel, God chose to begin his plan of redemption for the entire world with them. The Genesis description of their experiences demonstrates the interruption and reality of God's blessing in their lives.

Central to God's blessing was his covenant with Abraham. (Genesis 12:1–13; 15:1–21) God, the creator of the entire universe, freely chose to make everlasting promises to Abraham and his descendants. These promises in the Abrahamic covenant were the foundation for all of God's subsequent promises and covenants in the Bible. Genesis is not merely a beginning; it provides the foundation for the rest of the biblical narrative.

Certain scientists would like the world to believe that the first person was created purely through chance. Such belief takes far greater faith than to simply believe the creation story in the Bible. To believe that everything took place with no creator, no grand designer, and no one saying, "Runners take your mark," requires a great deal of confidence in pure speculation. The Bible says from the opening verse that God created.

PEOPLE TO KNOW

Very little is known about Eve, the first woman in the world, yet she is the mother of us all. She was the final piece in the intricate and amazing puzzle of God's creation. Adam now had another human being with whom he could fellowship and share equally in God's image. Here was someone for Adam to have a relationship with. Together they were greater than either of them could have been alone. Eve's story is told in Genesis 2:18–4:26, but her death is not recorded in Scripture.

In order for there to be a beginning, it requires a creator or some power to put the process into motion. The opening chapter of the Bible makes it clear that God was not created. He was the Creator and started to make the earth. The Nicene Creed (used throughout the Christian world since A.D. 325, when the First Council of Nicea was held by the Church fathers) begins, "I believe in God the Father almighty, the Maker of heaven and earth." These words are only the beginning of this book of beginnings.

GOD THE CREATOR

The first verse of the Bible tells us that there was someone whose voice sounded in the vast emptiness: "Runners to your mark." The Scriptures do not say, "In the beginning …" but God's Word makes it clear that in the beginning God was. He was not the result of his own conception. Clearly he was separate from his creation and apart from it. He was the Creator.

Small children often like to argue about the decisions that affect them. Sometimes after a parent unsuccessfully attempts to build his case, he simply says, "It's going to be this way just because it *is*." In the same way, the fact of Creation and the reality of the Creator are true just because they are. Given the alternatives to the truth—like natural selection or the Big Bang—my sincere hope is that you will simply come to the point of believing that God is and that he was the Creator … just *because*. For there to be a beginning, there must be something or someone who has the power of being itself first to start the cosmic process in motion.

ACT OF CREATION

In the beginning God did something. This God of action did something. What God did here is the most fantastic work that has ever been done, work that will never be done again. The word *create* is used to describe the work of architects with buildings or entrepreneurs with businesses, or artists with painting or music. Although some people would call what the world's greatest artists do with their paints "creative," it's not truly that at all, not in the Genesis sense of the creative acts of God. These world-class painters are taking something that already exists and rearranging it into something different. This activity is not true creativity but actually mediated creativity. The biblical view of Creation is more startling than this.

Creativity in a biblical sense presents an act of creation where there is no medium except the sound of someone's voice. God did not come down with his palette and began to mix paint and draw. There was no paint. There were no brushes. There was not even a blank canvas. There was only endless emptiness.

Because of this extraordinary creation, theologians use a special phrase to discuss God's creative works: *ex nihilo*. These words, literally meaning "out of nothing," explain that there was no preexistent matter that God used to create. All his art, all that which we know as tangible and intangible reality, did not come from rearranging anything. It came from scratch.

Creation or re-creation? While most Bible students believe that Genesis is an account of creation, some scholars believe that Genesis provides an account of both creation and re-creation. Those who believe in the two accounts contend that Genesis 1:1 tells of the original creation, then Genesis 1:2 ("Now the earth was [became] form-less and empty") describes a time subsequent to the initial creation when God re-created the heavens and the earth after they had become formless and void, perhaps because of some catastrophic event. The Hebrew word for "was" used here in the original text is translated "became" where it appears elsewhere in the Bible.

No amount of study that describes those things that are going on around us can account for creation *ex nihilo*. This action goes beyond the natural, and into the realm of the supernatural. Much to our chagrin, the Bible does not give us a scientific description of how God did this work, the specific times, or how many watts of power were needed. The Scriptures say that God spoke the world into existence. *In the beginning*, God *created*. These are foundational words of Scripture because they point us to right thinking. God is the all-powerful, all-wise Creator of the universe. His creative act begins our journey.

MAN AND WOMAN ARE CREATED

After God created the animals, the birds, the fish, and the brilliantly colored vegetation, the earth teemed with his creation. Then God looked down and saw that nothing in his creation bore his image. While everything was pro-nounced "good," nothing was made in his likeness. God wanted one of his creations to display his likeness, have a special understanding of God, and amazingly please God through loving and worshipping him. The Bible unfolds on every page a divine purpose for mankind to love and worship God.

"Then God said, 'Let us make man in our image, in our likeness, and let them rule over the fish of the sea and the birds of the air, over the livestock, over all the earth, and over all the creatures that move along the ground.'" (Genesis 1:26)

Various epics of creation have been found in the ruins of Babylon, Nineveh, Nippur, and Ashur, which are strikingly similar to the creation account in Genesis. These epics were written on clay tablets from before the time of Abraham. For example, the sequence of the creative acts: expanse (firmament), dry land, celestial lights, and humans.

Notice how God creates with action and a purpose. Also God says "us." The plural means Father, Son, and Holy Spirit were in agreement to create man and it didn't happen through accidental circumstances. No portion of God's creation is an accident. Like Albert Einstein said, "God does not play dice." With all other creatures, God simply spoke them into existence. With humankind, God made man in his image, which allowed man the ability to think, reflect, decide, learn, feel, and know.

Also from creation, man was given the ability to know right from wrong. God created intelligent, moral creatures. Finally God gave man the ability to be in relationship. The Sovereign God is three persons—Father, Son, and Holy Spirit—who enjoy perfect communication, flawless empathy, and eternal relationship. Man mirrors this capacity to be in relationship with another person, and the best example is through the holy relationship of marriage.

> So God created man in his own image, in the image of God he created him; male and female he created them. God blessed them and said to them, "Be fruitful and increase in number; fill the earth and subdue it. Rule over the fish of the sea and the birds of the air and over every living creature that moves on the ground." Then God said, "I give you every seed-bearing plant on the face of the whole earth and every tree that has fruit with seed in it. They will be yours for food.
>
> "And to all the beasts of the earth and all the birds of the air and all the creatures that move on the ground—everything that has the breath of life in it—I give every green plant for food." And it was so. (Genesis 1:27–30)

JUST A MINUTE

Were the days of creation literal, 24-hour days? The scholars who answer affirmative believe in a "young earth," which is thousands of years old rather than billions of years. Others accept such scientific evidence as fossil records and carbon dating. These scholars view the "days" of creation as time periods of undetermined length. They also argue that the sun wasn't even created to determine a "day" until day four.

Man and woman were created, put in charge of the animals and plants, then given a wonderful place to live called the Garden of Eden.

> Now the Lord God had planted a garden in the east, in Eden; and there he put the man he had formed. And the Lord God made all kinds of trees grow out of the ground—trees that were pleasing to the eye and good for food. In the middle of the garden were the tree of life and the tree of the knowledge of good and evil. A river watering the garden flowed from Eden; from there it was separated into four headwaters.

The name of the first is the Pishon; it winds through the entire land of Havilah, where there is gold. (The gold of that land is good; aromatic resin and onyx are also there.) The name of the second river is the Gihon; it winds through the entire land of Cush. The name of the third river is the Tigris; it runs along the east side of Asshur. And the fourth river is the Euphrates. The Lord God took the man and put him in the Garden of Eden to work it and take care of it. (Genesis 2:8–15)

Throughout this vast garden, God only made one requirement of man and woman: "And the Lord God commanded the man, 'You are free to eat from any tree in the garden; but you must not eat from the tree of the knowledge of good and evil, for when you eat of it you will surely die.'" (Genesis 2:16–17) Like a little child told not to step over the line, how quickly man tests the boundary with the Creator God.

Man Leaves the Garden

In the first two chapters of the Bible, everything is declared "good." Even when God created Adam, he then recognized that Adam felt alone and lonely, which was not a good thing. Then God created woman to be Adam's companion, which was a good thing.

Man Sins

Suddenly at the beginning of the third chapter of Genesis, the mood shifts and interrupts the calm and stress-free life in the Garden.

Now the serpent was more crafty than any of the wild animals the Lord God had made. (Genesis 3:1a)

Adam and Eve had never met such a sly creature. The sinister nature of the serpent is evident from his first words to the woman:

He said to the woman, "Did God really say, 'You must not eat from any tree in the garden'?" (Genesis 3:1b)

The cleverness of the question is evident because Eve knew that God had not said that. Her response makes it clear that Eve knew what God had said.

"We may eat fruit from the trees in the garden, but God did say, 'You must not eat fruit from the tree that is in the middle of the garden, and you must not touch it, or you will die.'" (Genesis 3:2b–3)

CULTURAL FACT

Other cultures also have a story about a fall of mankind. No doubt Adam told the original story to Methuselah, then Methuselah told the story to Noah, and Noah told his sons. In later cultures it was modified.

- Greek: The first people, in the golden age, were naked, free from evil and trouble, and enjoyed communion with the gods.
- Chinese: There was a happy age, when people had an abundance of food and were surrounded by peaceful animals.
- Persian: Our first parents, innocent, virtuous, and happy, lived in a garden, where there was a tree of immortality, until an evil spirit in the form of a serpent appeared.
- Hindu: In the first age, people were free from evil and disease, they had everything they wished for, and lived long.

In a few words, Eve successfully defended the character of God. But notice the subtle power of suggestion that the serpent raised in his question. He implied that God had placed one thing out of bounds and that if God says "no" at any one point, he might as well have taken away all freedom. The serpent implied that if man doesn't have total freedom, then he is no more than a slave. The serpent, or Satan, had come to Eve with an innocent concern that God had not given Adam and Eve a balanced diet to eat all of the fruit in the garden. Eve successfully defended God's command, then the serpent said to the woman …

"You will surely not die," the serpent said to the woman. "For God knows that when you eat of it your eyes will be opened, and you will be like God, knowing good and evil." (Genesis 3:4–5)

The serpent stopped being subtle and launched a full-on attack on the boundary set by God. The attack shows the subtle temptation that anyone faces from Satan. Will man serve God or will he pursue personal power, selfish purposes, and sensual desires? Who will prevail? Eve unfortunately failed the test for very familiar reasons—it looked good and she wanted to be wise.

When the woman saw that the fruit of the tree was good for food and pleasing to the eye, and also desirable for gaining wisdom, she took some and ate it. She also gave some to her husband, who was with her, and he ate it. Then the eyes of both of them were opened, and they realized they were naked; so they sewed fig leaves together and made coverings for themselves. (Genesis 6–7)

Adam and Eve were created to live in the presence of God and enjoy the Lord forever. When they violated God's Law, they received more knowledge than they expected—they discovered they were naked little creatures, far less when compared with a Holy God. The knowledge drove them to shame. When God walked in the cool of evening through the garden, he called for them but they hid in shame like frightened animals. Because of their disobedience, God put them out of the Garden of Eden and man has been running from the gaze of God ever since.

Mankind has the capacity and desire to love God because he first loved us. (1 John 4:19) Love for God is the only appropriate response to God's aggressive pursuit of man. This amazing story of God's love reaching out to mankind is repeated throughout the Bible.

PEOPLE TO KNOW

Noah was the only follower of God left in his generation. The world in Noah's day was flooded with evil and the number of people who remembered God's creation and love had dwindled to one—Noah. In response, God gave the world a 120-year last chance while Noah built the ark as a graphic illustration of his life message. For Noah, obedience meant long-term sticking with a particular project. Noah is also the second father of the human race because the world was destroyed in the Great Flood. Noah's story is told in Genesis 5:28–10:32. He is also mentioned in the Heroes of Faith chapter of Hebrews 11:7.

GOD'S PROMISE TO ABRAHAM AND THE PATRIARCHAL BLESSING

Some people have called the entire Old Testament the autobiography of God. Although God has no beginning or end and cannot be known fully by man, it is accurate to say the first 39 books of the Bible give a thin slice of God's story. Without a doubt, the most important character in the Old Testament is Abraham, the father of God's chosen people, the Jews. He is so significant that 2,000 years after he is introduced in the Old Testament, Mary, the soon-to-be mother of Jesus Christ, mentions his name. As Mary accepts her role and privilege of bearing God's son, she compares her call from God to her obedient ancestor Abraham.

"He has helped his servant Israel, remembering to be merciful to Abraham and his descendants forever, even as he said to our fathers." (Luke 1:54–55)

Also Zacharias, the father of John the Baptist, spoke through the prompting of the Holy Spirit and said:

"[God has promised] to show mercy to our fathers and to remember his holy covenant, the oath he swore to our father Abraham." (Luke 1:72–73)

Other catastrophic floods are found in the literatures of many ancient cultures:

- Egyptian tradition: The gods at one time purified the earth by a great flood, from which only a few shepherds escaped.
- Greek tradition: Deucalion warned that the gods were going to bring a flood upon the earth because of its great wickedness; he built an ark, which rested on Mount Parnassus. A dove was sent out twice.
- Hindu tradition: Manu, warned, built a ship in which he alone escaped from a deluge that destroyed all creatures.
- Mexican tradition: One man and his wife and children were saved in a ship from a flood that overwhelmed the earth.
- Native American tradition: Various legends, in which one, three, or eight persons were saved in a boat above the waters on a high mountain.

God Calls Abram to Move

Have you ever been drawn to do something different? It's an impulse that surges through your mind and heart, and then if you act, you change the direction of your life. Possibly you have picked up your family and moved, changed careers, started a new business on a shoestring, or given away a large amount of money, after feeling this compelling impulse, which some refer to as a "call."

The Bible gives no record of Abram until his call; suddenly 4,000 years ago, this prosperous man told his neighbors and friends he was pulling his family and moving to some place that he had never been before. Abram moved not on an urge or impulse but the Bible says Abraham *heard* God's voice.

The Lord had said to Abram, "Leave your country, your people and your father's household and go to the land I will show you. I will make you into a great nation and I will bless you; I will make your name great, and you will be a blessing. I will bless those who bless you, and whoever curses you I will curse; and all peoples on earth will be blessed through you." (Genesis 12:1–3)

God's speaking to Abram was more than just a call. The Bible calls this type of arrangement a covenant, or a contractual arrangement between two parties. As he often did throughout Scripture, God repeated his promise to Abraham. Through these affirmations, God answered Abraham's most difficult question, "How do I know you will do these things?"

"After this, the word of the Lord came to Abram in a vision: 'Do not be afraid, Abram. I am your shield, your very great reward.'" (Genesis 15:1)

Abraham's story continues:

When Abram was ninety-nine years old, the Lord appeared to him and said, "I am God Almighty; walk before me and be blameless. I will confirm my covenant between me and you and will greatly increase your numbers." (Genesis 17:1–2)

The Almighty Creator of the Universe took an oath upon his own life that whatever he promised he would fulfill. Talk about a guaranteed promise! In this same passage, God changed Abram's name to Abraham and Sarai's name to Sarah. God's covenant with Abraham had three components:

- **The gift of land.** God would give Abraham the Promised Land, also called Canaan or the land of Israel.

- **Abraham would become the father of a great nation.** Abraham probably pictured many children, but God gave Abraham and Sarah only one son. Over the next 2,000 years, Abraham's heirs would number in the millions.

- **All the nations of the earth would be blessed.** God in his foreknowledge saw ahead to a time when one of Abraham's descendants would be Jesus Christ, who would redeem the sins of the world.

CULTURAL FACT

At Hebron, in the city gate, Abraham purchased the cave of Machpelah to bury his wife, Sarah. Today, in the older parts of Hebron is a large structure called the Cave of Machpelah, a place sacred to Jews, Christians, and Muslims and currently inaccessible to all. The exterior of the structure is composed of large Herodian stones (37–4 B.C.) and inside that enclosure are the remains of a Byzantine/Crusader church, a mosque, and a synagogue. There are three pairs of above ground monuments: a pair for Abraham and Sarah; a pair for Isaac and Rebecca; and a pair for Jacob and Leah. The underground chambers have not been completely investigated or reported on, but the visible stone work there also seems to be Herodian.

God's covenant wasn't about the worthiness of the recipient, Abraham. Nor was there immediate evidence of God's pledge. Covenants are always about the faithfulness of the one (God) who made the promise. The Lord faithfully fulfilled every promise to Abraham.

THE PATRIARCHAL BLESSING

From the moment when God lifted his starter pistol and squeezed the trigger, time began. With the Abrahamic covenant, the format of the race changed to a relay. In a spiritual sense, God handed the baton (his blessing) to Abraham. Abraham passed it to Isaac, his son. Finally, Isaac passed the baton of God's blessing to his son Jacob. These three runners are often called the Patriarchs.

These Patriarchs had authority over their extended families plus over the entire tribe. Beyond providing traveling directions, these leaders set the religious course by example of which Deity the people would reverence. The Bible often refers to the Lord as the God of Abraham, Isaac, and Jacob. When a patriarch died, the lion's share of the inheritance passed to the firstborn son. Isaac's inheritance was not Abraham's animals or his treasures, but the anointing of God. As Genesis 25:11a says, "After Abraham's death, God blessed his son Isaac."

Isaac's wife, Rebecca, had twin sons, Esau and Jacob. In this case, the blessing didn't pass to the firstborn Esau. Through deceit and lying, Jacob received the blessing. Why, you may ask, did God allow it? Whether we like it or not, Jacob was the person that God selected for his blessing and God always gets his way. Long after Jacob deceived his father and thinking that he had stolen the blessing, Jacob suddenly found himself wrestling with a messenger from God:

Jacob was left alone, and a man wrestled with him till daybreak. When the man saw that he could not overpower him, he touched the socket of Jacob's hip so that his hip was wrenched as he wrestled with the man. Then the man said, "Let me go, for it is daybreak." But Jacob replied, "I will not let you go unless you bless me." The man asked him, "What is your name?" "Jacob," he answered. Then the man said, "Your name will no longer be Jacob, but Israel, because you have struggled with God and with men and have overcome." Jacob said, "Please tell me your name." But he replied, "Why do you ask my name?" Then he blessed him there. So Jacob called the place Peniel, saying, "It is because I saw God face to face, and yet my life was spared." (Genesis 32:24–30)

JUST A MINUTE

One of the key Old Testament covenants between God and man is called the Abrahamic Covenant. God burst into the lives of an older, childless couple, Abram and Sarai, with the words of strong determination: "I will make you into a great nation and I will bless you." (Genesis 12:2) The Lord's gracious promise was unconditional. God would multiply Abram's descendants and give them the land of Canaan. (Genesis 13:14–17) God formalized his promise to Abram as a formal agreement between a superior king and an inferior servant. (Genesis 15:1–21) Finally, the Lord swore by himself that he would do it. (Genesis 22:15–18) His word was irrevocable.

Although God selected Jacob to receive the blessing, he wasn't exempt from the pain of self-examination or conflict. Years before his blind father, Isaac, had asked a lying Jacob for his name. "I am Esau, your firstborn," Jacob had answered. Now, another man asks the blessing-seeking Jacob for his name and this time he tells the truth, "I am Jacob." For possibly the first time, Jacob told the truth about himself. He was a changed man and God changed his name to Israel.

CULTURAL FACT

It is not known exactly when the Patriarchs lived. Estimates for dating Abraham, Isaac, and Jacob range from 2100 to 1800 B.C. These dates would locate the patriarchal period before, or simultaneous with, the Mari tablets, which have been placed between 1813 and 1760 B.C. Mari was a powerful city, halfway between Babylon and the Mediterranean Sea on the banks of the Euphrates. It became rich through trading, and although it is not mentioned in the Bible, it is well known today because of the large archive of official documents discovered there. More than 20,000 clay tablets were dug up at the excavation site. The Mari tablets frequently mention the cities of Nahor and Haran. Abraham (Genesis 11:31) and Jacob (Genesis 27:43; 28:10) lived in Haran, and Abraham's servant traveled to Nahor (Genesis 24:10). Much of what is written in the Mari tablets may reflect aspects of culture known by the Patriarchs.

The Patriarchs were not selected because they were perfect in their lifestyles or lives (they weren't), but in spite of these imperfections, God chose them. These men carried the blessing from generation to generation. In a microcosm, these men are illustrated of a truth of all of Scripture, a perfect Creator, an image bearing but fallen mankind, a promise-making God, and a generation-to-generation blessing sealed by the free gift of redemption.

THE ELEVENTH SON OF JACOB, JOSEPH

Joseph began life as a shepherd. As the firstborn son of Jacob's beloved wife, Rachel, his father foolishly gave him special attention and a multicolored, long-sleeve cloak. Joseph's 10 older brothers seethed with jealousy over how their father gave the little brother special treatment.

CULTURAL FACT

It is ironic that Joseph was sold to a band of Midianites (Genesis 37:28), because the Midianites were distant relatives to Joseph and his brothers through Abraham's concubine Keturah. (Genesis 25:1–2) The Midianites lived as nomads in the desert region southeast of Canaan, along the northern coast of the Red Sea. They were often linked with the Ishmaelites (Genesis 37:27–28; Judges 7:25, 8:24), with whom they apparently shared the slave trade to Egypt.

One day the brothers had enough and threw their brother into a pit to die, then spilt blood on his cloak to show to Jacob. They said, "'Come now, let's kill him and throw him into one of these cisterns and say that a ferocious animal devoured him.'" (Genesis 37:20b) Then when some traders from Midian passed the brothers as they traveled to Egypt, they took Joseph out then sold him as a common slave. When he reached Egypt, Joseph was sold again to the household of Potiphar, captain of Pharaoh's guard. The young Hebrew found favor with his master, but then Potiphar's wife falsely accused Joseph of attempted rape and Joseph was thrown into prison.

The Lord was with him [in prison]; he showed him kindness and granted him favor in the eyes of the prison warden. So the warden put Joseph in charge of all those held in the prison, and he was made responsible for all that was done there. The warden paid no attention to anything under Joseph's care, because the Lord was with Joseph and gave him success in whatever he did. (Genesis 39:21–23)

While Joseph was in prison for almost 10 years, God demonstrated his sovereignty and prepared him to bring about a great blessing. While in prison, Joseph interpreted Pharaoh's dream and was finally released. He outlined a plan for guiding Egypt through a devastating famine, and Pharaoh elevated Joseph to become a prince of the land.

CULTURAL FACT

In Joseph's day, everyone had a robe or cloak. The people used their robes for warmth, to bundle belongings for a trip, to wrap babies, to sit on, or even use as security for a loan. Most of these robes were knee length, or short sleeved and plain. In contrast, Joseph's robe was probably the type which royalty wore—long-sleeve, ankle length, and colorful. The robe became a symbol of the favoritism Jacob had toward Joseph and it strained the already difficult relationship between Joseph and his brothers.

Because Joseph obeyed God and forgave his undeserving brothers, God brought the entire nation of Israel, which numbered hundreds of thousands, from Canaan to Egypt. Because of Joseph's leadership, the Jewish people were treated as guests.

As Jacob (known as Israel) was near his death, he called his children together to bless his sons as his last will and testament. And who would receive the covenant blessing, which was passed on from father to father? Jacob not only bypassed Reuben, his firstborn, but he passed the blessing to Judah, his *fourth* son:

"Judah, your brothers will praise you; your hand will be on the neck of your enemies; your father's sons will bow down to you … The scepter will not depart from Judah." (Genesis 49:8,10a)

Jacob was following the will of God because thousands of years later, Jesus Christ would be born into the tribe of Judah.

Years later, right after Jacob died, Joseph helped his surviving siblings understand how God had guided them to Egypt for their preservation.

His brothers then came and threw themselves down before him [Joseph]. "We are your slaves," they said. But Joseph said to them, "Don't be afraid. Am I in the place of God? You intended to harm me, but God intended it for good to accomplish what is now being done, the saving of many lives." (Genesis 50:18–20)

What Joseph didn't imagine was that it would be 400 years before the Jewish people would be released from Egypt through the Exodus and the leadership of Moses. One day after Joseph was gone from the memory of the Egyptian people, a ruler saw the Jews as a political threat so he enslaved them. This enslavement of Abraham's descendants marks the transition point from the history of the Patriarchs to the most important redemptive act in the Old Testament: the Exodus and the giving of the Law on Mount Sinai. In the next hour, you will learn how God miraculously provided a man to lead the Jewish people out of Egyptian bondage.

HOUR'S UP!

Genesis is a book of beginning God's great message of love to mankind. This beginning is more than a simple learning experience. The message is relevant to everyday life. In the next few questions, let's consider what application this hour will mean for your life.

1. Sometimes it's easy to feel like the world is so big and you are only one person, yet what encouragement and strength do you get from looking at Abraham and Sarah and how their lives began a movement of God that continues today?

2. When God created, he did something that will never be repeated. Pause for a moment and consider your unique role in the world. Spend a few moments of thanksgiving that God broke the mold when he created the unique person that you are.

3. When God created man, he gave each of us a bit of himself and his image. How are you fulfilling your God-given destiny to worship God and love him forever? List several ways you are fulfilling this desire from God.

4. Pause to consider the distinctions of man from the animals (any animal). Our ability to think, reflect, decide, learn, feel, and know is different from any other creature on the planet. List several reasons why your distinction is important (that is, it allows you to have a relationship with the Creator).

5. God drew a boundary in the tree of the knowledge of good and evil. When you have a boundary in your life, are you quick to test the boundary or simply accept it?

6. The serpent's lies to Eve and Adam show the cleverness of Satan's temptation even today. What aspects are used as temptation in your life? What steps can you take to be proactive against temptation (such as spending time reading the Bible or memorizing Scripture)?

7. While Noah was building the ark, God gave the world a 120-year chance to repent and change. What does this story show of God's long suffering and grace for aspects of your life?

8. Abraham faithfully believed the promise of God and God responded through blessing Abraham. Open your Bible and take a step of faith with one of God's promises (such as Matthew 6:33). Reflect on this promise or verse over the course of several days. What difference did it make in your life?

9. The Patriarchs passed God's blessing from generation to generation. How are you passing God's blessing in your life to your children or other relationships? Plot a course of action to make sure you are passing God's blessing from generation to generation.

10. While in prison for 10 years, Joseph probably didn't always feel like God was guiding his life. Yet after the fact, Joseph could reflect that what his brothers meant for evil, God meant for good and to save the entire nation of Israel. Take a moment to reflect on a bad experience from your past. How is God using that bad experience as a source of strength for today? If not, ask God to show you how it will be transformed.

HOUR 3

Out of Egypt—More Than a Movie

CHAPTER SUMMARY

LESSON PLAN:

In this hour, you will learn about …

- The three stages of Moses' life: prince, shepherd, leader.
- The miracle of nine plagues in Egypt.
- The final blow to the Egyptians through the Passover and the Angel of Death.

How often people forget a hero and his actions in only a few short years. Joseph, son of Jacob, had saved Egypt from famine and destruction. The Egyptian Pharaoh raised Joseph from a slave in prison to being second only to Pharaoh. During seven years of famine, Joseph brought his family (the entire race of Jews) to some of the finest land in Egypt, Goshen. A few generations later, Joseph had died and was long forgotten. The Jewish people were multiplying and the current Pharaoh was concerned about their growing population. The crafty leader said, "Look, the Israelites have become much too numerous for our Egyptian army to overcome. Come, we must deal shrewdly with them or they will become more numerous and, if war breaks out, will join our enemies, fight against us, and escape." The Pharaoh forced the Jewish people into slave labor. They built various cities across Egypt.

HISTORICAL FACT

> Who was the Pharaoh of Egypt? According to the biblical data, Jacob and his family entered Egypt around 1876 B.C. or during the reign of King Sesostris III of the Twelfth Dynasty. The ruler during the time of Moses who didn't know about Joseph was probably one of the kings of the Hyksos Dynasty, a Semitic line of conquerors from Asia.

To the amazement of the Egyptian Pharaoh, when he challenged the Jewish people with hard labor, their population increased even more. The ruler ordered the Hebrew midwives to kill all the boys and let the girls live, but the midwives obeyed God instead of Pharaoh. A Levi man and his wife had a son, and for three months they hid him. Then, one day, his mother floated the baby in the Nile in a papyrus basket. When Pharaoh's daughter drew the baby out of the water, she called him "Moses" and he became a prince in her home.

How did this young prince of Egypt become the leader of the Jewish people and a man whose face shone with radiance from his time in God's presence? You probably have seen Charlton Heston portraying Moses in *The Ten Commandments*. In this chapter, you will begin to learn more details about the true Moses who walked the face of the earth centuries ago and led the Jewish people out of captivity.

MOSES: PRINCE, SHEPHERD, LEADER

As the Hebrew people were challenged with hard labor, their population increased even more. Pharaoh gathered the Hebrew midwives and told them, "When you help the Hebrew women in childbirth and observe them on the delivery stool, if it is a boy, kill him; but if it is a girl, let her live." (Exodus 1:16) Yet the Bible tells us that these Jewish midwives feared God more than man, so they let the baby boys live. After a short period of time when the boy babies were not killed, Pharaoh called the midwives and asked, "Why have you done this? Why have you let the boys live?" The midwives answered Pharaoh, "Hebrew women are not like Egyptian women: they are vigorous and give birth before the midwives arrive."

So God was kind to the midwives and the people increased and became even more numerous. And because the midwives feared God, he gave them families of their own. Then Pharaoh gave this order to all the people, "Every boy that is born you must throw into the river, but let every girl live." (Exodus 1:16–22)

In the midst of such violence toward babies, a Levi man and his wife had a son. For the first three months, his mother managed to hide him successfully, and then she put him in a papyrus basket and floated him into the Nile River. She had his sister, Miriam, watch her brother and see what would happen to him. Pharaoh's daughter came to the river to bathe and discovered the basket and sent her slave girl to get it. Opening the basket, she discovered a crying baby boy and felt sorry for him. The daughter called the baby Moses, because she "drew him out of the water." He became a prince in the house of Pharaoh.

PEOPLE TO KNOW

Levi (Hebrew for "joined") was the third son of Jacob and Leah. (Genesis 29:34) Levi's three sons formed the three main divisions of the Levitical priesthood: the Gershonites, the Kohathites, and the Merarites. (Genesis 46:11) Moses and Aaron came from the tribe or family of Levi, which means they were descendants of Levi. As God gave the law to Moses, the members of the Levi tribe became the priesthood. They had no land allocation when they reached the Promised Land because God selected this tribe to serve the Lord.

PRINCE

Moses was raised as a grandson of the Pharaoh in the halls of the Egyptian palace. Moses' older sister, Miriam, was standing nearby watching her baby brother. She asked Pharaoh's daughter, "Shall I go and get one of the Hebrew women to nurse the baby for you?" "Yes, go," she answered. So Miriam went and brought Moses' mother to care for baby Moses in his early days. As the child grew older, his mother took him to Pharaoh's daughter and he became her son.

Although raised as an Egyptian prince, Moses never forgot his Jewish people. He watched as the Hebrew people labored as slaves. Instead of giving blind allegiance to the pagan culture of Egypt, Moses was drawn to the plight of the Jews and secretly mourned their burdens.

BIBLICAL FACT

Many scholars believe that Moses had probably reached the age of 40 while in Pharaoh's household. (Exodus 2:11–24)

One day while walking among the Jewish people, Moses saw an Egyptian mercilessly beating a slave. Filled with rage, Moses killed the Egyptian and buried the man's body in the sand (Exodus 2:12), looking around and hoping that no one had seen this act of violence. Like a kid sneaking cookies from the cookie jar, Moses' conscience knew that killing was wrong and he was burdened with guilt. A day later, he came across two Hebrews who were fighting and he attempted to intervene and break up the fight. One of the men confronted Moses saying, "Who made you ruler and judge over us? Are you thinking of killing me as you killed the Egyptian?" (Exodus 2:14)

The comment frightened Moses because he instantly realized that many people knew of his violence toward an Egyptian. Soon, Pharaoh heard of the death and tried to have Moses killed, but Moses fled the area and traveled hundreds of miles to the east. Moses was banished from the palace to the desert.

SHEPHERD

When Moses arrived in the desert of Midian, he sat down at a well. Seven daughters of a Midian priest came to draw water for their father's flock. Some shepherds came along to water their flocks and drove the women away from the well. Typically in the ancient East, unmarried women with no brothers had little protection from this type of practice. Moses stood up for the women and came to their rescue. Once again Moses demonstrated his sensitivity to injustice.

When the girls returned home, their father asked, "Why have you returned so early today?" They answered, "An Egyptian rescued us from the shepherds. He even drew water for us and watered the flock." "Where is he?" he asked his daughters. "Why did you leave him? Invite him to have something to eat." Moses agreed to stay and joined the household of the man for 40 years. He became a shepherd and raised the flocks of Jethro, another Midian priest. Moses married one of Jethro's daughters and they began to raise a family.

While Moses was learning the skill of raising sheep, the Pharaoh of Egypt died and the Jewish people continued to be oppressed in their slavery. However, God showed his faithfulness to the Jewish people. As they cried out, the Lord heard their despair (Exodus 2:24) and remembered his promise to Abraham, Isaac, and Jacob. After Moses had prepared for almost 80 years, the Lord was ready to move Moses into high-profile service.

One day while watching his father-in-law's sheep, Moses led the flock to the far side of the desert and came to the Mountain of Horeb. Then he spotted something strange—a burning bush that, although on fire, wasn't destroyed. Curious, Moses went to examine it more closely. From inside the flame, Moses heard his name, "Moses, Moses." Calling out in response, Moses exclaimed, "Here I am."

God commanded Moses to remove his sandals, as he was standing on holy ground. From the flame, God explained his listening ear to the Jewish people and how Moses would lead them out of Egypt to a land flowing with milk and honey. (Exodus 3:8) Then God said, "I know the king of Egypt will not let you go unless a mighty hand compels him. So I will stretch out my hand and strike the Egyptians with all the wonders that I will perform among them. After that, he will let you go. And I will make the Egyptians favorably disposed toward this people, so that when you leave you will not go empty-handed. Every woman is to ask her neighbor and any woman living in her house for articles of silver and gold and for clothing, which you will put on some of your daughters. And so you will plunder the Egyptians." (Exodus 3:19–22)

JUST A MINUTE

At the burning bush, Moses made four common excuses about why he couldn't serve God. He told about his personal shortcomings, his fear that the people would not believe him, his lack of experience, and his request that God send someone else. Does that sound familiar? (Exodus 3 and 4)

Because God had not spoken to the Jewish people for hundreds of years, Moses questioned the sanity of returning to Pharaoh and making a demand to release his people. Moses asked, "What if they don't believe me or listen to me or if they say, 'The Lord has not appeared to you'?" Then the Lord said, "What is that in your hand?" "A staff," Moses replied. The Lord said, "Throw it on the ground." Moses threw it on the ground and it became a snake, and he ran from it. (Wouldn't you run from a snake?) Then the Lord said to him, "Reach out your hand and take it by the tail." So Moses reached out and took hold of the snake and it turned back into a staff in his hand. "This," the Lord said, "is so that they may believe that the Lord, the God of their fathers—the God of Abraham, the God of Isaac, and the God of Jacob— has appeared to you." (Exodus 4:1–5)

Then the Lord gave Moses a second sign to perform for the Jewish leaders in Egypt. "Put your hand inside your cloak," the Lord said. So Moses put his hand into his cloak and when he took it out, it was leprous, like snow. These types of skin diseases were incurable during the time of Moses and the sure sign of death. "Now put it back in your cloak," the Lord said. So Moses put his hand back into his cloak and when he took it out, it was restored, like the rest of his flesh.

Then the Lord said, "If they do not believe you or pay attention to the first miraculous sign, they may believe the second. But if they do not believe these two signs or listen to you, take some water from the Nile and pour it on dry ground. The water you take from the river will become blood on the ground." (Exodus 4:6–9)

Moses was now armed with signs from God to show to the Jewish people and the Egyptians, but he mounted another objection, "O, Lord, I have never been eloquent, neither in the past nor since you have spoken to your servant. I am slow in speech and tongue." The Lord said to him, "Who gave man his mouth? Who makes him deaf or dumb? Who gives him sight or makes him blind? Is it not I, the Lord? Now go: I will help you speak and will teach you what to say." Then Moses told God another objection to returning to Pharaoh in Egypt. "O Lord, please send someone else to do it."

And what was God's response to this final objection? "Then the Lord's anger burned against Moses and he said, 'What about your brother, Aaron the Levite? I know he can speak well. He is already on his way to meet you, and his heart will be glad when he sees you. You shall speak to him and put words in his mouth; I will help both of you speak and will teach you what to do. He will speak to the people for you, and it will be as if he were your mouth and as if you were God to him. But take this staff in your hand so you can perform the miraculous signs with it.'" (Exodus 4:14–17)

With the concession that Moses could use his brother, Aaron, as a speaker or mouthpiece, Moses returned to Egypt to confront Pharaoh and lead the Jewish people out of the land.

LEADER

From the burning bush, God appointed Moses to deliver the Jewish people from the bondage of slavery to Pharaoh. First, he went to the Israelites, but no one believed that Moses spoke for God. Next Moses appeared before the ruler of Egypt, Pharaoh, in the famous scene where he said, "Let my people go." The Bible relates that God hardened Pharaoh's heart so that he didn't listen to Moses.

BIBLICAL FACT

When Moses spoke to Pharaoh, he was 80 years old. Aaron, who accompanied Moses, was 83 years old. (Exodus 7:6)

While the Jewish people didn't appoint Moses as a leader, God's power moved through Moses in various signs. For example, Moses commanded his walking staff to become a snake. The Egyptian magicians also made their staffs into snakes. Then God showed the leadership of Moses when the snake from Moses swallowed all of the other snakes.

The leadership of Moses began where his life started—in the palace of Pharaoh. The leadership carried forward for another 40 years in the wilderness and toward the promise land. In the next chapter, we will learn how Moses spent hours in the presence of God. His face glowed with the radiance of God. When he talked with the Jewish people, he wore a veil over his face. When he talked with God, he removed the veil and talked face to face. His leadership and guidance of the Jewish people is one of the hallmarks of the early Old Testament books.

THE LESSER NINE PLAGUES (A PREFACE TO THE FINAL BLOW)

In the court of the most powerful man in Egypt, Moses stood and asked for the release of the Jewish people. Through this resounding "no" from Pharaoh, the ruler brought a curse on his nation and his own household, which would exceed his wildest dreams. In a series of divine actions, commonly referred to as the 10 plagues, God performed wonders not only to free the Jews but also to judge the wicked and arrogant ruler of a godless nation.

BIBLICAL FACT

The 10 plagues represent a unique period in Old Testament history. It shows the greatest concentration of miracles. God methodically humiliates the gods of Egypt through his supernatural power.

WATER CHANGED TO BLOOD

God sent Moses and Aaron down to the Nile River to wait for Pharaoh. Moses carried the staff that had changed into a snake. While Pharaoh was trying to bathe, Moses raised his staff over the Nile. As a sign that God was with Moses, the water turned to blood. (Exodus 7:14–25) Pharaoh called his own magicians to see whether they could turn water into blood. His sorcerers were also able to make the transformation. Pharaoh was unwilling to release the Jews. The fish in the Nile died and the Egyptians had to dig wells to get drinking water.

FROGS

After waiting seven days, the Lord sent Moses again to Pharaoh with the demand, "Let my people go, so they may worship me." In response to the ruler's refusal, Aaron stretched his hand and staff. Then frogs came out of the streams and ponds into the land. (Exodus 8:1–15) Pharaoh's magicians were also able to produce frogs. Yet the ruler turned to Moses for relief and asked him to remove the frogs. "Tomorrow," Moses promised. The dead frogs were piled in large heaps across the land and it reeked with them. (Exodus 8:14) When the king saw the relief from this plague, he again refused to release the people.

GNATS

The Lord told Moses to have Aaron strike the earth with his staff and stir up the dust. Every bit of dust throughout the land of Egypt became gnats and quickly covered the people and animals. (Exodus 8:16–18) Once again, Pharaoh's magicians tried to duplicate the plague—yet they were unable. They appealed to their ruler saying, "This is the finger of God." (Exodus 8:19) But Pharaoh refused to listen or to release the Jews.

FLIES

God told Moses to confront Pharaoh with another plague: "If you don't let the people go, then I will make a distinction between the Egyptians and the land of Goshen where my people live." Flies poured into the Egyptian houses but not among the Jewish people. (Exodus 8:20–32) The ruler brought Moses back and said the people could sacrifice but only within the boundaries of Egypt. Moses objected and Pharaoh agreed to let the people leave—if Moses prayed for the flies to leave. When Moses left Pharaoh, he prayed and the flies disappeared—but Pharaoh changed his mind and didn't release the people.

PLAGUE OF LIVESTOCK

For the next plague, God revealed his power over Apis, the Egyptian bull god, who was the living personification of Ptah (the creator god) and the symbol of fertility. Again Moses predicted that Pharaoh would see a distinction between the Egyptian and the Hebrew people. All living animals of the Egyptians, including cattle, donkeys, horses, sheep, and goats, died in Egypt while not a single animal died among the Jewish people. (Exodus 9:1–7) Pharaoh sent men to investigate but was unyielding in not allowing the people to leave Egypt.

BIBLICAL FACT

With the plagues, God systematically showed his power over the Egyptian gods. With the frogs, God was greater than Heqt, the god of resurrection who assisted women in childbirth and who appeared in the form of a frog. When the hail destroyed the crops, God showed his greatness over Isis, the goddess of life, and Seth, the protector of the crops.

BOILS

For the sixth plague, God commanded Moses to take soot from a furnace and toss it into the air. The soot made the people and animals of Egypt break out in boils. (Exodus 9:8–12) Even the magicians couldn't appear before Pharaoh because of these sores—yet the ruler continued in his stubborn ways and didn't release the people.

HAIL

A seventh time, Moses went to confront Pharaoh and ask for the release of the Jewish people. Moses declared that because the ruler had set himself against God, the Lord would send the worst hailstorm ever to fall on Egypt. (Exodus 9:13–25) In his warning, Moses suggested that every animal and person stay inside or risk death. Some of the officials in the court hurried and brought their animals inside. Some people left their slaves and animals in the fields. When Moses stretched out his staff toward the sky, the thunder, lightning, and hail began to fall. No hail fell on the land of Goshen where the Jewish people were living. As the barley and flax were ripe for harvest, the hail destroyed these crops across Egypt along with all the trees. Egypt was left in ruins. Still Pharaoh refused to release the Jewish people.

HISTORICAL FACT

Wheat and barley have been grown in Egypt since 5000 B.C., and in Palestine since about 8000 B.C. Egyptians grew flax primarily for its fibers used to make linen. All Egyptian agriculture depended on water from the Nile River. Egypt was historically the wealthiest nation in the region because it produced more food than any other country.

LOCUSTS

From the seven previous plagues, Moses' reputation increased among the Egyptians as well as among the Jewish people. Pharaoh would have killed Moses if he could have done so. With each plague, Moses' status and prestige among the people increased. Despite the destruction of the land, Pharaoh refused to let the slaves go because of their vast economic impact on the country.

No one knows how long the plagues lasted, and yet they were influencing the country. The eighth plague was one of the worst. Moses threatened Pharaoh with the release of locusts, which would eat everything green and cover the earth. (Exodus 10:1–20) The court officials encouraged the ruler to listen to Moses and to release the Jews. They said, "Don't you know the country is in ruin?" (Exodus 10:7) Yet Pharaoh refused and the locusts came and destroyed anything green in the country—but there were no locusts in Goshen.

Pharaoh quickly summoned Moses and Aaron, acknowledging his sin and asking for prayer to remove the locusts. (Exodus 10:16–17) Moses agreed and prayed. Then in a quick about face, Pharaoh hardened his heart and refused to release the Hebrew people.

DARKNESS

The ninth plague was in direct confrontation to Ra or Re, Egypt's sun god. At the Lord's instruction, Moses stretched out his hand toward the sky and darkness covered all of Egypt for three days. (Exodus 10:21–29) However, the darkness didn't cover the land of Goshen. Then Pharaoh summoned Moses, saying that the Jewish people could go to worship in the desert although they had to leave their flocks and herds. Moses objected, "We need our livestock to sacrifice to God." And once again, Pharaoh hardened his heart and refused to release the Jews. He commanded Moses to leave his presence. Moses said, "As you say, I will never appear before you again."

THE FINAL PLAGUE: THE PASSOVER AND THE ANGEL OF DEATH

Egypt was ruined from the previous nine plagues. God moved in one final plague to release the Jewish people. The final plague and the events around it, called the Passover, comprise an event that the Jewish people continue to celebrate annually.

First, through God's instruction, Moses told the people to ask their Egyptian neighbors for articles of gold and silver. The Lord made the Egyptians willing to give these valuables to the Jews.

CULTURAL FACT

Before coins were introduced about 625 B.C., gold and silver were used as a way to exchange value. Ancient Egyptian bracelets and other items of gold jewelry were sometimes thick and heavy. A necklace recovered with Psusennes I in about 991 B.C. weighs more than 42 pounds.

Then God forewarned Moses that he was about to destroy the firstborn son of everyone in Egypt—from Pharaoh to the firstborn slave and also the firstborn animal. God was about to send an Angel of Death across the land. To prepare the Jewish people for the Angel of Death, God instructed that each man was to take a lamb for their family and slaughter it at twilight. The blood from the lamb was to be sprinkled on the doorposts and the tops of the doorframes. The Lord gave specific instructions about how to eat the lamb and to make bread without yeast. The people were to eat it and prepare for a journey with their staff. "Eat it in haste, it is the Lord's Passover." (Exodus 12:11b) This simple meal had numerous instructions and became the start of the Passover holiday, which the Jewish people continue to celebrate today.

The Jewish people prepared in the exact detail and timing that God had commanded Moses. Then the Angel of Death struck across Egypt—the wealthy and powerful or the poor and imprisoned. Every firstborn son and animal died. As the Bible says, "Pharaoh and all his officials and all the Egyptians got up during the night, and there was loud wailing in Egypt, for there was not a house without someone dead." (Exodus 12:30)

Suddenly the hard-hearted Pharaoh changed. The ruler summoned Moses and Aaron and asked the Jewish people to leave the land with their livestock. "And also bless me," he pleaded. (Exodus 12:32) The people left Egypt after exactly 430 years in that nation.

With Pharaoh's blessing, the Jewish people were released to travel toward the desert and begin an incredible journey, which is explained in the next chapter.

HOUR'S UP!

The stories about Moses and the 10 plagues are more than nice stories. While it's good to gain some factual knowledge about these events, what do they mean for today? The following questions will give you an opportunity to explore the applications from this hour—either individually or in a group setting.

1. Revisit the Hebrew midwives and how they feared God instead of obeying Pharaoh's command. What can you learn about the value of fearing God in everyday situations?

2. Recall how God protected the baby Moses from the earliest days of his life. Did Moses grow complacent or comfortable with God's protection as a prince? How can you keep your relationship with God fresh and not grow complacent? List a new discipline such as daily prayer or worship or Bible reading that you will incorporate into your life to continually grow in your relationship with God.

3. Prince Moses thought no one had seen him kill the Egyptian who was punishing the Hebrews. Are there areas in your life that you guard from others because you think no one knows? Meditate on how God constantly cares and watches every portion of our daily lives. How can you be more aware of his presence every day?

4. For 40 years, Moses cared for sheep in the desert of Midian, then suddenly he saw a burning bush and his life took a new direction. Has your life been in training? Could it possibly take a new direction? Begin to dream about the possibilities.

5. At the burning bush, Moses made one excuse after another about his deficiencies. Consider your current life. Are you giving God excuses rather than moving ahead in faith? Make a commitment to stop your excuses.

6. The plagues teach us about the stubbornness of Pharaoh. What application can you learn about the fruit of stubbornness from the repeated actions of the ruler of Egypt?

7. Each plague attacked an Egyptian god such as the river god or the sun god. What gods are you facing in your own life (materialism, hunger for power or position, or _____)? Celebrate God's power over the gods in your life and rejoice in the example of God's power through the plagues.

8. During several of the plagues, Pharaoh tried to bargain with God. He attempted to move God to lower the terms (complete release of the people). Are you bargaining with God over some daily situation? Are you asking for God to lower his standard (the Bible)? What can you do to accept God's conditions and move ahead with your life?

9. The plague of darkness covered the earth for three days. What is the difference between darkness and light?

10. The final plague had the greatest impact on Pharaoh and the people of Egypt. They lost their firstborn sons—who were the primary heirs. Reflect on the devastation of the people. When did God sacrifice his firstborn, only son for the world? Allow gratitude for this sacrifice to fill your heart.

HOUR 4

Journey Through the Wilderness

CHAPTER SUMMARY

LESSON PLAN:

In this hour, you will learn about …

- The importance of God's Laws and Commandments.
- How the Tabernacle helped the Jewish people to worship God.
- Key points in the Books of Laws: Leviticus, Numbers, and Deuteronomy.
- The reason behind the Old Testament system of sacrifice.

When the nation of Egypt reeked from the death of every firstborn, stubborn Pharaoh relented and permitted the slave population of Jews to leave the country. Then suddenly he forgot about the 10 plagues and the troublesome Moses and realized that he had released the economic essence of his nation. He had second thoughts and decided to pursue the Jews.

The Israelites had taken the southern route out of Egypt. During the night, a pillar of fire led them, and during the daylight, they followed a cloud. The armies of Pharaoh chased the Jews and they ran to the edge of the Red Sea. Escape looked hopeless. Then the Lord told Moses to raise his staff over the sea. The wind blew a path through the water and the waters separated, heaving up a wall of water on the left and another on the right. The Jewish people were able to walk across on dry ground.

The Egyptian army chased the people and also tried to cross the sea. But God threw the army into confusion and the wheels of their chariots began to fall off. Some of the Egyptians began to flee, saying "The Lord is fighting for the Israelites against Egypt." (Exodus 14:25) Then Moses stretched out his hand again and the waters flowed over the Egyptians. The entire army of Pharaoh died in one moment. While the Jewish people celebrated God's release, they quickly forgot this display of power. During the next 40 years, the Jewish people wandered in the wilderness. God provided for them physically, emotionally, and spiritually.

This chapter covers the laws of God to the Jewish people. While the details were important to the Jewish people, we will examine some of the critical elements that remain applicable to today's culture. You will gain an overview of Exodus, Leviticus, Numbers, and Deuteronomy, which are important books in the Bible.

BIBLICAL FACT

The dividing of the Red Sea is one of the most well-known miracles in the Bible. God supernaturally intervened into the natural order to bring glory to his name. At the Red Sea, God made the waters temporarily disobey the natural laws of gravity so that the Jewish people could cross on dry ground.

GOD'S COMMANDMENTS

Despite the miracles of the 10 plagues, the Jewish people soon forgot about God's power. After about a month of wandering in the wilderness, they began to complain. They began to long for the past, saying, "Oh, remember those meat pots in Egypt. If only we had died in Egypt." (Exodus 16:3) Similar to when they cried out to God in their slavery, God heard their cry for food. He provided a small, round bread, which looked like coriander seed. The people called it "manna," which sounds like the Hebrew word meaning, "What is it?" Each person gathered about two quarts each day. Yet the people continued to grumble and ask for meat beyond the manna.

One day after the people were complaining, God sent quail. (Exodus 16:10–13) While the quail was a one-time experience for the Jewish people, overall the Lord fed the people with manna—and not just for a few days—but throughout the 40 years of their wandering in the wilderness. (Exodus 16:33)

With the food situation under control, the people continued to mark their relationship with God through their complaining. When they traveled through the desert of Sin, they went from place to place and finally camped at Rephidim; however, there wasn't any water. The people came to Moses and demanded, "Give us water to drink."

Moses replied, "Why do you quarrel with me? Why do you put the Lord to the test?" The people continued to be thirsty for water and grumbled against Moses saying, "Why did you bring us up out of Egypt to make us and our children and our livestock die of thirst?" Do you hear the whiny tone in their voices as they complained? The situation was increasing in intensity and possible danger for Moses. He cried out to the Lord and said, "What am I to do with these people? They are almost ready to stone me." (Exodus 17:4)

The Lord answered Moses, "Walk on ahead of the people. Take with you some of the elders of Israel and take in your hand the staff with which you struck the Nile, and go. I will stake there before you by the rock at Horeb. Strike the rock, and water will come out of it for the people to drink."

So Moses did this in the sight of the elders of Israel. And he called the place Massah and Meribah because the Israelites quarreled and because they tested the Lord saying, "Is the Lord among us or not?" (Exodus 17:1–7) Repeatedly in this early period of their wandering in the desert, the Jewish people were testing the Lord (and Moses) to see God's guiding hand in their daily lives.

ATTACK!

About this time, the Amalekites, who were descendants of Amalek, a grandson of Esau (Genesis 36:15–16), came out to attack the Israelites. It was their first battle since the Lord defeated the Egyptian army at the Red Sea. In an unusual battle plan, Moses turned to his assistant, Joshua, and said, "Choose some of our men and go out to fight the Amalekites. Tomorrow I will stand on top of the hill with the staff of God in my hands." (Exodus 17:9) What a strange plan! Joshua went out into battle to fight the enemy. Holding his staff, Moses stood on the top of the hill with Aaron and Hur.

PEOPLE TO KNOW

Hur was one of Israel's leaders who, during the time in the wilderness, helped govern the people at Sinai in Moses' absence (Exodus 24:14) and helped support Moses' arms during the battle with the Amalekites. He was evidently the same Hur who was a descendant of Judah and grandfather of Bezalel, the craftsman who built the Tabernacle. (Exodus 31:2; 1 Chronicles 2:19)

"As long as Moses held up his hands, the Israelites were winning, but whenever he lowered his hands, the Amalekites were winning. When Moses' hands grew tired, they took a stone and put it under him and he sat on it. Aaron and Hur held his hands up—one on one side, one on the other—so that his hands remained steady till sunset. So Joshua's army overcame the Amalekite army with the sword." (Exodus 17:11–13)

The Amalekites suffered a severe punishment for attacking the Jewish people. "Then the Lord said to Moses, 'Write this on a scroll as something to be remembered and make sure that Joshua hears it, because I will completely erase the memory of the Amalekites from under heaven.' Moses built an altar and called it The Lord Is My Banner. He said, 'For hands were lifted up to the throne of the Lord. The Lord will be at war against the Amalekites from generation to generation.'" (Exodus 17:14–16)

DELEGATION

While the Israelites were moving around in the wilderness, Jethro, Moses' father-in-law, heard about all God had done for Moses and how he had brought the people out of Egypt. When Moses left Midian for Egypt to free the people, he had left behind his wife and two sons. Now Moses had sent for his wife, Jethro's daughter, and his two sons. With this visit, Jethro returned Moses' wife and two sons to him. The next day, as usual, Moses began to serve as the judge for the people from morning until night.

Jethro watched Moses render small and large decisions for the Jewish people. Then Jethro asked, "What is this you are doing for the people? Why do you alone sit as judge, while all these people stand around you from morning till evening?"

Moses answered him, "Because the people come to me to see God's will. Whenever they have a dispute, it is brought to me, and I decide between the parties and inform them of God's decrees and laws." From his observation, Jethro knew that the people would wear out Moses and that the burden of such judgment day in and day out was too much. He began to teach Moses the skill of delegation and to use capable men to teach the law, whereupon Moses would take only the most difficult cases. "That will make your load lighter, because they will share it with you. If you do this and God so commands, you will be able to stand the strain, and all these people will go home satisfied." (Exodus 18:13–27) The story is the beginning of an organized system of the law and government, which continues in today's society.

HISTORICAL FACT

Biblical scholars debate about which mountain in the Sinai Peninsula is Mount Sinai. The two most likely possibilities are Jebel Musa and Ras es-Salsafeh, both located on a granite ridge of about three miles. Most traditional scholars accept Jebel Musa, at the foot of which is St. Catherine's monastery where Friedrich Tischendorf discovered the Codex Sinaiticus, the fourth-century manuscript of the Greek Bible.

SUMMIT

For three months, the Jewish people wandered in the desert until they came to the foot of Mount Sinai, located in the southwestern region of the Sinai Peninsula. God called Moses to go up the mountain to make Israel into a "kingdom of priests and a holy nation." For 40 days and 40 nights, Moses met face to face with God and received the covenant commonly called the Ten Commandments. The Jewish people were camped at the base of the mountain for almost 11 months. (Numbers 10:11) The people only moved when the Lord commanded them to move with a cloud during the day and a pillar of fire at night. The Lord kept them at the base of the mountain for this period of time.

Without their leader, the mountain was capped with flames of fire, thunderstorms, earthquakes, and supernatural trumpet blasts as God spoke and delivered the commandments. The commandments were engraved on both sides of two large stone tablets. These commands are the basis of the Hebrew law. Four of them are about our attitude toward God; six of them are about our attitude toward humankind. (Exodus 20:1–17) God gave the law to set apart the Jewish people from the other nations. The law emphasizes the sinful nature of humans and how changes need to be made to be in the presence of a holy God.

BIBLICAL FACT

Five hundred years after the Jewish people received the Ten Commandments, Mt. Sinai is once again a place to meet God. On the mountain, Elijah the prophet learns what God can accomplish not in fire or earthquakes but in a still small voice. (1 Kings 19:11–12)

Moses had a strong presence of leadership among the Jewish people. When he disappeared for an extended period to Mt. Sinai, the people came to Aaron and said, "Come, make us gods who will go before us. As for this fellow Moses who brought us up out of Egypt, we don't know what has happened to him."

Bowing to the pressure of leadership, Aaron responded, "Take off the gold earrings that your wives, your sons, and your daughters are wearing, and bring them to me." Aaron made the earrings into an idol cast in the shape of a calf, fashioning it with a tool. He designed the calf to look like the Egyptian god, Apis, the bull god, who was the living personification of Putah (the creator god) and the symbol of fertility. How did the people react to the golden calf idol? They said, "These are your gods, O Israel, who brought you out of Egypt." (Exodus 32:4)

When Aaron observed the response of the people, he declared the next day a festival to the Lord. Throughout the day, the people offered sacrifices and fellowship offerings to the golden calf. While the people were turning away from the One God, Moses was up on Mt. Sinai meeting face to face with God and writing the Ten Commandments. God asked Moses to leave the mountain because the people had become corrupt and were sacrificing to man-made gods. The act of disobedience so angered the Lord that he wanted to destroy the people.

Moses interceded for the people: "'O Lord,' he said, 'why should your anger burn against your people whom you brought out of Egypt with great power and a mighty hand? Why should the Egyptians say, "It was with evil intent that he brought them out, to kill them in the mountains and to wipe them off the face of the earth"? Turn from your fierce anger, relent and do not bring disaster on your people. ... Then the Lord relented and did not bring on his people the disaster he had threatened.'" (Exodus 32:11–12, 14)

Moses walked down the mountain and his assistant, Joshua, rejoined him. At the noise outside the camp, Joshua suggested that possibly it was the sounds of war. Moses said it wasn't war but the sound of rejoicing and singing. As they entered the camp and saw the people worshipping the calf, Moses' anger burned against the people. He broke the two stone tablets that told the law. Then he destroyed the idol and ground it into powder and mixed it into water, then made the Israelites drink the water. Moses saw that Aaron had let the people run wild and out of control so he rallied the Levites to his side. He commanded the Levites, "This is what the Lord, the God of Israel, says: 'Each man strap a sword to his side. Go back and forth through the camp from one end to the other, each killing his brother and friend and neighbor.'" The Levites obeyed Moses' command and about three thousand people died. (Exodus 32:27–28)

THE COMMANDMENTS

Then Moses returned to the mountain for another 40 days and 40 nights. On this occasion, he engraved the stones with the commandments of God. Through the experience, his face was transformed so that it shone with the light of God's presence. (Exodus 34:29–35)

Moses received more than the Ten Commandments. The Lord also gave a series of laws to the Jewish people on every aspect of daily life. These laws covered the scope of life—from the death penalty for murder, to kindness to widows and orphans, to how to show hospitality to strangers. While many of the specific laws don't apply to our lives today, the principles behind the laws are certainly relevant. Qualities such as mercy, fairness, and justice are the bedrock of Israel's law and make the Jewish people distinct from any other nation.

BIBLICAL FACT

Moses wore a veil when he was not in God's presence because his face was so radiant. (Exodus 32:29, 35) One other person in the Bible had a face, which "shined like the sun." Jesus had a shining face when he was transfigured in the New Testament. (Matthew 17:2)

THE TABERNACLE TO WORSHIP GOD

Beyond the specific laws instituted to move the Jewish people toward a Holy God, the Lord instructed Moses how to build a place of worship called a Tabernacle or tent of meeting. God would continue to be present everywhere, but the sanctuary or tent of meeting was a place where people could especially encounter God.

Notice the detailed instructions that are included about the tabernacle in Exodus 25–27, 30–31, and 35–40. "And let them make Me a sanctuary that I may dwell among them." (Exodus 25:8, NKJV) Each item of the tent of meeting was portable so the people could carry this place of God's presence as they wandered through the wilderness. Exact measurements were given for the linen border of the tabernacle. Worshippers entered from the east and in the western court stood a bronze altar for the priests to wash themselves in preparation to enter the Holy Place. Only the priests could enter the Holy Place and once a year on the Day of Atonement, the high priest could enter the inner area called the Most Holy Place.

Inside the Holy Place were three pieces of furniture. On the north side, a table held the bread of the Presence, which was 12 cakes of unleavened bread representing the 12 tribes of Israel. On the south side stood a pure gold lampstand with seven branches and seven lamps, which the priests filled with oil each evening. Finally, an altar of incense made of acacia wood and covered with gold was three feet high and one and a half feet square.

CULTURAL FACT

The tabernacle and the Ark of the Covenant (Exodus 25:10, 36:20) were built from the wood of the acacia tree, an orange-brown, hard-grained, and insect-repellent wood. Many varieties of acacia grew in the Sinai Desert, Egypt, and southern Canaan. These trees produced round, fragrant clusters of yellow blossoms.

Inside the Most Holy Place in the tabernacle, the Ark of the Covenant dominated the area. While movies have created a fictional picture of this ark, the Bible tells us the true details of this ark. It contained the two tablets on which Moses wrote the Ten Commandments, a pot of manna, and Aaron's staff, which contained buds. Exodus documents numerous rebellions and grumbling from the Jewish people. At one point some tribes wondered why Moses and Aaron and the Levite people should be chosen as priests. The Lord commanded each tribe to put a staff in the ground. The next morning Aaron's staff had budded. (Numbers 17)

The four items in the ark—two tablets, manna, and staff—served as a constant reminder of the most important elements to God: his Covenant with his people (the tablets), his constant and loving material provision (manna), and God's means of provision to him through the priesthood (the staff).

The cover to the ark was called the mercy seat and represented the presence of God. On each end of the mercy seat stood a cherub made of one piece with the mercy seat cover. These two cherubim of gold faced each other with their wings outstretched above the mercy seat.

Throughout their travels in the wilderness, the Jewish people carried the elements of the tabernacle and assembled it whenever they stayed in one place. Later, in the days of Solomon, the various elements of the tabernacle were moved into the temple. Scholars speculate that the Ark of the Covenant was probably lost in the Babylonian captivity.

Books of Laws

Leviticus, Numbers, and Deuteronomy constitute the Laws for the Hebrew Nation and the Journey to the Promised Land. Leviticus and Deuteronomy contain the laws and Numbers is comprised of a series of events to document the journey to Canaan.

Leviticus

When reading through the Bible, many people will quit somewhere in Leviticus. The name of this book comes from the Septuagint or the ancient Greek translation of the Old Testament. The word means "about, or relating to, the Levites."

After the final plague of Egypt, God redeemed the firstborn sons of the Jewish people. The Lord killed all of the firstborn sons of Egypt but through the blood of the Passover lamb, the Angel of Death skipped the Jewish firstborn and preserved their lives. Through this preservation, God redeemed the firstborn sons of the Israelites and claimed them as the Lord's sons. In substitution for these firstborns, God appointed the Levites, or the descendants of the tribe of Levi, to serve God as priests. Aaron and Moses were members of this tribe, who were charged to care for the tabernacle and later the temple. They were also the musicians, officers, judges, scribes, and teachers of the law. This book contains the bulk of the system of laws for the Hebrew nation. The Levite priesthood administered these laws. The laws covered some of the basic issues of life such as warfare, housing and furniture, diet and foodstuffs, dress, and family life. In addition, other issues were covered such as slavery, manslaughter, theft and injury, treatment for the helpless, and education.

Another key portion of Leviticus details the garments for the priest. These members of the tribe of Levi were mediators between the people and a Holy God. The priests wore long white linen coats with belts or girdles with scarlet, blue, and purple woven into the design. Under their coats, the priests wore linen breeches and a plain cap. Aaron, the first of numerous high priests, had distinctive dress. Besides his regular dress, he wore a two-piece apron called an ephod, which was ornamented. He also wore a breastplate with twelve precious stones engraved with the names of each of the tribes of Israel. In the pocket of the breastplate, two stones called Urim and Thummim (Exodus 28:30) were directly over the priest's heart. The high priest also wore a turban (mitre) or headdress with an attached gold plate inscribed with the words, "Holiness to the Lord." The words served as a reminder to the priest that they served a pure and Holy God.

BIBLICAL FACT

The Urim and Thummim, the two gem stones that mean "perfection" and "light," were used as a divine guidance for Israel. No scholars agree on how they worked. Some believe the stones were like a pair of dice while others think they were engraved with symbols which meant yes and no, or true and false. Before the Scriptures were written or collected, these stones were used to seek God's guidance.

Leviticus also provides the Jewish people with a series of major festivals to celebrate and remember the workings of God. (Leviticus 23–25) Specific regulations are given for the following:

- The Sabbath
- The Passover
- The Feast of Unleavened Bread
- The Feast of First Fruits (Harvest)
- The Feast of Weeks or Pentecost

- The Feast of Trumpets (later known as Rosh Hashanah)
- The Day of Atonement (the most holy day of the year)
- The Feast of Tabernacles (also called the Feast of Booths)

Every seventh sabbath year, or 50 years, the people were to celebrate the Year of Jubilee, where they cancelled all debts and set free any slaves. The Year of Jubilee prevented any long-term poverty within families.

BIBLICAL FACT

The number seven probably represented completeness and perfection. This number was significant throughout the Mosaic Law. Every seventh day was the Sabbath. Every seventh year was the sabbath year. Every seventh sabbath year followed a Year of Jubilee. Every seventh month was especially holy, with three feasts. There were seven weeks between Passover and Pentecost. The Passover feast lasted seven days. The Feast of Tabernacles lasted seven days.

NUMBERS

The Book of Numbers describes the events of the Jewish people before they enter the Promised Land. The chapters contain long lists of names and numbers, which sometimes discourage readers. The ancient Israelites celebrated the contents of Numbers as the final roll call before the battle. God protected the Jewish people as they wandered the desert for 40 years. The book contains two main sections and each begins with a numbering or a census. A member of each tribe was sent into Canaan to report. (Numbers 13) The men returned with the report that the land was rich and flowed with milk and honey. Yet their report also stirred fear in the hearts of the people as they described powerful cities and giants. Caleb from the tribe of Judah and Hoshea or Joshua from the tribe of Ephraim wanted the people to trust God and move ahead. Instead they rebelled and said, "Wouldn't it be better for us to go back to Egypt?" (Numbers 14:3)

The anger of the Lord burned at the response of the people to his promise. In his glory, the Lord told Moses that he would strike the Jewish people with a plague, then rebuild them through Moses. The great leader pleaded with God to spare the people. God answered Moses' prayers, but with a price for the people. They would wander 40 years in the desert, and no one except Joshua and Caleb would be allowed to enter the land. Disappointed, the Jewish people decided to try to conquer the land under their own strength. Without God's hand of protection, the people were quickly defeated.

As the people wandered and died in the desert, the Bible is silent until the first month of the fortieth year. (Numbers 33:38) Again the people face a water shortage and once again the entire community rises up against Moses and Aaron. God commands Moses to speak to a rock for the water to flow. Perhaps in exasperation from the continual grumbling from the people, Moses instead lifts his staff and strikes the rock twice and it gushes with water for the people. Because Moses struck instead of spoke, the Lord tells Moses that he and Aaron will not be allowed into the Promised Land. Only Joshua and Caleb will have this privilege.

The second major portion of Numbers also begins with a census. (Numbers 26:1–65) Who will lead the people into Canaan? God declares Joshua the successor to Moses. "Then he laid his hands on Joshua and commissioned him, as the Lord instructed through Moses." (Numbers 27:23)

DEUTERONOMY

The fifth book in the Bible is the final book attributed to Moses as the writer. Deuteronomy means "second law." Now a second generation was ready to enter Canaan. Deuteronomy recounts some of the history of the people and the various laws. At this time, the Jewish people didn't have a king although the king was required to make a copy of this book for himself. Most Bible scholars believe the book is a series of addresses, which Moses delivers during the final months of his life. This narrative contains several key themes:

- The importance of remembering God's Word (Deuteronomy 6:4–12)
- The riches of divine provision and the dangers of forgetfulness and idolatry (Deuteronomy 8)
- The blessings of obedience and the curses of sin (Deuteronomy 28)

One of the most touching stories in Deuteronomy is the final chapter. Moses, who has faithfully led the people around the wilderness for 40 years, is permitted to climb Mount Nebo to survey the land that Israel will conquer. (Deuteronomy 34) Moses comes down the mountain, then dies, and is greatly mourned. The final verse summarizes Moses' life, "For no one has ever shown the mighty power or performed the awesome deeds that Moses did in the sight of all Israel." (Deuteronomy 34:12)

THE OLD TESTAMENT SYSTEM OF SACRIFICE

A major section of these three books (Leviticus, Numbers, and Deuteronomy—and particularly Leviticus) is the system of sacrifice. Through detailed laws, God established five sacrifices:

- The *burnt offering* was with a bull, ram, or male bird and used for the atonement of unintentional sin in general and the expression of complete surrender to God.

- The *grain offering* used grain, fine flour, olive oil, incense, baked bread, or salt to recognize and celebrate God's goodness and provisions.

- The *fellowship offering* involved an animal without defects or a variety of breads as a voluntary act of worship, thanksgiving, and fellowship.

- The *sin offering* used different sacrifices according to the status of the person offering it: young bull (high priest and congregation), male goat (leader), female goat or lamb (common person), dove or pigeon (the poor), and a tenth of an ephah of fine flour (the very poor). The sin offering was for specific unintentional sin yet also for confession of sin, forgiveness of sin, and cleansing from defilement.

- The *guilt offering* involved a ram or a lamb and was mandatory atonement for unintentional sin which required restitution; cleansing from defilement; to make restitution; and to pay a 20 percent fine.

The sacrificial system with the unceasing sacrifice of animals and the never-ending glow of altar fires were designed to burn their sinfulness into the hearts of the Israelites. Without God's forgiveness, it was impossible to approach a holy God. The sacrificial system pointed to the sacrifice of Christ on the cross. Because of the sacrifice of Jesus Christ, the animal sacrifices are no longer necessary. Jesus Christ became the High Priest and mediator between God and mankind.

Hour's Up!

The Laws of God, the Commandments, the construction of the Tabernacle, and the sacrificial system are more than simply rules in the Bible, they teach us lessons for today. In the next few minutes, consider some questions which return to the information in this hour and cause you to consider how these passages will apply to your life.

1. Consider how the Lord guided the Israelites with the cloud in the day and fire in the night. How does God guide your day-to-day life?

2. The Israelites passed through the Red Sea on dry ground and were rescued from the clutches of Pharaoh's army. Yet how soon did they begin grumbling? Do you celebrate God's rescue and then quickly grumble? What signposts can you create in your life as reminders of God's faithfulness?

3. Revisit how Jethro, Moses' father-in-law, taught him the skill of delegation. (Exodus 18) What practical application can you make in your daily life? Are there skills you are hoarding that you could pass on to family or co-workers so they could learn from the experience?

4. Reread the Ten Commandments. (Exodus 20:1–17) Four of these commands are about our attitude toward God and six are about our attitude toward humankind. Are there several that stand out for you? Pause and ask God to teach you how to become more like him and move toward increased holiness.

5. While Moses went up Mt. Sinai to receive the commandments, what happened among the people? How easily did they forget about God and create a golden calf? What does this story teach us about our need for vigilance in guarding our relationship with God? How can you strengthen your vigilance this coming week?

6. Detailed instructions were included about the Tabernacle. God created the Tabernacle as his dwelling place. Note the irony where a wandering people without a homeland would call God their dwelling place. The people needed a physical place to symbolize their relationship with God. Where does God dwell in your life? Can you celebrate the in-dwelling Spirit of God in your life? How?

7. The Ark of the Covenant was filled with reminders of God's faithfulness. What "symbols" are in your life to remind you of God's leading and guidance and faithfulness? (A worn Bible? A necklace? An old church bulletin?)

8. The priest had elaborate garments and the High Priest had additional garments. The New Testament calls Jesus our High Priest and mediator between God and man. (Hebrews 9:15) Reflect on Jesus' role as the High Priest in your life. What does this mean to you?

9. The various festivals were to celebrate and remember God's working in the lives of the Jewish people. How do you look at holidays like Easter and Christmas? Are they celebrations of remembrance? How can you increase your Biblical understanding of these holidays for the future? Make plans today.

10. Return to the various sacrifices. These sacrifices are not needed today because of the New Testament role of Jesus Christ. How has Jesus taken the place of each of these sacrifices? Reflect and celebrate.

HOUR 5

Conquering the Land

CHAPTER SUMMARY

LESSON PLAN:

In this hour, you will learn about ...

- Joshua and the battles for Canaan.
- The judges of Israel— Deborah, Gideon, Samson, and Samuel.
- The Israelites' demand for a king.

For years, the Jewish people wandered in the desert. Moses, the leader of the Jewish nation, was not allowed to enter into the new land, so Joshua and Caleb led a new generation of people into the Promised Land. Canaan was a land that flowed with milk and honey and had many cities. Against all odds, the Jewish people began to fight against fortified cities with inexperienced warriors and low-quality weapons. As they followed God's laws and obeyed his will, they conquered the land.

The odds against winning these battles took incredible leadership from Joshua. Joshua's faith in the power of God guided the people to incredible feats. Joshua stood in the shadow of Moses for years and learned from this leader. He knew the importance of staying close to the Book of the Law. In a key verse, Joshua says, "Do not let this Book of the Law depart from your mouth; meditate on it day and night, so that you may be careful to do everything written in it. Then you will be prosperous and successful. Have I not commanded you? Be strong and courageous. Do not be terrified; do not be discouraged, for the Lord your God will be with you wherever you go." (Joshua 1:8–9)

BIBLICAL FACT

As the Jewish people entered the Promised Land, the Lord repeated the miracle of the parting of the Red Sea and God confirmed the leadership of Joshua to take the mantle of Moses. The waters parted and the people entered on dry land. (Joshua 3:14–17) Years later the prophet Elisha was confirmed as the successor to the prophet Elijah with a similar miracle. (2 Kings 2:14)

JOSHUA AND THE BATTLES FOR CANAAN

Some of the most violent chapters in the Bible are contained in the Book of Joshua. As God gave the Jewish people the land, they destroyed once-mighty nations and eliminated the memory of these people from the face of the earth. Throughout these battles, Joshua displayed great faith as he led his army against some impossible odds.

JERICHO

In one of the first chapters of the Book of Joshua, a short story indicates from where Joshua drew his daily strength and courage. As Joshua stood near the fortified city of Jericho, he looked up and saw a man standing with a drawn sword. "Are you for us or for our enemies?" (Joshua 5:13) "Neither," he replied, "but as a commander of the army of the Lord I have now come."

Joshua fell with his face to the ground and worshipped, then asked, "What message does my Lord have for his servant?" The commander of the Lord's army replied, "Take off your sandals, for the place where you are standing is holy."

When this passage was originally translated, the scholars capitalized the reference to this person, believing that he was a possible Christophany (an Old Testament visitation by Jesus Christ). Joshua's lack of protest to the man and his act of worship is strong evidence to this fact. The commander of the Lord's army told Joshua that he was neither friend nor enemy but on the Lord's side. This supernatural encounter early in the days of his leadership provided Joshua with strength and faith to affirm the power for his conquests came from the living God.

HISTORICAL FACT

One of the oldest cities in Palestine, Jericho was located on the west bank of the Jordan River almost 10 miles north of the Dead Sea. After Joshua conquered the city, it was abandoned until the time of King Ahab, when Hiel the Bethelite rebuilt it at the cost of his two sons, who fulfilled Joshua's curse that death would follow anyone who tried to rebuild it. (Joshua 6:26; 1 Kings 16:34)

One of the best-known stories in the Bible is the fall of Jericho. The number seven is prominent in the fall of the city. Seven priests were to carry seven rams' horns or trumpets in front of the Ark of the Covenant for seven days around the city. Each day the people were commanded to silently follow the priests and the Ark around the city, then return to their camp. Imagine the people of Jericho watching this huge band of people circle their city in silence.

CULTURAL FACT

> Jericho had a double wall around the city. The city was built on a mound, with the first wall, made of stone, surrounding it. The first wall held in place a flat rampart, above which stood the second wall, made of mud brick, that was Jericho's proper city wall. When the stone wall fell, the mud brick wall collapsed and slid down the slope, creating a pile of rubble that the attackers could climb over.

On the seventh day, the Jewish people walked around the city six times. On the seventh circuit, the priests sounded the trumpet and Joshua commanded the people, "Shout! For the Lord has given you the city! The city and all that is in it are to be devoted to the Lord. Only Rahab the prostitute and all who are with her in her house shall be spared, because she hid the spies we sent. But keep away from the devoted things, so that you will not bring about your own destruction by taking any of them. Otherwise you will make the camp of Israel liable to destruction and bring disaster on it. All of the silver and gold and the articles of bronze and iron are sacred to the Lord and must go into his treasury." (Joshua 6:16–19)

During the final trip around the city, the walls crumbled and Joshua's army destroyed every living thing—men and women, young and old, cattle, sheep, and donkeys. The people celebrated God's power in the destruction of Jericho and believed they could conquer the land of Canaan.

CULTURAL FACT

> In the narrative of the falling of Jericho and other Bible stories, a trumpet or shophar sounds. The *shophar* is an animal horn and typically from a goat or a ram. The instrument is used as a signal for warfare (Judges 3:27) and for assembling the people for religious festivals such as the Day of Atonement. (Leviticus 25:9)

The Lessons from Sudden Defeat

Bolstered with confidence from the destruction of Jericho, the Israelites turned their attention to the city of Ai. Joshua did not send all the people to Ai but only 2,000 or 3,000. Instead of achieving victory, the Jewish army faced resistance from the men of Ai; the Jewish army fled and 36 men died. In response to his defeat, Joshua tore his clothes and fell face down with the elders of Israel in front of the Ark of the Covenant where they remained until evening.

Then the Lord told them, "Stand up. Israel has sinned. ... They have taken some of the devoted things. They have stolen, they have lied, they have put them with their own possessions." (Joshua 7:11) God commanded the people to consecrate themselves, and tribe by tribe they appeared before the Lord. To claim the promised land, the Israelites had to maintain their devotion to God. Then the tribe of Judah came forward clan by clan and the Lord selected the Zerahites. Next the various families within the Zerahites clan came forward and the Lord selected the family of Zimri. Within Zimri, the Lord selected Achan. Standing before the commander of Israel, Joshua, Achan confessed to stealing a beautiful robe, 200 shekels of silver, and a wedge of gold, which weighed 50 shekels. Gathering everything that Achan owned (including his sons and daughters and animals), they took him to the Valley of Achor and stoned him, then burned his remains and heaped a large pile of stones over him. In clear demonstration, God showed the Israelites that the only way they could reclaim the land of Canaan was to maintain a holy devotion to God. Any other possible action was nonnegotiable.

With the Lord's blessing, the people went on to conquer Ai and other cities across the promised land. In his farewell address to the people, Joshua reminded his people to renew their covenant with God and declared, "As for me and my house, we will serve the Lord." (Joshua 24:15b) Joshua was buried in the Promised Land. The people also buried the bones of Joseph, which the Israelites had brought out of Egypt. After years of homelessness and wandering, the people found rest.

Remember how Moses passed the mantle of leadership to Joshua? Not all of the land of Canaan was conquered and, with Joshua's death, the people wondered who would lead them. The nation of Israel moved into a new era.

THE JUDGES OF ISRAEL—A STUDY IN CONTRASTS

Judges covers the 350-year period of Israel's history with 14 different judges. The book contrasts God's continual faithfulness to the Jewish people while they repeatedly fall away from God. The book has seven different cycles where the people sin, become slaves, and then experience deliverance or salvation. These leaders were not judges in long black robes, but leaders who God appointed to guide the people through some dark period of their history. This section examines four of the best-known judges—Deborah, Gideon, Samson, and Samuel.

DEBORAH

One of five women in the Old Testament called a prophetess, Deborah decided cases under a palm tree. (Judges 4:4–5) The Israelites were summoned to battle and Barak was supposed to lead them but lacked nerve, so Deborah took the role of leadership. She instructed Barak in the strategy of battle (Judges 4:9, 14) and is called the "mother of Israel." (Judges 5:7) Deborah was a good role model for a leader in Israel because she stood for God and integrity. From her leadership, "the land had peace for forty years." (Judges 5:31)

GIDEON

Have you heard the expression "putting a fleece before the Lord"? To "put out a fleece" is to test God's will and ask the Lord to respond one way or another.

This expression comes from the story of Gideon, another one of Israel's judges. Once again the people had swung from obedience to disobedience. The Lord chose his deliverer or judge—Gideon from the Abierzite clan of the tribe of Manasseh. To illustrate the depth of disobedience among the Israelite people, Joash, the father of Gideon, built an altar to Baal and, beside it, an Asherah pole to another god. To purge Israel of its disobedience to the Lord, Gideon began with his own father. One night, he destroyed the altar to Baal and the Asherah pole, built a new altar to the Lord God, and sacrificed on it. The next morning the people wanted to retaliate against Gideon. His father, Joash, said, "If Baal is really a god, he can defend himself when someone breaks down his altar." (Judges 6:31) The people began to call Gideon by a new name—Jerub-Baal, or "Let Baal contend with him"—because he broke the altar of Baal.

That night, Gideon asked the Lord whether he was going to use Gideon to rescue Israel. Gideon put a fleece in the threshing floor and asked God to make the fleece wet and the ground dry the next morning. The following morning, he squeezed out a bowl of water from the fleece. Then he posed the opposite test to the Lord. Again Gideon put out the fleece; this time, he asked that the ground be wet but the fleece remain dry if he was to attack the Midianites for Israel. "That night God did so. Only the fleece was dry; all the ground was covered with dew." (Judges 6:40)

Gideon sounded a call to gather Israel to fight the Midianites. Thirty-two thousand men were ready to fight. The Lord told Gideon that he had too many men. The Lord, through Gideon, announced, "Anyone who trembles with fear may turn back and leave Mount Gilead." (Judges 7:3) Twenty-two thousand men left, and ten thousand men remained to fight. Again the Lord said there were too many men for the fight. Gideon took the men down to the water. The men who lapped the water with their tongues like a dog were separated from the men who kneeled down to drink the water. Three hundred men lapped like dogs while the others knelt to drink. "The Lord said to Gideon, 'With the three hundred men that lapped I will save you and give the Midianites into your hands. Let all the other men go each to his own place.'" (Judges 7:7) The number of fighting men had slipped from 32,000 to 300!

What a dramatic reduction and something that only God could engineer. Gideon positioned the men with torches and clay jars and trumpets. They surrounded the camp, blew their trumpets and broke the clay jars so the torches were clearly seen. The Lord caused such confusion that the Midianites turned on each other and killed each other with their swords. It was a remarkable victory for Israel and Gideon.

SAMSON

Samson was born during another difficult cycle for the Jewish people. They had been under the Philistines' rule for 40 years. An angel appeared to his mother saying she would have a child who should be a Nazirite from birth for the rest of his life. All Nazirites, whether male or female, made a voluntary vow of separation to God, which included three rules:

- They abstained from wine or any strong drink.
- They didn't cut their hair.
- They had no contact with the dead. (Numbers 6:3–8)

Samson and his mother were both to follow the regulations. Samson's service was remarkable in several ways. He did not take the vow himself but it happened before his birth. He served throughout his lifetime and he eventually broke every stipulation for a Nazirite. He drank at his wedding, he associated with the dead, and his head was sheared (in the famous story of Samson and Delilah).

Samson was an unusual judge because often it seemed he did whatever he wanted (like marrying a Philistine woman), yet his life shows again God's faithfulness to stay with his people even when they rebel. After a number of events, Samson fell to the wiles of Delilah who coaxed Samson to tell his secret of his hair. She secretly cut his hair, thus eliminating Samson's strength. With his strength gone, Samson was captured by the Philistines, who gouged out his eyes and took him as a slave. One day during a celebration to Dagon, the Philistine god, the Philistines brought out Samson as a prized slave. He gripped two pillars of the stadium, prayed for God's strength, and brought down the roof, killing more than 3,000 people, including himself. In his life and death, Samson showed how the Lord empowers people to meet the challenges of life.

BIBLICAL FACT

Samson seemingly broke every rule. He violated his prohibition to touch the dead. (Judges 14:19) He probably drank wine. He revealed the secret that his strength was from his hair and it was cut. (Judges 16:13–17) In this way, his involvement with Delilah caused his downfall. Despite this bad boy image, Samson is listed as a hero of the faith. (Hebrews 11:32) His life is a sobering reminder that great abilities are not the same as great faith.

SAMUEL

Judges shows the moral, political, and spiritual corruption of the Jewish people after the leadership of Joshua. The next section of the Bible shows how Israel is brought back into a worship relationship with the Lord of the Universe.

The story begins with a woman struck with a horrible cultural crisis—she was childless. Each year, Hannah came to the temple of Jerusalem to pray and plead with God for a child. One day the high priest, Eli, spotted this woman in fervent prayer and accused her of being drunk. She confessed to praying in great pain and anguish so Eli asked the Lord to grant her petition. The next year, Hannah was pregnant and she named her newborn Samuel. Because of God's divine intervention, Hannah gave Samuel to Eli after Samuel was weaned for continual service in the temple.

PEOPLE TO KNOW

For 40 years, Eli served as a judge and priest for Israel. Eli's sons committed immorality with women in the temple. (1 Samuel 2:12–17, 22) As a leader, Eli was in a position of authority to stop these abuses but he did not do so. The one bright spot for Eli's household was the boy Samuel, who became one of the greatest judges of Israel.

Eli's sons were wicked and displeased the Lord through their corrupt actions regarding the animal sacrifices. When Samuel was a young boy, one night the Lord called out to Samuel. God had been silent for many years. Samuel ran to Eli because he thought the priest called for him. After the third time Samuel said he heard his named called, Eli realized God was speaking to the boy and told him to respond, "Speak, Lord, for your servant is listening." This story marked the first time that God spoke through the prophet Samuel.

The Israelites went out to fight the Philistines but in their battle, they were defeated and 4,000 Jews were killed. The elders thought maybe the battle results would turn in their favor if they brought the Ark of the Covenant. Eli's two sons, Hophni and Phinehas, entered the battle with the Ark. When the Ark entered the Hebrew camp, the people shouted and the Philistines wondered, "What's all the shouting about?" They learned that the Ark of the Lord entered the camp and the Philistines said, "We're in trouble! Nothing like this has ever happened before. Who will deliver us from the hand of these mighty gods? They are the gods who struck the Egyptians with all kinds of plagues in the desert. Be strong, Philistines! Be men, or you will be subject to the Hebrews, as they have been to you. Be men and fight!" (1 Samuel 4:8–9)

While the Israelites brought the Ark, which was a symbol of God's presence, they were living in disobedience to the commands of God. In the battle, the Philistines defeated Israel, killed 30,000 men, and captured the Ark of the Covenant. They also killed Eli's two sons and when the battle news reached Eli, he fell off a wall and died. (1 Samuel 4)

With the captured Ark, the Philistines entered into Dagon's temple. The next morning, the stone god, Dagon, was lying face down on the ground. They put the statue upright; the following morning, Dagon was again on the ground with his head and hands broken and lying on the threshold. Because the ungodly Philistines had the Lord's Ark, the Philistines broke out in tumors and decided to ask their rulers what to do about it. The rulers recommended moving the Ark to different Philistine cities. The change didn't help because then the people in the new city broke out with tumors. So they moved the Ark to a third city and its people, too, broke out with tumors. After seven months of terror, the Philistines turned to their priests and diviners, who recommended returning the Ark to Israel. The Ark was returned to Israel.

After the deaths of Eli and his sons, Samuel became the leader among the people and spoke on behalf of God for many years. As Samuel grew old, he appointed his sons as the judges for Israel. "But his sons did not walk in his ways. They turned aside after dishonest gain and accepted bribes and perverted justice." (1 Samuel 8:3) It's almost unbelievable, but Samuel's sons were as wicked as the sons of Eli. The Jewish people were about to enter a new era in their history.

THE ISRAELITES DEMAND A KING

One day the elders of Israel came to Samuel at Ramah and said, "You are old, and your sons do not walk in your ways; now appoint a king to lead us, such as all the other nations have." (1 Samuel 8:5) This request displeased the Lord; since his people left Egypt, God had served in the role of a leader or king, albeit one not visible to his subjects. Now the people wanted a human king. Speaking for God, Samuel warned the people that a king would create many hardships. A king would take young men to fight in wars and to farm his fields. Also a king would draft young women to serve in his palace and serve his court. Then a king would tax the people and take the best of their flocks and crops. Finally a king would take away the people's personal freedoms.

The people listened to Samuel's warnings, then responded "No! We want a king over us. Then we will be like all the other nations, with a king to lead us and to go out before us and fight our battles." Reluctantly the Lord allowed the Israelites to have their king. The people wondered, who would be this king?

Samuel waited for the arrival of a 30-year-old man named Saul, "an impressive young man without equal among the Israelites—a head taller than any of the others." (1 Samuel 9:3) In a private ceremony, Samuel anointed Saul as king.

CULTURAL FACT

Anointing with oil was a widespread Old Testament practice. Oil was a means of personal cleansing and a mark of honor to a distinguished guest. The practice of anointing had particular significance with figures in public office. Kings, priests, and prophets were anointed as a sign of being chosen by God. The word *Messiah* means "one who is appointed" and became the sense of "one appointed by God" for the salvation of His people.

After Samuel anointed Saul, he received the Spirit of the Lord. (1 Samuel 10:9–11) Saul confirmed his leadership through a successful offensive against the invading Ammonite army. (Samuel 11:1–11) Then Samuel publicly installed Saul as king of Israel in Gilgal, the site of Joshua's campaigns during the conquest of Canaan. (Samuel 11:12–15)

The Israelites prepared to battle the Philistines. Saul and his troops waited seven days at Gilgal for Samuel to arrive and sacrifice before they went into battle. When Samuel failed to appear on schedule, the men lost their motivation to fight, and some scattered. To solve this situation, Saul took the sacrifice into his own hands and made the offerings. As the king finished the burnt offerings, Samuel arrived, saying, "You have acted foolishly. You have not kept the command the Lord your God gave you; if you had, he would have established your kingdom over Israel for all time. But now your kingdom will not endure; the Lord has sought out a man after his own heart and appointed him leader of his people, because you have not kept the Lord's command." (1 Samuel 13:13–14) For 42 years, Saul reigned over Israel; the history of the Jewish people, however, would take another significant turn, as detailed in the next hour.

HOUR'S UP!

Joshua leading the people into the Promised Land, the various judges, and the beginning of the kings are more than "nice" stories. These stories are recorded for your personal growth and application to everyday life. Take a few minutes to explore how these stories are relevant to you in the following questions.

1. Consider Joshua and his leadership of the Jewish people. What can you learn about God's demands for holy living and how the Lord will bless those who follow his law? How have you been following God's laws?

2. To tumble the walls of Jericho, the Jewish people walked in faith for seven days and did some unusual things—like walking silently around the city with the Ark of the Covenant. Take a moment and pause with the Scriptures. Is God asking you to take some unusual measures with a family member, co-worker, or neighbor? Write it down, and then commit to following God's leading this coming week and trusting him for the results.

3. During the days of Joshua, God initiated a firm policy regarding "devoted things" or things which were to be given to God. Today, the Lord still doesn't want us to make our "things" a higher priority than a relationship with God. Take a moment and consider if you've fallen into a cultural, material trap. In what areas? List them in the margin, then make a plan to break from them and replace them with a deeper desire for holiness.

4. As you revisit the life of the judge Deborah, what can you take away about her integrity and consistency? Is this something you need in your own life? Take a few moments in prayer and ask God to bring a person or action into your life that will help in these areas.

5. The Book of Judges reveals a vicious cycle of sin, slavery, repentance, and salvation—seven times! It also shows the deep and abiding compassion and love of God no matter how far you've failed. Consider a failure in your life during the past week (everyone has at least one). Take a moment to celebrate God's faithful love, yet also to plan a course of action to halt this failure in the future and grow from this experience.

6. Think about the life of Samson. His strength and deeds are something commonly known in the Bible. Consider Samson's disconnect between his great ability and his lack of faith in God. List several of your abilities. Are you using these abilities for God in some capacity? How could you in the future? Pause and ask God to increase your faith, then consciously watch to see how God will begin to work in your daily life.

7. Hannah persisted in prayer for years and asked God for a child. What can her example teach us about prayer? Do you expect God to instantly answer your prayers or do you labor in prayer for a long-term solution like Hannah?

8. As a young boy, Samuel listened to God and heard his voice. He became the first of the prophets in the Bible. Samuel made a daily priority to turn to God. What can you learn from his example?

9. Consider the lack of spiritual training in the sons of Eli and Samuel. When these sons perverted the Law of God before the Jewish people, the fathers could have been proactive in cutting short this action—but they didn't. Is there some area in your child's life where you need to continue to parent? Even when they are adults, can you do it gently?

10. When Israel wanted a king, the Lord selected Saul for the job. Yet Saul was interested in his own agenda more than God's plans. God knew Saul's heart and withdrew his blessing. The Israel monarchy would continue but in the hands of another family. Is there a lesson about your agenda versus God's agenda that you can draw from Saul's life?

PART II

The Kings and the Prophets

HOUR 6

The Kings

CHAPTER SUMMARY

LESSON PLAN:

In this hour, you will learn about ...

- The life of King David, a man after God's own heart.
- The events of King Solomon, the wisest man who lived on earth.
- How the kingdom of Judah and Israel was divided.

As a result of the Israelites' demand to have a king "like the other nations," the Jewish nation moved into a new period of its history. Instead of following an invisible God and king, the people wanted a human being. Immediately in their first king, Saul, they began to see the failure of a human king.

This hour emphasizes two key kings in the history of Israel—David and his son Solomon. The final portion of the hour will examine the divided kingdom and how as a result of disobedience to God, the people are divided.

DAVID, A MAN AFTER GOD'S OWN HEART

Different Bible leaders wear key names. Abraham was a friend of God. Moses was a man who talked with God face to face. David holds a distinction in Scripture of being a man after God's own heart. As a boy, David spent hours caring for sheep in the fields. In those quiet moments, David learned to play the harp and created songs and psalms to the Lord. The psalms will be covered later in this book but they show the range of emotions that David had in his relationship with God. Look carefully at the emotion words in a short psalm of ascents from David (Psalm 131):

- "My heart is not proud, O Lord, my eyes are not haughty.
- I do not concern myself with great matters or things too wonderful for me.

- But I have stilled and quieted my soul, like a weaned child with its mother; like a weaned child is my soul within me.
- O Israel, put your hope in the Lord both now and forevermore."

The prophet Samuel was old and gray, looking for the Lord to provide a new leader for Israel. While he anointed Saul, Samuel knew another would stand in Saul's place because Saul had been disobedient. The old prophet continued to mourn for Saul and the Lord was sorry he had ever made Saul king of Israel. (1 Samuel 15:35)

Then one day the Lord told Samuel, "How long will you mourn for Saul, since I have rejected him as king over Israel? Fill your horn with oil and be on your way; I am sending you to Jesse of Bethlehem. I have chosen one of his sons to be king." (1 Samuel 16:1) Samuel knew Saul would be watching him so he asked the Lord how to deceive the king. God told him to take a heifer to sacrifice and invite Jesse to the sacrifice.

Arriving in Bethlehem, Samuel carefully examined each of the sons of Jesse and tried to determine which person God had selected as the new king of Israel. When the oldest son, Eliab, arrived, Samuel thought, "Here's the new king." Yet the Lord said something key to his character and all of Scripture, "Do not consider his appearance or his height, for I have rejected him. The Lord does not look at the things man looks at. Man looks at the outward appearance, but the Lord looks at the heart." (1 Samuel 16:7)

Samuel continued to look at Jesse's sons for the new king. Seven sons walked in front of the prophet but none of them were chosen. Samuel asked Jesse, "Are these all the sons you have?" The father replied, "There is still the youngest but he is tending the sheep." Samuel said, "Send for him; we will not sit down until he arrives." (1 Samuel 16:11) Everyone waited for the arrival of the final son. As David entered the room, the Lord said, "Rise and anoint him, he is the one." From this anointing, God's Spirit rested with power on David, the son of Jesse.

With the selection of David as the future king, the Spirit of God left King Saul. An evil spirit tormented Saul. A servant suggested David could play the harp and soothe the king. David became one of King Saul's armor bearers. The appointment to the king's court was clearly not permanent as David continued to tend his father's sheep.

THE GIANT AND FIVE STONES

During one of Saul's periodic battles with the Philistines, a nine-foot giant named Goliath confronted Saul and the Israelites. He challenged Israel to choose a single man and battle him; whichever survived would conquer the entire nation of his enemy. No one wanted to fight Goliath and the men were terrified of his shouting. For 40 days, Goliath came out in the morning and the evening shouting his challenge for a fight.

BIBLICAL FACT

> Goliath's armored coat was made of overlapping plates of bronze, which were sewn on the leather. His armor weighed about 120 pounds. The giant's spear was like a long sword; it was used in hand-to-hand combat and weighed about 15 pounds.

Jesse asked David to take some bread and cheese to his brothers who were in the Israelite army. The father wanted some reassurance of the health and condition of his sons in battle so he asked David for a report. When David arrived at the camp, he heard the challenge from Goliath and responded, "Who is this uncircumcised Philistine that he should defy the armies of the living God?" (1 Samuel 17:26)

David's oldest brother, Eliab, confronted his youngest brother's courageous statement and questioned why he had come to the camp. David's defiance was reported to Saul and the king sent for him. The king admired his courage but said, "You are only a boy, and he has been a fighting man since his youth." David told the king about defending his sheep from a bear and a lion with the Lord's help. Saul permitted David to represent Israel in the fight and tried to fit him with armor but David wasn't used to such equipment.

Instead, he selected five smooth stones and went to fight Goliath. At first, Goliath mocked David's small size, then moved to attack him. David quickly put a stone in his sling and struck Goliath's forehead with such force that it sank in his face. The giant fell to the ground and David rushed to get his huge sword and then cut off his head. With the Philistine champion defeated, the enemy turned and ran with the Israelites pursuing. (1 Samuel 17)

SAUL CHASES DAVID

After such a great victory, the people sang, "Saul has slain his thousands, and David his tens of thousands." (1 Samuel 18:7) King Saul saw David's success and was afraid of David because he could tell the Lord was with the young man. Saul's jealousy of David grew as David continually succeeded in other battles. Finally, King Saul attempted to have David killed, but Saul's son, Jonathan, who was fond of David, warned him of the plot. Saul tried to kill David himself and David escaped, becoming a nomad with his own small army of men. Saul continued to chase David, and yet with God's protection, David escaped every time. During this time, David had two opportunities to kill Saul, but David spared the king because Saul was the anointed king of Israel.

JUST A MINUTE

Twice David spared Saul's life—once in the cave at En Gedi (1 Samuel 24:1–7) and again in the wilderness of Ziph (1 Samuel 26:2, 7–12). Although Saul was bent on destroying David, and Saul often acted demented and unfit for office, David refused to kill Saul because he respected the office of the king. David's example serves as a model for how God's people should respect their government leaders—even though they may not care for their actions or policies.

With Saul acting like a madman, David took his small army of 600 men and settled in Ziglag, a Philistine city. He agreed to serve the Philistine king on demand. When the Philistines prepared to go to battle with Saul and the Israelites, the Philistine leaders sent David away from the battle because they didn't feel they could trust his allegiance. King Saul was wounded during the battle and committed suicide on his sword.

DAVID ESTABLISHES HIS DYNASTY

David lamented the death of Saul and his son, Jonathan, who was a close friend of David's and then became king of Israel. (2 Samuel 4:1–5:5) After David was established as the king, he captured Jerusalem and renamed it "the city of David."

Because the country was stabilized from the military action, David brought the Ark of the Covenant into Jerusalem. The king wanted to build a permanent home for the Ark, or a temple, in Jerusalem. Because of David's love and devotion for God, the Lord spoke through Nathan the prophet, saying, "The Lord declares to you that the Lord himself will establish a house for you: When your days are over and you rest with your fathers, I will raise up an offspring to succeed you, who will come from your own body, and I will establish his kingdom." (2 Samuel 7:11b–12) King David's heirs would rule Israel.

This prophecy from Nathan points to the arrival of a Messiah—Jesus Christ, who was a direct descendant of King David. Because David was a man of many battles, the Lord didn't permit David to build the temple. Because David had been a man of war and bloodshed, God didn't permit him to construct the Lord's temple. Instead David prepared the various building supplies for the temple and gave the plans to his successor.

DEVOTED YET IMPERFECT

One spring, when the king normally went off to fight battles, David stayed behind in Jerusalem. One evening while walking on the roof of his palace, he saw a beautiful woman named Bathsheba, who was bathing. Bathsheba was married to Uriah, the Hittite. David sent for Bathsheba and slept with her. A few weeks later, she sent word to David that she was pregnant.

To cover his sin, David sent for Uriah, expecting the soldier to come back from war and sleep with his wife. Instead Uriah slept in the entrance to the palace. When David questioned him about it, Uriah replied, "How can I sleep with my wife, when the Ark of the Covenant and the soldiers are in tents?" (2 Samuel 11:11) To cover his own sin, David sent word to his commander to place Uriah at the front of the battle so he would be killed. After an appropriate period of mourning, David sent for Bathsheba and she became David's wife. Bathsheba gave birth to David's son.

However, not all was well after Uriah's demise. David's sin did not go unnoticed by God. Nathan the prophet came and visited David and told a parable about a rich man who stole a little lamb from a poor man. David was furious and said the man should be punished. Nathan told David, "You are the man! ... Why did you despise the word of the Lord by doing evil in his eyes?" (2 Samuel 12:7, 9)

In punishment, the Lord struck the child. During the illness, the king prayed and fasted. On the seventh day, the child died and David noticed his servants were whispering. He asked, "Is the child dead?" And the servants answered, "Yes." David changed his clothes, went into the house of the Lord and worshipped, and then ate. As long as the child lived, David hoped for the Lord's graciousness but when the child died, David knew there was nothing else to be done. He comforted his wife, Bathsheba, slept with her, and she became pregnant with a son, whom they named Solomon.

David ruled Israel 40 years until he was an old man. His life wasn't perfect and some of his judgments were flawed. Despite his weaknesses, God took and used David's life so it became a standard for later generations. He was a man after God's own heart. (1 Samuel 13:13–14)

SOLOMON, THE WISEST MAN WHO LIVED ON EARTH

In the final days of David's reign, the king appointed his son, Solomon, as his successor with this advice, "So be strong, show yourself a man, and observe what the Lord your God requires: Walk in his ways, and keep his decrees and commands, his laws and requirements, as written in the Law of Moses, so that you may prosper in all you do and wherever you go, and the Lord may keep his promise to me." (The promise was for continual heirs on the throne.) (1 Kings 2:3–4)

JUST A MINUTE

King David's farewell words to his son and successor, Solomon, are recorded in 1 Kings 2:1–9. Charges of this type were a fairly common way in the ancient world for fathers to pass some final instructions to their children. The key elements are as follows: (1) an acceptance and blunt reminder of death (2:2), (2) a charge to act responsibly (2:2), (3) a reminder of the Lord's covenant with Israel and the house of David (2:3), and (4) instructions to honor David's commitments and to serve with justice.

In Gibeon, King Solomon offered a thousand burnt offerings to the Lord. That night, God appeared in a dream, "Ask for whatever you want me to give you." Solomon confessed insecurity about youth and his inexperience to lead the Jewish people and then made his request, "So give your servant a discerning heart to govern your people and to distinguish between right and wrong. For who is able to govern this great people of yours?" (1 Kings 3:9)

God was pleased that Solomon asked for wisdom and not long life or wealth. God promised to grant Solomon wisdom but also would give him riches and honor "so that in your lifetime you will have no equal among kings." Finally God gave Solomon a conditional promise, "And if you walk in my ways and obey my statutes and commands as David your father did, I will give you long life." (1 Kings 3:14) In the next few pages, you will see how Solomon both did and did not fulfill this commandment for obedience during his lifetime.

HISTORICAL FACT

Under Solomon's leadership, Israel's borders grew and were extended. This growth, combined with extensive building and commercial projects, meant that Solomon needed increased revenues. He divided Israel into 12 districts then appointed governors over each district. These leaders were charged to levy and collect taxes to provide for the increased needs of Jerusalem and the royal family. Judah, the tribe of David and Solomon, was exempt of paying taxes, which provided a major source of tension.

Soon after Solomon returned to Jerusalem, two prostitutes came to the king. The women lived in the same house. One woman had a baby and then three days later the other woman had a baby. During the night, one woman laid on her child and smothered the baby. According to the woman talking to the king, this woman got up and took the other's baby and put it next to her breast. When the woman awoke, she thought her baby died but she looked at him closely and saw it wasn't her son. The other woman who was listening protested saying, "No, the living son is mine and the dead one is yours." They argued before King Solomon.

The king stopped the argument and said, "Bring me a sword. Cut the living baby in two and give half to one and half to the other." The woman whose son was alive was filled with compassion for her son and pleaded for his life to the king saying, "Please, my lord, give her the living baby! Don't kill him!" The woman whose son was dead said, "Neither I nor you shall have him. Cut him in two!"

Observing the responses, King Solomon made his ruling: "Give the living baby to the first woman. Do not kill him; she is his mother." (1 Kings 3:24–27) The entire nation of Israel heard about this decision and held it in awe because they knew Solomon had wisdom to administer divine justice from God.

CULTURAL FACT

The parched landscape of Lebanon today stretches the imagination to consider that 3,000 years ago, the area was covered with massive cedar trees—the cedars of Lebanon. King Solomon sent thousands of laborers to cut cedar and transport it to Jerusalem where it was used for various buildings including his residence called The Forest of Lebanon. (1 Kings 7:2)

Four years into Solomon's reign, he began building the Lord's temple. King David prepared for this project by gathering some of the stones and materials. The temple would provide a permanent home for the Tabernacle and the Ark of the Covenant, which had been built in the desert as the Israelites journeyed away from Egypt.

It took about seven years to build the temple. Chapters 6 and 7 of 1 Kings provide a detailed description of the building and the specialized ornaments. For example, the sea of cast bronze was one piece and set upon 12 bronze oxen to replace the basin of washings for the tabernacle. (1 Kings 7:23–26) This bronze sea held about 11,500 gallons of water. While these remarkable works of art were built to the glory of God, during the construction, the Lord reminded his builder about the importance to keep the law. Keeping the law was more important than the material of cedar and gold. (1 Kings 6:11–13)

After the temple was completed, the priests carried the Ark of the Covenant into the Holy of Holies for Solomon's temple. "When the priests withdrew from the Holy Place, the cloud filled the temple of the Lord. And the priests could not perform their service because of the cloud, for the glory of the Lord filled his temple." (1 Kings 8:10–11)

CULTURAL FACT

The entire Mediterranean region, including Israel, is prone to earthquakes. Serious earthquakes occur about every 50 years. To make the temple earthquake proof, the builders used three courses of cut stones and one of cedar beams, which enabled the building to absorb more shock.

Solomon prayed a prayer of dedication. He reminded the people that God dwells in people—and that despite this remarkable temple in Jerusalem, humankind can't build a house to contain the Lord of the Universe. (1 Kings 8:27) Solomon said that God was a God of all the earth. He stressed the faithfulness of God and also stressed how the king and the Jewish people also needed to follow God faithfully to enjoy his continued blessing.

Also Solomon understood that the Lord wasn't a personal possession of the Jewish people but a God for all peoples. He asked that when the Gentiles pray in the direction of this house that their prayers would be answered as well. King Solomon asked God to create a house of prayer for all nations. (1 Kings 8:41–43)

After a dedication prayer, the priests began a round of sacrificial offerings; according to the sacred historian (2 Chronicles 7:5), a total of 22,000 cattle and 120,000 sheep and goats were sacrificed. The number of animals seems unbelievably large yet the sacrifice involved thousands of priests who used auxiliary altars. (1 Kings 8:4) The dedication of the temple was at the same time as the Feast of Weeks and the usual one-week celebration was extended for two weeks. (2 Chronicles 7:9) A large number of people were customarily fed with fellowship meals after the sacrifices. When the ceremony was over, the people returned home thankful for God's presence in the temple and a new sense of divine guidance for King Solomon and the country.

Whereas this magnificent temple took 7 years to build, the king's palace took 13 years and was even grander than the temple. Solomon's palace served as the administrative hub of his kingdom with five buildings: the House of the Forest of Lebanon, the hall of pillars, the throne room, a palace for Pharaoh's daughter, and a palace for Solomon. Solomon's throne was made of wood and inlaid with ivory. Six steps approached the throne, which was situated on the seventh level. At either end of the 6 steps stood 12 lions. (1 Kings 10:18–20)

Word about Solomon and the splendor of his kingdom spread throughout the earth. The queen of Sheba heard about Solomon's wisdom, and she journeyed to Jerusalem. She came to ask hard questions (also known as riddles or perplexing sayings) to satisfy her own mind. Sheba was the homeland of Sabeans, a people who dealt with precious commodities such as gold, perfumes, and rare spices.

The queen brought a large caravan of camels carrying these precious items. "Solomon answered all of her questions; nothing was too hard for the king to explain to her." (1 Kings 10:3) The queen marveled at King Solomon's organization, the design of his palace, and even the food on his table. "The report I heard in my own country about your achievements and your wisdom is true. But I did not believe these things until I came and saw them with my own eyes. Indeed, not even half was told me; in wisdom and wealth you have far exceeded the report I heard." (1 Kings 10:6–7)

BIBLICAL FACT

Underlying each of King Solomon's accomplishments was his God-given wisdom. His wisdom surpassed all the other known wise men of his day. (1 Kings 4:30–31) He gave 3,000 proverbs, many of which are contained in the Book of Proverbs. He composed 1,005 songs, including Psalm 72 and Psalm 127. (1 Kings 4:32)

Throughout his reign, Solomon accumulated tremendous wealth. As the Bible says, "King Solomon was greater in riches and wisdom than all the other kings of the earth." (1 Kings 10:23)

Beyond his possessions, Solomon also accumulated many foreign women as wives. His wives came from nations where God had specifically commanded the Israelites not to intermarry because it would turn their hearts away from God. (1 Kings 11:2; Deuteronomy 7:1–3) He had 700 wives of royal birth and 300 concubines who led Solomon astray. (1 Kings 11:3)

The king turned away from God as he loved these foreign wives. "As Solomon grew old, his wives turned his heart after other gods, and his heart was not fully devoted to the Lord his God, as the heart of David his father had been. He followed Ashtoreth the goddess of the Sidonians, and Molech, the detestable god of the Ammonites. So Solomon did evil in the eyes of the Lord." (1 Kings 11:4–5) Because of the change in his heart and attitude of following the Lord, God was angry at Solomon and raised up enemies against him. In Jerusalem, Solomon reigned 40 years over Israel. (1 Kings 11:42)

THE DIVIDED KINGDOM—JUDAH AND ISRAEL

Rehoboam succeeded Solomon as the next king. Solomon, in the final years of his rule, had imposed a policy called *corvee* (pronounced *cor-vey*), which forced men and women (including some Jews) into slave labor camps. Solomon used these laborers to build the magnificent storage cities, the temples, and the various royal dwellings.

With Solomon's death, the people wanted corvee to end. They were tired of watching their sons and daughters forced into labor and giving their productive years to government projects. Jeroboam, a leader who had rebelled against Solomon, came to the new king in front of a large assembly from Israel and asked King Rehoboam, "Your father put a heavy yoke on us, but now lighten the harsh labor and the heavy yoke he put on us, and we will serve you." (1 Kings 12:4) Understanding the importance of such a decision, King Rehoboam asked for three days to consider his course of action.

The new king turned to the elders and wise men who served his father, Solomon. They provided wise counsel saying, "If you serve the people as their king and give them a favorable answer, then they will serve you." Unfortunately, the young king, who was full of himself, turned to his companions in the royal court to get a second opinion. These young men answered King Rehoboam with the response he liked saying, "Tell these people … My father laid on you a heavy yoke; I will make it even heavier. My father scourged you with whips; I will scourge you with scorpions." (1 Kings 12:10–11) Of course, King Rehoboam followed the foolish advice of the young men and spoke his response to Jeroboam and the Israel people. The Jewish people rebelled against the house of David.

"When all the Israelites heard that Jeroboam had returned, they sent and called him to the assembly and made him king over all Israel. Only the tribe of Judah remained loyal to the house of David." (1 Kings 12:20) To squelch this rebellion, King Rehoboam assembled 18,000 men from Judah and Benjamin and they prepared for what would have been the bloodiest civil war in the history of Israel. The Bible says that the Word of the Lord came to Shemaiah, who was called a "man of God." With great courage and obedience to God, Shemaiah appeared before King Rehoboam and said, "This is what the Lord says: Do not go up and fight against your brothers, the Israelites. Go home, every one of you, for this is my doing." (1 Kings 20:24) The people obeyed and returned home.

In that moment of Jewish history, the north and south divided forever. The South included the tribe of Judah and the city of Jerusalem. The 10 tribes in the north kept the name Israel and were ruled by Jeroboam. King Jeroboam faced a tremendous opportunity to tear the bulk of the Jewish people away from the godlessness of King Rehoboam, Solomon's son. Instead of drawing the people to God, King Jeroboam moved the people away from the Lord. He created two golden calves for the people to worship and established one in Bethlehem and the other in Dan. He announced to the people, "It is too much for you to go up to Jerusalem. Here are your gods, O Israel, who brought you up out of Egypt." (1 Kings 12:28)

God did not overlook this idol worship. When the son of Jeroboam fell ill, he asked his wife to disguise herself and go to the Lord's prophet Ahijah for help. Now Ahijah had become blind because of his age but the Lord revealed it was King Jeroboam's wife and he said, "I tore the kingdom away from the house of David and gave it to you … You have done more evil than all who lived before you. You have made for yourself other gods, idols made of metal; you have provoked me to anger … Because of this, I am going to bring disaster on the house of Jeroboam." (1 Kings 14:8–10) King Jeroboam ruled for 22 years and led Israel into idolatry and repeatedly turned away from God.

For the remainder of the Old Testament, the kingdom is divided into north and south. The golden age of David and Solomon had ended. More kings would arise in the north and south, but none like David and Solomon.

Israel, the northern kingdom, had 20 kings and 9 dynasties over a 200-year period before the kingdom fell to the Assyrians in 722 B.C. In contrast, Judah, the southern kingdom, also had 20 kings from 1 dynasty and this kingdom lasted 350 years before falling to the Babylonians in 586 B.C.

THE KINGS OF ISRAEL

Let's briefly examine each of Israel's kings with a few details about what happened during their reigns.

- **Jeroboam** (1 Kings 11:26–14:20)   To prevent the people from worshipping in Jerusalem, Jeroboam set up two golden calves. Despite several warnings from God, Jeroboam refused to repent.

- **Nadab** (1 Kings 15:25–28)   The son of Jeroboam. Nadab's name means "generous." Nadab followed in the evil ways of his father. Baasha, a military commander, killed Nadab, then succeeded him as king.

- **Baasha** (1 Kings 15:27–16:7)   In continuation of the sins of Jeroboam, Baasha ruled 24 years and warred with Judah. A prophet named Jehu predicted the downfall of his entire family.

- **Elah** (1 Kings 16:6–14)   The son of Baasha, Elah reigned two years and was prone to a wild lifestyle. One day Zimri, one of his chariot officers, killed Elah when he was drunk, then killed his entire family.

- **Zimri** (1 Kings 16:9–20)   This military officer had a short reign of seven days and his accomplishment was killing the Baasha dynasty. He set his palace on fire and committed suicide.

- **Omri** (1 Kings 16:15–28)   The people selected Omri king and he reigned 12 years. The Bible says that he was more evil than the other kings of Israel who came before him.

- **Ahab** (1 Kings 16:28–22:40; 2 Kings 9:30–37)   This king claimed the title of the most wicked king of Israel. He reigned 22 years and married Jezebel. Among his evil acts, Ahab initiated Baal worship. Both Ahab and Jezebel died bloody deaths.

- **Ahaziah** (1 Kings 22:40–2 Kings 1:18)   The son of Ahab, this king fell through the lattice of his upper room and instead of calling out to God, Ahaziah sought the help of Baal and died from his injuries.

- **Jehoran** (Joram; 2 Kings 3:1–9:25)   He reigned for 12 years and faced a rebellion from Moab who had paid tribute to Ahab. Jehu killed Jehoran.

- **Jehu** (2 Kings 9:1–10:36) A military officer in Ahab's bodyguard, Jehu was anointed by the prophet Elisha to eliminate Baal worship. He killed Jehoran, the king of Israel; Jezebel; Ahaziah, the king of Judah; Ahab's 70 sons; the brothers of Ahaziah; all the friends of Ahab's house; and all the priests and worshippers of Baal. He reigned 28 years but did not follow God and instead allowed golden calves to be worshipped.

- **Jehoahaz** (2 Kings 13:1–9) The son of Jehu, Jehoahaz reigned 17 years and Israel was dominated during his rule by the Syrians.

- **Jehoash** (Joash; 2 Kings 13:10–14:16) King Jehoash fought with Syria and retook the land his father lost. He reigned 16 years and also fought Judah and plundered Jerusalem.

- **Jeroboam II** (2 Kings 14:23–29) This son of Jehoash continued the wars of his father against Syria and reigned for 41 years. The abominable social conditions of the country and the idolatry were challenged by Amos and Hosea.

- **Zechariah** (2 Kings 14:29–15:12) His short reign lasted six months before he was publicly assassinated.

- **Shallum** (2 Kings 15:10–15) After a one-month reign, Menahem assassinated Shallum and took over as the new king.

- **Menahem** (2 Kings 15:14–22) This cold-blooded, evil man was a brutal king who reigned 10 years and taxed the wealthy people of Israel.

- **Pekahiah** (2 Kings 15:22–26) King Pekahiah reigned two years before he was assassinated by one of his chief officers, Pekah.

- **Pekah** (2 Kings 15:27–31) A powerful military officer who reigned 20 years, Pekah was eventually assassinated by Hoshea.

- **Hoshea** (2 Kings 15:30–17:6) This final king of Israel reigned for nine years and paid tribute to the king of Assyria but was secretly forming an alliance with the king of Egypt. The Assyrians came and conquered the northern kingdom and led Israel into captivity.

THE KINGS OF JUDAH

While the kings of Israel were leading their people away from God, the smaller southern kingdom of Judah was a bit better following the Lord—but not much. Here's a brief look at their kings.

- **Rehoboam** (1 Kings 11:42–14:31)   This son of Solomon split the kingdom and allowed the worship of other gods. During the first five years of his reign, an Egyptian king carried off the treasures in the temple and the palace. He reigned for 17 years.
- **Abijam** (1 Kings 14:31–15:8)   King Abijam was wicked like his father but in his battle with King Jeroboam of Israel, Abijam turned to the Lord and won. He reigned three years.
- **Asa** (1 Kings 15:8–24)   Under King Asa, a wave of reform swept the land and he tore down the foreign altars and high places. He reigned 41 years and served the Lord with zeal. Late in his life, he had foot problems and refused to ask the Lord for help. (2 Chronicles 16:12)
- **Jehoshaphat** (1 Kings 22:41–50)   This son of Asa also served the Lord, appointed godly judges, and lived in peace with the kings of Israel. He reigned 25 years.
- **Jehoram** (2 Kings 8:16–24)   Despite a godly father and grandfather, King Jehoram was ruined from his marriage to Athaliah, the daughter of Jezebel. He reigned eight years and died of a horrible intestinal disease, perhaps an extreme form of dysentery. (2 Chronicles 21:18–19)
- **Ahaziah** (2 Kings 8:24–9:29)   The grandson of Jezebel and the son of Athaliah, King Ahaziah reigned one year and was killed by Jehu from Israel.
- **Athaliah** (2 Kings 11:1–20)   The queen for eight years, then the queen mother for one year, Athaliah reigned for eight years and was evil. She had a fanatical devotion to Baalism and massacred her own grandchildren.
- **Joash** (2 Kings 11:1–12:21)   King Joash reigned 40 years. As a child he was hidden in the temple from his wicked grandmother Athaliah. His uncle, Jehoiada, the high priest, engineered the removal of the wicked queen Athaliah. Joash, who became king at age seven, served the Lord as long as Jehoiada, the priest, was alive. During the final years of his life, King Joash set up the idols again in Judah. He was assassinated in his bed in revenge for killing Zechariah, the son of Jehoiada.
- **Amaziah** (2 Kings 14:1–20)   He reigned for 29 years and followed the Lord until toward the end of his life when he worshipped the Edomites' gods and was assassinated.

- **Azariah** (Uzziah; 2 Kings 15:1–7)   Uzziah reigned for 52 years and part of this time probably coregent with his father, Amaziah. He increased his kingdom and followed the Lord for the bulk of his years, then tried to assume the role of a priest and God inflicted Uzziah with leprosy.

- **Jotham** (2 Kings 15:32–38)   Served as a coregent with his father most of his 16-year reign. He followed the Lord, and the leprosy of his father served as a warning of God's possible wrath.

- **Ahaz** (2 Kings 16:1–20)   For part of his reign, Ahaz served as co-regent with his father but as a young king, Ahaz set himself against the practices of his forefathers. He reintroduced Baal worship and revived Molech worship—even sacrificing his own son in a fire. He reigned for 16 years.

- **Hezekiah** (2 Kings 18:1–20:21)   King Hezekiah inherited a disorganized realm but reigned with great reformation for 29 years. He destroyed the idols of Ahaz, reopened and cleansed the temple, and restored worship of God. During his reign, Israel fell to Assyria but Judah was spared.

- **Manasseh** (2 Kings 21:1–18)   King Manasseh was the most wicked of the kings of Judah—and also reigned the longest, for 55 years. He rebuilt the idols and reestablished Baal worship. Tradition says he had the prophet Isaiah sawed in half. In the final days of his life, Manasseh repented and turned to the Lord God. (2 Chronicles 33:12-16)

- **Amon** (2 Kings 21:19–26)   Like his father, Amon was wicked and reigned two years before his officials killed him in his palace.

- **Josiah** (2 Kings 22:1–23:30)   King Josiah was eight years old when he became king and he reigned 31 years. He steadfastly followed the Lord. His discovery of the Book of the Law in the temple led to sweeping religious reform. He reinstituted the Passover, which Israel had neglected for about 300 years. He was killed in battle at Megiddo.

- **Jehoahaz** (2 Kings 23:31–34)   After reigning for three months, King Jehoahaz was overthrown by Pharaoh and taken to Egypt where he died.

- **Jehoiakim** (2 Kings 23:34–24:5)   Pharaoh put Jehoiakim on the throne and he reigned for 11 years. Then he revolted and the king of Babylon came and carried him off to Babylon to die or be killed.

- **Jehoiachin** (2 Kings 24:6–16) The son of Jehoiakim reigned for three months until he was forced to surrender Jerusalem and was carried off to Babylon where he lived at least 37 years.
- **Zedekiah** (2 Kings 24:17–25:30) King Nebuchadnezzar of Babylon put King Zedekiah into power. Zedekiah was a weak king and eventually tried to rebel. The Babylonians crushed King Zedekiah and carried him off in chains, and he died in prison.

The Book of 1 Kings begins with the glory of King Solomon's reign and 2 Kings ends with the Jewish people in captivity: Israel in the hands of the Assyrians and Judah in the control of the Babylonians. These historical books show the strong spiritual decline of the nation.

HOUR'S UP!

David and Solomon and their ancestors are more than historical figures. Their lives and relationship to God have relevance to our lives today. Take a few minutes and consider these questions and discover the relevance for you.

1. Reread Psalm 131. Look at the emotions in this psalm. Are you experiencing some of these same emotions in your relationship with God? Reflect on David's honest relationship with God the Father.

2. Consider how Samuel waited to see which of Jesse's sons would be anointed king. He learned the lesson that God looks at the heart and not like man at the outward appearance. How are you looking at others? On the inside or out? And how do others look at you? On the inside or out?

3. Notice the soothing role of music for King Saul from David. What role does music play in the life of your spirit? Soothing? When do you use it?

4. Note David's sensitivity to leadership—even when he didn't agree with King Saul. How do you respond to such leadership in your life (church, work, home)? Do you seek God for his leadership in your life?

5. David longed to build a temple for the Lord but God didn't allow it. The Lord permitted David to make preparations for his son, Solomon. What are some longings in your heart and how is God preparing these longings to come to fruition or not?

6. While David was a man after God's own heart, he was also human in his frailty and sin with Bathsheba. Often the Bible characters are put on a pedestal. What part is sin playing in your own life and how are you asking God to heal or remove these areas from your life?

7. King Solomon recognized his inexperience and asked the Lord for wisdom. Are there areas in your life where you feel inexperienced? How are you handling it? With your own strength or are you asking for divine guidance and wisdom from God?

8. Solomon built a magnificent temple for God. These passages also tell us that God dwells throughout the earth—not in a particular place or church. Reflect on the presence of God everywhere in the world. What can you do to increase your awareness of God's presence?

9. Reflect on the decision of Rehoboam. He could have made a wise decision and kept the northern and southern kingdoms as one. Where in your life have you made a rash and unwise decision? Have you been in the spiritual desert life for years before you find your way? What happened to make this change? How can you increase your use of Godly wisdom?

10. Twenty kings of Israel and twenty kings of Judah show the up and down pattern of a national relationship with their Heavenly Father. Sometimes they trusted God and other times they turned away. How can you lend more consistency to your daily walk with God? List several ways you can do this such as daily Bible reading, increased prayer, attendance at church, and so on.

HOUR 7

The Major Prophets: Part One

CHAPTER SUMMARY

LESSON PLAN:

In this hour, you will learn about ...

- The significance of two prophets with similar names: Elijah and Elisha.
- Isaiah, who is generally regarded as the greatest of the Old Testament prophets.
- The dark days of Judah and the message of Jeremiah, known as the weeping prophet.

Have you ever had an anchor in your life? Possibly that anchor is a parent, significant teacher, mentor, or friend. Imagine what happens when that person disappears from your life. For a period of time, you lose your way. The Israelites had experienced the miracles of God as they escaped through the dry ground of the Red Sea and fled the grasp of Pharaoh. The Hebrews came into the Promised Land, conquered the region, and then built a magnificent temple to the Lord.

Take a moment and scan through the 40 kings of Israel and Judah in the previous chapter. It's quickly evident the Jewish people had lost their anchor in the Lord. Disobedience had grown to a new level. They had stopped entering the temple for worship. They no longer waited and entered God's presence. The people decided to continue in their immoral ways and to worship other gods such as from the Amorites or Edomites, people from Canaan who they supposedly conquered with the hand of the Lord.

In the midst of this massive disobedience to the Lord, the Old Testament prophets suddenly appeared. These men were given the task to stand in front of the people and tell them what they didn't want to hear. The prophet began with "Thus says the Lord," then usually challenged the people head-on to change their disobedient behavior. This heavenly assignment was filled with danger. The prophets were attacked, tortured, and thrown into prison and pits, and they faced overwhelming loneliness. The prophets were relentless in their confrontation of the people.

CULTURAL FACT

Worshipped throughout the Middle East because of his association with powerful forces, Baal was a pagan god of storms and fertility. In Canaanite literature, the name literally means "husband," "owner," or "master." Worship of these pagan gods involved infant sacrifice, self-mutilation, and ritual prostitution. Despite these evil practices, the Israelites adopted the worship of Baal, which led to God's judgment.

The first five prophets listed in the Old Testament—Elijah, Isaiah, Jeremiah, Ezekiel, and Daniel—are often referred to as the "major" prophets. All other prophets who are included in the Bible are called "minor" prophets. The distinction between major and minor only refers to the amount of Bible material that chronicles the lives of these men. It doesn't refer to their impact on the people of Israel or Judah. The Lord distinctly called each prophet for his service, and each prophet called the people to repentance. The word *prophet* doesn't mean someone who predicts the future like a fortune-teller. Instead these prophets were bold and courageous spokesmen of God's unbending truth.

This hour examines four major prophets and how the Lord used them in the history of Jewish people.

ELIJAH AND ELISHA

Some prophets seem to appear in history for their particular moment, whereas others tend to grow in importance as time passes. Elijah is the latter type of prophet and his role in history grows as time passes. He is the first and the greatest of God's messengers to the Israelite people. He is a part of the final prophecy of the Old Testament in Malachi 4:4–6, "Remember the law of my servant Moses, the decrees and laws I gave him at Horeb for all Israel. See, I will send you the prophet Elijah before that great and dreadful day of the Lord comes. He will turn the hearts of the fathers to their children, and the hearts of the children to their fathers; or else I will come and strike the land with a curse." This reference to Elijah marked the final words for 400 years of silence between the Old Testament and the New Testament.

Another affirmation of the importance of Elijah came in the New Testament. On the Mount of Transfiguration, Elijah appears with Moses and Jesus. (Matthew 17:1–8; Mark 9:2–8; and Luke 9:28–36) Three of the disciples— Peter, James, and John—accompanied Jesus Christ to see a glimpse of his glory and holiness. In this sort of surreal moment, a voice sounded from heaven and the three disciples saw Elijah talking with Jesus and Moses.

These three common disciples were seeing three uncommon men: Jesus, the Son of God; Moses, the giver of the Law; and Elijah, the prophet of God to proclaim God's message to the people.

PEOPLE TO KNOW

In the New Testament, the people asked John the Baptist, "Are you Elijah, the prophet?" (John 1:21) From the final prophecy of Malachi in the Old Testament about Elijah, the Jewish people were watching for the return of the prophet to herald the arrival of the Messiah. The transfiguration of Christ in the New Testament and the inclusion of Elijah confirmed the fact that Jesus is the Messiah.

No information is given about Elijah's parents. He dressed in rugged clothing and suddenly he appeared before King Ahab of Israel, saying, "As the Lord, the God of Israel, lives whom I serve, there will be neither dew nor rain in the next few years except at my word." (1 Kings 17:1) The prophet spoke this warning, left, and hid in the Kerith Ravine to the east of the Jordan River. The Lord told Elijah to drink from the brook and sent ravens to feed the prophet. In the mornings and in the evenings, the ravens brought Elijah bread and meat.

CULTURAL FACT

Zarephath was in the Phoenician territory, seven miles south of Sidon, which was the stronghold of Baal. Because of the agricultural society, many widows were exceptionally poor and had few options. The widow that Elijah met was in a desperate plight and about to die when she met the prophet.

After a period of time, from the lack of rain, the brook dried up. The Lord told Elijah to move at once to Zarephath of Sidon and a widow would supply him with food. When Elijah walked into the town gate of Zarephath, a widow was gathering sticks. Elijah asked her for a little water and a piece of bread.

The widow answered, "As surely as the Lord lives, I don't have any bread—only a handful of flour in a jar and a little oil in a jug. I am gathering a few sticks to take home and make a meal for myself and my son, that we may eat it—and die." (1 Kings 17:12)

Elijah had good news for the widow about God's protective hand. He told her not to be afraid but to go home and make him a cake of bread, then to make bread for herself and her son. "For this is what the Lord, the God of Israel says: 'The jar of flour will not be used up and the jug of oil will not run dry until the day the Lord gives rain on the land.'" (1 Kings 17:14) And through this prophecy, the Lord provided every day for Elijah, the widow, and her son.

Later the son grew ill, and finally he stopped breathing. The widow asked Elijah whether he had come to reveal her sins. The prophet carried the boy to an upper room where he was staying and pleaded with God for mercy and healing. He stretched out on the boy three times and the boy's life returned. The widow said to Elijah, "Now I know that you are a man of God and that the word of the Lord from your mouth is the truth." (1 Kings 17:24)

King Ahab was one of the most wicked kings in Israel and was married to Jezebel, a princess from Sidon who was a determined and devilish woman. For a moment, stand in the shoes of King Ahab. This roughly dressed prophet appears in court and announces a drought as God's judgment, then disappears. Wouldn't Ahab be searching the kingdom for Elijah? Three years later, the Lord came to Elijah and said, "Go and present yourself to Ahab and I will send rain on the land." (1 Kings 18:1) In obedience, Elijah went to see Ahab.

HISTORICAL FACT

Most scholars recognize Ahab as the most evil king of Israel, who at times displayed courage and even humility (1 Kings 21:29), yet Ahab never served the Lord wholeheartedly. Jezebel, his well-known wife, led King Ahab into wickedness. The King rejected God and openly served Baal and built an altar, a temple, and a wooden image. His lasting legacy was negative and he died in a tragic battle, and, as prophesied, the dogs licked his blood.

Obadiah, a believer in the Lord, was in charge of Ahab's palace. Ahab and his queen Jezebel had been killing the Lord's prophets but Obadiah had preserved 100 prophets and hidden them in two caves where he supplied them with food and water. King Ahab sent Obadiah out to search the land for grass and water to keep his animals alive. As Obadiah walked the land, he came to Elijah. When he recognized the prophet, Obadiah bowed to the ground and asked what he had done wrong to deserve death from Ahab. For the last few years, King Ahab had been searching the earth for Elijah and yet hadn't found him anywhere. Obadiah told Elijah about hiding the prophets of the Lord and continuing to worship God since his youth.

Elijah tried to calm down Obadiah and said, "As the Lord Almighty lives, whom I serve, I will surely present myself to Ahab today." (1 Kings 18:15)

ONE OF THE GREATEST CONTESTS IN THE BIBLE

When King Ahab went out to meet the prophet, he called him "the troubler of Israel." Elijah immediately took issue with the name and said that Ahab had caused the trouble because of leaving the God of his fathers and turning to follow Baal. Elijah challenged King Ahab to gather together the 450 prophets of Baal along with the people of Israel.

Everyone assembled at Mount Carmel and Elijah spoke to the people, saying, "How long will you waver between two opinions? If the Lord is God, follow him; but if Baal is God, follow him." Then Elijah suggested a contest between himself and the 450 prophets of Baal. Elijah asked for two bulls. The Baal prophets would chose one bull and prepare it for sacrifice. Elijah would prepare the other bull. Neither Elijah nor the Baal prophets would set fire to their bulls. Elijah and the prophets of Baal would each call on their respective god to light the fire. "The god who answers by fire—he is God." (1 Kings 18:25)

The prophets of Baal selected their sacrifice and began to call on Baal from morning until noon. These prophets danced around the altar and shouted but no one answered. About noon, Elijah began to taunt Baal's prophets saying, "Shout louder! Surely he is a god! Perhaps he is deep in thought, or busy, or traveling. Maybe he is sleeping and must be awakened." The taunting made these prophets shout even louder and cut themselves with their swords and spears until they bled. The contest continued until the evening sacrifice—yet there was no answer.

Finally Elijah called the people to watch him. He repaired the altar of the Lord, which was in ruins. He dug a large trench around the altar, enough to hold about 15 quarts of water. Then he asked the people to fill four large jars of water and pour it over the offering and the wood. They filled these jars three times until the water ran over the altar and filled the trench.

With the drama increasing, Elijah stepped forward and prayed, "O Lord, God of Abraham, Isaac and Israel, let it be known today that you are God in Israel and that I am your servant and have done all these things at your command. Answer me, O Lord, answer me, so these people will know that you, O Lord, are God, and you are turning their hearts back again." (1 Kings 18:36–37)

Then the fire of the Lord fell from heaven and burned the sacrifice, the wood, the stones, and the soil, including taking all of the water from the trench. When the people saw the fire, they fell to the ground on their faces and cried out to the Lord.

Elijah commanded the people to seize the Baal prophets and kill them in the Kishon Valley. The people seized the Baal prophets and killed them. King Ahab witnessed the hand of God, and Elijah turned to him and said, "Go, eat and drink, for there is the sound of a heavy rain." (1 Kings 18:41) Ahab went off to eat but Elijah climbed to the top of Mount Carmel and bowed low to the ground with his head on the ground. He asked his servant to look toward the sea. Seven times he asked him to look for something. The seventh time, the servant reported, "A cloud as small as a man's hand is rising from the sea." (1 Kings 18:44)

The prophet told his servant to go and tell Ahab to hitch up his chariot before the rain stopped him. The sky grew dark and the wind rose and a heavy rain came as Ahab was riding to Jezreel. And look what happened to Elijah: "The power of the Lord came upon Elijah and tucking his cloak into his belt, he ran ahead of Ahab all the way to Jezreel." (1 Kings 18:46)

When King Ahab returned home, he told his wife, Jezebel, about the events on Mount Carmel and the death of the Baal prophets. Years earlier, Jezebel introduced Ahab to the Baal prophets and when she learned the news of their deaths, Jezebel sent a messenger to Elijah threatening to take his life. Afraid for his life, Elijah ran to Beersheba, left his servant, and traveled on another day into the desert. He prayed for the Lord to take his life. Suddenly an angel of the Lord appeared and gave Elijah food and water. The prophet fell asleep again and the angel appeared a second time to give Elijah food and water. Strengthened from the food, Elijah traveled 40 days and 40 nights to Horeb and entered a cave to spend the night.

Notice how Elijah fled from Jezebel without seeking guidance from the Lord. That night as Elijah slept in the cave, the word of the Lord came to him and asked, "What are you doing here, Elijah?" (1 Kings 19:9) Through his response, the prophet revealed that he didn't understand the question. He said, "I have been very zealous for the Lord God Almighty. The Israelites have rejected your covenant, broken down your altars, and put your prophets to death with the sword. I am the only one left, and now they are trying to kill me too." (1 Kings 19:10)

To gain his attention, the Lord asked Elijah to go outside to the mouth of the cave and watch for the Lord's presence. The mountain had a fierce wind but the Lord wasn't in the wind. Then there was an earthquake but the Lord wasn't in the earthquake. Next fire broke out but the Lord wasn't in the fire. Finally a gentle whisper came. Elijah pulled his cloak over his face and stood—because he knew the whisper was the presence of the Lord. Again the Lord asked why he was there. Elijah made the same answer as before. God commanded Elijah to travel to Damascus and to anoint Hazael king over Aram, Jehu to be king of Israel, and Elisha son of Shaphat to succeed Elijah as a prophet. Then the Lord answered the prophet's concern about being the only one left, saying, "I reserve seven thousand in Israel—all whose knees have not bowed down to Baal and all whose mouths have not kissed him." (1 Kings 19:18)

JUST A MINUTE

Elijah had a deep relationship with the younger prophet, Elisha. In today's terms, such a relationship is called mentoring a prospective leader. Eventually when Elisha took up the mantle of Elijah (2 Kings 2:13), he took over Elijah's role as the main prophet of Israel.

Elijah found Elisha, son of Shaphat, plowing in the field. The older prophet placed his cloak on the young man to indicate that Elisha was called to be his successor. Later, Elijah appeared in the vineyard of Naboth. The prophet found King Ahab taking possession of the vineyard for which the king murdered Naboth. Ahab was not pleased to see the prophet and Elijah proclaimed God's judgment against the King and his wicked wife, Jezebel. In response, King Ahab tore his clothes and fasted. From the king's response, the Lord decided to bring about disaster not on Ahab himself but instead on the rule of his son. (1 Kings 21:27–29)

Elijah's final appearance in the Bible is filled with drama. Elijah tried to leave Elisha, his attendant, at different places but the younger man insisted on accompanying the prophet. Elijah rolled up his cloak and struck the water of the Jordan River; it divided and the pair walked across on dry ground. Elijah asked Elisha, "Tell me, what can I do for you before I am taken from you?" (2 Kings 2:9) Elisha asked for a double portion of his spirit. The older prophet replied that it would be difficult yet possible if Elisha saw the prophet go to heaven. Suddenly as they walked together, a chariot of fire and horses appeared and Elijah went up to heaven in a whirlwind. In mourning for his friend and mentor, Elisha tore his own robe and then wore the cloak of his friend Elijah. When he reached the Jordan River, Elisha struck the water with his cloak and the waters separated so he could walk across on dry ground. (2 Kings 2:8–14)

Elisha has some significant stories in the Bible. For extra reading, turn to these stories:

- Elisha heals the poisoned water (2 Kings 2:19–22)
- Elisha calls a curse on boys who tease him (2 Kings 2:23–25)
- The prophet Elisha increases a widow's food supply (2 Kings 4:1–7)
- Elisha raises a widow's son from the dead (2 Kings 4:18–35)
- Elisha pronounces sentences on kings (1 Kings 21:19–22; 2 Kings 8:7–10)

The prophet Elijah and his successor Elisha have some of the most remarkable stories in the Bible from the prophets.

ISAIAH

Known as the messianic prophet, Isaiah is quoted in the New Testament more than any other prophet. He is called the messianic prophet because he was a man with a singular mission to proclaim to Israel about a Messiah who would one day bring peace, healing, and justice to the world.

God called Isaiah a prophet during the year of Uzziah's death. He was a prophet of the southern kingdom of Judah, during a period when the Assyrians had already destroyed the northern kingdom of Israel. Isaiah lived during the reigns of kings Uzziah, Jotham, Ahaz, and Hezekiah. According to Jewish tradition, King Manasseh executed Isaiah.

Isaiah wrote the mission statement for Jesus Christ and his ministry as Messiah in Isaiah 61:1–2, "The Spirit of the Sovereign Lord is on me, because the Lord has anointed me to preach the good news to the poor. He has sent me to bind up the brokenhearted, to proclaim freedom for the captives and release from darkness for the prisoners, to proclaim the year of the Lord's favor and the day of vengeance of our God." Seven centuries later, Jesus Christ entered the temple and read the Scriptures. He opened the scroll of Isaiah and read the same words from Isaiah 61:1–2, then sat down. "The eyes of everyone in the synagogue were fastened on him, and he began saying to them, 'Today this scripture is fulfilled in your hearing.'" (Luke 4:20–21)

BIBLICAL FACT

The seraphim, which are celestial beings, are mentioned twice in the Bible—and both of these times are in Isaiah 6. The noun is based on the Hebrew word *seraph* and means "to burn with fire." The seraphim relate to purification and conduct continual worship of God in heaven.

The first few chapters of Isaiah are a clarion call to the Jewish people concerning their blatant disregard for God and the surety of their punishment. The prophet was probably a bit proud of his accomplishments when he entered the temple in Isaiah chapter 6. He faced a life-changing moment in the temple:

In the year that King Uzziah died, I saw the Lord seated on a throne, high and exalted, and the train of his robe filled the temple. Above him were seraphs, each with six wings: With two wings they covered their faces, with two they covered their feet, and with two they were flying. And they were calling to one another: "Holy, holy, holy is the Lord Almighty; the whole earth is full of his glory."

At the sound of their voices, the doorposts and thresholds shook and the temple was filled with smoke. "Woe to me!" I cried. "I am ruined! For I am a man of unclean lips, and I live among a people of unclean lips, and my eyes have seen the King, the Lord Almighty." Then one of the seraphs flew to me with a live coal in his hand, which he had taken with tongs from the altar. With it he touched my mouth and said, "See, this has touched your lips; your guilt is taken away and your sin atoned for." Then I heard the voice of the Lord saying, "Whom shall I send? And who will go for us?" And I said, "Here am I. Send me!" (Isaiah 6:1–8)

Immediately following the Lord's call for Isaiah to proclaim his message to the Israelites, God predicted the people's negative reaction: "Go and tell this people, 'Be ever hearing, but never understanding; be ever seeing, but never perceiving,'" (Isaiah 6:9) Like the experience of almost every prophet, the people would not listen to Isaiah.

Some of the most-often-quoted passages in the Old Testament about Jesus Christ are in the words of Isaiah:

- **Virgin birth.** "Therefore the Lord himself will give you a sign: The virgin will be with child and will give birth to a son, and you will call him Immanuel!" (Isaiah 7:14)

- **Character of the Messiah.** "For to us a child is born, to us a son is given, and the government will be on his shoulders. And he will be called Wonderful Counselor, Mighty God, Everlasting Father, Prince of Peace." (Isaiah 9:6–7)

- **Death by crucifixion.** "He had no beauty or majesty to attract us to him, nothing in his appearance that we should desire him. He was despised and rejected by men, a man of sorrows, and familiar with suffering. ... He was pierced for our transgressions, he was crushed for our iniquities; the punishment that brought us peace was upon him, and by his wounds we are healed." (Isaiah 53:2–3, 5)

HISTORICAL FACT

In 1947, a shepherd was looking for a stray goat and stumbled on some clay jars in a cave in Qumran that contained some ancient scrolls. Although these documents were from the first century A.D., they were remarkably preserved in the dry and hot climate of the Dead Sea. Known as the Dead Sea Scrolls, one of the most significant discoveries was a complete Book of Isaiah. This discovery helped confirm the authenticity of the later manuscripts.

One of Isaiah's greatest achievements came in the deliverance of Jerusalem from the Assyrian army. In the fourteenth year of King Hezekiah, the Assyrian army was camped around Jerusalem. The army commander told the people that their god was no better than the other nations' gods and that the Assyrians would be victorious. The prophet urged King Hezekiah to resist the Assyrians. Then Isaiah prayed and the Lord said through him, "Do not be afraid of what you have heard—those words with which the underlings of the king of Assyria have blasphemed me ...." (Isaiah 37:5) Then the prophecy came that the Assyrian leader would be called back to his country. This same night, a disaster befell the encamped Assyrians. Through divine intervention, the leader withdrew to Nineveh, where his own sons killed him. The prophecy was fulfilled. (Isaiah 36–37)

Many modern scholars call the Book of Isaiah among the finest in literature.

JEREMIAH

After Isaiah saved Jerusalem from the Assyrians, the prophet Jeremiah came along about 100 years later. He attempted to save Jerusalem from the Babylonian army—but failed. During 40 terrible years of war in Jerusalem, the prophet Jeremiah stood strong and proclaimed the words of God. Known as "the weeping prophet," Jeremiah had a tender heart and wrote the longest book in the Bible.

Listen to his words, yet read behind the words to imagine his weeping and tears over the sins of the Jewish people, "Hear and pay attention, do not be arrogant, for the Lord has spoken. Give glory to the Lord your God before he brings the darkness, before your feet stumble on the darkening hills. You hope for light, but he will turn it to thick darkness and change it to deep gloom. But if you do not listen, I will weep in secret because of your pride; my eyes will weep bitterly, overflowing with tears, because the Lord's flock will be taken captive." (Jeremiah 13:15–17)

The heart of Jeremiah was broken because he understood the sinful nature of his people's hearts, which was breaking the heart of God. Jeremiah heard God's call on his life at a young age. In fact, Jeremiah heard God's voice before he drew his first breath. "The word of the Lord came to me, saying, 'Before I formed you in the womb I knew you, before you were born I set you apart; I appointed you as a prophet to the nations.'" (Jeremiah 1:4–5)

HISTORICAL FACT

Jeremiah became a prophet during a three-way struggle for world supremacy between Assyria, Babylonia, and Egypt. For 300 years, Assyria, with Nineveh as its capital, had ruled the world. Now Assyria was growing weak as Babylonia became more powerful. About midway through Jeremiah's ministry of prophecy, Babylonia broke Assyria (610 B.C.) and a few years later crushed Egypt (605 B.C.). For 70 years, the Babylonians ruled the world.

Set apart as God's chosen instrument to the Jewish people before birth, as a young man of 20, Jeremiah heard his first divine summons:

"Ah, Sovereign Lord," I said, "I do not know how to speak; I am only a child." But the Lord said to me, "Do not say, 'I am only a child.' You must go to everyone I send you to and say whatever I command you. Do not be afraid of them, for I am with you and will rescue you," declares the Lord. Then the Lord reached out his hand and touched my mouth and said to me, "Now, I have put my words in your mouth. See, today I appoint you over nations and kingdoms to uproot and tear down, to destroy and overthrow, to build and to plant." (Jeremiah 1:6–10)

A great deal of the prophet's work was doom and gloom—a message of repentance and change to the Jewish people. Yet notice how God added words of hope to Jeremiah's message. He encouraged the people not only to tear down and destroy but to build and to plant.

MOLDED LIKE A POTTER AND CLAY

One of the most famous series of incidents from Jeremiah's ministry came at the potter's house. Following God's guidance, Jeremiah visited a potter and watched him work. While making a pot, the craftsman was dissatisfied with the results so he reworked the clay until the potter was finally satisfied with the outcome. Jeremiah explained the potter and the clay were a parable of how God deals with the Jewish people. Like the potter has liberty to rework his creation, the Lord is equally at liberty to break and remold the people of Judah. (Jeremiah 18:1–17)

Due to his prophecy, Jeremiah faced increasing hostility and threats from the people, yet he faithfully followed the Lord. "Let a cry be heard from their houses when you suddenly bring invaders against them, for they have dug a pit to capture me and have hidden snares for my feet. But you know, O Lord, all their plots to kill me. Do not forgive their crimes or blot out their sins from your sight. Let them be overthrown before you; deal with them in the time of your anger." (Jeremiah 18:22–23)

Then the Lord told Jeremiah to go again to the potter's house and buy a clay jar. The prophet was to gather the leaders of the Jewish people and take them to the Valley of Ben Hinnom and say:

"… beware, the days are coming, declares the Lord, when people will no longer call this place Topheth or the Valley of Ben Hinnom, but the Valley of Slaughter. In this place, I will ruin the plans of Judah and Jerusalem. I will make them fall by the sword before their enemies, at the hands of those who seek their lives, and I will give their carcasses as food to the birds of the air and the beasts of the earth. I will devastate this city and make it an object of scorn; all who pass by will be appalled and will scoff because of all its wounds. …" (Jeremiah 19:6–8)

His prophecy was not the way to win the affection of the Jewish leadership. Then Jeremiah smashed the pot as a public sign of how God would smash the Jewish people because of their pagan worship.

And how did the people react to the prophet's words? The chief officer of the temple had Jeremiah publicly beaten and thrown into stocks. (Jeremiah 20:1–2) The young prophet was a fearless reformer.

Imagine a television evangelist who constantly called people sinners and announced that the capital of your country was about to be destroyed because of your sin. Wouldn't this person be attacked and criticized and ridiculed—especially when his predictions didn't become immediately true?

Jeremiah was in the middle of this type of situation. He was constantly going straight to the temple and confronting the religious leaders. He consistently told people that Jerusalem was about to be destroyed. The religious leaders were furious, and how did Jeremiah react to this criticism? Jeremiah said, "O Lord, you deceive me, and I was deceived, you overpowered me and prevailed. I am ridiculed all day long; everyone mocks me." (Jeremiah 20:7) The discouragement grew for Jeremiah to the point that he was about to walk away from his office as a prophet of God. It was just too difficult to maintain.

Then Jeremiah was encouraged in his faith and said, "But the Lord is with me like a mighty warrior; so my persecutors will stumble and not prevail. They will fail and be thoroughly disgraced; their dishonor will never be forgotten. O Lord Almighty, you who examine the righteous and probe the heart and mind, let me see your vengeance upon them, for to you I have committed my cause." (Jeremiah 20:11–12) As with many tenderhearted people, Jeremiah's moods swung from joy to despair. In almost the next breath, he turned and said, "Cursed be the day I was born! May the day my mother bore me not be blessed! Cursed be the man who brought my father the news, who made him very glad saying, 'A child is born to you—a son!'" (Jeremiah 20:13–14)

BIBLICAL FACT

Besides the potter and the clay pot, Jeremiah used other symbols in his preaching and attempts to capture the attention of the Jewish people. He used a ruined belt (chapter 13), abstinence from marriage (chapter 16), the yoke of straps and crossbars (chapter 27), and the purchase of a field (chapter 32).

As a prophet Jeremiah served the Lord. His loneliness isn't too different from the lonely experience of every minister. Yet Jeremiah knew that the daily experience was temporal compared to the eternal perspective. He knew firsthand the daily challenges of living in a world filled with pain and proclaiming a heavenly message. The prophet's hope was fixed also on the coming of the Messiah. Jeremiah proclaimed, "'The days are coming,' declares the Lord, 'when I will raise up to David a righteous Branch, a King who will reign wisely and do what is just and right in the land. In his days Judah will be saved and Israel will live in safety. This is the name by which he will be called: The Lord Our Righteousness.'" (Jeremiah 23:5–6) Jeremiah knew that a day of hope and redemption was coming, and he looked expectantly toward that day.

The small Book of Lamentations is composed of five poems of "lament" about when the Babylonians destroyed Jerusalem. While scholars can't prove Jeremiah wrote this book, tradition and the style of the book is definitely like the prophet. Some of the best-known verses from Lamentation are "Because of the Lord's great love we are not consumed, for his compassions never fail. They are new every morning; great is your faithfulness." (Lamentations 2:22–23)

Hour's Up!

The prophets like Elijah, Elisha, Isaiah, and Jeremiah had fascinating stories and proclaimed truth from God. Yet where is the relevance of their message for today? The following 10 questions will help you in the process of applying the Bible to everyday life.

1. The prophets were fearless in their proclamation of God's truth. What can you learn from their fearlessness and apply to your daily life of faith?

2. Although Baal isn't worshipped today, our culture worships sex, beauty, money, and other deities. How is your life ensnared in these other "gods" and what steps can you take to escape and return to the true God?

3. Note how Elijah and God cared for the widow and her son during the drought in Israel. Are there widows in your neighborhood or life where you could be God's instrument of care and protection? How can you begin such a relationship if you don't have one now?

4. The people at Mount Carmel wavered between Baal and God. How is today's world also wavering between following the culture and God? Can you list some ways that you have slipped in your faith and need to recommit?

5. After a great spiritual victory, it's easy to forget that victory. Notice how Elijah forgot to pray and simply fled after the victory of Mount Carmel. How have you sometimes slipped after a great step of faith?

6. Where does God speak? He speaks through the Scriptures, through prayer, and through teaching from others. Notice that God isn't in the fire or earthquake but is in a still small voice. Take some time today to open your Bible, pray, and listen to God's voice.

7. Elijah took the time to groom the prophet Elisha to take his place. How are you preparing others to follow after you—possibly a family member or a co-worker? Make a conscious effort to be involved in this type of mentoring relationship with someone.

8. The prophet Isaiah felt great about his call as a messenger of God. Then how did he react in God's temple when he caught the heavenly vision? You may not have a vision, and yet how can you catch a heavenly glimpse of God from Isaiah's vision? What does it do to your daily relationship with God?

9. Isaiah lived in faithfulness to God. Despite the Assyrian army commander telling the people that the Lord wouldn't rescue them, Isaiah continued to proclaim faithfulness. How has your faith slipped in recent weeks? Rededicate yourself to learning more about God and the Bible.

10. Jeremiah wept and was discouraged as a prophet. Does it sound familiar? The life of faithfulness does involve highs and lows. Jeremiah clung to God's faithfulness and protection despite his feelings. What lessons can you apply from this experience to your everyday life?

HOUR 8

The Major Prophets: Part Two

LESSON PLAN:

In this hour, you will learn about ...

- How God turns his back on the Jewish people and they are exiled.
- The unusual imagery and mysterious nature of the prophet Ezekiel.
- Daniel, a captive in Babylon who became the Babylonian prophet.

When the farmer plants seeds, he doesn't see immediate results. Only with water, fertilizer, and time do seedlings pop out of the ground and plants begin to grow. Images of the seed and the farmer often appear in different places throughout the Bible. Seeds illustrate an important principle throughout the Scriptures: for every action, there is a consequence.

For centuries, the Jewish people had rebelled against God. Despite messages from prophets, the people continued to worship false gods and run away from a righteous relationship with the Lord of the Universe. God has mercy but eventually he judges the actions of the people. The seeds of wickedness had sprouted and the Lord decided to remove the people from the Promised Land. Just like the parent who warns his child, "One more time and I'll have to take you outside …," God had to remove his people after they continued in wickedness.

In this hour, you will examine what life was like for the Jewish people in exile. Then you will study the lives of two more major prophets—Ezekiel and Daniel.

THE ASSYRIANS CAPTURE THE JEWISH PEOPLE

In 722 B.C., the northern kingdom, Israel, fell to the Assyrians. All 12 tribes of Israel—except for the tribes of Judah and Levi—fell to the enemy. Any cities that did not hold future value were leveled and the Assyrians killed the people who were not captured. Overall, the Assyrians wanted the people to live so that they would carry out their building projects and use the skilled Jewish workmen. Some people were sent to rural areas to cultivate the land and raise crops.

Scholars have shown that the Assyrians took good care of their captives. They fed their captives adequately on the journey, provided footwear to protect their feet during the march, and did not break up families but kept whole communities as a group.

CULTURAL FACT

Assyrian scribes, administrators, and foreign interpreters functioned in multiple languages. Assyria controlled a number of countries and conquered many lands. The archeological records left behind show the Assyrian inscriptions for the number of prisoners, battle accounts, and even tax receipts. Their command of different languages is reflected in the fact the Assyrian officials knew about the internal affairs of Judah and also spoke Hebrew. (2 Kings 18:26–35)

The Assyrians also planned to overtake the southern kingdom of Judah; however, Judah survived almost 140 years until the Babylonians destroyed it in 586 B.C.

The Assyrian king Sennacherib attacked Jerusalem during the fourteenth year of the reign of King Hezekiah. When Sennacherib warned the Jewish people, they didn't surrender. The king of Assyria sent his field commander to speak to the people in the common language saying, "This is what the great king, the king of Assyria, says: 'On what are you basing this confidence of yours? You say you have strategy and military strength—but you speak only empty words. On whom are you depending, that you rebel against me?'" (2 Kings 18:19–20)

Then Eliakim, son of Hilkiah, said to the field commander, "Please speak to your servants in Aramaic, since we understand it. Don't speak to us in Hebrew in the hearing of the people on the wall." (2 Kings 18:26)

But the commander replied, "Was it only to your master and you that my master sent me to say these things, and not to the men sitting on the wall—who, like you, will have to eat their own filth and drink their own urine?" The people, however, did not reply because the king had commanded, "Do not answer him." (2 Kings 18:27, 36)

When he heard the news, King Hezekiah tore his robe in sorrow and went into the temple of the Lord. The prophet Isaiah came and told King Hezekiah that the Lord had heard his prayer. "Therefore this is what the Lord says concerning the king of Assyria: 'He will not enter this city or shoot an arrow here. He will not come before it with shield or build a siege ramp against it. By the way that he came he will return.'" (2 Kings 19:32–33)

During that night the angel of the Lord walked through the camp of the Assyrians, and the next morning 185,000 men were dead. Assyrian King Sennacherib broke camp and withdrew. One day while worshipping his gods, two of his sons killed the Assyrian king and the prophetic words of Isaiah became truth.

THE STRANGE GIFT

Later, King Hezekiah became ill and near death. Again Isaiah visited and told him to put his house in order because he would not recover. Once again the King repented and prayed to the Lord. Before Isaiah left the court, the Lord told him to return and tell him that the Lord would add 15 years to his life. (2 Kings 20:6) Then, Merodach-Baladan, son of Baladan, king of Babylon, sent King Hezekiah a gift and letters because he heard that the king was sick. King Hezekiah received the messengers from Babylon and showed them all of his storehouses and treasures. "There was nothing in his palace or in all his kingdom that Hezekiah did not show them." (2 Kings 20:13)

Isaiah went to King Hezekiah and the prophet inquired about the messengers such as where did they come from and what did they see? Then Isaiah said to the king, "Hear the word of the Lord. The time will surely come when everything in your palace, and all that your fathers have stored up until this day, will be carried off to Babylon. Nothing will be left, says the Lord. And some of your descendants, your own flesh and blood, that will be born to you, will be taken away, and they will become eunuchs in the palace of the king of Babylon." (2 Kings 20:16–18)

And what self-centered response did King Hezekiah say about this warning from Isaiah? "The word is good because I will have peace and security in my lifetime, the king said." (2 Kings 20:19–20)

HISTORICAL FACT

King Manasseh encouraged the Israelites into idolatry by building altars of worship for Baal, the Canaanite fertility god.

When King Hezekiah died, his son Manasseh ruled for 55 years and he led the people away from God. "He did evil in the eyes of the Lord, following the detestable practices of the nations the Lord had driven out before the Israelites." (2 Kings 21:2) King Manasseh filled Jerusalem with innocent blood and then his son Amon succeeded him as king.

Amon also did evil, but his son Josiah became king at eight years old. King Josiah followed the Lord as had his great-grandfather, King Hezekiah. The high priest during King Josiah's reign was Hilkiah, who opened the temple of the Lord, which had been neglected, and found the Book of the Law and read it to the king. Hearing the Book of the Law, King Josiah led a nation-wide revival and turned to the Lord.

The small son of Hilkiah also heard the words of the law. His name was Jeremiah. Years later as a grown man, the prophet Jeremiah reflected on this day of excitement when the Book of the Law was discovered and said, "When your words came, I ate them; they were my joy and my heart's delight, for I bear your name, O Lord God Almighty." (Jeremiah 15:16)

Yet Josiah's reign of following the Lord was short-lived. At age 39, Josiah went out to battle King Neco of Egypt. The king of Egypt warned Josiah not to fight him, saying, "I'm not here to fight you …." But Josiah didn't listen and died from an Egyptian arrow in battle. Josiah's son, Jehoahaz, reigned for three months until the king of Egypt replaced him with his own brother, Jehoiakim.

King Jehoiakim showed great contempt for the words of God and even burned the scroll of Jeremiah. Seven years later, Babylon invaded Jerusalem and carried Judah's king and noblemen to Babylon. Along with these noblemen went the prophet Ezekiel. As for King Jehoiakim, his children were killed in his presence and his eyes were gouged out and he was carried away in chains. The Lord brought about the words of Isaiah's prophecy and affirmed the reality of the lesson from the seed. When seeds of idolatry and distrust are planted, they grow into rebellion and bondage for a nation. (Jeremiah 36–39)

HISTORICAL FACT

Nebuchadnezzar became king of Babylon in 605 B.C. and conducted several campaigns in Palestine. He squelched Jehoiakim's rebellion in about 602 B.C., deported Jehoiachin in 597 B.C., and destroyed Jerusalem in 586 B.C.

EZEKIEL

The third major prophet, Ezekiel, centers his book on the great issues of sin and apostasy (abandonment of faith or rebellion from Israel) and exile that dominate the books of Isaiah and Jeremiah. Ezekiel was younger than Jeremiah and lived his early years in Judah. Then the Babylonians took over the country and exiled Ezekiel to Babylon. At age 30, God called Ezekiel to become a prophet in Babylon. He and Daniel were contemporaries and in the country at the same time. More than 60 times, Ezekiel used a phrase that dominates his message to the Jewish people, "that they might know that I am the Lord."

HISTORICAL FACT

Ezekiel received revelations from the Lord while living in exile in Babylon between 593 and 571 B.C. Everything scholars know about Ezekiel is contained in his written prophecy. No compelling data exists for the acceptance of any other author than the one named in the book: Ezekiel, son of Buzi (a priest), who was taken captive with Jehoiachin and other Hebrews in 597 B.C.

Born into a priestly family, the Book of Ezekiel has two purposes:

- First, in his role as a prophet, the book confronts the people about their sinfulness and their life apart from God.
- Second, in his role as a priest, the book pleads with the sovereignty of God for these same people as a priest would do for his people.

God sent Ezekiel to the people to explain that their oppression and captivity in Babylon were signs not of God's abandonment but of their sin:

"Son of man, I am sending you to the Israelites, to a rebellious nation that has rebelled against me; they and their fathers have been in revolt against me to this very day. The people to who I am sending you are obstinate and stubborn. Say to them, 'This is what the Sovereign Lord says.' And whether they listen or fail to listen—for they are a rebellious house—they will know that a prophet has been among them. And, you son of man, do not be afraid of them or their words." (Ezekiel 2:3–6)

For 22 years, Ezekiel lived what he preached. He told the people about the forthcoming judgment of God. The Lord told Ezekiel to illustrate his messages with some dramatic object lessons. For example, the Lord told Ezekiel to lie on his side for 390 days during which he could only eat one 8-ounce meal cooked over manure. He faithfully obeyed God's directions.

The most dramatic obedience to the Lord involved the death of Ezekiel's wife. In the fourth year of his prophetic ministry, he learned, "The word of the Lord came to me, 'Son of man, with one blow I am about to take away from you, the delight of your eyes. Yet do not lament or weep or shed any tears. Groan quietly; do not mourn for the dead. Keep your turban fastened and your sandals on your feet; do not cover the lower part of your face or eat the customary food of mourners'." (Ezekiel 24:15–17) Then Ezekiel's wife died and the prophet followed the instructions of the Lord not to mourn. The Jewish people were amazed at the actions of this priest. Yet the prophet's actions were a symbol of how the Jewish people had effectively killed their relationship with God and acted as if he didn't exist.

HEAVENLY VISIONS

Throughout the Book of Ezekiel, Ezekiel uses dramatic word pictures to get his point across to the Jewish people in Babylon. One of the most dramatic is a wheel with eyes: "I looked, and I saw a windstorm coming out of the north—an immense cloud with flashing lightning and surrounded by brilliant light. The center of the fire looked like glowing metal, and in the fire was what looked like four living creatures. In appearance their form was that of a man, but each of them had four faces and four wings. ... As I looked at the living creatures, I saw a wheel on the ground beside each creature with its four faces.

This was the appearance and structure of the wheels: They sparkled like chrysolite, and all four looked alike. Each appeared to be made like a wheel intersecting a wheel. As they moved, they would go in any one of the four directions the creatures faced; the wheels did not turn about as the creatures went. Their rims were high and awesome, and all four rims were full of eyes all around. When the living creatures moved, the wheels beside them moved; when the living creatures rose from the ground, the wheels also rose." (Ezekiel 1:4–6, 15–19)

Wheels? Eyes? Creatures who moved around? This dramatic vision was a representation of God's judgment seat. The judgment throne of God was mobile, just as the Jewish people followed the light of God's presence in the fire and the cloud across the wilderness for 40 years. Because the Israelites have turned away from God, the Lord would have a mobile place of chastisement for the people. It's a somber message of God's forthcoming judgment on the sin of the people.

JUST A MINUTE

Do you have any skeletons in your closet? Israel had many skeletons or things to hide from God. They had grown proud with their reputation. Through the prophet Ezekiel, the Lord confronted three secrets to call into question their proud self-image: They were born to Canaanite parents (Ezekiel 16:3), they were abandoned at birth (Ezekiel 16:4–5), and they were adopted (Ezekiel 16:6–7). Without a measure of God's grace in their lives, the Israelites couldn't belong to God.

The prophet's next vision is even stranger than his spinning wheel with eyes. Ezekiel steps into his role as a priest with this vision. "Then I looked, and I saw a hand stretched out to me. In it was a scroll, which he unrolled before me. On both sides of it were written words of lament and mourning and woe. And he said to me, 'Son of man, eat this scroll; then go out and speak to the house of Israel.' So I opened my mouth, and he gave me the scroll to eat. Then he said to me, 'Son of man, eat this scroll I am giving you and fill your stomach with it.' So I ate it, and it tasted as sweet as honey in my mouth." (Ezekiel 2:9–3:3)

Imagine eating a document filled with the sins of Israel that Ezekiel called lament, mourning, and woe. This scroll must have been horrible. Then the Lord tells the prophet to eat the scroll—to literally put it in his mouth and eat the paper. The prophet should have been sick from the contents and the paper—then came the wonderful twist to the vision. The scroll was sweet and didn't sicken the prophet. Instead it tasted like honey. As a priest in the service of God, Ezekiel was charged to bring the sins of the people to God and plead their case of mercy before a Righteous Judge. Through this vision, Ezekiel experienced the Lord's assurance that ultimately God's grace would be extended to the Jewish people.

Restoration is a major theme of the Book of Ezekiel. The climax of this theme is a third vision about dry bones, which is his most famous passage:

The hand of the Lord was upon me, and he brought me out by the Spirit of the Lord and set me in the middle of a valley; it was full of bones. He led me back and forth among them, and I saw a great many bones on the floor of the valley, bones that were very dry. He asked me, "Son of man, can these bones live?" I said, "O Sovereign Lord, you alone know." Then he said to me, "Prophesy to these bones and say to them, 'Dry bones, hear the word of the Lord! This is what the Sovereign Lord says to these bones. I will make breath enter you, and you will come to life. I will attach tendons to you and make flesh come upon you and you will come to life. Then you will know that I am the Lord.'" (Ezekiel 37:1–6)

As Ezekiel stood and watched, a loud rattling sound filled the valley and the bones were covered with flesh but they didn't move because they had no breath. Then the Lord commanded the prophet to breathe on the bodies and suddenly a vast army came to life and stood on their feet. This vision was a weird sight for the prophet Ezekiel, yet the interpretation was filled with a serious message. God was comparing the Israelite people with a valley of dry and lifeless bones. The Jewish people in God's eyes were dead and their bones were scattered. But when the people heard God's word again, then the Lord promised restoration and new life. God would take the dead and bring them to life.

The final vision from Ezekiel must have given hope to the Jewish people who were exiled in Babylon. The temple of the Lord in Jerusalem had been ransacked and destroyed. The glory of the Lord, which filled the Holy of Holies in the temple, had departed. Then Ezekiel saw a new temple built in Jerusalem. As he stood and watched in Jerusalem, Ezekiel said, "I saw the glory of the God of Israel coming from the east. His voice was like the roar of rushing waters, and the land was radiant with his glory. … The glory of the Lord entered the temple through the gate facing east. Then the Spirit lifted me up and brought me into the inner court, and the glory of the Lord filled the temple." (Ezekiel 43:1–2, 4–5)

Ezekiel concludes his prophecy with his theme of restoration and how the Lord will bring the Jewish people back to a relationship with God. The city of Jerusalem will have a new name. "And the name of the city from that time on will be: The Lord Is There." (Ezekiel 48:35)

DANIEL

The fourth and final major prophet is Daniel. This book deals with events that take place in Babylon as the Jewish people are living away from Jerusalem in exile. As mentioned earlier, Daniel and Ezekiel were contemporaries and it's likely that they knew each other. Daniel shows through graphic stories what can happen to a person who is wholly committed to following the God of Israel.

The Babylonian King Nebuchadnezzar commanded that the best and brightest young men from Israel be assembled and brought into the palace. The king planned to teach these young men the language and literature of the Babylonians. The selection process was specific: "Israelites from the royal family and the nobility—young men without any physical defect, handsome, showing aptitude for every kind of learning, well informed, quick to understand, and qualified to serve in the king's palace." (Daniel 1:3–4)

JUST A MINUTE

Daniel and his three friends understood that eating the king's food would result in defilement. They refused to "go along to get along." Instead, in faith, they took a stand and God honored their stand, giving them strength to not compromise their moral backbone and to carry out their plan with tough-minded resolve.

Soon after entering the palace, Daniel and his Jewish friends resolved not to defile themselves eating the king's rich food and wine. Daniel asked permission to eat vegetables and drink water from the chief steward, but the steward was worried about the result. If the king thought the steward wasn't properly handling his job, then it could mean the steward's death. Daniel proposed a test: Give the Jewish boys nothing but vegetables and water for 10 days, and then compare their appearance with the other young men who were eating the royal food. The steward agreed to the test.

"At the end of the ten days, they [Daniel and his friends] looked healthier and better nourished than any of the young men who ate the royal food. So the guard took away their choice food and the wine they were to drink and gave them vegetables instead." (Daniel 1:15–16)

As these four young men committed their lives to the service of God and following him, look at the results:

To these four young men God gave knowledge and understanding of all kinds of literature and learning. And Daniel could understand visions and dreams of all kinds. At the end of the time set by the king to bring them in, the chief official presented them to Nebuchadnezzar. The king talked with them, and he found none equal to Daniel, Hananiah, Mishael and Azariah [Shadrach, Meshach, and Abednego]; so they entered the king's service. In every matter of wisdom and understanding about which the king questioned them, he found them ten times better than all the magicians and enchanters in his whole kingdom. (Daniel 1:17–20)

Because of God's clear blessing on their lives, Daniel and his friends were 10 times better than anyone else in the kingdom!

INTERPRETER OF DREAMS

During the second year of King Nebuchadnezzar's reign, the king had a disturbing dream—so disturbing that he couldn't sleep. He assembled all of the magicians and wise men in his kingdom and announced that he had a troublesome dream. These astrologers answered, "O King, tell us your dream that we may tell you the meaning." But the king refused to tell them the dream, saying that beyond interpretation, the astrologers also had to tell him the dream in the first place. What a challenge from the king! And if the wise men failed to respond to the challenge, then the penalty would be death. Furious at the astrologers, the king issued a decree that all the wise men should be executed.

From the commander of the king's guard, Daniel received the death notice from the king and he asked, "Why did the king issue such a harsh decree?" (Daniel 2:15) After the commander explained, Daniel went to the king and asked for time to interpret the dream. Then Daniel appealed to his friends for prayer. The young Daniel wanted to place his entire future in the hands of God.

That night, the Lord answered and Daniel had a vision and saw the king's dream and the interpretation. Then in front of the king and the wise men, Daniel told the dream and the interpretation.

Notice the response from the king: "Then King Nebuchadnezzar fell prostrate before Daniel and paid him honor and ordered that an offering and incense be presented to him. The king said to Daniel, 'Surely your God is the God of gods and the Lord of kings and a revealer of mysteries, for you were able to reveal this mystery.'" (Daniel 2:46–47) Daniel's interpretation involved a summary of political and military powers that would rise over the next several centuries. Daniel attributed his abilities to God: "Praise be to the name of God for ever and ever, wisdom and power are his." (Daniel 2:20)

A WALK IN THE FIERY FURNACE

While Daniel and his friends were given prominent positions of leadership, King Nebuchadnezzar's verbal honor to the Lord was with his voice but not with his whole being. The Chaldeans worshipped many other gods and they plotted to trap Daniel and his friends.

PEOPLE TO KNOW

The Chaldeans were people who lived in a region at the head of the Persian Gulf. Detailed astronomical cuneiform records provide information valuable for reconstructing historical events, and confirm the Chaldeans' reputation as astrologers and astronomers.

King Nebuchadnezzar made an image of gold, 90 feet high and 9 feet wide, and set it up on the plain of Dura in the province of Babylon. Then he summoned the officials to come to the dedication of the image he had set up. ... Then the herald loudly proclaimed, "This is what you are commanded to do, O peoples, nations and men of every language: As soon as you hear the sound ... you must fall down and worship the image of gold that King Nebuchadnezzar has set up. Whoever does not fall down and worship will immediately be thrown into a blazing furnace." (Daniel 3:1–2, 4–6)

See the trap? The other wise men were jealous of the Jewish leaders and knew the Jews would not bow to an idol. So they announced to King Nebuchadnezzar, "... [t]here are some Jews whom you have set over the affairs of the province of Babylon—Shadrach, Meshach and Abednego—who pay no attention to you, O king. They neither serve your gods nor worship the image of gold you have set up." (Daniel 3:12)

The arrogant king didn't take this type of public display of disobedience lightly. He was furious and commanded the furnace to be heated seven times its normal temperature. The guards firmly tied the three men and threw them into the fire. King Nebuchadnezzar was watching the burning and asked his advisers in amazement, "Wasn't it three men that we tied up and threw into the fire?" They replied, "Certainly, O king." He said, "Look! I see four men walking around in the fire, unbound and unharmed, and the fourth looks like a son of the gods." (Daniel 3:24–25)

HISTORICAL FACT

Who was the fourth person in the fire with Shadrach, Meshach, and Abednego who looked "like the Son of God"? (Daniel 3:25 in some translations) King Nebuchadnezzar understood this figure was divine (Daniel 3:28). These appearances of Christ in the Old Testament are known as Theophanies or "appearances of God." They include the angel who comforted Hagar (Genesis 16:7–13), the visitor who appeared to Abraham and Sarah (Genesis 18:1–15), the Lord with Moses in the burning bush (Exodus 3), and the glimpse of God by Moses on Sinai (Exodus 33:11). These appearances of God were temporary, yet pointed to the arrival of Christ.

The king called for the men to come out of the furnace and, to his amazement, the fire hadn't harmed a single hair on their heads or their clothing nor did they smell like the fire. From this miracle, the king declared, "'Praise be to the God of Shadrach, Meshach and Abednego, who has sent his angel and rescued his servants! They trusted in him and defied the king's command and were willing to give up their lives rather than serve or worship any god except their own God. Therefore, I decree that the people of any nation or language who say anything against the God of Shadrach, Meshach and Abednego be cut into pieces and their houses be turned into piles of rubble, for no other god can save in this way.' Then the king promoted Shadrach, Meshach and Abednego in the province of Babylon." (Daniel 3:28–30) Instead of punishment for not bowing down to the king's statue, Shadrach, Meshach, and Abednego were promoted for their faithfulness to the God of the Universe.

GOD'S FINGER ON THE WALL

After King Nebuchadnezzar's death, his son, Belshazzar, succeeded him as king. One night during a drunken celebration, King Belshazzar ordered the silver and gold goblets from the temple in Jerusalem to be brought out. While they were drinking from these goblets, they praised the gods of gold, silver, bronze, iron, wood, and stone. "Suddenly the fingers of a human hand appeared on the wall and wrote on the plaster of the wall, near the lamp stand in the royal palace … Then all of the king's wise men came in, but they could not read the writing or tell the king what it meant. So King Belshazzar became even more terrified and his face grew more pale. His nobles were baffled." (Daniel 5:5–6, 8–9) Then the queen, who some scholars say was the queen mother, remembered Daniel and told the king that Daniel could tell the meaning.

King Belshazzar called for Daniel and told him if he read the writing, he would become the third highest ruler of the land. Daniel told the king to keep his gifts and said the king had not followed in the humility of his father, but taken the Lord's goblets from the temple and hailed the gods of gold, silver, bronze, iron, wood, and stone. "You did not honor the God who holds in his hand your life and all your ways. Therefore he sent the hand that wrote the inscription." (Daniel 5:23–24) The inscription told King Belshazzar that he would die that very night and his kingdom would be divided. The prophecy came true and Darius the Mede took over the kingdom of Babylon.

INTO THE LIONS' DEN

Through these various incidents, Daniel's role in the kingdom was increasing. Despite different rulers and kings, each of them knew the importance of Daniel and his connection to the Lord of the Universe. The kingdom had been divided into three provinces and Daniel ruled one of these three areas.

Darius even considered putting Daniel over the entire kingdom. The king's advisers were horrified at the thought of a Jew ruling over them. Because of their jealousy of Daniel, they plotted to trap Daniel:

So the administrators and the satraps went as a group to the king and said, "O King Darius, live forever! The royal administrators, prefects, satraps, advisers and governors have all agreed that the king should issue an edict and enforce the decree that anyone who prays to any god or man during the next thirty days, except to you, O king, shall be thrown into the lions' den." (Daniel 6:6–7)

The men appealed to the king's ego and he issued a law, which could not be revoked or appealed.

The jealous leaders knew Daniel prayed three times each day in an open window that faced Jerusalem. Despite knowing of the decree against prayer, Daniel went home and prayed and the leaders caught Daniel in the violation. They told the king about the violation and King Darius was greatly distressed and determined to rescue Daniel. Yet because of the unchangeable nature of this law, King Darius had to carry out his own order. He threw Daniel into the lions' den and said, "May your God, whom you serve continually, rescue you!" (Daniel 6:16)

They sealed the lions' den with a stone and the king's own signet ring so no one could open it. That night was filled with worry and concern for King Darius. He couldn't eat or sleep. At the first light of day, he rushed to the den and removed the stone and called out, "Daniel, servant of the living God, has your God, whom you serve continually, been able to rescue you from the lions?"

Daniel answered, "O king, live forever! My God sent his angel, and he shut the mouths of the lions. They have not hurt me, because I was found innocent in his sight. Nor have I ever done anything wrong before you, O king." (Daniel 6:20–21) The king was overjoyed at the news and had Daniel released from the lions' den. Then the men who had falsely accused Daniel, along with their wives and children, were thrown into the lions' den—and they were overpowered and killed before they even reached the floor.

The last six chapters of Daniel are prophecies about the future. Scholars have disagreed with the interpretation of these prophecies. Some believe they point to the birth of Jesus Christ, whereas others attest they point to events that occurred during the reign of Antiochus Epiphanes (175–164 B.C.). Daniel's prophecies hammer home the same truth from the stories in the first part of this book: God is in control of daily life and history.

HOUR'S UP!

The Jewish people falling into exile, the mysterious prophecy and visions of Ezekiel, and the stories and prophecies of Daniel are more than interesting stories. Each of these stories and prophecies have relevance to our world and life today. Take a few moments with these 10 questions to consider how the Scriptures are applicable to your life.

1. Throughout the time of the prophets (and especially in this hour) the people continue to rebel, yet God continues to warn his people about the results of rebellion. In what areas of your life are you in rebellion? With your family or something personal? What steps can you take to run to God instead of away from God?

2. King Hezekiah was ill and near death. Isaiah told him to put his house in order, then Hezekiah repented and the Lord said he would have 15 more years. The story illustrates how God chooses his timing for prayer and to resolve the conflicts and difficulties in our lives. What are you facing? How can you turn these areas into the hands of God?

3. Revisit some of the history of the kings and how Hezekiah's great-grandson, Josiah, was so righteous. What impact are you having on the children who are in your life? Is it to increase their faith in God? What steps can you resolve to take today to increase your impact on the children in your family or relationships?

4. In the life of the prophet Ezekiel, God used dramatic incidents to underscore his message—like not mourning the death of his wife. How have you "killed" an area of relationship with God in your life? Possibly it's an area like prayer, Bible reading, church attendance, or _____. Ask the Lord to reveal this area, then take some steps to rekindle your love relationship with God.

5. Recall Ezekiel's vision of the creatures with eyes and wheels that turn. The judgment of God is coming for the earth. What do you need to do in your life to confess or ask for forgiveness? Resolve to change at least one area of your life.

6. Ezekiel saw a valley of dry bones spring to life. God promises restoration and new life to each person. Are there areas of your life that need restoration and new life? Name a couple and then ask God to restore these areas of your life.

7. While living in exile in Babylon, Daniel resolved to continually follow the Lord. As a young man, he asked the king's steward to change his food so he didn't have to eat the king's food (offered to pagan gods). How are you daily continually following the Lord in your life? Can you take a step to strengthen your daily resolve in this area?

8. Shadrach, Meshach, and Abednego refused to bow down to worship other gods. While your life might not include a physical idol, consider the idols in your life such as money, success, possessions, etc. How are these "desires" or "idols" dominating your life? Learn from Shadrach, Meshach, and Abednego's resolve.

9. Daniel's experience with the finger of God on the wall points out the ever-watching eye of God. He knew King Belshazzar was drunk and had called for the temple goblets and used them to worship false gods. How can you increase your consciousness of God's watching presence in your life?

10. Daniel in the lions' den is a famous Bible story. Consider this story again and how it involves jealous leaders who laid a trap for Daniel. He knew about the trap, yet the prophet continued to serve and follow his God—even though it meant being thrown into the lions' den. What can you learn from Daniel's example as you seek to avoid the various spiritual traps in your life?

HOUR 9

The Minor Prophets: Part One

LESSON PLAN:

In this hour, you will learn about …

- Hosea, the prophet who married a prostitute to give an example of Israel's unfaithfulness.
- Joel, the prophet who proclaimed the coming day of God's judgment.
- The prophet Amos, who predicted God's judgment on Israel and the future glory of David's kingdom.
- The short book of Obadiah, who prophesied the doom of Edom.

In Hours 7 and 8, you learned about the four major prophets (Isaiah, Jeremiah, Ezekiel, and Daniel). In Hours 9 and 10, you will learn about the 12 men who comprise the "minor prophets." These prophets are known as minor not because of their importance but because their writings are considerably shorter than the writings of Isaiah or Jeremiah. Hosea and Amos were sent to Israel, while Obadiah, Jonah, and Nahum prophesied regarding the enemies of Israel and Judah. The other prophets spent their time in Judah: four prior to the exile and three afterward. Let's consider all of these prophets as different players on the same team. They made a major impact on their world.

JUST A MINUTE

There is nothing minor about the minor prophets—or the final 12 prophets of the Old Testament. In modern culture, bigger is seen as better and celebrity is often mistaken for significance. The longer books of Isaiah and Jeremiah "could" be mistaken to elevate their message. It's far from the truth. These short books from the "minor" prophets help us gain additional perspective on the sins God hates and the faith he honors.

How do you react when someone in your life has been unfaithful? Do you abandon this person to his or her own difficulties and push on to another person? Or do you try repeatedly to restore the unfaithful relationship? The little Book of Hosea examines these issues through the life of Hosea. The book has three parts: the unfaithfulness of Israel, Israel's disobedience and punishment, and the promise of restoration.

In the eighth century B.C., the prophet Hosea began his ministry during the reign of King Uzziah (Azariah) of Judah (792–740 B.C.) and King Jeroboam II of Israel (792–753 B.C.). Hosea's career as a prophet spanned the reigns of Judean kings Jotham (752–736 B.C.) and Ahaz (736–720 B.C.) and concluded during the rule of Hezekiah (729–699 B.C.). During the prophet's lifetime, he witnessed the reigns of the last six kings of Israel but in his prophecies, Hosea didn't mention any of their names.

THE UNFAITHFULNESS OF ISRAEL

God called the prophet to experience the message before he preached it to Israel. What did God think about the continual unfaithfulness of Israel? In Hosea, the Lord showed the prophet a personal example. "When the Lord began to speak through Hosea, the Lord said to him, 'Go, take to yourself an adulterous wife and children of unfaithfulness, because the land is guilty of the vilest adultery in departing from the Lord.'" (Hosea 1:2) In response, Hosea married Gomer, daughter of Diblaim, who was already guilty of adultery. Gomer had a son with Hosea, and then two more children from another man. These children are symbols of the past and present unfaithfulness of Israel to the Lord.

Hosea wrote, "Sound the trumpet in Gibeah, the horn in Ramah." (Hosea 5:8) The ram's horn sounded an emergency and called the fighting men to defend the land. These towns were north of Jerusalem and within or near the borders of Benjamin. The text implies the enemy had already swept through the north and was about to invade Judah. The prophetic words affirm how the Lord was bringing judgment on the people because of their disobedience.

The last two children were given names that symbolized the different problems between the Jewish people and the Lord. The second child, a daughter, was called Lo-Ruhamah (which literally means "not loved"). The name pointed out the Lord's exasperation at the disobedience and rebellion of Israel. God declared, "for I will no longer show love to the house of Israel, that I should at all forgive them. Yet I will show love to the house of Judah; and I will save them—not by bow, sword or battle, or by horses and horsemen, but by the Lord their God." (Hosea 1:6–7)

The third child showed God's final decision to reject Israel. This child was called Lo-Ammi (which literally means "not my people"). One covenant from God is prominent throughout the Bible: God declared to Israel that they were his people and he was their God. Now in Hosea, this consistent covenant formula was reversed: "Then the Lord said, 'Call him Lo-Ammi, for you are not my people and I am not your God.'" (Hosea 1:9)

The prophet Hosea proclaimed to the Israelites how they had abandoned God and chased after other gods. Canaanite religious practices had crept into every aspect of the national life and compromised the Jewish people's relationship with God. Yet the Lord was relentless in his love of Israel and declares, "I will betroth you to me forever. I will betroth you in righteousness and justice, in love and compassion." (Hosea 2:19)

Gomer, the adulteress wife, ran off from Hosea. God commanded the prophet to go to the market and buy her. Hosea's actions symbolized God's desire for reconciliation with his faithless people. They were also a statement of hope that some day people who are faithless will return again to the Lord of the Universe.

ISRAEL'S DISOBEDIENCE AND PUNISHMENT

Idolatry was the key crime in Israel. Jewish priests were feeding on the sins of the people. (Hosea 4:4–10) Young women were harlots, married women were having sexual relations with other men, and men were visiting prostitutes. (Hosea 4:11–14) Because the priests, king, and the people were rebelling against God, "their deeds do not permit them to return to their God. A spirit of prostitution is in their heart and they do not acknowledge the Lord." (Hosea 5:4) The prophet described the possibility of irreversible rejection from God. Hosea listed a series of charges against an unrepentant Israel.

JUST A MINUTE

For a minute consider the fog. It's a vapor, which covers the earth then the sun comes out and burns it off. Hosea used fog as a metaphor of Israel's faithlessness. (Hosea 6:4) Israel's commitment to God was empty and fleeting like fog. When the people felt the "heat" of moral and spiritual conflict, their loyalty to God evaporated. Hosea preached against this sort of fleeting faith, which evaporates like fog when the sun hits it.

Although the people had turned away from God, the Lord had endless compassion and desire for his people. God wanted to bind the wounds of Israel and restore His wounded people. "Come, let us return to the Lord, he has torn us into pieces but he will heal us; he has injured us but he will bind up our wounds. After two days he will revive us; on the third day he will restore us, that we may live in his presence." (Hosea 6:1–2) The prophet envisioned the Jewish people returning to the Lord, but then Hosea woke up and understood it was a dream. Because the Jewish people continued in their actions and were unrepentant, God's judgment followed on the people.

Have you heard the expression "reap the whirlwind"? The origin of the expression is likely found in Hosea. "They sow the wind and reap the whirlwind." (Hosea 8:7) In the early days of Israel, they turned to the Lord, but as they grew prosperous and more materialistic, the people relied less and less on God and turned instead to worthless idols.

THE PROMISE OF RESTORATION

While the bulk of Hosea preaches against the sins of Israel, the final chapters turn with a promise of restoration. The horrible acts of sin against the Lord are worthy of God's judgment. Justice demanded that Israel should be punished. Yet in the Lord's great compassion, he was reluctant to turn against his own people and instead looked forward to a day of restoration. "How can I give you up, Ephraim? How can I hand you over, Israel? … My heart is changed within me; all my compassion is aroused. I will not carry out my fierce anger." (Hosea 11:8–9)

Despite the catalog of sins and the proclamation of judgment, Hosea could foresee a day when Israel would admit it needed God and would turn to him. Then the Lord in great compassion would heal the wounds of the people and restore them to fellowship. Speaking of God, Hosea said, "I will heal their waywardness and love them freely, for my anger has turned away from them. I will be like the dew to Israel; he will blossom like a lily … Who is wise? He will realize these things. Who is discerning? He will understand them. The ways of the Lord are right; the righteous walk in them, but the rebellious stumble in them." (Hosea 14:4–5a, 9)

Hosea had a specific message for the people of Israel—yet with universal applications. A faithful God relentlessly loves his unfaithful people. Everyone who reads these words can draw strength from the prophet Hosea.

JOEL

This prophet carried a name meaning "Jehovah is God." Repentance is a word that many people avoid—even Christians. When someone repents, they turn away from a particular act and never repeat it again. It's much more in-depth than a simple "Hey, I'm sorry" prayer tossed on the run. Look at the depth of emotion in Joel's words, "Mourn like a virgin in sackcloth grieving for the husband of her youth." (Joel 1:8) The theme of this little book is "The Day of the Lord" or the day of God's judgment on Israel. It's not an easy message, but the message sounds clear even in today's world. The message from Joel breaks into four parts: an invasion of locusts, the Lord's answer, the day of the Lord, and the promise of future blessings.

HISTORICAL FACT

The Book of Joel doesn't have any indication about when it was written. Scholars have offered various dates for the writing from early pre-exile times to as late as 530 B.C. Some believe the internal evidence indicates the book was written during the reign of Joash king of Judah (835–796 B.C.) and in the time of Jehoida the high priest.

AN INVASION OF LOCUSTS

Remember that one of the 10 plagues in Egypt involved locusts? These flying insects ate everything green in their path. For a rural economy, which is heavily dependent on crops for human and animal feed, a plague of locusts is devastating. A locust resembles a large grasshopper and vast clouds come and swarm over the earth. Listen to Joel's specific warning: "What the locust swarm has left the great locusts have eaten; what the great locusts have left the young locusts have eaten; what the young locusts have left other locusts have eaten." (Joel 1:4) The invasion of these insects would be far worse for Israel than anything they had faced from any other enemy and Joel saw this swarm as a clear sign of God's pending judgment.

HISTORICAL FACT

An adult locust is able to live four days without eating and survive on stored fat. A locust swarm can cover more than a square mile, with 50 million insects capable of devastating 100 tons of vegetation a day. Locust swarms have been known to blanket 2,000 square miles and trigger epidemics as they die and rot. It's estimated that a swarm of locusts can eat in one day what 40,000 people eat in one year.

The Lord's Answer

Is repentance something outward or does it involve a change of heart? The prophet Joel answered this question in his charge to Israel. When it came to repentance, the Lord wanted more than tearing clothes, which the Jewish people used as a symbol of repentance. Joel proclaimed, "Rend your heart, and not your garments. Return to the Lord your God, for he is gracious and compassionate, slow to anger and abounding in love, and he relents from sending calamity." (Joel 2:13) Even in this late day, when the locust is headed to eat everything, it's not too late to repent and turn to God's compassion, says Joel. While sin leaves scars, God wants to restore people to usefulness in spite of their past disobedience.

Some people wonder if turning to God can restore the wasted years from their past. Here's a tiny promise of restoration which is slipped into Joel: "I will repay you for the years the locusts have eaten … you will have plenty to eat, until you are full, and you will praise the name of the Lord your God, who has worked wonders for you; never again will my people be shamed." (Joel 2:25–26)

The Day of the Lord

Beyond a miracle of restoration, the prophet Joel promised even greater hope: the Spirit of the Lord would be poured out on the entire world—young and old, male and female. Everyone who calls on the name of the Lord will be saved. This prophecy of Joel points to the arrival of Jesus Christ.

Many years later on Pentecost, this prophecy was fulfilled (Acts 2:16–21): "And afterward, I will pour out my Spirit on all people. Your sons and daughters will prophesy, your old men will dream dreams, and your young men will see visions … And everyone who calls on the name of the Lord will be saved." (Joel 2:28, 32) Because of his resurrection, Jesus Christ has been declared Lord. As a result, anyone who calls on the name of Jesus will be saved. Joel declared judgment against the various nations around Israel who didn't follow God but declared restoration and hope for those who turned to God.

Thirteen of the sixteen prophets address the topic of the Day of the Lord. The concept isn't a single event in human history but a reference to future events. In some Bible passages, the term describes a day when the Lord will account for past judgments and release Godly wrath. In other accounts such as Joel, the Day of the Lord isn't only about judgment but also includes a future hope, restoration, and blessing.

PROMISE OF FUTURE BLESSINGS

The final chapter of Joel looks ahead to a day when all the nations around Israel will be brought to judgment. The prophet lists some of the sins of these nations such as selling children into prostitution. Joel ends on a hopeful note forecasting the day when the Lord will bless the people. "The Lord will roar from Zion and thunder from Jerusalem; the earth and sky will tremble. But the Lord will be a refuge for his people, a stronghold for the people of Israel." (Joel 3:16) In three short chapters, the prophet Joel moves from the threat of locusts, to restoration, to the promise of God's salvation and blessing. These words written long ago can provide strength for trials.

HISTORICAL FACT

It's sobering to hear the prophet Amos describe the nation of Israel: "'They do not know how to do right,' declares the Lord, 'who hoard plunder and loot in their fortress.'" (Amos 3:10) The nation lost its national consciousness and was no longer able to distinguish between right and wrong. It's frightening when a nation is on the verge of moral collapse, yet unaware. In the case of Israel, its enemies were standing and waiting for it to fall: "Therefore this is what the Sovereign Lord says: 'An enemy will overrun the land; he will pull down your strongholds and plunder your fortresses.'" (Amos 3:10)

AMOS

Are you easily intimidated? What is your natural response to confrontation? While the natural tendency of the prophet Amos was to avoid confrontation, the Lord gave this prophet incredible boldness. Little is known about the background of the prophet Amos. Although born in the southern kingdom of Judah, Amos ministered primarily in the northern kingdom of Israel during the reigns of Uzziah, king of Judah (792–740 B.C.) and Jeroboam II, king of Israel (793–753 B.C.). In the opening verse, Amos calls himself a shepherd from Tekoa. (Amos 1:1) Some scholars believe Amos was a wealthy farmer who left his home in Judah to prophesy in Israel. Being a prophet is often a lonely occupation. The priest Amaziah from Bethel accuses Amos of conspiracy against Israel and says, "Get out, you seer! Go back to the land of Judah. Earn your bread there and do your prophesying there. Don't prophesy anymore at Bethel, because it is the king's sanctuary and the temple of the kingdom." (Amos 7:12–13)

Look at the bold tone of Amos' reply to Amaziah:

"I was neither a prophet nor a prophet's son, but I was a shepherd, and I also took care of sycamore-fig trees. But the Lord took me from tending the flock and said to me, 'Go, prophesy to my people Israel.' Now then, hear the word of the Lord. You say, 'Do not prophesy against Israel, and stop preaching against the house of Isaac.' Therefore this is what the Lord says: 'Your wife will become a prostitute in the city, and your sons and daughters will fall by the sword. Your land will be measured and divided up, and you yourself will die in a pagan country. And Israel will certainly go into exile, away from their native land.'" (Amos 7:12–17)

HISTORICAL FACT

Although Amos was a simple shepherd, the Lord gave him knowledge of lands and nations that were far beyond his Judean pastures. Because of his prophetic words, he knew about the tragic futures of Damascus (Amos 1:5) and also the nearby Philistine city of Gaza (Amos 1:6). His words of condemnation and doom encompassed the Edomites in the dry lands of the south and the Phoenicians in the seacoast town of Tyre.

It was like the shepherd told the priest, "Hey, I was minding my own business tending my flocks and taking care of my fruit trees. I didn't ask for this assignment, but God called me to it." During this period of Israel's history, there were professional prophets known as "seers" who were traveling preachers. Amos made it clear that he was not a "prophet for hire" but a real prophet called and set apart by the Lord of the Universe.

Like several of the other prophets, Amos called Israel to seek God in repentance:

"For I know how many are your offenses and how great your sins. You oppress the righteous and take bribes and you deprive the poor of justice in the courts. Therefore the prudent man keeps quiet in such times, for the times are evil. Seek good, not evil, that you may live. Then the Lord God Almighty will be with you, just as you say he is. Hate evil, love good; maintain justice in the courts. Perhaps the Lord God Almighty will have mercy on the remnant of Joseph." (Amos 5:12–15)

Like several other prophets, Amos used distinct visions to proclaim God's truth to the Israelites and show them the future for Israel. In simple word pictures, Amos described five distinct visions for the future: locust, fire, a plumb line, a basket of ripe fruit, and a stricken sanctuary. Two of the images are particularly important.

What tool is the most critical for any builder? It's not a hammer, saw, or tape measure. For any builder or carpenter, the most distinct tool is his level. If his walls and flooring are not level or "plumb," then he will soon be out of business. A building that is not level is a complete waste of time and materials. The prophet Amos didn't mince words about his vision. The shepherd-turned-prophet began talking about an important tool—the plumb line:

"This is what he showed me: the Lord was standing by a wall that had been built true to plumb, with a plumb line in his hand. And the Lord asked me, 'What do you see, Amos?' 'A plumb line,' I replied. Then the Lord said, 'Look, I am setting a plumb line along my people Israel; I will spare them no longer. The high places of Isaac will be destroyed and the sanctuaries of Israel will be ruined; with my sword I will rise against the house of Jeroboam.'" (Amos 7:7–9)

CULTURAL FACT

Amos wrote, "He who made the Pleiades and Orion...." (Amos 5:8) Pleiades refers to the cluster of stars within the constellation of Taurus, one of the signs of the Zodiac. Orion is a prominent constellation in the southern sky in the shape of a hunter. Amos is confronting the astral worship among the Israelites who had drifted far from God in their idolatry. The prophet was calling them to leave behind astrology and belief in the Zodiac and instead turn their beliefs and allegiance back to the Lord of the Universe.

For a moment, imagine a wall and God is standing on the top. The wall itself represented the people of Israel and the structure was not straight but crooked. To make his point, God dropped a plumb line with a heavy weight at one end along the side of the wall. To the casual observer, this wall probably looked straight but when against the plumb line, the wall was not perfect.

The prophet proclaimed this message to the nation of Israel, "Woe to you who long for the day of the Lord! Why do you long for the day of the Lord? That day will be darkness, not light. It will be as though a man fled from a lion only to meet a bear, as though he entered his house and rested his hand on the wall only to have a snake bite him. Will not the day of the Lord be darkness, not light—pitch-dark, without a ray of brightness?" (Amos 5:18–20)

Because of the sin of the Israelite people, Amos proclaimed God's pending judgment. He was going to tear down the wall (the people) and rebuild it so it would be plumb or level. The city was measured for destruction. Twice the Lord had measured, punished, and forgiven, but his grace and patience had run its course and the nation would be completely destroyed.

The future of Israel was also told through a fruit basket, which was likely to have been full of figs. Amos declared, "This is what the Sovereign Lord showed me: a basket of ripe fruit. 'What do you see Amos?' he asked. 'A basket of ripe fruit,' I answered. Then the Lord said to me, 'The time is ripe for my people Israel; I will spare them no longer. In that day,' declares the Sovereign Lord, 'the songs in the temple will turn to wailing. Many, many bodies—flung everywhere! Silence!'" (Amos 8:1–3)

The vision is further clarified with the prophet declaring how the Lord would hunt down the rebellious people and not one of the Israelites would be able to escape judgment. Israel might have felt special and protected from such danger because the Lord brought them out of Egypt, but God no longer chose to regard Israel as distinct and special. He said, "All the sinners among my people will die by the sword, all those who say 'Disaster will not overtake or meet us.'" (Amos 9:10)

CULTURAL FACT

"As a grain is shaken in a sieve, but not a pebble will reach the ground." (Amos 9:9) When grain was gathered into storage, the final stage was to clean the grain and sift it in a sieve. As it was winnowed, the chaff was blown away and only pebbles and small clumps of mud remained with the grain. A sieve had holes, so when it was shaken, the grain would fall through and the pebbles and other things would remain in the sieve. According to the prophet, the nation of Israel would be shaken with a sieve so fine that even the smallest grain would not come through—instead everything would be destroyed.

While much of Amos is a wake-up call to the Israelites to change their sinful ways, the final portion of the book looks ahead to the days of restoration of Israel and foreshadows the arrival of a Messiah, Jesus Christ. "'The days are coming,' declares the Lord, 'when the reaper will be overtaken by the plowman and the planter by the one treading grapes. New wine will drop from the mountains and flow from all the hills. I will bring back my exiled people Israel; they will rebuild the ruined cities and live in them. They will plant vineyards and drink their wine; they will make gardens and eat their fruit. I will plant Israel in their own land, never again to be uprooted from the land I have given them,' says the Lord your God." (Amos 9:13–15)

OBADIAH

This little book is the shortest one in the Old Testament, yet little is known from the text about the prophet or the circumstances for his prophecy. The prophet doesn't refer to any historical circumstances tied to an exact date. Scholars speculate the book was written between 605 and 586 B.C. The theme of the book centers on the ancient feud between Edom and Israel.

South of the Dead Sea stretching about 100 miles north and south and about 20 miles east and west was a rocky mountain range known as Edom. The land was well watered and abundant in pasture. Periodically the Edomites would go on raiding expeditions against Israel then retreat to their mountain strongholds. These descendants of Esau (Genesis 25:23; 27:41) were in perpetual conflict with the Jewish people. Edom refused to grant Israel a passageway through its land. In response to this action, the prophet predicted, "Because of the violence against your brother Jacob, you will be covered with shame; you will be destroyed forever." (Obadiah 1:10)

While Edom continued to commit violence against the Jewish people, God would protect Israel and eternally punish anyone who opposes them. He said, "'But on Mount Zion will be deliverance, it will be holy, and the house of Jacob will possess its inheritance. The house of Jacob will be a fire and the house of Joseph a flame, the house of Esau will be a stubble, and they will set it on fire and consume it. There will be no survivors from the house of Esau.' The Lord has spoken." (Obadiah 1:17–18)

CULTURAL FACT

Petra, the capital of Edom, was in a mountain stronghold about 5,000 feet above sea level. Because the town was virtually impregnable, the people became arrogant with their sense of security.

History bears witness to the truth behind the short Book of Obadiah. The Edomites disappeared from the face of the earth. "Deliverers will go up on Mount Zion to govern the mountains of Esau. And the kingdom will be the Lord's." (Obadiah 1:21) The final words of the prophet were against anyone who brings arrogance, pride, and rebellion. In their mountain fortress, Edom believed they were indestructible but the Lord humbled this nation and restored Israel.

Hour's Up!

As prophets of the Lord, Hosea, Joel, Amos, and Obadiah each held a significant role for the Jewish people during their lifetimes. The prophecies are more than "stories" but relevant to our lives today. Take a few moments and consider the following 10 application questions.

1. Hosea's marriage to the prostitute Gomer is a stirring example of God's faithfulness to us when we are unfaithful. Consider a time in your life—recently or farther in the past—when you were unfaithful. How can you lean on the faithfulness of God in this situation in the future?

2. Hosea preaches against the idolatry in Israel. The Jewish people weren't simply worshipping other gods but they were consciously turning away from the God of the Universe and unrepentant. Repentance means turning away from the behavior in the past. Are there gods of idolatry in your life (money, family, success, things, or add your own to this list)? Make a detailed plan to turn from these "idols" and turn toward God in your life.

3. Fog or sunshine. How do you compare your commitment to the Lord of the Universe? Is it fleeting and temporary like fog or is it firm and hot like sunshine?

4. Return to the prophet Joel and the locust. Consider the thoroughness of locusts to eat everything in their path. How in a spiritual sense is sin eating into your life? What do you need to do to repent and make a change in your life?

5. What have locusts eaten in your life? Have the years slipped away or money or family or what? Take a moment and pause in prayer and claim the promise of Joel 2:25–26.

6. The prophet Joel mentions "the Day of the Lord." In our daily lives, it's easy to forget the coming judgment of God on our world. The prophets like Joel bring us back to the point of reality—God eventually will destroy the world. Consider this concept. How does a consciousness of this reality change your plans for the day? How does it change your speech and what you talk about? Plan a couple of changes as you meditate on the Day of the Lord.

7. Revisit the prophet Amos's response to intimidation. How do you respond when someone tries to intimidate you? How can you learn from Amos and claim the boldness and the strength and wisdom to have a godly response and calm your fears?

8. The image of a plumb line or level is one that can stick with you. Consider your life next to the standard of God's truth in the Bible (your plumb line). Every day, we grow in our relationship with God and the Bible shines new truth into our life. What truth has bubbled to the surface of your life from this study? What steps can you take to consciously change?

9. Consider the overripe fruit in a basket. How does rotting fruit show you a tiny bit of God's perspective on the sins or failures of your own life? A tiny bit of sin can permeate your entire life—like a single rotten fruit corrupts a whole fruit basket. Ask God to work on your life and help you to live a more Godly life.

10. Like Edom, many people believe they are beyond the reach of God's hand, until God brings them low. Then when they humble themselves, he restores them—just like the Israelite people. Have you ever experienced a second chance or restoration from God in your life? Turn to a friend and make a point of telling someone about this restoration experience and how it was a blessing in your life.

HOUR 10

The Minor Prophets: Part Two

CHAPTER SUMMARY

LESSON PLAN:
In this hour, you'll learn about ...

- The missionary Jonah, who took a detour in the belly of a large fish.
- The prophet Micah, who forecasted the impending fall of Israel and Judah but also foretold the birthplace of the Messiah.
- Nahum, who prophesied a message of doom for Nineveh.
- Habakkuk, the prophet who taught Judah that the righteous will live by faith.
- The final four minor prophets: Zephaniah, Haggai, Zechariah, and Malachi, who each played a role in the history of the Jewish people and have relevant messages for today.

Imagine a modern-day prophet. Likely it would be a man walking down the street wearing a sandwich-board sign. The front of the sign proclaims, "Beware the world ..." and the back would say "... is coming to an end. Repent." While the image of such a man makes us smile, repentance is no laughing matter. Through the message of the minor prophets, God continually talked with the Jewish people about their destiny if they didn't change their current course of action. Prophets were lonely people because their message wasn't often kindly received. Their messages weren't just something for long ago but also stir chords in our lives today. In the next few pages, you will learn more details about some of these remarkable men.

FISH TALE OR TRUTH?

One of the better-known Bible stories almost appears too fantastic. A large fish swallows a rebellious prophet. The prophet spends three days and three nights in the belly of this large fish, before the fish throws up the prophet and he lands on the beach.

When someone tells you an amazing-wonder-if-it-really-happened type of story, how do you determine that you've heard the truth? You look for a second opinion to confirm the story. The best source for the story about Jonah is Jesus Christ. Jesus unmistakably believed Jonah's story was a historical fact. A scholar would have to strain considerably to make anything else from the language of Jesus in the New Testament when he says, "For as Jonah was three days and three nights in the belly of a huge fish, so the Son of Man will be three days and three nights in the heart of the earth. The men of Nineveh will stand up at the judgment with this generation and condemn it; for they repented at the preaching of Jonah and now one greater than Jonah is here." (Matthew 12:40–41)

Jesus called the story of Jonah a "sign" of his own resurrection. As Jesus told the story, he put his resurrection, the fish, the repentance of the Ninevites, and Judgment Day in the same category. It was reality that Jesus was talking about his own resurrection, so he also believed and accepted the story of Jonah. The story occurred exactly as it was recorded. It reveals several key principles: the danger in running away from duty, how the Lord uses imperfect men as channels of God's truth, and the expansive nature of God's mercy.

THE RELUCTANT PROPHET

The first verse of Jonah explains the prophet's mission and call from God: "The word of the Lord came to Jonah son of Amittai: 'Go to the great city of Nineveh and preach against it, because its wickedness has come up before me.'" (Jonah 1:1) Instead of heading for Nineveh, Jonah went in the opposite direction toward Tarshish, which was the farthest end of the known world. Because Jonah fled from God, the Lord sent a violent storm on the sea, which threatened to break the ship. The sailors were terrified, threw out any empty cargo, and were praying to their gods. As these sailors looked around they knew one of their passengers was missing—Jonah. The captain found Jonah asleep below deck and demanded, "How can you sleep? Get up and call on your god! Maybe he will take notice of us and we will not perish." (Jonah 1:6)

JUST A MINUTE

Many people have read children's stories about Jonah and the whale. The Hebrew word for *whale* means "great fish" or "sea monster." Many "sea monsters" have been found that are large enough to swallow a man. Jonah's three days and nights in the "great fish" was a miracle to reach the people of Nineveh with God's message. Jesus Christ referred to this miracle in Luke 11:29–30: "This is a wicked generation. It asks for a miraculous sign, but none will be given it except the sign of Jonah. For as Jonah was a sign to the Ninevites, so also will the Son of Man be to this generation." Without the miracle of the "great fish," the people of Nineveh might not have paid attention to the prophet.

As the storm continued to break at the ship, the sailors increased their intense effort to do something, so they decided to cast lots and see who was causing the storm. The lot fell to Jonah. The sailors' suspicion about Jonah increased and they asked him questions like, "What did you do?" and "Where do you come from?"

Jonah responded: "I am a Hebrew and I worship the Lord, the God of heaven, who made the sea and the land." (Jonah 1:9) His answer terrified the men; they knew Jonah was running from the Lord because he had already told them. Asking what to do, Jonah suggested that he be thrown into the sea and it would be calm because he knew the storm was his fault. Firsthand, Jonah knew the weight of guilt. Trying not to throw Jonah overboard, the men rowed against the wind and the storm grew wilder. They asked the Lord not to hold them accountable for killing Jonah, and then threw him overboard. Immediately "the raging sea grew calm." (Jonah 1:15) A great fish swallowed Jonah, and he spent three days and three nights inside the fish.

CULTURAL FACT

Scholars aren't certain where Tarshish is located, but it could be Tartessus on the south coast of Spain. The city represented the most distant city known to the Israelites. Jonah got on a ship in Joppa, a non-Israelite port town, located west of Jerusalem and about 50 miles southwest of Jonah's hometown of Gath Hepher.

Inside the fish, Jonah prayed. He showed his familiarity with the Psalms and his prayer sounds as if it could have come from this book, "In my distress I called to the Lord, and he answered me. From the depths of the grave I called for help, and you listened to my cry." (Jonah 2:2) He acknowledged his failure to follow God's command to go to Nineveh and sought God's forgiveness; then the Lord commanded the fish and "it vomited Jonah onto dry land." (Jonah 2:10)

The Lord gave Jonah a second command: "Go to the great city of Nineveh and proclaim to it the message I give you." (Jonah 3:2) Do you dare disobey God's command twice? The next verse says, "Jonah obeyed the word of the Lord and went to Nineveh."

It took Jonah three days to cross the city and proclaim his message of repentance. The prophet told the city that in 40 days, the city would be destroyed. The king proclaimed a fast and urged everyone to repent, saying, "Who knows? God may yet relent and with compassion turn from his fierce anger so that we will not perish." (Jonah 3:9) Notice the result of true repentance: "When God saw what they did and how they turned from their evil ways, he had compassion and did not bring upon them the destruction he had threatened." (Jonah 3:10)

Jonah was not surprised at the result and the change of God's plans to destroy the city. He went east and sat in the shade to see what would happen. The Lord provided a vine for shade but the next day a worm ate the vine and Jonah felt like he might die in the heat and sunshine. He was angry at God's provision of the shade, then its removal. God showed his care and compassion for the people of Nineveh saying, "You have been concerned about this vine, though you did not tend it or make it grow. It sprang up overnight and died overnight. But Nineveh has more than a hundred and twenty thousand people who cannot tell their right hand from their left, and many cattle as well. Should I not be concerned about that great city?" (Jonah 4:10)

The words of Jonah celebrate the results of true repentance and give a practical example of how to obey God's voice and follow His guiding hand.

Micah

This little book is in contrast to most of the other prophets. Instead of pronouncing doom and gloom, Micah is an impassioned plea between proclaiming impending judgment and the promise of future blessing for Israel and Judah.

Little is known about Micah beyond his name and his place of origin. The prophet was born in the rural village of Moresheth Gath in the lowlands of Judah, near the region of Philistia. The place of birth sets Micah apart from his contemporary prophets, Isaiah, who was from Jerusalem, and Hosea, who was from Israel.

Sometimes people try to make a lifetime of following God into a simple formula. Like the infomercials that promise instant hair growth or instant weight loss, these simple prescriptions often look suspicious. Is it really that easy?

Micah has a simple formula for following God's will: "He has showed you, O man, what is good. And what does the Lord require of you? To act justly and to love mercy and to walk humbly with your God." (Micah 6:8) Although the words of instruction may be simple, it takes a lifetime of discipline and self-denial to learn and absorb these three dimensions of obedience. Social injustice according to Micah is not optional for a person who follows the Lord. Each person has an obligation to do the right thing.

The second quality or discipline is to love mercy. The Hebrew word translated "mercy" also means "loyal or steadfast love." In the New Testament, Jesus Christ admonishes his followers to "love your enemies, do good to those who hate you, bless those who curse you, pray for those who mistreat you." (Luke 6:27) The challenge to love mercy is much more than difficult. It's impossible without the measure of God's grace and the empowering of God's Spirit.

The third measure of obedience from Micah called the people to walk humbly with God. The rulers of Israel had demonstrated no humility in their service of God. The prophet exhorts the people to walk humbly with God which keeps a person dependent on the Lord's resources rather than trusting in mere human solutions. A lifetime of work and effort is captured in three simple phrases.

NOSE TO NOSE WITH THE LEADERS

Like several of the other prophets, Micah didn't hold back his words when it came to confrontation about the forthcoming judgment of God on the sins of the people. He especially challenged leaders who had abandoned the call on their life from God:

But as for me, I am filled with power, with the Spirit of the Lord, and with justice and might, to declare to Jacob his transgression, to Israel his sin. Hear this, you leaders of the house of Jacob, you rulers of the house of Israel, who despise justice and distort all that is right; who build Zion with bloodshed, and Jerusalem with wickedness. Her leaders judge for a bribe, her priests teach for a price, and her prophets tell fortunes for money. Yet they lean upon the Lord and say, "Is not the Lord among us? No disaster will come upon us." Therefore because of you, Zion will be plowed like a field, Jerusalem will become a heap of rubble, the temple hill a mound overgrown with thickets. (Micah 3:8–12)

While Micah forecasts the destruction of Israel, he also holds out hope for the people. He gives one of the most famous prophecies about Jesus Christ and predicts the place of His birth. "But you, Bethlehem Ephrathah, though you are small among the clans of Judah, out of you will come for me one who will be ruler over Israel, whose origins are from of old, from ancient times." (Micah 5:2) This prophet told exactly where the Christ would be born and gave a clear anticipation of his birth.

Nahum

Reconsider Nineveh after the proclamation from Jonah. The entire city changed the direction of their lives and followed God. Scholars generally agree the prophet Nahum spoke about 120 years after Jonah (650 B.C.). Little is known about the person Nahum, whose name means "comfort."

BIBLICAL FACT

The Bible calls Nahum an "Elkoshite." Since the sixteenth century, an Arab tradition has identified Elkosh with Al Ovosh, a village near modern Mosul in Iraq. Many have speculated that the New Testament Capernaum (or "Town of Nahum") was his home, but no proof exists to substantiate this theory.

The prophet pictures the city of Nineveh in full idolatry and turned away from following God. In likely reference to the work of Jonah, Nahum says, "The Lord is slow to anger and great in power; the Lord will not leave the guilty unpunished. His way is in the whirlwind and the storm, and clouds are the dust of his feet." (Nahum 1:3) Because of Nineveh's sin, the city will be completely destroyed. The purpose of this book is to show the utter destruction of those who don't follow God and also to encourage Israel about their future restoration and relief. The prophet says, "Look at your troops—they are all women! The gates of your land are wide open to your enemies; fire has consumed their bars." (Nahum 3:13)

Habakkuk

Ever felt the injustice in the world and wanted to cry out to God for help and mercy? An intense prophet, Habakkuk had a passion about his cries to the Lord. In the opening of his book, he complained to the Lord, "How long, O Lord, must I call for help, but you do not listen? Or cry out to you, 'Violence!' but you do not save? Why do you make me look at injustice? Why do you tolerate wrong? Destruction and violence are before me; there is strife, and conflict abounds. Therefore the law is paralyzed, and justice never prevails. The wicked hem in the righteous, so that justice is perverted." (Habakkuk 1:2–4)

A simple look at the newspapers or news magazines shows the injustice and violence in the world and it doesn't seem to ever stop. The prophet complained, wondering whether God was active among the people. In light of his goodness and power, how could God allow such evil to continue? Habakkuk pledged to stand in the watchtower and wait for God's answer saying, "I will stand at my watch and station myself on the ramparts; I will look to see what he will say to me, and what answer I am to give to this complaint." (Habakkuk 2:1)

THE LORD'S ANSWER ABOUT INJUSTICE

God was not silent with the prophet's outcry but answered his pleadings: "Then the Lord replied: 'Write down the revelation and make it plain on tablets so that a herald may run with it. For the revelation awaits an appointed time; it speaks of the end and will not prove false. Though it linger, wait for it; it will certainly come and will not delay.'" (Habakkuk 2:2–3) The Lord asked Habakkuk to be patient. "My answer will come in due time," God said to the prophet.

JUST A MINUTE

Consistently throughout the Old Testament and New Testament, the Bible explains the sovereign control of God across the universe. His timing is perfect, and patience is something that has to be acquired in the face of injustice and evil. As the writer of Hebrews said, "Let us hold unswervingly to the hope we profess, for he who promised us is faithful." (Hebrews 10:23)

INTO GOD'S PRESENCE

In the tradition of Abraham, Moses, and Elijah, the prophet Habakkuk had the opportunity to know God face to face and enter into his Holy Presence. He wrote about his experience, saying, "God came from Teman, the Holy One from Mount Paran. His glory covered the heavens and his praise filled the earth. His splendor was like the sunrise; rays flashed from his hand, where his power was hidden … I heard and my heart pounded, my lips quivered at the sound; decay crept into my bones, and my legs trembled. Yet I will wait patiently for the day of calamity to come on the nation invading us." (Habakkuk 3:3–4, 16)

Because the prophet had entered God's presence, Habakkuk found answers to his pressing questions (often called *complaints* in the Bible). In the final portion of this book, Habakkuk wrote one of the most stirring passages in the Bible about faith. Notice the dismal results of life and the prophet's response: "Though the fig tree does not bud and there are no grapes on the vines, though the olive crop fails and the fields produce no food, though there are no sheep in the pen and no cattle in the stalls, yet will I rejoice in the Lord, I will be joyful in God my Savior. The Sovereign Lord is my strength; he makes my feet like the feet of a deer, he enables me to go on the heights." (Habakkuk 3:17–19)

As the prophet waited in God's presence, Habakkuk finally learned an important truth about God. He could wait patiently for the justice of God against the evil in the world. He could wait for God's blessings and be of good courage because the timing for all of life is in the hands of a sovereign and caring Lord.

The Final Four: Zephaniah, Haggai, Zechariah, and Malachi

The Old Testament ends with books from four more prophets. Each of these prophets proclaims a unique message to a unique audience. Because the books are short, let's look at these final four as a group.

Zephaniah, the Royal Prophet

A direct descendant of King Hezekiah of Judah (715–686 B.C.), Zephaniah was a part of the royal family. He prophesied during one of the most important periods of religious reform in Judah or during the reign of King Josiah (640–609 B.C.). During the reign of Manasseh, Josiah's father, the Israelites declined into idolatry and evil. When Josiah became king, he reopened the temple and rediscovered the Book of the Law. It led to a major corporate renewal of the covenant with the Lord. Some scholars believe Zephaniah uttered his prophecy near the beginning of Josiah's reign and before the religious revival swept across Judah.

The theme of Zephaniah is his search for the judgments of God. Most of the book has a somber, grim, condemning tone. In the final chapter of the book, Zephaniah foretells a glad day when the Jews will become a praise among all the earth:

On that day they will say to Jerusalem, "Do not fear, O Zion; do not let your hands hang limp. The Lord is with you, he is mighty to save. He will take great delight in you, he will quiet you with his love, he will rejoice over you with singing." … "At that time I will gather you; at that time I will bring you home, I will give you honor and praise among all the peoples of the earth when I restore your fortunes before your very eyes," says the Lord. (Zephaniah 3:16–17, 20)

HAGGAI, THE PROPHET OF THE TEMPLE

Scholars believe that Haggai was born in captivity during the 70 years of exile in Babylon and he returned to Jerusalem with King Zerubbabel. He was a contemporary of Zechariah. (Ezra 5:1, 6:14) Imagine the excitement to return to the homeland, then discover the temple of the Lord lies in ruin. Cyrus gave permission to rebuild the temple, yet this reconstruction was stalled. Haggai proclaimed, "'Is it a time for you yourselves to be living in paneled houses, while this house remains a ruin?' ... Now this is what the Lord Almighty says: 'Give careful thought to your ways. Go up into the mountains and bring down timber and build the house, so that I may take pleasure in it and be honored,' says the Lord." (Haggai 1:4, 7–8)

CULTURAL FACT

Cyrus the Great, the conqueror of the Babylonian empire, decided to allow the Jewish people who had been deported to return to their homelands. (Ezra 1:2–4) While born in Babylon, the prophet Haggai was allowed to return to Jerusalem. From 605 to 586 B.C., Jerusalem had been burned and the temple demolished. (2 Kings: 24–25) After 70 years, the people were allowed to return to Jerusalem and began to rebuild the temple, but when the enemies complained, the work stopped for 15 years. From the preaching of Haggai and Zechariah, work was resumed and completed in four years.

While the words of the prophet Haggai contain some sharp remarks about his call to build a House of the Lord, the second chapter contains some beautiful promises about the continued faithfulness of God: "'This is what I covenanted with you when you came out of Egypt. And my Spirit remains among you. Do not fear ... The glory of this present house will be greater than the glory of the former house,' says the Lord Almighty. 'And in this place I will grant peace,' declares the Lord Almighty." (Haggai 2:5, 9)

ZECHARIAH, PROPHET OF THE LONG VISION

Zechariah was a contemporary with Haggai but scholars generally agree that Zechariah was a young man because he was the grandson of Iddo, who had returned to Jerusalem 16 years earlier. (Nehemiah 12:4, 16) For a couple months, Haggai had been preaching and the people started rebuilding the temple before Zechariah began preaching. Haggai's preaching lasted less than four months but Zechariah preached for about two years. The Book of Zechariah is longer than Haggai and includes numerous Messianic details about the life and work of Christ.

Initially, Zechariah called the people to repentance (sound familiar?), then he launched into eight night visions. The primary importance of this book is the series of Messianic prophecies concerning Christ. Each of the following statements is in plain and specific language. They are not only about the great doctrines of the coming Messiah's death for sin and his deity, but they also include details about his life such as entering Jerusalem riding a donkey and the betrayal of Jesus for 30 pieces of silver:

- Christ's atoning death for the removal of sin (Zechariah 3:8–9, 13:1)
- The Triumphal Entry (Zechariah 9:9, quoted in Matthew 21:5 and John 12:15)
- Jesus' universal reign as King and Priest (Zechariah 6:13, 9:10)
- Jesus' betrayal for 30 pieces of silver (Zechariah 11:12, quoted in Matthew 27:9–10)
- His deity (Zechariah 12:8)
- His pierced hands on the cross (Zechariah 12:10, 13:6, quoted in John 19:37)

The final chapter of Zechariah proclaims the return of the Lord to reign in Jerusalem in stirring words, "The Lord will be king over the whole earth. On that day there will be one Lord, and his name the only name." (Zechariah 14:9)

MALACHI, THE FINAL OLD TESTAMENT PROPHET TO A DISOBEDIENT PEOPLE

Most scholars believe that Malachi is the last prophet of the Old Testament who proclaims to a disobedient nation. The exact date is not known, but it is generally accepted that Malachi lived nearly a century after Haggai and Zechariah and also that Malachi worked with Nehemiah and Ezra for their reforms. His life is generally placed at 450 to 400 B.C. This book represents an important transition between the Old Testament and the New Testament.

CULTURAL FACT

The Jews had been home from Babylon for about 100 years and had given up their idolatry because of their exile yet still were neglecting the house of the Lord. The priests had grown lax, and the sacrifices were inferior, plus tithes were neglected. The people had reverted to their old practice of intermarrying with idolatrous neighbors. (Ezra 9)

What happens when you forget about the love of God? When someone forgets about God's love, it affects the home, worship, and attitudes. If God's love and loyalty are in doubt, a sacred commitment is no longer sacred. The Lord sent the prophet Malachi to shake the Jewish people from their spiritual stupor and to come back to the Lord. Malachi reveals a people who question the reality of their sin and the faithfulness of God. They are hardened in their attitudes through and through.

Just listen to some harsh and frank words from Malachi, which are rarely quoted in today's culture yet are still relevant (speaking about marriage):

Has not the Lord made them one? In flesh and spirit they are his. And why one? Because he was seeking godly offspring. So guard yourself in your spirit, and do not break faith with the wife of your youth. "I hate divorce," says the Lord God of Israel, "and I hate a man's covering himself with violence as well as his garment," says the Lord Almighty. So guard yourself in your spirit, and do not break faith. (Malachi 2:15–15)

Repeatedly the prophets have exhorted the people about "The Day of the Lord." Like those before him, Malachi returns to this theme in the final words of the book, "Remember the law of my servant Moses, the decrees and laws I gave him at Horeb for all Israel. See I will send you the prophet Elijah before that great and dreadful day of the Lord comes. He will turn the hearts of the fathers to their children, and the hearts of the children to their fathers; or else I will come and strike the land with a curse." (Malachi 4:4–6) The book ends with a confrontation between a disappointed God and a disappointed people. These are the final words from a prophet of God for 400 years.

HOUR'S UP!

As you've completed this hour, you've studied through all of the prophets—major and minor. While each of these men prophesied for their period of Jewish history, the Scriptures have application to our lives today as well. Take a few minutes and ponder these questions, which will help you see the relevance of the minor prophets to your everyday life.

1. When God told Jonah to go to Nineveh, the prophet headed in the opposite direction. Isn't that human nature to be contrary and opposite from what we know to do? How is this happening in your own life? Where are you stubborn and resisting the direction of God in your life? Be honest and then turn toward the Lord.

2. Jonah shows us how God uses imperfect people as channels of truth and mercy. How is God using you as a channel of truth and mercy in your home? Your office? Your neighborhood? Are there steps you need to take to increase your witness for God in these places? Make some concrete plans.

3. Jonah uses some verses from the Psalms for his prayers inside the great fish. Take a moment to turn to the Psalms and use them in your prayers. They will give you some fresh insight in how to pray and praise God.

4. The prophet Micah provides a formula for following the will of God: Act justly, love mercy, and walk humbly. Consider each of these traits in your life. How can you learn more about God's will and follow these three traits? Make a recommitment in one area in particular to grow in this area of your life.

5. Nahum shows the continual need to return to God in repentance. It's not a one-time action, and Nineveh had returned to their godless actions from the time of Jonah. Name an area of your life where you have to continually work: anger, temper, impatience—to name a few common ones. Select one and make a commitment to repent and renew your effort in prayer and God's grace in your life.

6. Injustice surrounded Habakkuk. This prophet pledged to stand in the gap for the injustice of his nation. How does injustice affect your current life? Think about the violence in your city, in our nation and world. What steps can you take to increase your time in prayer for these areas of injustice?

7. Habakkuk learned the value of entering God's presence. Through prayer, we can enter into a conversation with God. We talk, then sit in silence and listen to his guidance. Maybe the guidance will be a still small voice of reminder or possibly a verse from the Bible. Too often in our hurried world, we don't take the time to listen to God. Take a few moments today to sit in God's presence. Reread Habakkuk 3:17–19.

8. In the short Book of Zephaniah, we are reminded, "The Lord is with you, he is mighty to save. He will take great delight in you, he will quiet you with his love, he will rejoice over you with singing." (Zephaniah 3:16) Meditate on God's mighty power to intervene in your life and quiet you with his love. In faith, trust God with a difficulty in your life (everyone has at least one).

9. Zechariah's small book is filled with Messianic prophecies about Jesus Christ. Take a few minutes and look up each of the Scriptures in this section about Jesus. They were written many years before Jesus walked the earth. How do these Messianic prophecies strengthen your faith and belief in Jesus as the Christ?

10. The final book in the Old Testament, Malachi, reminds readers to focus on the love of God. Take a small piece of paper and write the words, "God loves me." Put the paper in your pocket, on your desk, or on the dashboard of your car. Let the words sweep over you, and celebrate God's love in your life.

HOUR 11

The Israelites Return Home

CHAPTER SUMMARY

LESSON PLAN:

In this hour, you'll learn about ...

- The priest Ezra and the power of God's word in human life.
- The trusted official of King Artaxerxes, Nehemiah, who rebuilt the walls of Jerusalem.
- Queen Esther, who saved the Jewish people from destruction.

Imagine for a moment that today's political climate in Cuba changes. The Cubans, who have been living in Miami, Florida, are given the opportunity to return to Havana, which has become a dilapidated and poverty-stricken countryside. How many of the people would return? Would they have the patience to rebuild their old countryside? What would be the people's reaction if pockets of Communists attacked the Cubans and waged guerrilla warfare?

In many ways, the imaginary scene with Cuba actually happened with the Jewish people. Babylon and Assyria had taken the people away from Jerusalem and Judah into captivity in their lands. For 70 years, the people had settled into an economic and social situation in a new place. The life in exile healed the people of their idol worship and gave them a new devotion to the Lord Jehovah. In the providence of God and in answer to the prophecy from Isaiah (Isaiah 44:28), the Jewish state was reborn.

There were three returns from Babylonian exile as recorded in the books of Ezra and Nehemiah. Under Zerubbabel as the governor, the first group of Jews returned and the temple was rebuilt in 538 B.C. Ezra led the second return in 458 B.C. and when Nehemiah was governor he led the third return in 444 B.C. Under the second and third return (Ezra and Nehemiah), the walls of Jerusalem were rebuilt. While in the Bible the Book of Esther is after Nehemiah, the events in the book took place about 30 years before Nehemiah. Esther and her marriage to the king gave the Jewish people prestige in the nation and made possible the later work of Nehemiah. During this hour, you will learn about three books written about the same period of history: Ezra, Nehemiah, and Esther.

EZRA

The priest Ezra, according to persistent Jewish tradition, wrote 1 and 2 Chronicles, Ezra, and Nehemiah. Tradition says that originally the four books were one work. Some scholars believe that Nehemiah wrote the Book of Nehemiah. As the great-grandson of Hilkiah, the priest who 160 years earlier had directed King Josiah's reformation, Ezra returned to Jerusalem in 457 B.C., which was 80 years after Zerubbabel returned and 13 years before Nehemiah.

The final two verses of 2 Chronicles are the same as the first two verses of Ezra, which explains why some people think they were originally one book and written by the same person. The prophet Daniel probably showed King Cyrus the prophecies concerning the return of the people and also the prophecies of Isaiah who 200 years before had called Cyrus by name.

It's no wonder that Cyrus had high regard for the Jews. Listen to the opening words of Ezra to see this high opinion from Cyrus: "This is what Cyrus king of Persia says: 'The Lord, the God of heaven, has given me all the kingdoms of the earth and he has appointed me to build a temple for him at Jerusalem in Judah. Anyone of his people among you—may his God be with him, and let him go up to Jerusalem in Judah and build the temple of the Lord, the God of Israel, the God who is in Jerusalem.'" (Ezra 1:2–3)

HISTORICAL FACT

One hundred forty years before Cyrus issued the decree allowing the Jewish people to return to Israel, the prophet Isaiah said a man named Cyrus would issue this order. (Isaiah 44:28) Josephus, a first-century Jewish historian, later asserted that Cyrus was shown Isaiah's prophecy and that the king had an earnest ambition to fulfill what was written. If the story is true, it is possible that Daniel was the one who showed Cyrus the Isaiah prophecy. (Daniel 6:28, 9:1–2; 10:1)

With this invitation from the king to return to their homeland, the 42,360 people (not counting their 7,337 servants and 200 men and women singers) packed their belongings and headed for Jerusalem. Each of these people traveled home with a vision inside their mind of what God's temple would look like. Here's what they found after seven months of traveling:

When the seventh month came and the Israelites had settled in their towns, the people assembled as one man in Jerusalem. Then Jeshua son of Jozadak and his fellow priests and Zerubbabel son of Shealtiel and his associates began to build the altar of the God of Israel to sacrifice burnt offerings on it, in accordance to what is written in the Law of Moses the man of God. Despite their fear of the peoples around them, they built the altar on its foundations and sacrificed burnt offerings on it to the Lord, both morning and evening sacrifices. Then in accordance with what is written, they celebrated the Feast of Tabernacles with the required number of burnt offerings prescribed each day. (Ezra 3:1–4)

HISTORICAL FACT

Ezra was called a scribe. (Ezra 7:6) He had the qualities of a scribe, which included a detailed, technical knowledge of the Law and the ability to teach it. (Ezra 7:10) Officials known as scribes were mostly secretaries and recorders.

EZRA AND HIS COMPANIONS ARRIVE IN JERUSALEM

The Jewish people had traveled many days to reach the site of the Lord's temple. Although their parents and forefathers had been guilty of idolatry and disobedience for generations, they gathered as a single group or "one man" in the place of ruin that was formerly called Solomon's Temple. The grandeur and beauty of the place was gone, yet the people wanted to celebrate their arrival in the land and at the Temple of God.

Within a short time, they began to rebuild the temple with great fanfare and celebration:

When the builders laid the foundation of the temple of the Lord, the priests in their vestments and with trumpets, and the Levites (the sons of Asaph) with cymbals, took their places to praise the Lord, as prescribed by David king of Israel. With praise and thanksgiving they sang to the Lord: "He is good; his love to Israel endures forever." And all the people gave a great shout of praise to the Lord, because the foundations of the house of the Lord was laid. (Ezra 3:10–11)

The celebration was for more than simply a foundation. The people renewed their covenant with the God of Israel and were committing themselves to the completion of a beautiful temple in God's name and also honoring the Lord every day with their lives. And witness their reaction to the laying of the temple foundation, "But many of the older priests and Levites and family heads, who had seen the former temple, wept aloud when they saw the foundation of this temple being laid, while many others shouted for joy. No one could distinguish the sound of the shouts of joy from the sound of weeping, because the people made so much noise. And the sound was heard far away." (Ezra 3:12–13) These elder leaders had seen the former temple, dreamed of rebuilding the temple, and now wept with joy as it was about to be rebuilt.

While King Cyrus was in power, the reconstruction temple work was steady, and then his successor, Artaxerxes (see the following section on Esther), took the throne of Persia and for a time the temple building was halted. The priest Ezra had to return to Babylon to settle a dispute about the Israelites rebuilding the temple. Eventually the dispute was settled and the temple completed. Ezra writes:

Then the people of Israel—the priests, the Levites and the rest of the exiles—celebrated the dedication of the house of God with joy. For the dedication of this house of God they offered a hundred bulls, two hundred rams, four hundred male lambs and, as a sin offering for all Israel, twelve male goats, one for each of the tribes of Israel. And they installed the priests in their divisions and the Levites in their groups for the service of God at Jerusalem, according to what is written in the Book of Moses. (Ezra 6:16–18)

Because the people had rebuilt the physical structure of the temple, they restarted the various offices of the priesthood and also began the sacrifices—or their means to enter into God's presence through worship. Also for the first time in many years, the people began to celebrate the Passover. "So the Israelites who had returned from exile ate it, together with all who had separated themselves from the unclean practices of their Gentile neighbors in order to seek the Lord, the God of Israel. For seven days they celebrated with joy by changing the attitude of the king of Assyria, so that he assisted them in the work on the house of God, the God of Israel." (Ezra 6:21–22)

Ezra Exhorts the People to Religious Renewal

The stage was set in Israel for a new religious renewal. While the Book of Ezra isn't precise about the dates, Ezra returned to Babylon, set out for Jerusalem in April 458 B.C., and arrived in August of that year. The priest was well versed in the Law of Moses (the first five books of the Bible) and a large body of Jews returned with Ezra to Jerusalem. The book takes a shift at the beginning of chapter 8 and switches to first person for chapters 8 and 9.

When Ezra arrived in Jerusalem, various representatives approached him about the lapse in standards from the leadership. The priests and other leaders had married foreigners. This development shocked Ezra because he saw those marriages as being in direct violation to God's laws. He said, "When I heard this, I tore my tunic and cloak, pulled my hair from my head and beard and sat down appalled ... And I sat there appalled until the evening sacrifice." (Ezra 9:3–4) The priest fell on his face before God in prayer and said, "O my God, I am too ashamed and disgraced to lift up my face to you, my God, because our sins are higher than our heads and our guilt has reached the heavens." (Ezra 9:6)

CULTURAL FACT

Tradition says that Ezra was the originator of synagogue worship and the president of the Great Synagogue. Nehemiah was said to have organized the Great Synagogue in about 410 B.C., and Ezra served as the president. The Great Synagogue or Great Assembly was a body in Nehemiah 8–9, which organized various legal and ritual enactments. Scholars disagree about the exact nature of this institution. The Great Synagogue had the purpose to rebuild the religious life of the returned Israelites. Tradition says that the Great Synagogue played an important role in gathering, grouping, and restoring the books in the Old Testament.

Why was intermarriage such a problem for Ezra as he called the people to righteousness? From the Jewish history before their exile, intermarriage with non-Jews almost invariably led the people into idolatry and worship of foreign gods. The exile to Babylon was seen as a purification of Israel and the people had affirmed their desire to follow God's law, which prohibited marriage to non-Jews.

While the people had sinned, Ezra called the people of Jerusalem to assemble. Scholars generally agree that Ezra called them during the rainy season (November to December 458 B.C.). When the priest set the issue before the people, he received overwhelming support and a committee of investigation was established. Three months later, the committee reported that over a hundred men, including a number of Levites, had married foreign wives. All those men were required to divorce their wives, even if they had children with these women. While this method of reestablishing the purity of the Jewish people sounds severe, it was effective.

The book ends with a list of the men who committed the sin of marriage to foreign wives, and then abruptly ends. As mentioned earlier, most scholars believe the books of Ezra and Nehemiah were part of a larger book (along with the books of Chronicles), which explains the lack of conclusion.

NEHEMIAH

The story of Nehemiah, a civil governor, begins in far-off Persia where he was a cupbearer for the king:

In the month of Kislev in the twentieth year, while I was in the citadel of Susa, Hanani, one of my brothers, came from Judah with some other men, and I questioned them about the Jewish remnant that survived the exile, and also about Jerusalem. They said to me, "Those who survived the exile and are back in the province are in great trouble and disgrace. The wall of Jerusalem is broken down, and its gates have been burned with fire." When I heard these things I sat down and wept. For some days I mourned and fasted and prayed before the God of heaven. (Nehemiah 1:1b–4)

Nehemiah was a man of prayer and persistence. He prayed for four months before making a request to the king. Look at Nehemiah's broken spirit as he prayed:

"O Lord, God of heaven, the great and awesome God, who keeps his covenant of love with those who love him and obey his commands, let your ear be attentive and your eyes open to hear the prayer your servant is praying before you day and night for your servants, the people of Israel. I confess the sins we Israelites, including myself and my father's house, have committed against you. We have acted very wickedly toward you. We have not obeyed the commands, decrees and laws you gave your servant Moses." (Nehemiah 1:5–7)

PEOPLE TO KNOW

A part of the royal court and a highly trusted individual, Nehemiah was a cupbearer to King Artaxerxes I, son of Xerxes, and, thus, the stepson of Queen Esther, the Jewess. Esther became queen of Persia about 60 years after the Jews returned to the city of David, Jerusalem. Because of Esther, the Jews must have had prestige in the Persian court. Many scholars believe that Esther was still alive and an influential person when both Ezra and Nehemiah went to Jerusalem.

In exile, Nehemiah understood the reason Jerusalem had been destroyed and how the people had been carried off into a foreign land. He and others had sinned. Also through prayer, Nehemiah knew the Lord was calling him to return to Jerusalem and direct the rebuilding of the walls around the City of David. As he continued praying, Nehemiah asked God to soften the heart of King Artaxerxes for his request of a leave of absence:

In the month of Nisan in the twentieth year of King Artaxerxes, when wine was brought to him, I took the wine and gave it to the king. I had not been sad in his presence before; so the king asked me, "Why does your face look so sad when you are not ill? This can be nothing but sadness of heart." I was very much afraid, but I said to the king, "May the king live forever! Why should my face not look sad when the city where my fathers are buried lies in ruins, and its gates have been destroyed by fire?" The king said to me, "What is it you want?"

Then I prayed to the God of heaven, and I answered the king, "If it pleases the king and if your servant has found favor in his sight, let him send me to the city of Judah where my fathers are buried so I can rebuild it." Then the king, with the queen sitting beside him, asked, "How long will your journey take, and when will you get back?" It pleased the king to send me; so I set a time. (Nehemiah 2:1–6)

The king's heart was prepared for Nehemiah's conversation because of his time spent in prayer. In fact, the king initiated the conversation asking, "What's wrong, Nehemiah? You look sad." The comment from the king appears tender and kind, yet why do the verses say that Nehemiah felt afraid? In the court of the Medo-Persian kings, the people were forbidden to show any negative emotion. The punishment was death. Because of his prayers, Nehemiah was filled with courage and told the king exactly what was bothering him.

When the king heard his difficulty, Artaxerxes asked what he could do to help. Nehemiah shot up a quick prayer, "Help me, God." It was a miracle that the king granted Nehemiah's request. The cupbearer and his companions were given safe passage from Babylon to Jerusalem and they had papers that identified them as on a mission from the king. Along their route to Jerusalem, they were given permission to gather any building materials.

After arriving, Nehemiah faced the physical challenge of rebuilding the broken walls but then he had another difficulty:

When Sanballat heard that we were rebuilding the wall, he became angry and was greatly incensed. He ridiculed the Jews and in the presence of his associates and the army of Samaria, he said, "What are those feeble Jews doing? Will they restore their wall? Will they offer sacrifices? Will they finish in a day? Can they bring the stones back to life from those heaps of rubble—burned as they are?" Tobiah the Ammonite, who was at his side, said, "What they are building—if even a fox climbed up on it, he would break down their wall of stones." (Nehemiah 4:1–3)

The words of these opponents hurt Nehemiah and his men but they were determined to continue. The cupbearer prayed, "Hear us, O our God, for we are despised. Turn their insults back on their own heads. Give them over as plunder in a land of captivity ... So we rebuilt the wall till all of it reached half its height, for the people worked with all their heart." (Nehemiah 4:4, 6)

PEOPLE TO KNOW

Sanballat was a leading opponent of the Jews after their return from captivity. He tried to hinder the work of Nehemiah to rebuild the walls of Jerusalem. His designation as a Horonite probably indicates the town of his origin, possibly Horonaim of Moab. In papyri found at the Jewish settlement in Elephantine, Egypt, Sanballat is called the governor of Samaria. His daughter married "one of the sons of Joiada, the son of Eliashib the high priest." (Nehemiah 13:28) Nehemiah viewed such a "mixed marriage" as a defilement of the priesthood.

Tobiah was an Ammorite official who tried to prevent the Jews from rebuilding the wall of Jerusalem. (Nehemiah 2:10; 4:3; 6:1–19) Tobiah is shown in high favor with leading men in Jerusalem who were bound to him by marriage relationships. During Nehemiah's absence in Babylon, Eliashib, the priest, gave Tobiah a special room in the Temple, from which Nehemiah ejected him. (Nehemiah 13:4–6) It is clear that Tobiah was a man of considerable influence.

When Sanballat and Tobiah saw their ridicule didn't stop any of the work on the wall, they conspired to attack the workers and even kill them. Nehemiah got word about this possible attack and set guards for the workmen. Also he made a short speech:

After I looked things over, I stood up and said to the nobles, the officials and the rest of the people, "Don't be afraid of them. Remember the Lord, who is great and awesome, and fight for your brothers, your sons and your daughters, your wives and your homes." When our enemies heard that we were aware of their plot and that God had frustrated it, we all returned to the wall, each to his own work." (Nehemiah 4:14–15)

Despite the opposition, the reconstruction of the wall moved rapidly ahead. "So the wall was completed on the twenty-fifth of Elul, in fifty-two days. When all our enemies heard about this and all the surrounding nations saw it, our enemies lost their self-confidence, because they realized that this work had been done with the help of our God." (Nehemiah 6:15–16)

To celebrate the completion of the wall, Nehemiah and Ezra knew the people needed reformation again. Ezra brought out the Book of the Law of Moses and read it to the people. "He read it aloud from daybreak till noon as he faced the square before the Water Gate in the presence of the men, women and others who could understand. And all the people listened attentively to the Book of the Law." (Nehemiah 8:3–4) As they heard God's words, the people realized corruption again had invaded the priesthood. Nehemiah persevered in cleansing the Temple of these disobedient priests. This final act from Nehemiah shows how everyone needs a leader or Savior. The people would have to wait 400 years before the Messiah arrived.

JUST A MINUTE

In the presence of the Jewish people, Nehemiah read the entire Book of the Law. (Nehemiah 8:3–4) As a result of his faithfulness, Nehemiah cleansed the Temple of disobedient priests, yet the people lacked a consistent leader or guide or priest for the next 400 years until Jesus Christ arrived and began his three years of teaching and ministry at the age of 30. Until Jesus began his ministry, the Jewish people were waiting and watching expectantly for the arrival of their Savior or Messiah the prophets had foretold.

ESTHER

Some have said the Book of Esther contains the first recorded beauty pageant. This short book has all of the elements of a great novel: A beautiful young orphan girl who is not known rises to become the queen of the land. She hides a secret, which could mean her death. The story includes an ambitious villain with a passion to destroy the innocent and become the king's top counselor. This story includes romantic love, a power struggle, and a startling expose.

The overriding point of the story is clear: The God of the Universe steps into a difficult situation to rescue the Jewish people and save them from certain destruction. The book is unusual in the respect that God is not mentioned in the entire book. Scholars agree the writer assumed the presence of God and the activity of God to guide human events, which make the book more than simply a "nice" story.

Although the Book of Esther follows the Book of Nehemiah in the Bible, the events in this book occur about 30 years before Nehemiah. The first group of Jews returned to Jerusalem in 538 B.C. Twenty years later, the temple was completed. (Ezra 1–6) About 40 years later, the story of Esther takes place.

ORPHAN GIRL BECOMES QUEEN

The story opens with a wild celebration in Susa, the Persian kingdom of Cush. King Xerxes had gathered the leaders for a banquet. "For a full 180 days, he displayed the vast wealth of his kingdom and the splendor and glory of his majesty." (Esther 1:4) The men and the women had separate banquets of celebration. During the seventh day, when King Xerxes was in high spirits from wine, he commanded his servants to "bring before him Queen Vashti, wearing her royal crown, in order to display her beauty to the people and nobles, for she was lovely too look at." (Esther 1:11)

Yet when the queen refused to appear, the king burned with anger. Not normally refused anything, the king asked the wise men what to do about this situation. These scholarly men understood the importance of this refusal: It could potentially open the door for many wives throughout the nation to refuse their husbands. They proposed a solution to the king: to issue a royal decree, which could not be repealed, commanding Vashti never to appear in his presence again. "Also let the king give her royal position to someone else who is better than she. Then when the king's edict is proclaimed throughout all his vast realm, all the women will respect their husbands, from the least to the greatest." (Esther 1:19b–20)

The edict from the king created a vacancy, and a search for a beautiful wife was begun. The story turns and introduces the exiled Jews living in the city of Susa. "Mordecai had a cousin named Hadassah, whom he had brought up because she had neither father nor mother. This girl, who was also known as Esther, was lovely in form and features, and Mordecai had taken her as his own daughter when her father and mother died." (Esther 2:7)

At the king's order, the young girls of the kingdom were brought to the palace and Esther entered the harem for preparation to meet the king. Mordecai forbade Esther to say anything about her family or nationality. Each girl had 12 months of beauty treatments before they were brought to the king. "Now the king was more attracted to Esther than to any of the other women, and she won his favor and approval more than any of the other virgins. So he set a royal crown on her head and made her queen instead of Vashti." (Esther 2:17)

After Esther had become the queen, she continued not saying anything about her Jewish heritage. Cousin Mordecai, while sitting at the king's gate, uncovered a plot to assassinate the king and told Esther. The queen told the king and the two officials were hanged. Mordecai received the credit for stopping the assassination. (Esther 2:19–23)

HAMAN'S PLOT TO DESTROY THE JEWS

King Xerxes honored and elevated Haman, the Agagite. The king commanded all royal officials and noblemen to kneel and pay him honor. Mordecai would not kneel or pay honor to Haman and it enraged him. Haman learned that Mordecai was a Jew and plotted to destroy all of the Jews throughout the nation. Going to the king, Haman talked about the different customs and habits of the Jewish people, how they didn't obey the king's laws and it was in his interest to destroy them. To sweeten the offer, Haman offered to give the king ten thousand talents of silver for the royal treasury. The king listened and said, "Keep the money and do with the people as you please." (Esther 3:11) Then the king issued a decree with his royal seal to kill all of the Jews—young and old, men and women, including little children—on a single day and to plunder their goods.

As Mordecai learned of this death decree from the king, he tore his clothes and mourned bitterly sitting at the king's gate. No one was allowed to enter the palace in mourning. Queen Esther heard about her cousin and sent a servant to find out why he was in sackcloth. Mordecai told the servant everything about the plot to destroy the Jews and her cousin urged Esther to enter the king's presence and beg for mercy.

Listening to the message, Esther described her possible death sentence if she were to enter the king's presence without an invitation. She had not been called to the king for 30 days. When the servant brought this news, Mordecai told his adopted daughter, the queen, "Do not think that because you are in the king's house you alone of all the Jews will escape. For if you remain silent at this time, relief and deliverance for the Jews will rise from another place, but you and your father's family will perish. And who knows but that you have come to royal position for such a time as this?" (Esther 4:13–14) In reply to her cousin, Esther requested the Hebrews fast for three days before she tried to reach the king and she concluded, "When this is done, I will go to the king, even though it is against the law. And if I perish, I perish." (Esther 4:16)

JUST A MINUTE

The Book of Esther is distinctive in three ways. First, the central figure of the book is a woman. It's striking to find a female playing the central role in a story set in the most public of domains, the royal court. Second, instructions from the Torah define Jewish life, for example in matters of diet, Sabbath, and marriage, are notable in their absence from Esther. Finally, God is not directly mentioned in this story of deliverance from danger in an alien land. Mordecai has an oblique reference to deity in 4:14, but if Esther is read within the larger biblical context, hints of providential design are reinforced.

ESTHER'S REQUEST TO THE KING

On the third day, Queen Esther put on her royal robes and walked to the inner court of the palace. The king sat on his throne facing the entrance and held out his royal scepter. She had risked her life and pleased the king. "What is it, Queen Esther? What is your request? Even up to half of the kingdom and it will be given to you?"

Esther said, "If it pleases the king, let him come with Haman today to a banquet for him." Later the king and Haman came to Esther's banquet, and the king asked his question again, "What do you want, Queen Esther? Ask and it will be given to you, up to half of the kingdom." She replied, "If it pleases the king, let the king and Haman come tomorrow for a banquet; then I will answer the king's question."

Haman left the queen's banquet in high spirits but burned with anger when he passed the king's gate and saw Mordecai, the Jew who refused to bow down to him. At his home, Haman gathered his wife and friends to tell about the queen's banquet and the Jew who refused to honor him. He asked their advice about what to do. His wife and friends suggested that Haman build a 75-foot gallows and ask the king to hang Mordecai on it, and then go to Queen Esther's dinner. (Esther 7)

That night the king could not sleep, so he ordered the book of chronicles of his reign to be read to him (good falling-asleep material). During the reading, he learned about how Mordecai had foiled an assassination plot. "What honor and recognition has Mordecai received?" the king asked. "Nothing has been done for him," his attendants answered.

The king asked, "Who is in the court?" Haman had arrived to ask the king to hang Mordecai on the gallows. Invited into the king's chamber, the king asked Haman, "What should be done for the man the king delights to honor?" Self-centered Haman believed that he would be the man the king mentioned, so he suggested that the honoree receive a royal horse from the king and a royal robe and have a noble prince walk before him, proclaiming, "This is what is done for the man the king delights to honor!" The king commanded Haman, "Get the robe and the horse and do this at once for Mordecai. Don't neglect to do anything you mentioned."

For the next day, Haman walked the streets and honored Mordecai. Rushing home to prepare to attend the queen's second banquet, Haman described his day to his wife and friends. They warned him, "Since Mordecai, before whom your downfall has started, is of Jewish origin, you cannot stand against him—you will surely come to ruin!" (Esther 6:13)

At the queen's banquet with Haman and the king, the king again asked Queen Esther what she wanted. She pleaded for the king to spare the lives of her and her people. Then the king asked for clarification, "Who is he? Where is the man who has dared to do such a thing?" Queen Esther answered, "The adversary and enemy is this vile Haman." (Esther 7:5–6) Angry, the king hanged Haman on the gallows prepared for Mordecai.

PURIM CELEBRATED; THE GREATNESS OF MORDECAI

Although the enemy of the Jews, Haman, had been killed, the king's edict against the Jews still needed to be overturned. King Xerxes wrote another command for the Jews to assemble and protect themselves and to kill and destroy anything which might attack them. Queen Esther had saved the lives of the Jewish people in Persia. In commemoration, the Jews continue to celebrate the Feast of Purim.

The story concludes with a stirring accounting of Mordecai. "Mordecai the Jew was second in rank to King Xerxes, preeminent among the Jews, and held in high esteem by his many fellow Jews, because he worked for the good of his people and spoke up for the welfare of all the Jews." (Esther 10:3)

JUST A MINUTE

The story of Esther is not just one with a moral. This historical event is about the Jewish deliverance from complete destruction during the days following the Babylonian captivity. What if the nation of Israel had been completely wiped out 500 years before Christ arrived into the world? It would have made a radical difference in the rest of history: no Jewish people, no Messiah; no Messiah, no lost world. The beautiful girl Esther paved the way for the coming of Jesus Christ to the world. Through Queen Esther, God preserved the lives of the Jewish people and in the big picture of human history moved so that Jesus Christ could eventually rescue a lost world.

HOUR'S UP!

During this hour, you've learned about the priest Ezra, the civil governor Nehemiah, and Queen Esther. These historical figures had impact on their culture and people, yet they are also relevant to our lives today. The Bible is more than knowledge, the information has spiritual application to our everyday lives. The following 10 questions will guide you in moving from your head knowledge about these historical figures to enhancing your spiritual journey.

1. Ezra says when the Jewish people traveled from exile to Jerusalem, they gathered in the ruined area of Solomon's Temple as "one man." Note the focus they had on a single goal—to rebuild the temple. What goals are you facing in your life? Name one or two, then pick one to focus on and see whether you can make some solid progress—operating as "one man" to meet the objective of this goal.

2. As the Jews laid the foundation stone for the new temple in Jerusalem, they celebrated with praise and thanksgiving. Praise and thanksgiving isn't for a single holiday, but it's something that is to be a part of our regular worship of God. Take some steps to increase your daily praise and thanksgiving. It might be as simple as listening to some praise and worship music on the way to work or in your kitchen.

3. When Ezra arrived in Jerusalem, he didn't hesitate to confront the Jewish leaders about their intermarriage in direct violation of God's Law. He forced the people to make difficult decisions to gain purity. Sometimes we have to make difficult choices to recommit our lives to a pure and holy relationship with God and our fellow man. Is there some area of your life that needs this rededication to purity and following God's Law? Plan a course of action to change and follow God's Law.

4. Nehemiah was a man of prayer and persistence. As a member of the royal court, he prayed four months before asking the king for his release. Are there decisions in your life that need to be made but involve prayer and persistence? Follow the example of Nehemiah as you rise to these challenges of life.

5. When King Artaxerxes asked Nehemiah what he could do to help, the cupbearer sent up a one-second prayer, "Help me, God." When you face a sudden need, where do you turn? A one-second prayer or do you simply move ahead on your own strength and energy? Do something physical to remind you to try more one-second prayers. Possibly it's writing the word "Pray" on the mirror of your bathroom or some other creative solution. Pray and ask God to show you.

6. After Nehemiah arrived in Jerusalem, he faced some severe opposition. The spiritual life of following God is not without opposition. As you reflect on how Nehemiah handled this conflict, what lessons can you learn for your own life?

7. Note how Esther followed the advice of her cousin Mordecai in the text. The Scriptures speak of honoring father and mother and one of those ways is to listen to their advice. How are you honoring a family member in your life? If you are not, then what steps can you take to begin to honor this family member?

8. King Xerxes had a book that was read to chronicle his reign. He learned Mordecai had overthrown an assassination plot, yet was not honored for it. Not that we should be honored for every good deed, but is there a co-worker or family member you could honor for their good deeds and efforts? Draw some plans to become an instrument of honor and blessing for that person.

9. In Esther, Haman began a wicked plot to kill the Jews. God intervened through the life of Queen Esther to save her people. Take a few moments and celebrate God's protection and guidance in your life.

10. In the final chapter of Esther, we learn about the elevation of Mordecai to become second only to the king. Each of us has an opportunity daily to help the broader good around us. How can you reach out to a neighbor or friend and do something for their welfare? Make a point to try and do this action in secret so you will get no credit but in God's eyes alone.

PART III

The Old Testament
Wisdom Books

HOUR 12
Wisdom Books: Part One

CHAPTER SUMMARY

LESSON PLAN:

In this hour, you will learn about ...

- The background of Hebrew poetry and wisdom literature.
- The national hymnbook of Israel, the Book of Psalms.
- Proverbs, which captures some of the wisdom of Solomon.

In the Old Testament, poetry and wisdom literature are closely related. In general, wisdom literature is in a poetic form, but the reverse isn't true. Five Old Testament books are clearly poetic: Job, Psalms, Proverbs, Ecclesiastes, and the Song of Songs. Of these five books, four are considered wisdom (Job, Proverbs, Ecclesiastes, and Song of Songs), while the Book of Psalms is not considered wisdom but is considered Hebrew poetry. Over the next two hours, let's examine some of the major points of these books.

HEBREW POETRY AND WISDOM LITERATURE

Almost one third of the Old Testament may be poetry. At times, it's difficult to know where the Hebrew poetry ends and the prose begins. Only a few Old Testament books contain almost no poetry: Leviticus, Ruth, Ezra, Nehemiah, Esther, Haggai, and Malachi—but even these books have an occasional poetic form. While the majority of English poetry is expected to rhyme, Hebrew poetry doesn't rhyme. Instead, Hebrew poetry contains two easily recognized characteristics: parallelism and imagery.

PARALLELISM IN POETRY

The poetry contains three types of parallelism:

- Synonymous
- Antithetical
- Synthetic

Synonymous parallelism is where a concept is expanded and magnified in successive sentences. For example, "Lord, who may dwell in your sanctuary? Who may live on your holy hill?" (Psalm 15:1) Both of the sentences in this verse express the same idea with different words. This type of parallelism provides God's wisdom in understandable form and is beautiful in any language.

Antithetical parallelism is often used in Proverbs: "Folly delights a man who lacks judgment, but a man of understanding keeps a straight course." (Proverbs 15:21) The second portion of the verse is in direct contrast to the first portion. First, the psalmist writes, "A fool lacks judgment." Then he tells the opposite truth: "A wise man keeps to a straight course of action." Through the contrasts, the reader learns a deeper truth than either concept on their own.

Synthetic parallelism takes the first thought and magnifies it with a second statement: "Do not swerve to the right or the left; keep your foot from evil." (Proverbs 4:27) Although it is important to understand the precepts of the Bible, it's also critical to understand the movement in the hearts of people who follow God. This type of movement can be learned through the poetic books in the Old Testament.

IMAGERY IN POETRY

Hebrew poetry is also filled with figurative language and imagery. Often similes and metaphors are used:

> "I am like an olive tree flourishing in the house of God." (Psalm 52:8a, simile)

> "The Lord is my shepherd ..." (Psalm 23:1a, metaphor)

Other times, Hebrew poetry uses inanimate objects as though they were alive: "Let the fields be jubilant, and everything in them. Then all of the trees of the forest will sing for joy." (Psalm 96:12, personification) Finally, Hebrew poetry also uses exaggeration or hyperbole: "With your help I can advance against a troop; with my God I can scale a wall." (Psalm 18:29)

BIBLICAL FACT

Seventy-one times in Psalms and three times in Habakkuk, the term *selah* is used (see Psalm 3:2). Scholars don't agree on the meaning of the word, but it could indicate a musical interlude or transition. The root word for *selah* is believed to come from the root "to lift up." Some scholars believe *selah* marks a climax in the music where singers and musicians lift up their praise to God. Other scholars believe the word indicates a change in voice or to repeat from the beginning. Clearly there is no agreement about the meaning of this mysterious word in Psalms.

WISDOM LITERATURE

In English, there is a fairly defined meaning for "wisdom." In Hebrew, the word has broader meaning and includes skill in making things, akin to the English concept of craftsmanship. Wisdom includes the willingness and ability to rightly relate to and perceive the world in all of its aspects. Because God created the world in a certain way, wisdom involves living in accordance to the basic structure of the universe. Wisdom literature is geared to teach practical aspects of life and the wisdom literature is the Old Testament's "instruction manual for life."

The Jews recognize three books in the Old Testament as poetry: Psalms, Proverbs, and Job. These books are plainly written in Hebrew verse. Contemporary Biblical scholars recognize a group of Bible books and call them Wisdom Literature: Job, Proverbs, Song of Songs, and Ecclesiastes. Each of these books focuses on practical love of wisdom.

Three Old Testament books are clearly poetic: Psalms, Proverbs, and Job. Four are considered wisdom (Job, Proverbs, Ecclesiastes, and Song of Songs), while the Book of Psalms is not considered wisdom but Hebrew poetry.

PSALMS

In many Bibles, the book naturally opens to Psalms and the person begins reading there. There are many psalms, which are much loved and are the basis of many great hymns in the Church. For the Jewish people, Psalms became their hymnbook and prayer book. David, a man after God's own heart and the king of Israel, wrote the majority of Psalms—73 of them. Asaph wrote 12 psalms, the sons of Korah wrote 11 psalms, Solomon wrote 2 psalms (Psalms 72, 172), Moses wrote 1 (Psalm 90), Ethan wrote 1 (Psalm 89), and 50 of the psalms are anonymous.

Jesus Christ loved Psalms and said that many things in this book referred to him. (Luke 24:44) It's evident the words of the psalms became such a part of the life of Christ that he quoted Psalms during his final words on the cross. (Matthew 27:46 and Luke 23:46) Of the 283 Old Testament quotations that appear in the New Testament, 116 (more than 40 percent) came from Psalms.

SHAPED LIKE THE BOOKS OF MOSES

Like the first five books of the Bible from Moses, called the Pentateuch, the Book of Psalms is organized into five sections:

- Book I (Psalms 1–41)
- Book II (Psalms 42–72)
- Book III (Psalms 73–89)
- Book IV (Psalms 90–106)
- Book V (Psalms 107–150)

Each book ends with a doxology, which is an affirmation of praise to God found in the last verse or two of the concluding psalm. For the final book (V), the entire final psalm is a concluding doxology:

Praise the Lord. Praise God in his sanctuary, praise him in his mighty heavens. Praise him for his acts of power: Praise him for his surpassing greatness. Praise him with the sounding of the trumpet, praise him with the harp and lyre, praise him with tambourine and dancing, praise him with the strings and flute, praise him with the clash of cymbals, praise him with resounding cymbals. Let everything that has breath praise the Lord. Praise the Lord. (Psalm 150)

The reason for this organization is unclear. Most likely it had something to do with how the Jews used the psalms in temple worship. Books I and II are composed primarily of psalms written by King David; Book III includes psalms of Asaph (Psalms 73–83) and the psalms of the sons of Korah (Psalms 84–88). Books IV and V include anonymous psalms along with a few by David and others.

THEMES OF THE PSALMS

From their theme, many psalms can be identified as one of the seven basic types of psalms:

- Psalms of praise
- Psalms of wisdom
- Lamentation psalms
- Messianic psalms
- Penitential psalms
- Thanksgiving psalms
- Imprecatory psalms

PSALMS OF PRAISE

Sacrifice was the center of worship in the Old Testament. Repeatedly the Scriptures say a heart filled with praise is more important than a big ram or a perfect sheep for sacrifice. A Holy God wants praise and adoration from his people. "O Lord, our Lord, how majestic is your name in all the earth!" (Psalm 8:1) Other examples of psalms of praise include Psalms 113–118 and 145–150.

PSALMS OF WISDOM

To gain wisdom, the wisdom psalms make clear the need to meditate on Scripture. If you want to perish, these psalms also make it clear that you should ignore the truth of God's word and you will not be able to stand before God's judgment. Wisdom psalms make a sharp contrast between the wicked and the righteous, address God's blessing and cursing, and often focus on righteous living. These psalms often focus on many of the same issues found in the Book of Proverbs. There are several subcategories of wisdom psalms including creation psalms (which call for the believer to celebrate God's creation of the universe and the Savior of his people), torah psalms (which focus on the sufficiency, truth, and beauty of God's law), and finally history psalms (which review the history of Israel and call for a recommitment to God—even in the face of rebellion). "Blessed is the man who does not walk in the counsel of the wicked or stand in the way of sinners or sit in the seat of mockers but his delight is in the law of the Lord, and on his law he meditates day and night." (Psalm 1:1–2) Other examples of wisdom psalms include Psalms 19, 37, 49, 127, 133, and 138.

LAMENTATION PSALMS

Some people believe it's unspiritual to lament. The Jewish people understood the importance of godly sorrow and included lamentation psalms. As the people were hurting, they brought their pain to the throne of God. It took spiritual strength to express deep sorrow before the Lord. "Hear my prayer, O Lord; let my cry for help come to you. Do not hide your face from me when I am in distress. Turn your ear to me; when I call, answer me quickly." (Psalm 102:1–2) Other examples of lamentation psalms include Psalms 12, 25, 39, 86, 120, and 129.

JUST A MINUTE

Lamentation psalms are written for real people in difficult situations. These sufferers know that God will not be angry with their honesty toward him—even if they scream at God, it is a scream of faith. Here's the basic structure of a lamentation psalm:

An introductory cry
The lament proper such as "I am hurting" or "You do not care"
A confession of trust
Reasons for God to act
Petitions like "Hear me" or "Save me" or "Punish them"
A vow to praise God

These lamentation psalms are a model of godly response to suffering.

MESSIANIC PSALMS

Messianic psalms promised royal authority to one who was both David's offspring and David's Lord. They are also called the royal psalms or coronation psalms, emphasize God as king, and often use the words "the Lord reigns." These psalms speak of God's rule as Creator, Savior of Israel, and the Coming King. "The Lord says to my Lord: 'Sit at my right hand until I make your enemies a footstool for your feet.'" (Psalm 110:1) Other examples of messianic psalms include Psalms 2 (the deity and universal reign of the Messiah), 16 (his resurrection from the dead), 22 (his suffering), 45 (his royal bride), 72 (the glory of his reign), 110 (his role as eternal king and priest), and 118 (his rejection by His nation's leaders).

PENITENTIAL PSALMS

The penitential psalms are poems where the writer confesses sin to the Lord, asks for and receives forgiveness, and then praises God for the provision of a renewed relationship after God's forgiveness. "Have mercy on me, O God, according to your unfailing love; according to your great compassion blot out my transgression. Wash all my iniquity and cleanse me from my sin." (Psalm 51:1–2) Other examples of penitential psalms include Psalms 6, 38, 102, 130, and 143.

THANKSGIVING PSALMS

Thanking God for his goodness is a primary concern in the Book of Psalms. Thanksgiving psalms sometimes follow lamentation psalms. The psalmist pours out his sorrow and grief to the Lord, and then follows it with a time of praise and rejoicing at God's faithfulness. "Give thanks to the Lord, for he is good. His love endures forever. Give thanks to the God of gods. His love endures forever. To him who alone does great wonders. His love endures forever." (Psalm 136:1–4) Other examples of thanksgiving psalms include Psalms 18, 66, 108, 118, 119, and 135.

IMPRECATORY PSALMS

Some of the most troubling psalms are the ones which contain prayers asking God to curse the wicked and call down his holy wrath on our enemies. These imprecatory psalms accurately reflect God's abhorrence of evil. "May the table set before them become a snare; may it become retribution and a trap. May their eyes be darkened so they cannot see, and their backs be bent forever." (Psalm 69:22–23) Other imprecatory psalms include Psalms 35, 88, 109, 137, and 140.

PSALMS WERE WRITTEN FOR SINGING

Singing occurs throughout the Bible as an act of worship, an expression of gratitude, and even as acts of lamentation or sorrow. The Israelites used string instruments (harp and lyre), wind instruments (trumpet, flute, pipe, and horn), and percussive instruments (cymbal and tambourine). David had an orchestra of 4,000, for which he made each instrument. (1 Chronicles 23:5)

Since their creation, the psalms have been one of the most-loved portions of the Bible. People often read them in times of celebration and times of grief for comfort. With 150 psalms to cover, this hour can't cover all the psalms but here's a running list of some favorites:

Psalm 1 uses poetic language to contrast wickedness and godliness.

Psalm 10 probes the question: Where is God when times are tough?

Psalm 19 celebrates the wonder and glory of creation and how God is made known to man through the Scriptures. The closing prayer (verses 13–14) is one of the best prayers in the Bible.

Psalm 22 begins with ancient words which Jesus Christ repeats on the cross, "My God, my God, why have you forsaken me?" (verse 1) Although written 1,000 years before the days of Jesus, it is a vivid description of the crucifixion.

Psalm 23 is one of the most beloved passages in the Bible and often called The Shepherd's Psalm.

PEOPLE TO KNOW

David composed Psalm 23 and kept sheep when he was a boy. When Samuel came to find the King of Israel, David was watching the family sheep. (1 Samuel 16:11) God selected David as the king, and he was taken from the sheepfolds to shepherd the nation of Israel.

Psalm 46 confirms God is always with us. It is the basis for Martin Luther's famous hymn "A Mighty Fortress Is Our God."

Psalm 55 shows how David responds when close friends betray him. It's a foreshadowing of when Judas betrays Jesus in the New Testament and an example to each of us about how to respond to a friendship betrayal with the overriding message to trust in God.

Psalm 90 may have been the first psalm. Moses, the author, lived 400 years before David. The psalm is about asking for compassion from an all-powerful God.

JUST A MINUTE

One of David's favorite expressions in Psalms is the word picture of sitting in the shadow of God's wings. (Psalms 17:8, 36:7, and 63:7) The wings of a bird symbolized protection, refuge, and defense. Faced with danger or a fire, a prairie chicken will gather her chicks under her wings for protection. In the same way, God offers his protection for those who follow him.

Psalm 100 connects the act of giving thanks with praise, worship, and joy. Often this Psalm is read at Thanksgiving Day worship services.

Psalm 117 stands out as the shortest Biblical chapter and the shortest psalm. It is also the middle chapter of the Bible. "Praise the Lord, all you nations; extol him, all you peoples. For great is his love toward us, and the faithfulness of the Lord endures forever. Praise the Lord."

Psalm 119 is the longest chapter in the Bible with 22 stanzas. Each stanza begins with a letter of the Hebrew alphabet in sequence. Each stanza is eight lines and each of the eight-line stanzas begins with the same letter from the Hebrew alphabet. It's a remarkable look at Hebrew poetry and a celebration of the importance of the Word of God.

Psalms 120–134 are called the songs of ascents. Scholars believe pilgrims traveling to the religious festivals in Jerusalem sang these psalms *a cappella* on the road.

Psalm 137 was sung in captivity and longs to return to Jerusalem and the certain retribution for those who captured them and hauled them into exile. It is not a psalm of gratitude but stands in contrast to Psalm 126, written after the Jews returned from Babylon, which is filled with gratitude.

Psalm 139 is an intensely personal consideration of the intimate knowledge of God about his people. The final verse is one of the most needed prayers in the Bible: "See if there is any offensive way in me, and lead me in the way everlasting." (verse 24)

Whatever the mood, it can likely be found in a psalm. As readers meditate on the honest expressions throughout this book, they hopefully learn to become more honest in their personal relationship with God.

What Is a Proverb?

A proverb is a brief statement that expresses a general truth (such as "money is the root of all evil"—these exact words are not found in the Bible). The majority of Proverbs is a series of disconnected proverbs. The Hebrew word meaning "proverb" allows for longer exhortations such as chapter 2, which describes the moral benefits of wisdom. The majority of proverbs express a statement with an elaborate consequence: "He who answers before listening—that is his folly and his shame." (Proverbs 18:13) Or the proverb expresses a contrast: "He who obeys instructions guards his life, but he who is contemptuous of his ways will die." (Proverbs 19:16) Many proverbs use figurative language: "Pleasant words are a honeycomb, sweet to the soul and healing to the bones." (Proverbs 16:24)

Like the Book of Psalms and the first five books of the Bible (the Pentateuch), this book is also divided into five sections:

- Solomon's way of wisdom (chapters 1–9)
- The main collection of Solomon's proverbs (chapters 10–24)
- Hezekiah's collection of Solomon's proverbs (chapters 25–29)
- The words of Agur (chapter 30)
- The words of King Lemuel (chapter 31)

Because this book has 31 chapters and most months have that many days, some people cover a proverb each day for devotional reading and a daily dose of the wisdom from this book.

Teaching is the primary design of the proverbs and especially for the young—to give them compact practical statements, which will stick in their minds and hearts. Proverbs cover a broad range of subjects: wisdom, fear of God, righteousness, morality, chastity, knowledge, diligence, self-control, trust in God, proper use of riches, control of the tongue, consideration of the poor, training of children, honesty, idleness, laziness, justice, common sense, and more. As bits of wisdom, proverbs aren't laws that must be strictly followed. Proverbs provide practical guidance about how someone may act in a particular circumstance. Human relationships are complex; true wisdom and discernment are necessary to deal with these relationships.

JUST A MINUTE

Common sense reveals the value of good advice. When someone listens to those who are wiser, they benefit from the other person's hard-earned experience. Growing up, getting along with others, and holding a job would all be impossible without the guidance from others who have walked the same path.

Proverbs specializes in practical advice, but it's more than simply a collection of tips and tricks. The book passes on a core of knowledge that God says everyone must have for successful living. Because the words in this book concern human nature and God's ways, they speak to the modern problems as much as the ancient ones. Although our landscapes and gadgets have changed since the time of Solomon, human nature has not changed nor has God's nature.

A Passion for Wisdom

King Solomon wrote the majority of Proverbs. As a young man, Solomon had a consuming passion for wisdom and knowledge. (1 Kings 3:9–12) During his day, he was the literary prodigy of his day. Leaders and kings from the ends of the earth came to listen as Solomon lectured on botany and zoology. As a businessman, he had vast enterprises and a reputation as a poet, moralist, preacher, and scientist—besides his role as a political ruler.

CULTURAL FACT

The Hebrew word meaning "foolish" is used exclusively in Proverbs except for two occurrences in Psalms. It means the "absence of wisdom." Foolishness characterizes the speech of fools and the reactions of the impulsive person. Foolishness affects the lifestyle of a person and is often identified with sin and iniquity. While Proverbs doesn't hold out much hope for the adult fool, the rod of correction is identified as the remedy for children. (Proverbs 22:15, 26:11, and 27:22)

Practical Everyday Help

Proverbs succinctly details some of the overall principles scattered throughout the Bible. The teachings of Proverbs are not expressed with the words like the prophets or Moses saying, "This is what the Lord says"; instead the proverbs are given from the practical experience of a man who is tested and tried in the experience. This book is like an owner's manual for life. Any owner's manual will explain what needs to be done to avoid serious problems but doesn't promise or guarantee that nothing will go wrong. The best guarantee for the life of faith is to read and learn the wisdom in this book.

A Sampling of Proverbs

Here's a small sample of the wisdom from Proverbs, which are commonly known in the book:

"Trust in the Lord with all your heart and lean not on your own understanding, in all your ways acknowledge him, and he will make your paths straight." (Proverbs 3:6–7)

"Honor the Lord with your wealth, with the first fruits of all your crops, then your barns will be filled to overflowing, and your vats will brim over with new wine." (Proverbs 3:9–10)

"Go to the ant, you sluggard; consider its ways and be wise! It has no commander, no overseer or ruler, yet it stores its provisions in summer and gathers its food at harvest." (Proverbs 6:6–8)

"Ill-gotten treasures are of no value, but righteousness delivers from death." (Proverbs 10:2)

"Whoever loves discipline loves knowledge, but he who hates correction is stupid." (Proverbs 12:1)

"A gentle answer turns away wrath, but a harsh word stirs up anger." (Proverbs 15:1)

"A cheerful look brings joy to the heart, and good news gives health to the bones." (Proverbs 15:30)

"In his heart a man plans his course, but the Lord determines his steps." (Proverbs 16:6)

"Wine is a mocker and beer a brawler; whoever is led astray by them is not wise." (Proverbs 20:1)

"A good name is more desirable than great riches; to be esteemed is better than silver or gold." (Proverbs 22:1)

"Train a child in the way he should go, and when he is old he will not turn from it." (Proverbs 22:6)

"He who oppresses the poor to increase his wealth and he who gives gifts to the rich—both come to poverty." (Proverbs 22:16)

"Listen to your father, who gave you life, and do not despise your mother when she is old. Buy truth and do not sell it; get wisdom, discipline and understanding. The father of a righteous man has great joy, he who has a wise son delights in him. May your father and mother be glad, may she who gave you birth rejoice." (Proverbs 23:22–25)

"An honest answer is like a kiss on the lips." (Proverbs 24:26)

"Do not answer a fool according to his folly, or you will be like him yourself." (Proverbs 26:4)

"As iron sharpens iron, so one man sharpens another." (Proverbs 27:17)

Here are some of the obscure proverbs, which also contain kernels of wisdom:

"As vinegar to the teeth and smoke to the eyes, so is a sluggard to those who send him." (Proverbs 10:26)

"Like a gold ring in a pig's snout is a beautiful woman who shows no discretion." (Proverbs 11:22)

HISTORICAL FACT

> Proverbs 25–30 reflect the important reforms, which King Hezekiah enacted in Judah. (Proverbs 25:1) Hezekiah's father, King Ahaz, had turned away from the Lord and served idols and even practiced child sacrifices. (2 Chronicles 28:1–4) From the turning away from God, Judah suffered devastating losses to the Assyrians and the Israelites of the northern kingdom. Hezekiah restored temple worship and resumed nationwide observance of the Passover. It was probably during this period that the scribes found and copied these proverbs of Solomon, which are included in the Book of Proverbs.

Toward the end of the book, Agur includes his sayings (Proverbs 30) and includes wisdom such as, "There are three things that are too amazing for me, four that I do not understand: the way of an eagle in the sky, the way of a snake on a rock, the way of a ship on the high seas, and the way of a man with a maiden." (Proverbs 30:18–19)

Proverbs concludes with an epilogue about the wife of noble character. "A wife of noble character who can find? She is worth far more than rubies. Her husband has full confidence in her and lacks nothing of value." (Proverbs 31:10–11) The modern culture praises women who have initiative and education and independence. Look at the independence of this wife: "She considers a field and buys it; out of her earnings she plants a vineyard … She sees that her trading is profitable, and her lamp does not go out at night." (Proverbs 31:16, 18)

For the various writers of Proverbs, wisdom isn't something elusive, which can't be secured. As a person faithfully and consistently follows the advice in this book, they will walk with the wise.

HOUR'S UP!

During this hour, you've learned some details about Hebrew poetry, then more specifics about Psalms and Proverbs. While the information is good, how does this material relate to your life today? Take a few minutes to ponder these 10 application questions and move to a deeper level than simply learning for learning's sake.

1. The parallelism in Hebrew poetry has a purpose to emphasize a truth from the Scriptures. Read Psalm 15:1–5. List three qualities of a righteous person from this text. How can you absorb more of these qualities in your life?

2. Take a psalm like Psalm 23 and personalize the psalm when you read it. "Because the Lord is (your name) Shepherd, …" What personal insight or blessing do you receive from this personalization of the psalm?

3. Wisdom is used in a broad sense in these books. Previously wisdom was defined as including "the willingness and ability to rightly relate to and perceive the world in all its aspects." Through daily reading of the psalms, how can you increase wisdom in your life and Godly insight?

4. Read Psalm 19; reflect on the Law and the psalmist's love of God's Law. What do you learn from this psalm about the love of the Law? Take some action to recommit to loving God's Laws in your everyday life and relationships.

5. Wisdom psalms are clearly designed to meditate on various aspects of God. Take a small portion of a psalm and read it out loud, and then write the verse on a small card and carry it with you throughout the day. In spare moments, turn to it and think repeatedly (or meditate) on the words.

6. Thanksgiving psalms are not just for a single holiday but are to be used throughout the year. Often the world is fairly thankless. How can you add more thanks into your life? With your family? With your co-workers? With your neighbors? Make a point today to express gratitude, thanks, and appreciation often. Consistent practice will make this attitude a daily habit.

7. Read Psalm 117. Is it in the middle of your Bible? It marks the middle chapter. Read it aloud today and celebrate God's faithfulness. Tell a friend or family member a specific way that God has been faithful in your life.

8. Many people have Proverbs 3:6–7 as a daily prayer or lifetime verse. It's a passage they turn to often for encouragement and strength. What encouragement do you gain from these proverbs to increase your trust of God?

9. The entire chapter of Proverbs 10 confronts laziness. Do you have a lazy attitude in your life? Where? What steps can you take today to plan change?

10. Reread Proverbs 15:1. Take the time today to memorize this verse and keep it in your mind. You will face conflict at some point soon in your life. What insight and wisdom can you gain from this proverb?

HOUR 13

Wisdom Books: Part Two

LESSON PLAN:

In this hour, you'll learn about …

- The meaninglessness of earthly life according to the Book of Ecclesiastes.
- A celebration of married love captured in the Song of Songs.
- The Godly perspective on suffering through the Book of Job.

In this hour, you will learn about three of the most misunderstood books in the Bible—Ecclesiastes, Song of Songs, and Job. Ecclesiastes and Song of Songs (or Song of Solomon, as the book is called in some translations) are often ignored or rarely read, yet they each contain insight into the Lord of the Universe from one of the wisest men who walked the earth—King Solomon. When you face pain and suffering (as all people do at some point in their lives), the wisdom in the book of Job will serve as a comfort and aid. Some scholars believe Job is one of the oldest books in the Bible. Let's jump into the hour and begin our second part on the wisdom books.

The Book of Ecclesiastes opens with this identification of its author, "The words of the Teacher, son of David, king in Jerusalem." (Ecclesiastes 1:1) Most scholars consider Solomon to be the author of this book. In his day, he was the most famous and powerful king in the world. He was noted for his wisdom, riches, and literary achievements (see 1 Kings 4 and 9). Solomon probably wrote this book toward the end of his life, after he repented of his pursuit of foreign wives and his idolatry. Some consider this book a monument to Solomon's recommitment to the living God and a guide for others through the pitfalls and perils of life.

What does it mean to fear God? In essence, to fear God is to repent from evil and turn in wonder to the living God with worship, reverence, and lifetime service. Dread isn't a part of fear with God if we approach God with proper respect and obedience for the Creator. We "fear" God because of the final verse of Ecclesiastes. In the final days, God will judge everyone—the righteous and the wicked. Life can't be lived with abandon as if God will not remember the deeds from the past or see these deeds. The exhortation for the reader to fear God and to expect divine judgment are two of the great themes of this book and provide a framework for it.

JUST A MINUTE

When reading a book, sometimes it's better to flip to the ending to be able to understand where the book is headed. Ecclesiastes is this type of book. Everything in the book should be interpreted with the conclusion in mind:

> Now all has been heard, here is the conclusion of the matter: Fear God and keep his commandments, for this is the whole duty of man. For God will bring every deed into judgment, including every hidden thing, whether it is good or evil. (Ecclesiastes 12:13–14)

MEANINGLESSNESS OF LIFE

Ever wondered if your life has meaning? Solomon, the wisest man on the face of the earth, also asked this question. The word *meaningless* occurs 37 times in Ecclesiastes and shows the writer was not a happy person. Unlike Solomon's father, David, who used words like *rejoice* and phrases like *shout for joy* and *praise God* throughout Psalms, Solomon wrote this book after the temple and palace were built. He sat on the throne in relative peace and security; because of his riches, everyone thought he should be happy. Instead, he began the book saying, "'Meaningless! Meaningless!' says the Teacher, 'Utterly meaningless! Everything is meaningless.'" (Ecclesiastes 1:2)

COMPETING WORLDVIEWS

Ecclesiastes contains two competing worldviews. One view is the perspective of mortal men (under the sun) and the other view is from a Sovereign God (under heaven). The conflict between the two worldviews is strongly presented in Ecclesiastes. Solomon gives a persuasive view of naturalism and opens with a cynical perspective about life:

Generations come and generations go, but the earth remains forever. The sun rises and the sun sets, and hurries back to where it rises. The wind blows to the south and turns to the north, round and round it goes, ever returning on its course. All streams flow into the sea, yet the sea is never full. To the place the streams come from, there they return again. All things are wearisome, more than one can say. The eye never has enough of seeing, or the ear its fill of hearing. (Ecclesiastes 1:4–8)

See the endless cycle of life and the cynical tone of the author? Life goes around and around as the sun circles the earth. According to the author, everything is going around in circles and the meaninglessness, hopelessness, and cynicism makes perfect sense.

If you've heard the expression "Life is a rat race," then you realize it's not an original expression; the concept was clear in Ecclesiastes. The Teacher looked at life and decided to explore every pleasure and to live with gusto:

I thought in my heart, "Come now, I will test you with pleasure to find out what is good." But that also proved meaningless. "Laughter," I said, "is foolish. And what does pleasure accomplish?" … I denied myself nothing my eyes desired; I refused my heart no pleasure. My heart took delight in all my work, and this was the reward for all my labor. Yet when I surveyed all that my hands had done and what I had toiled to achieve, everything was meaningless, a chasing after wind; nothing was gained under the sun. (Ecclesiastes 2:1–2, 10–11)

From the text, it's unclear whether the author participated in all the activities mentioned or whether he is making an illustration. If the stories are true, then the Teacher lived a wild life of pleasure in his early years. These activities are consistent with what the Bible tells about the early years of Solomon. The sensuality of ancient times matches the hedonism of modern days. And what is the consequence of living for self without any consciousness of eternity? "What does a man get for all the toil and anxious striving with which he labors under the sun? All his days his work is pain and grief, even at night his mind does not rest. This too is meaningless." (Ecclesiastes 2:22–23)

The Teacher acknowledges everything has a season and a time. This passage is one of the best known in Ecclesiastes:

There is a time for everything, a season for every activity under heaven: a time to be born and a time to die, a time to plant and a time to uproot, a time to kill and a time to heal, a time to tear down and a time to build, a time to weep and a time to laugh, a time to mourn and a time to dance, a time to scatter stones and a time to gather them, a time to embrace and a time to refrain, a time to search and a time to give up, a time to keep and a time to throw away, a time to tear and a time to mend, a time to love and a time to hate, a time for war and a time for peace. (Ecclesiastes 3:1–8)

Each of us has experienced these different opposites in life. Then the Teacher draws some conclusions, "What does a worker gain from his toil? I have seen the burden God has laid on men. He has made everything beautiful in time. He has also set eternity in the hearts of men; yet they can not fathom what God has done from beginning to end." (Ecclesiastes 3:9–11)

Eternity in the hearts of humankind is a key thought in this book. At this point in history, God had not revealed much about eternal things. That revelation will come later in the arrival of Jesus Christ. Solomon seemed to know that the Messiah would be coming and would make sense of a senseless world.

The Teacher continues throughout Ecclesiastes to explore the greatest indulgences of life. Yet the Teacher concludes that God has created humankind to be restless until they find their rest in the Lord. He concludes wisdom is the best course. "The quiet words of the wise are more to be heeded than the shouts of a ruler of fools." (Ecclesiastes 9:17) Finally, the Teacher gives some hope, "Remember your Creator in the days of your youth, before the days of trouble come and the years approach when you will say, 'I find no pleasure in them.'" (Ecclesiastes 12:1)

Early in this section, you learned about the end of this book. Here's the conclusion the Teacher drew after his search, "Not only was the Teacher wise, but he imparted knowledge to the people. He pondered and searched out and set in order many proverbs. The Teacher searched to find just the right words, and what he wrote was upright and true. The words of the wise are like goads, their collected sayings like firmly embedded nails—given by one Shepherd. Be warned, my son, of anything in addition to them. Of the making of books, there is no end, and much study wearies the body." (Ecclesiastes 12:9–12)

JUST A MINUTE

Young people often think and act as if they will live forever. The final chapter of Ecclesiastes (chapter 12) paints a clear picture of old age and introduces it to young people with the warning, "Remember your Creator in the days of your youth." Clearly, there are many elderly people who defy this portrait. Yet for the majority of elderly, the conditions mentioned in the book are typical. Ecclesiastes warns young people to remember God before their earthly life ends. Although most people don't like to consider it, each human being is moving daily closer toward death—no matter what our age. Ecclesiastes challenges young people to live unto God, for life is empty and meaningless without him.

The stirring conclusion of this book is in the phrase, "Fear God and keep his commandments, for this is the whole duty of man." (Ecclesiastes 12:13) Because of the fear of God, life contains meaning. Fearing God will provide the discernment about what is valuable in life and what is not.

WHY IS ECCLESIASTES IN THE BIBLE?

This book is one of the most misunderstood books in the Bible. Christians tend to ignore the message of the book or consider it simply as the testimony of a man who is living apart from God. While some people have questions about this book, the contents lead the reader to understand the importance of fearing God.

The Lord gave King Solomon a remarkable opportunity to observe and explore every avenue of earthly life. Because of the depth of his experimentation and research, Solomon concluded that, overall, humankind finds little happiness in life and an unending yearning for something eternal. Solomon's search for meaning finds fulfillment in the New Testament. Joy is one of the key words in the New Testament. Through Jesus Christ, man discovers the desire of the ages: abundant life.

SONG OF SONGS: IN PRAISE OF MARRIAGE

Do you enjoy a love song? This ancient book celebrates the blossoms of springtime and some believe Solomon wrote it to celebrate his marriage to his favorite wife. Called the Song of Songs, it possibly indicates King Solomon believed this song was the most marvelous of the 1,005 songs which he created. (1 Kings 4:32) This passage shows the setting for this book, "See! The winter is past; the rains are over and gone. Flowers appear on the earth; the season of singing has come, the cooing of doves is heard in our land. The fig tree forms its early fruit; the blossoming vines spread their fragrance. Arise, come, my darling; my beautiful one, come with me." (Song of Songs 2:11–13)

Solomon, son of King David and third king of Israel, is the author of this book. He is named as the author and his name appears seven times. (Song of Songs 1:1, 1:5, 3:7, 3:9, 3:11, 8:11–12)

THE SPEAKERS

Old Testament scholars familiar with the structure of Hebrew poetry believe this complex book is a superb composition. The entire book is filled with sudden shifts from one speaker to another and from one place to another with no explanation of the shifts, making it difficult to follow. In Hebrew, the speaker changes are indicated with gender and in some Bible translations this change in speaker is indicated with some extra space on the actual printed page.

Song of Songs includes three speakers:

- The bride, called the Shulamite (Song of Songs 6:13)
- The king
- A chorus of women called the "daughters of Jerusalem"

At this point, Solomon's harem is relatively small—only 60 wives and 80 concubines with numerous virgins on a waiting list. (Song of Songs 6:8) In later years, Solomon's harem grew to include 700 wives and 300 concubines (see 1 Kings 11:3).

The key person throughout this book is the bride. A common opinion is that the Shulamite was Abishag of Shunem, the most beautiful woman in all of Israel. During the last days of King David, Abishag attended the king. (1 Kings 1:1–4) After Solomon assumed the crown, Abishag became his wife because if she had married someone else, it might have endangered his throne. (1 Kings 2:17, 22)

PEOPLE TO KNOW

Who was the Shulamite? In one place in Song of Solomon, the bride of the poem is identified as "the Shulamite," (Song 6:13) and no other references reveal her identity. Who was this young woman who was such a passionate pursuit for King Solomon? Several suggestions have been made:

- She may have been Abishag, the Shunammite maiden who was at David's side in his old age. (1 Kings 1:1–4, 15) After David's death, one of his sons, Adonijah, requested that he be given Abishag. But this was improper in that Solomon, David's successor, was entitled to her along with David's other wives and concubines. (1 Kings 2:17–22)
- She may have been a woman from Shunem, a town in the territory of Issachar near Jezreel. (Joshua 19:18) If so, she would have been known as a Shunammite, but by interchanging the Hebrew letters lamed (l) and nun (n), which was commonly done, she could also have been known as a Shulamite.
- It may have been that "Shulamite" could also have been rendered "Shelomith," which would make the name of a feminine title related to the name of Solomon, "the Solomoness."

INTERPRETATIONS

Song of Songs is a moving love story between a young country girl and King Solomon. Using delicate poetry, the lovers express deep longing and intense passion for each other. Solomon likens the beauty of his bride to delicious fruit or scenic gardens. The young girl compares her love for her husband to the anticipation of a frantic search. In this eloquent passion between a bride and bridegroom, the book includes an exhortation to remain sexually pure before marriage. (Song of Songs 2:7) This book celebrates human sexuality in the context of marriage.

Not everyone has interpreted the book as about marriage. Both Christians and Jews have seen deeper meanings in this poem. Usually Christians have regarded the poem as a song of Christ and the Church. Throughout the New Testament, the Church is called the bride of Christ. (Matthew 9:15, 25:1; John 3:29; 2 Corinthians 11:2; Ephesians 5:23; Revelation 19:7, 21:2, 22:17) Adherents of this interpretation believe human marriage is a foretaste and the counterpart of the relationship between Christ and his Church.

On the other hand, Jews read this book at the Passover as an allegory referring to the Exodus, when God selected Israel for his bride. The intense passion and love for Israel is exemplified in the love of a king toward a humble young country girl. In several places in the Old Testament, Israel is called God's wife. (Jeremiah 3:1, Ezekiel 16, 23)

DETAILED LOOK AT SONG OF SONGS

In the first chapter, the bride expresses her love for the king and the king for his bride. It takes place in three different settings: the palace, the banquet table, and the bridal chamber. In the second and third chapters, the bride thinks about the king both day and night. "My lover is mine and I am his; he browses among the lilies. Until the day breaks and the shadows flee, turn, my lover, and be like a gazelle or like a young stag on the rugged hills." (Song of Songs 2:16–17)

In the fourth chapter, the king confesses that he cannot keep from thinking about his bride, who invites the king into her garden of marital delights. "You have stolen my heart, my sister, my bride; you have stolen my heart with one glance of your eyes, with one jewel of your necklace." (Song of Songs 4:9) In the fifth chapter, the bride recalls with delight their union; her love for the king almost overwhelms her. The sixth chapter captures the king's response to the bride's expressions of love and the bride's contentment with her husband. The final two chapters express the bride's frustration with the social customs and the king's official duties, which limit the bride's time with him. The book concludes with a final commitment of their love. "Come away, my lover, and be like a gazelle or like a young stag on the spice-laden mountains." (Song of Songs 8:14)

In beautiful poetical language, Song of Songs celebrates the union of marriage and the commitment between a man and a woman.

CULTURAL FACT

How could a man with a harem of 1,000 women have a love for any one of them that would be fit to be a portrait of Christ's love for the Church? A number of Old Testament figures were polygamists. Even though God's Law was against it from the beginning, as Christ so plainly stated, in the Old Testament times, God nevertheless seems to have accommodated himself to prevailing customs. Kings generally had many wives. It was one of the status symbols of royalty. And Solomon's devotion to this lovely girl seems to be genuine and unmistakable. Also, Solomon was a king in the family that eventually produced the Messiah. It seems fitting that his marriage should, in a sense, prefigure the Messiah's eternal marriage to his bride. (Revelation 19:6–9)

JOB

Almost everyone has felt like Job at one time or another. When someone goes through trials or times of suffering, self-pity often overwhelms the individual. The Book of Job examines the troubling questions, the reality of doubts, and the real anguish of a suffering person. The book delivers God's perspective on suffering. It asks a common question: If God is just and good, why do people suffer?

A UNIVERSAL PROBLEM

As individuals suffer with unexplained afflictions, it's easy to ask, "Why me? Why now? God, is this how you treat your friends?" Through the words in this book, individuals face some of the most profound of moral questions. To discover an answer requires a face-to-face encounter with a Holy God for answers. Pain and suffering is found throughout the Bible, but no book contains the perspective of Job.

AUTHOR OF JOB

Some scholars believe that Job was never intended to be a literal book of history and that it is only a story used to teach theological truths. As a highly artistic literary work, Job is more poetic than any other history in Scripture and contains scenes and dialogue. Throughout history, major conservative scholars believe this book is about a real man named Job, dramatized into an incredible work of art, as well as an ancient historical story.

HISTORICAL FACT

The Book of Job takes place during the patriarchal period, long before where the book appears in the sequence of Old Testament books. The exact date of the story isn't known, but the vocabulary and form suggest it may be the oldest book in the Old Testament, written 500 or more years before Moses received the Laws of God.

The opening words of this book provide a fascinating glimpse into the life of this man:

In the land of Uz there lived a man whose name was Job. This man was blameless and upright, he feared God and shunned evil. He had 7 sons and 3 daughters, and he owned 7,000 sheep, 3,000 camels, 500 yoke of oxen and 500 donkeys, and had a large number of servants. He was the greatest man among all the peoples of the East. His sons used to take turns holding feasts in their homes, and they would invite their three sisters to eat and drink with them. When a period of feasting had run its course, Job would send and have them purified. Early in the morning he would sacrifice a burnt offering for each of them, thinking, "Perhaps my children have sinned and cursed God in their hearts." This was Job's regular custom. (Job 1:1–5)

SATAN AND GOD TALK

Job was blessed with wealth beyond Abraham and also had a spiritual relationship with the Lord. It was an incredible combination of physical and spiritual blessing in Job's life. Then the scene of the book switches to heaven:

One day the angels came to present themselves before the Lord, and Satan also came with them. The Lord said to Satan, "Where have you come from?" Satan answered the Lord, "From roaming through the earth and going back and forth in it." Then the Lord said to Satan, "Have you considered my servant Job? There is no one on earth like him; he is blameless and upright, a man who fears God and shuns evil." "Does Job fear God for nothing?" Satan replied. "Have you not put a hedge around him and his household and everything he has? You have blessed the work of his hands so that his flocks and herds are spread throughout the land. But stretch out your hand and strike everything he has, and he will surely curse you to your face." The Lord said to Satan, "Very well, then, everything he has is in your hands, but on the man himself do not lay a finger." Then Satan went out from the Lord's presence. (Job 1:6–12)

The high drama of this story is unlike anywhere else in the Bible. Satan was bragging to God about his accomplishments and walking around the earth. The exception in Satan's domain was a man named Job, and the Lord reminded Satan that not everyone in the world was in his power—particularly the righteous. "Well, small wonder Job is righteous," Satan responds, "you've given the man anything that anyone could ever want or need."

God understood Job's faithfulness was not connected to the Lord's blessings. He turns Satan loose to attack Job's physical possessions and family. Yet Job remains faithful to God. When Job received the news that his livestock were gone and his children were killed, he responded to the news: "At this, Job got up and tore his robe and shaved his head. Then he fell to the ground in worship and said: 'Naked I came from my mother's womb, and naked I will depart. The Lord gave and the Lord has taken away; may the name of the Lord be praised.' In all this, Job did not sin by charging God with wrongdoing." (Job 1:21–22)

INSIGHT INTO SUFFERING

This story clearly demonstrates God's relationship to suffering in the world. Even in the decisions and actions of Satan, there are two wills and two motivations running side by side. God and Satan were both involved in the attack on Job's property. When the Lord removed his hedge of protection around Job, Satan used the Chaldeans to attack Job's livestock. The Chaldeans weren't coerced into attacking but freely chose to attack Job.

In the final days, God will judge the individual for his or her actions. He doesn't remove our responsibility for our actions and will judge evil in the final days. Pain and death are the direct consequences of living in a fallen world. Since Adam and Eve disobeyed God in the Garden of Eden, everyone is born into a world of suffering. The New Testament will detail God's plan to reunite mankind to himself and make the world free from suffering through an eternal relationship with God.

Job's physical possessions and his family were destroyed in the first test. During another day, Satan and the Lord were once again talking about the righteous actions of Job. Satan said Job continued to be righteous because of his health. "'Skin for skin!' Satan replied, 'A man will give all he has for his own life. But stretch out your hand and strike his flesh and bones, and he will surely curse you to your face!'"

"The Lord said to Satan, 'Very well, then, he is in your hands; but you must spare his life.' So Satan went out from the presence of the Lord and afflicted Job with painful sores from the soles of his feet to the top of his head. Then Job took a piece of broken pottery and scraped himself with it as he sat among the ashes. His wife said to him, 'Are you still holding on to your integrity? Curse God and die!' He replied, 'You are talking like a foolish woman. Shall we accept good from God, and not trouble?' In all this, Job did not sin in what he said." (Job 2:4–10)

In the face of suffering, Job's suffering increased through physical suffering. Despite the physical attack to his body and sores throughout his skin, Job refused to stop faithfully following the Lord.

With Friends Like These ...

You've probably heard the saying, "With friends like these, who needs enemies?" The expression probably found its origin in Job. Three of Job's "friends"—Eliphaz, Bildad, and Zophar—came and took turns trying to explain to Job why he was suffering. Job answered each one in turn. They went three rounds. (Job 4–14, 15–21, and 22–26) In the first two rounds, all three friends spoke; and in the final round, only Eliphaz and Bildad spoke. Apparently Zophar remained silent because he had given up on Job. As the well-known phrase "Job comforters" implies, these friends ended up making Job's misery and pain greater than when they started talking to him. Each friend operated under the assumption that Job suffered the results from sin in his life—something the reader knows not to be true from the information in the first three chapters.

In chapters 29 through 31, Job made a long speech in which he called for his vindication since he felt like his suffering was unjust. Then the reader meets a fourth friend, Elihu, who was clearly younger than the other men. He said that the others had not really met the issues. He believed Job had managed to justify himself, but failed to justify or explain the ways of God. (Job 32:12) Through four speeches, Elihu contended suffering was God's means to discipline his people. He said it was unthinkable for God to do anything that unjust and that nothing was hidden from God's eyes. Because God was aware of Job's suffering, Job must have sinned. Elihu linked suffering with hardness of heart and disobedience, which can only be remedied through repentance and a changed life. In many regards, Elihu echoed the concerns and feelings of the previous three friends.

PEOPLE TO KNOW

Let's look in detail at the four "friends" of Job: Eliphaz, Bildad, Zophar, and Elihu.

Eliphaz was the chief and oldest of Job's comforters. A very religious man, Eliphaz sought to uphold the holiness, purity, and justice of God. He became uneasy when Job questioned his understanding of God.

Bildad was the second of Job's comforters. In his three speeches, Bildad expressed the belief that all suffering is the direct result of one's sin. He had little patience with the questionings and searchings of Job. He is called "Bildad the Shuhite" (Job 2:11), which means he belonged to an Aramean nomadic tribe that lived in the Transjordan area southeast of Canaan.

Zophar was the third of Job's friends to speak and is called a Naamathite (Job 2:11), indicating he was from Naamah, in northern Arabia. Through Zophar's two discourses, he accused Job of wickedness and hypocrisy, urged Job to turn from his rebellion, and charged that God was punishing Job far less than his sins deserved. (Job 11:6)

Elihu was the youngest of Job's "comforters" and spoke after the three friends failed to give convincing answers to Job's questions. Elihu is called "the son of Barachel the Buzite of the family of Ram." (Job 32:2) Like Job's other friends, Elihu was probably from the Transjordan area southeast of Israel.

GOD FINALLY ANSWERS

Toward the conclusion of Job, God responded to Job's questions. The Lord's answers were not a two-way conversation but a monologue from God, and some of the most beautiful poetic words in Scripture about the character of God:

Then the Lord answered Job out of the storm. He said: "Who is this that darkens my counsel with words without knowledge? Brace yourself like a man: I will question you, and you shall answer me. Where were you when I laid the earth's foundation? Tell me, if you understand. Who marked off its dimensions? Surely you know? Who stretched a measuring line across it? On what were its footings set, or who laid its cornerstone—while the morning stars sang together and all the angels shouted for joy? ... Have you entered the storehouses of the snow or seen the storehouses of the hail, which I reserve for times of trouble, for days of war and battle? What is the way to the place where the lightning is dispersed, or the place where the east winds are scattered over the earth?" (Job 38:1–7, 22–24)

The questions from God carry through for two chapters. God told Job to take it like a man and questioned Job's right to question him. The theme of this section reminds us of Moses standing in front of God and the burning bush. God answered Job's questions saying, "Because I said so. Any questions?"

In response, Job waved a white flag in surrender to God's verbal assault. God made his holy presence known to Job and Job responded, "I am unworthy— how can I reply to you? I put my hand over my mouth. I spoke once, but I have no answer—twice but I will say no more." (Job 40:3–5) Job repented of his mistrust of God while suffering. Throughout the questions from Job and despite a direct conversation with the Lord of the Universe, Job never received answers to his questions.

JUST A MINUTE

The book calls the reader (and Job) to trust God and get to know the Lord in the middle of suffering. It will be enough. Eventually in the book, Job quits talking and listens to God. He received a revelation or knowledge that God is the omnipotent Creator. With this revelation, Job acknowledges that God can do all things. Then Job is able to see the awe-inspiring reality of God instead of his own suffering. He repents, and God delivers him from his suffering.

JOB'S RESTORATION

After Job repented, the Lord instructed him to pray for his friends. "After Job had prayed for his friends, the Lord made him prosperous again and gave him twice as much as he had before .... After this, Job lived a hundred and forty years; he saw his children and their children to the fourth generation. And so he died, old and full of years." (Job 42:16–17)

Although Job is the oldest book in the Old Testament, it clearly contains a message of redemption, which is amplified in the New Testament. Those who join in the redemptive suffering of Jesus Christ will one day be transported to a glorious place to live with God forever.

HOUR'S UP!

During this hour, you've learned some details about three unusual books in the Bible: Ecclesiastes, Song of Songs, and Job. While it's important to learn the details of the Scriptures, how do these books continue to have relevance in everyday life today? Explore your personal application of these books in the following 10 questions.

1. Ecclesiastes celebrates the whole duty of man—to fear God and keep his commandments. (Ecclesiastes 12:13–14) Take a moment and evaluate how you are keeping God's commandments. Honestly pick an area where you are weak. Plan some steps of change in your life.

2. Sometimes people feel like because they have not tried something, they can't believe it's wrong—like drugs or alcohol. Meditate on the detailed investigation of the writer of Ecclesiastes. He didn't deny himself any pleasure yet found it was meaningless. Does this research and insight help you for your own spiritual journey with God? How?

3. Return to Ecclesiastes 3:1–8, where the Teacher reflects about the different seasons of life. Name a season in your life (there may be several so list several of them). Now take a moment in prayer to celebrate this season. Ask God to bless and use this season in your life.

4. Solomon's search in the book of Ecclesiastes finds its fulfillment in the New Testament and the abundant life of following Jesus Christ. Have you found this abundant life in your own circumstances? If not, how can you find it through prayer or talking with a friend? Ask God to show you how to find fulfillment in your life.

5. Song of Songs is an often-neglected book in the Bible yet celebrates a beautiful love story. Read the book with the viewpoint of God wooing his bride, the Church. What insight does this viewpoint give you about God's continual love for the Church?

6. Song of Songs celebrates human sexuality and the sanctity of marriage. If you are married, take a verse in Song of Songs such as Song of Songs 4:9 and personalize it with your spouse. Make a point to celebrate your marriage and the love relationship. Take some guidance from Song of Songs, and incorporate this wisdom into your marriage and relationship.

7. Job addresses a universal question: Where is God in the midst of suffering? What insight do you gain about the workings of Satan in the earth through the opening chapters of this book? How can you increase your protection or guard against Satan? Prayer and Scripture are two weapons at your immediate disposal.

8. Take a moment to reflect on God's plan to redeem the world from suffering through Jesus Christ. Job is incomplete without understanding God's sacrifice through Jesus Christ. Celebrate God's plan and how it applies in your life.

9. Job's friends believe that suffering is a result of sin. This concept is put to rest through the book of Job. Our suffering doesn't come from sin in our life but is a part of the human experience. Think of a time when you have suffered (it might be at the moment). Rejoice in God's constant watch over your life and that he will give you the strength for each day.

10. Reread Job 38:1–24. Reflect on God's large perspective on our life. It's easy to get caught in the details of everyday life without an eternal perspective. Job learns that he needs to get to know and trust God in the middle of his suffering—not ask questions. What application can you make to your personal situation?

PART IV
Meet Jesus Christ

HOUR 14

Prediction and Preparation for the Messiah

LESSON PLAN:

In this hour, you will learn about ...

- The period of 400 silent years between the Old Testament and the New Testament.
- The one who heralded the arrival of Jesus Christ, John the Baptist.
- The miracles surrounding the birth of Jesus.
- The early years of Jesus Christ.

Intermission during a play at the theater is a chance for everyone to stretch and prepare for the next act. The curtain has dropped and with expectancy everyone waits for the play to continue. The prophet Malachi set the tone for the next act saying in his final words, "See, I will send you the prophet Elijah before that great and dreadful day of the Lord comes." (Malachi 4:5) See the expectancy in those words of waiting for Elijah? Yet the curtain was shut for 400 years.

In this hour, you will learn what happened in history during the 400 years of silence between the Old and New Testaments. Then you will explore what happened when "Elijah" (predicted to return to lead the way for the Messiah), or John the Baptist, arrived to herald the forthcoming Messiah. History was stirred at the birth of Jesus and the early years of his life. The birth of Jesus Christ changed the course of human history and remains a focal point of history and a division between B.C. (Before Christ) and A.D. (*Anno Domini*, in the year of our Lord).

The world of the New Testament was radically different from the Old Testament world. Over four centuries of changes took place, which changed every aspect of everyday life. Many of these changes are interrelated, yet for clarity, they've been divided into political, geographic, religious, and language changes.

POLITICAL CHANGES

Toward the end of the Old Testament, Ezra and Nehemiah rebuilt the temple and the city walls of Jerusalem and completed the reconstruction in 445 B.C. For the next 100 years, the Medo-Persians controlled Jerusalem. Media was the name of a place and people associated with Persia (especially in the books of Esther and Daniel). Media became a province of the Persian Empire in 549 B.C. when the Medan overlord was conquered by Cyprus the Great. In 331 B.C., Alexander the Great conquered the Medo-Persians.

HISTORICAL FACT

Alexander has a fascinating story. With the Bible stories of the young kings David and Josiah firmly in his mind, at age 24, Alexander was completing his conquest of the Persian Empire. Before Alexander's conquest, three Greek minds dominated the world: Socrates, Plato, and Aristotle. Aristotle had a famous pupil named Alexander. The young pupil dreamed of uniting the world under one political philosophy. Although Alexander only lived until the age of 33, his philosophy called Hellenism dominated the world for many centuries.

Ptolemies (Egyptian rule): Following Alexander's death, four of his generals divided the empire. Palestine lay between the two eastern sections of the empire, Syria and Egypt. Egypt went to Ptolemy (the first of the Ptolemies) and Syria went to Seleucus (who was the first of the Seleucid dynasty). Palestine went first to Syria, then passed to Egypt and remained under Egyptian control until 198 B.C. Mainly the Jews were peaceful under the Ptolemies' rule.

Seleucids (Syrian rule): King Antiochus the Great of Syria recaptured Palestine in 198 B.C. Initially, the Seleucids were tolerant toward the Jews but that soon changed. The Jewish refusal to give up their identity and religion frustrated Antiochus IV Epiphanes. He turned violent against them and made an effort to exterminate them and their religion. In 168 B.C., he desecrated the temple and offered a pig (an unclean animal) on its altar. He also built an altar to Zeus in the temple, prohibited temple worship, forbade circumcision on the threat of death, sold thousands of Jews into slavery, and destroyed every copy of the Scriptures that could be located. His actions against the Jews led to the famous Maccabean revolt.

The Maccabean Period: A priest with intense patriotism named Matthias rose in protest against Antiochus. With his five warlike sons, Matthias began a guerrilla war against the Seleucids. When he died in 166 B.C., his mantle fell to his son, Judas Maccabaeus, also known as Judas the Hammer.

Because of his bold raids, he became a hero to the Jewish people and remains so today. His efforts were so successful that he won concessions from the Greeks, which included reopening the temple for sacred worship. The Feast of Hanukkah commemorates the heroic acts of Judas the Hammer.

The Roman Period: In 142 B.C., the Jews gained their full freedom from domination, which lasted 80 years. In 63 B.C., General Pompey from Rome conquered Palestine. Twenty-three years later, Rome appointed Herod the Great as the local king over the Jews.

GEOGRAPHIC CHANGES

At the end of the Old Testament, Palestine was a Persian province. Four hundred years later in the time of Jesus, the land of Palestine was divided into three regions or provinces: Judea in the south, Samaria in the center, and Galilee in the north.

Galilee was a fertile area, which was crossed with major trade routes. When the kingdom of David and Solomon was divided into north and south, Galilee and Samaria comprised the northern kingdom. When the north fell to the Assyrians in 722 B.C., the population was deported to Assyria and pagan immigrants were settled in the area. Matthew's gospel calls this area Galilee of the Gentiles. (Matthew 4:15) The non-Jews impacted this area of the country and the people from Judea in the south looked down on the Galileans. The attitude explains Nathanael's question in John 1:46 about Jesus, "Nazareth! (in the Galilee region) Can anything good come from there?" Yet Jesus spent most of his ministry in Galilee.

Samaria is slightly smaller than Galilee. The Assyrians destroyed the city of Samaria in 722 B.C. and deported all of the inhabitants. During the time of Christ, Samaria had a mixture of Israelites who managed to escape deportation and immigrants not of Jewish origin. The people of Samaria developed their own type of God worship based on the five books of Moses. They built a temple on Mount Gerizim. When Ezra and Nehemiah wanted to rebuild the temple in Jerusalem, the Samaritans offered to participate but they were rebuffed. About this time a group of Jewish dissidents moved to Samaria. The combination of the temple and the dissidents made a rift between the Samaritans and the Jews. The Jews avoided traveling through Samaria if at all possible.

Judea was more or less the same area as the old kingdom of Judah (Judea is a Latinized version of the word Judah). The land was approximately 55 by 55 miles but its boundaries were never precisely fixed.

RELIGIOUS CHANGES

Wherever Alexander the Great conquered, he spread the Greek culture and language. Even after his death and his empire was divided and later absorbed into the Roman Empire, Greek spread and became the language of the civilized world. This spread of Greek culture, language, and thought is called Hellenism (from Hellas, the Greek name for Greece). Part of the Jewish culture endorsed Hellenism, while another portion strongly resisted it.

CULTURAL FACT

Samaria, the capital of the northern kingdom of Israel, was located on a 300-foot-high hill, 42 miles north of Jerusalem. Archaeologists have discovered the foundations of Omri's palace and the larger foundations and ruins of the palace of Ahab, his son, on the summit of the hill of Samaria. Just inside the north wall of the palace, they found several thousand fragments of ivory. These fragments give substance to the account in the first book of Kings (22:39), which lists the ivory house as one of the great achievements of Ahab.

From the Jews' struggle over Hellenism emerged two main parties of Judaism during the days of Jesus—the Pharisees and the Sadducees. With Hellenism spreading throughout the religious community, the Pharisees took the Scriptures and believed it was their responsibility to determine how the Law applied to new conditions. These Pharisees led to prominence of teachers of the Law or Scribes. In contrast, the Sadducees didn't try to adapt the Law to new situations but limited themselves to the first five books of Moses and nothing else—not the other Scriptures or the writings of the prophets.

LANGUAGE CHANGES

After the Babylonian exile, Aramaic replaced Hebrew as the common language in Palestine. Although Aramaic is a Semitic language related to Hebrew, it's different enough so the average Hebrew-speaker could not readily understand it. Aramaic was the language of commerce and diplomacy centuries before Alexander the Great. Several documents in Ezra were written in Aramaic instead of Hebrew. (Ezra 4:8–6:18 and 7:12–26)

Hebrew is the language of the Old Testament, but by the time of Christ, Hebrew had become mainly the language of the religious since the Hebrew Bible was written in Hebrew. Many people could still read and write in Hebrew but it was not their everyday language.

HISTORICAL FACT

Latin was the language of Rome and was used in official documents but not spoken throughout the Empire. Greek was the common language that connected the Roman Empire—like English in the modern world.

Jesus could read and perhaps speak Hebrew (Luke 4:17–19), but usually he spoke Aramaic. He probably also spoke at least some Greek, but there is no proof in the Bible. The Apostles wrote in Greek. Some scholars believe the Gospel of Matthew was written in Aramaic and later translated into Greek.

More than 400 years of silence from God after the prophet Malachi came to an end when God sent John the Baptist to announce the coming of his son.

John the Baptist

One of the most remarkable people in the New Testament is often under-rated: John the Baptist. Traditionally, Christian scholars and teachers have given him little credit. The writers of the four Gospels had a different perspective. Only two writers mention the birth of Jesus, but all four include details about the life and ministry of John the Baptist. Why does he garner so much attention?

Generation after generation passed without anyone hearing directly from God and speaking the words, "Thus says the Lord." Imagine the struggle for the priests to speak passionately about God week after week in the temple.

John's Unusual Birth

Then John the Baptist arrived on the scene and spoke God's word with authority. The Gospel of Luke details his unusual parents, Zechariah and Elizabeth. The couple had no children and were both well along in years. Zechariah was a priest and he was selected for the high honor of entering the temple and burning incense. To be selected was a once in a lifetime type of experience for Zechariah. Each of these priests typically had bells on the hem of their long robes so everyone could hear their movement into the temple with the incense.

As Zechariah was burning the incense, suddenly an angel appeared to him at the altar and the Bible says "he was gripped with fear." (Luke 1:12) It had been centuries (400 years) since God had appeared or spoken.

But the angel said to him, "Do not be afraid, Zechariah, your prayers have been heard. Your wife Elizabeth will bear a son, and you are to give him the name John. He will be a joy and delight to you, and many will rejoice because of his birth, for he will be great in the sight of the Lord. He is never to take wine or other fermented drink [he was to be a Nazarite like Samson], and he will be filled with the Holy Spirit even from birth. Many of the people of Israel will he bring back to the Lord their God. And he will go on before the Lord, in the spirit and power of Elijah, to turn the hearts of the fathers to their children and the disobedient to the wisdom of the righteous—to make ready a people prepared for the Lord." (Luke 1:11–17)

No messenger from God had appeared to the Jewish people for 400 years, so Zechariah's next question was logical, "How can I be sure of this? I am an old man and my wife is well along in years." (Luke 1:18) Yet the angel was disturbed with Zechariah's question and said, "I am Gabriel. I stand in the presence of God and I have been sent to speak to you and tell you this good news. And now you will be silent and not able to speak until the day this happens, because you did not believe my words, which will come true at their proper time." (Luke 1:19–20)

Zechariah had been in the temple for an extended period of time and the people were amazed when the priest came out and could not speak. Elizabeth, his wife, became pregnant. When the baby was born and to be named, she called her son John. They questioned her because no one in the family was named John. Turning to Zechariah, he called for a tablet and wrote, "His name is John." Instantly, Zechariah could speak and praised God. Look at the reaction to John's birth: "The neighbors were all filled with awe and throughout the hill country of Judea people were talking about these things. Everyone who heard this wondered about it, asking, 'What then is this child going to be?' For the Lord's hand was with him." (Luke 1:65–66)

JOHN PREPARES THE WAY

The Gospel of Mark begins with the story of John the Baptist preaching in the wilderness. Mark quotes the prophet Isaiah 40:3, "It is written in Isaiah the prophet, 'I will send my messenger ahead of you, who will prepare your way—a voice of one calling in the desert, prepare the way for the Lord, make straight paths for him.'" (Mark 1:2–3) Like the prophets from the Old Testament, John spoke for God and dressed a bit differently than his contemporaries. He wore camel hair clothing and a leather belt, plus he ate locusts and wild honey. (Mark 1:6) Also like the prophets, John often spoke of the "Day of the Lord." John proclaimed good news—that the Messiah was coming and he would use a tool like a farmer to separate the chaff from the wheat. The people were fed from the wheat but the chaff was only good for burning.

The crowds began to gather to hear John speak. Even the Jewish leaders were interested in knowing about the arrival of the Messiah. Herod the Great was pushing around the Jewish leaders, and for them the appearance of a Messiah would mean relief. But John even attacked the Jewish leaders: "But when he saw many of the Pharisees and Sadducees coming to where he was baptizing, he said to them, 'You brood of vipers! Who warned you to flee from the coming wrath?'" (Matthew 3:7) John's words didn't win him any friends among the religious leaders.

BIBLICAL FACT

Baptism is a sacred rite signifying purification, initiation, or identification of an individual with a leader, group, or teaching. There were several types of baptism in the Scriptures:

- Jewish baptism: a ceremonial cleansing prescribed for both people and articles. (Exodus 19:10–14; Leviticus 8:6; Hebrews 9:10)

- John's baptism: a preparatory act in which the Jews expressed their belief in the imminent coming of the Messiah and their desire to turn away from sin and live righteous lives. (Mark 1:4–8)

- Jesus' baptism: an act of ceremonial righteousness. By being baptized, Jesus was not admitting his sinfulness. Christ was consecrating himself to ministry. (Mark 1:9–11)

- Spirit baptism: the supernatural work of the Holy Spirit by which believers are joined to the body of Christ. (Romans 6:3–4; 1 Corinthians 12:13)

- Christian baptism: a ceremonial act instituted by Christ (Matthew 28:19) and practiced by the apostles (Acts 2:38) that depicts a believer's union and identification with Christ in his death, burial, and resurrection.

- Baptism by fire: a possible reference either to judgment at the Second Coming or to the coming of the Spirit at Pentecost. (Matthew 3:9–12; Luke 3:16–17)

Besides his courage to call the people to repentance, John began something called baptism. At that time in history, many other rabbis or teachers baptized their students in ceremonial baths. Also, Gentile converts to Judaism had to participate in a baptism. Now John called everyone to come and be baptized. His message was that everyone—Jews and Gentiles alike—were unclean and needed a ceremonial bath. John the Baptist's forceful actions created a stir and shouting match between John and the other rabbis. Yet he wasn't worried about the reactions to his message from God. John knew that the Messiah was about to enter the earth and he called everyone to be prepared.

John Wasn't the Messiah

John the Baptist had drawn a huge crowd at the river Jordan and caught the attention of the religious leaders. The Gospel of John describes more about John:

Now this was John's testimony when the Jews of Jerusalem sent priests and Levites to ask him who he was. He did not fail to confess, but confessed freely, "I am not the Christ." They asked him, "Then who are you? Are you Elijah?" He said, "I am not." "Are you a prophet?" He answered, "No." Finally they said, "Who are you? Give us an answer to take back to those who sent us. What do you say about yourself?" John replied in the words of Isaiah the prophet, "I am a voice of one calling in the desert, 'Make straight the way of the Lord.'" Now some Pharisees who had been sent questioned him, "Why then do you baptize if you are not the Christ, nor Elijah, nor the Prophet?" "I baptize you with water," John replied, "but among you stands one you do not know. He is the one who comes after me, the thongs of whose sandals I am not worthy to untie." (John 1:19–27)

John the Baptist knew that he was bearing witness for the arrival of the Messiah, Jesus Christ. He called the religious leaders of the day into question and didn't candy-coat any of his words. This prophet was called in his mother's womb and it was indicated when Mary, the mother of Jesus, visited Elizabeth, John's mother, when she was pregnant with John. (Luke 1:41)

One day while preaching and baptizing at the Jordan River, John looked up and saw Jesus coming toward him. John must have understood his divine calling because he said, "Look, the Lamb of God, who takes away the sin of the world! This is the one I meant when I said, 'A man who comes after me has surpassed me because he was before me.'" (John 1:29–30) He heralded the arrival of Jesus Christ, God's son, to the world.

The Birth of Jesus

The arrival of Jesus Christ on earth was one of the greatest acts of creation. God willingly sent his son to earth and capped an event that the prophets and others had forecast. The Lord of the Universe left his throne in heaven and became a tiny baby. The event is celebrated each year with Christmas, yet the details of Jesus' birth do not appear in the first Gospel, Matthew, but come in the Gospel of Luke.

THE ANNUNCIATION

Luke, the physician, has the greatest detail about the birth of Jesus. Mary, a virgin, was pledged to marry Joseph but they were not married yet. Remember, at this time God hadn't spoken through the prophets or anyone for 400 years. The angel Gabriel had appeared to Zechariah, John's father, in the temple but John had not been born. Elizabeth, John's mother, was in her sixth month of the pregnancy when the angel, Gabriel, appeared to Mary and said, "Greetings, you who are highly favored! The Lord is with you!" (Luke 1:28) Mary was unsure what was happening to her and wondered what the greeting meant. So Gabriel continued, "Do not be afraid, Mary, you have found favor with God. You will be with child and give birth to a son, and you are to give him the name Jesus. He will be great and will be called the Son of the Most High. The Lord God will give him the throne of his father, David, and he will reign over the house of Jacob forever; his kingdom will never end." (Luke 1:30–33) Mary knew she was going to have the baby of an important person but she was still confused. How could she, a virgin, have a baby?

HISTORICAL FACT

When Mary traveled into the Judean hill country to see her cousin Elizabeth, it was no leisurely stroll along a country road. She traveled along the mountainous terrain that contained a rugged beauty, desert yellows, a glimpse of the Dead Sea, and perhaps a few groves of fruit trees that grew in terraced slopes. One main north-south road linked the region's principal cities—Jerusalem to the north, Bethlehem, Bethzur, and Hebron to the south. The hill country was rather bleak. The eastern slopes were mostly impassable desert, stretching 10 to 15 miles from their highest point, 3,000 feet near Hebron, down to the Dead Sea—the lowest point on the earth at 1,300 feet below sea level. (Joshua 15:2) The vast wasteland was broken only by imposing cliffs and canyons and a few forts and oases. It was an area fit for fugitives, rebels, and hermits—but certainly not for a pregnant Mary.

Gabriel continued to answer her confusion, "The Holy Spirit will come upon you, and the power of the Most High will overshadow you. So the holy one to be born will be called the Son of God." (Luke 1:35) These words from the angel echo back to the Creation of the world and the words in

Genesis 1:2, "The Spirit of God was hovering over the waters." This same Spirit was about to create a fertilized egg inside Mary—Jesus, the Messiah. As confirmation, Gabriel told Mary that her cousin, Elizabeth—who was well past the childbearing years—was also pregnant. Then the angel includes a statement about the working of a Sovereign God: "For nothing is impossible for God." (Luke 1:37)

Mary hurried off to see her cousin, Elizabeth, and when she arrived, the baby inside of Elizabeth (John the Baptist) leapt for joy. Then Elizabeth told Mary, "Blessed are you among women, and blessed is the child you will bear!" (Luke 1:42) Even before Mary could tell Elizabeth about the angel Gabriel, Elizabeth used some of the same phrases that the angel had spoken in confirmation and reassurance.

THE MAGNIFICAT

Mary responded to her cousin with a song of praise, which is known as the Magnificat. The song demonstrates that Mary had an intimate knowledge of the prophets and the Old Testament:

And Mary said, "My soul praises the Lord and my spirit rejoices in God my Savior, for he has been mindful of the humble state of his servant. From now on all generations will call me blessed, for the Mighty One has done great things for me—holy is his name. His mercy extends to those who fear him, from generation to generation. He has performed mighty deeds with his arm; he has scattered those who are proud in their inmost thoughts. He has brought down rulers from their thrones but has lifted up the humble. He has filled the hungry with good things but has sent the rich away empty. He has helped his servant Israel, remembering to be merciful to Abraham and his descendants forever, even as he said to our fathers." (Luke 1:46–55)

Mary clearly understood that she would be giving birth to a king, the Son of David. The words of this song parallel many of the Old Testament prophecies about the Messiah.

THE ANGEL AND JOSEPH

While Mary is "with child," what about Joseph? He would have to deal with the news of his fiancée's pregnancy without the confirmation from a cousin (Elizabeth) or an angelic visitation:

Because Joseph her husband was a righteous man and did not want to expose her to public disgrace, he had in mind to divorce her quietly. But after he had considered this, an angel of the Lord appeared to him in a dream and said, "Joseph, son of David, do not be afraid to take Mary home as your wife, because what is conceived in her is from the Holy Spirit. She will give birth to a son, and you are to give him the name Jesus, because he will save his people from their sins." (Matthew 1:19–21)

From the beginning, Joseph did not believe Mary's story about the Holy Spirit. Who could blame him? Remember, God had not spoken directly to his people in 400 years. Rather than humiliate her in public, he decided to divorce her quietly. In his provision and mercy, God sent an angel to confirm what Mary reported. Joseph did what he was told. Scripture doesn't tell a lot of detail about Joseph, but we know he was a carpenter and deeply loved Mary, because he believed the angel and didn't quietly divorce Mary but supported her throughout her pregnancy.

THE SHEPHERDS AND ANGELS

The story of the birth of Jesus is commonly read from Luke 2:1–20. Caesar decreed that the entire Roman world should be counted; Joseph, who was from Nazareth in Galilee, had to travel with pregnant Mary to Bethlehem, because he was from the house of David, or a descendent of King David. Everyone had to be counted—even those people related to King David—so they had to return to their hometown. Arriving in Bethlehem, the couple could find no place to sleep so they stayed in a small stable and Jesus was born and placed in a manger.

That evening, shepherds were watching their flock in the fields when an angel appeared and announced the birth of Jesus, "Do not be afraid. I bring you good news of great joy that will be for all people. Today in the town of David a Savior has been born to you; he is Christ the Lord. This will be a sign to you: you will find a baby wrapped in cloths and lying in a manger." (Luke 2:10–12) Suddenly a host of angels appeared and praised God. The shepherds went to the stable and found the baby Jesus. The miracle of the angels again confirmed the arrival of the Messiah, Jesus.

THE EARLY YEARS OF JESUS

Little is recorded in the Bible about the early years of Jesus, but the few stories give some indication of the type of child and young man that he would become.

FOUR EYEWITNESS ACCOUNTS OF JESUS

If four different people witness the same event, they see it from four different angles and perspectives. The same is true with the four Gospels in the New Testament. Each man provides a unique perspective on the life of Jesus Christ. While each man covers the same portion of history, each writes from his unique vantage point.

Matthew, the tax collector, was concerned to write about how Jesus was the Messiah from a historical perspective. The book is filled with references to the Old Testament and even begins with a family tree to show how Jesus is from the lineage of King David.

Mark, a young man during the days of Jesus, wrote the shortest Gospel and the one that contains straight narrative of the various events in the life of Christ. He doesn't mention the birth of Jesus nor write about the early years of Jesus' life.

Luke, a physician, is the only non-Jew who writes for the New Testament. His Gospel contains the birth of Jesus, including some of the prebirth movements. His Gospel is the only one to mention Jesus as a young man.

John, the disciple or the Beloved, writes with the most theological perspective. His Gospel is arranged around different subjects or topics instead of chronologically. John's Gospel provides an intimate portrait of Jesus Christ.

HISTORICAL FACT

These four perspectives only show a small portion of the life of Christ. The writers divinely told the stories that were critical to understanding the life of Jesus. As John writes at the end of his Gospel, "Jesus did many other things as well. If every one of them were written down, I suppose that even the whole world would not have room for the books that would be written." (John 21:25)

Luke's is the only Gospel to include some information about the early years of Jesus' life. The Gospel is limited to one story about Jesus' bar mitzvah (an event which happened when a boy reached age 12).

Every year, his parents went to Jerusalem for the Feast of the Passover. When he was 12 years old, they went up to the Feast, according to the custom. After the Feast was over, while his parents were returning home, the boy Jesus stayed behind in Jerusalem, but they were unaware of it. Thinking he was in their company, they traveled on for a day. Then they began looking for him among their relatives and friends. When they did not find him, they went back to Jerusalem to look for him. After three days, they found him in the temple courts, sitting among the teachers, listening to them and asking them questions. Everyone who heard him was amazed at his understanding and his answers. When his parents saw him, they were astonished. His mother said to him, "Son, why have you treated us like this? Your father and I have been anxiously searching for you." "Why were you searching for me?" he asked. "Didn't you know I had to be in my Father's house?" But they did not understand what he was saying to them. Then he went down to Nazareth with them and was obedient to them. But his mother treasured all these things in her heart. And Jesus grew in wisdom and stature and in favor with God and man. (Luke 2:41–52)

The story is remarkable, and must be true. The early Church held Mary and Joseph, as the parents of Jesus, in high esteem and reverent awe. They were literally idolized and worshipped. This story shows them in a bad light as parents. Why didn't they know Jesus wasn't with them on the return trip home? The Passover Feast involved literally hundreds of people traveling, and families traveled in caravans. After the first day, they realized that Jesus wasn't with their group so they returned to Jerusalem to look for him. The young Jesus was in the temple and was drawn away from his earthly parents to his Heavenly Father. When his earthly parents, Mary and Joseph, arrived the young Jesus was obedient and returned home.

The final verse is an excellent means that Scripture uses to identify four areas of growth: wisdom, stature (physical), in favor with God (spiritual), and in favor with man (the ability to make friends). Even as a young man, Jesus is headed to balance in his life.

HOUR'S UP!

In this hour, you've studied the period between the Old Testament and the New Testament, then learned about the birth and early years of Jesus Christ. Are these simply "nice" stories, or do they have relevance to your life today? Take a moment to consider the following 10 questions to apply these Scriptures to your everyday life.

1. For 400 years between the Old Testament and the New Testament, the Jewish people only heard silence. How do you react to silence? Uncomfortably or comfortably? When you go through a silent period or a dry period when God doesn't seem to be active in your life, what can you do? Take the initiative to gain an increased awareness of God in your life (a Bible study, a new church, a new book, or a new Bible-reading program). See if these methods will pull you from the dry period.

2. As you understand the geographic changes in Palestine during the 400 years of silence, what insight do you gain about the Jews' opinion of Samaria? Turn to Luke 10:25–37 and read the Parable of the Good Samaritan. What do you learn about the meaning of the word *neighbor?*

3. Language was important in the period of silence and it is also important for us today. Take a moment and express appreciation for the ability to read the Scriptures in your own language.

4. Jesus talked about John the Baptist and his greatness (Matthew 11:11–15), yet the passage also challenges us to be open to the leading of God's spirit. Meditate on this passage and ask God to show you how to grow in your relationship with your Heavenly Father.

5. Imagine yourself in the shoes of Zechariah, John the Baptist's father, when he sees the angel Gabriel and doesn't believe. His reaction seemed fairly innocent but his punishment was eight months of silence. What insight can you have from Zechariah's experience to increase your trust of God every day?

6. When John the Baptist spoke to the people and the religious leaders of his day, he didn't pull any punches. He cried out to prepare the way for the arrival of Jesus. Take a moment and admire John's boldness. Ask God for some moments of boldness in your own life, then see what comes to mind—it might be as simple as an invitation or a relationship which needs mending or _____ (you fill in the blank). Ask God to show you, then act.

7. With Joseph, the angel Gabriel appeared in a dream and directed his steps. In primitive cultures and in biblical times, God often used dreams to direct people's steps. Today he uses more direct methods such as the Scriptures. Turn to Luke 1:37 and trust God for your impossibilities.

8. Reflect for a moment about why there are four Gospels in the New Testament. Each man gives a different perspective on the life of Jesus Christ. Are you drawn to a particular Gospel account more than another? Is it related to the perspective of the writer?

9. Reread the story of Jesus in the temple. (Luke 2:41–52) Jesus knew that he must be about the business of his Heavenly Father. In our daily life, it's easy to get caught in the business of life and not spiritual business. How can you commit to increasing your involvement in spiritual matters in your daily life?

10. "Jesus grew in wisdom and stature and in favor with God and man."
    (Luke 2:52) Notice the balance in the life of Christ—emotional, phys-
    ical, spiritual, and relational. Is your life in balance? Take a moment to
    evaluate. Which area in your life needs some reinforcements? What
    steps can you take to reinforce this area? Make a plan and set some
    goals to follow.

HOUR 15
Jesus Begins His Ministry

CHAPTER SUMMARY

LESSON PLAN:

In this hour, you will learn about ...

- The significance of the Baptism of Jesus.
- Why Jesus spent 40 days and 40 nights in the wilderness and faced temptation.
- How Jesus called the first five of his disciples.
- The details of the first miracle of Jesus—changing water to wine.
- Jesus delivering the Sermon on the Mount and his plunge into public ministry.

After 400 years of silence between the Old Testament and the New Testament, the history of the relationship between God and man takes a giant leap of improvement with the birth of Jesus Christ. Angels appear to shepherds and three wise men follow a star to visit the Christ child. The Gospel of Luke records one story about the boyhood of Jesus as his parents find him in the temple interacting with the religious leaders of his day. From age 12 until age 30, there is nothing in the Bible about Jesus—only silence. Jesus spent almost 20 years training for his earthly ministry. This hour details how Jesus Christ began his ministry with a baptism in the Jordan River, then spent 40 days and 40 nights in the desert facing temptation, before delivering his most famous sermon—the Sermon on the Mount.

In the eyewitness accounts of the life of Christ, three of the four Gospels record Jesus' baptism and the beginning of his earthly ministry. Now almost 20 years after Mary and Joseph lost Jesus in the temple, a 30-year-old Jesus weaves through the crowd and arrives on the banks of the Jordan River.

THE BAPTISM OF JESUS

John the Baptist had prepared the way for the arrival of Jesus Christ. The Gospel of Matthew records John the Baptist saying to the crowd, "I baptize you with water for repentance. But after me will come one who is more powerful than I, whose sandals I am not fit to carry. He will baptize you with the Holy Spirit and with fire. His winnowing fork is in his hand, and he will clear his threshing floor, gathering the wheat into the barn and burning up the chaff with unquenchable fire." (Matthew 3:11–12)

PEOPLE TO KNOW

If John the Baptist were alive today, would he be comfortable using today's media? Probably not. He was not an outward success. John wasn't the head rabbi of a large synagogue. Nor did he wear fine clothes or drive a chariot. John the Baptist was a simple man and wore simple clothes. He illustrates the truth of Paul's words in 1 Corinthians 1:27: "But God chose the foolish things of the world to shame the wise; God chose the weak things of the world to shame the strong."

John the Baptist had drawn tremendous crowds for his baptism of repentance. The Jewish leaders wondered whether John was the Messiah so they sent some priests and Levites to ask in person who he was representing. As the Gospel of John records:

He did not fail to confess, but confessed freely, "I am not the Christ." They asked him, "Then who are you? Are you Elijah?" He said, "I am not." "Are you the Prophet?" He answered, "No." Finally they said, "Who are you? Give us an answer to take back to those who sent us. What do you say about yourself?" John replied in the words of Isaiah the prophet, "I am the voice of one calling in the desert, 'Make straight the way for the Lord.'" (John 1:19–23)

As John the Baptist was standing in the Jordan River, suddenly Jesus Christ appeared on the banks and prepared for John to baptize him. In an instant, John knew who was in front of him and said, "Look, the Lamb of God, who takes away the sin of the world! This is the one I meant when I said, 'A man who comes after me has surpassed me because he was before me.' I myself did not know him, but the reason I came baptizing with water was that he might be revealed to Israel." (John 1:29–31)

For 400 years, God had not spoken to the Jewish people. Silence was the only response from heaven. Then the angels heralded the arrival of Jesus Christ in a stable, and his bar mitzvah was recorded, but then followed 18 years of silence. Now Jesus stood on the banks of the Jordan River and came for John to baptize him and begin his ministry. There were no angels but simply Jesus saying to John, "Baptize me."

"But John tried to deter him saying, 'I need to be baptized by you, and do you come to me?' Jesus replied, 'Let it be so now, it is proper for us to do this to fulfill all righteousness.' Then John consented." (Matthew 3:13–15)

JUST A MINUTE

Matthew 3:15 uses the phrase "to fulfill all righteousness." Jesus was not baptized because he had sinned. The Lord Jesus was without sin. (2 Corinthians 5:21, Hebrews 4:15, and Hebrews 7:26) Jesus' baptism served several purposes: (1) Jesus joined the believing remnant of Israel who John the Baptist baptized, (2) Jesus confirmed the ministry of John, and (3) Jesus fulfilled the will of his Heavenly Father, which was confirmed with the voice from heaven.

As John baptized Jesus in the water, something amazing happened. People who witnessed it must have recalled it their entire lives. When Jesus came out of the water, "at that moment heaven was opened, and he saw the Spirit of God descending like a dove and lighting on him. And a voice from heaven said, 'This is my Son, whom I love; with him I am well pleased.'" (Matthew 3:16b–17)

From his Heavenly Father, Jesus heard the words of love, "well-done, Son." With this baptism, Jesus Christ began his public ministry.

FORTY DAYS AND FORTY NIGHTS IN THE WILDERNESS

Jesus' opportunity to revel in the praise of his Heavenly Father was short lived. Immediately after his baptism, "Jesus, full of the Holy Spirit, returned from the Jordan and was led by the Spirit in the desert where for forty days and forty nights he was tempted by the devil. He ate nothing during those days and at the end of them he was hungry." (Luke 4:1–2)

Remember the second hour of this book where Adam and Eve were living in the Garden of Eden? In the middle of this paradise, Satan tempted Adam and Eve and as a result they were thrown out of the Garden of Eden. Now in the New Testament, one of the important themes is how Jesus fulfilled the role of a new Adam and became a new representative of God's people called the Son of Man. Since from the beginning of time Jesus was sent to achieve victory over Satan where Adam suffered defeat, it's not surprising that after Jesus' baptism, his first test of his power came from Satan in the desert.

Unlike Adam in a beautiful garden, Jesus had been in the dry desert for 40 days and 40 nights and, as the Scriptures said, Jesus was hungry. Scholars believe Jesus was tempted in the barren heights of the mountain region overlooking Jericho. For 40 days, Jesus fasted.

When Moses received the Ten Commandments on Mount Sinai, he fasted 40 days. (Exodus 34:28) In 1 Kings 19:8, the prophet Elijah also fasted 40 days on the way to the same mountain. Moses represented the Law and Elijah the prophets. Jesus, the Messiah, was the fulfillment of the Law and the Prophets. From the mountaintop where Jesus was fasting, he could look eastward across the Jordan and see the mountain ranges of Nebo where centuries before Moses and Elijah had been with God. Moses climbed Nebo to see the Promised Land and Elijah had been swept away on a chariot into heaven from the same mountain location.

TEMPTATION

When Jesus was hungry from fasting, the Devil appeared to him. The Bible doesn't describe Satan's form but Jesus was able to recognize that the suggestions came from Satan. The Devil came with a tempting offer, "'If you are the Son of God, tell this stone to become bread.' Jesus answered, 'It is written, man does not live on bread alone.'" (Luke 4:3–4)

Notice how Satan attacked Jesus with a tempting offer. As the Son of Man, Jesus had the power to change stones into bread, and after 40 days of fasting, the hunger pains must have been incredible. Instead of falling to the God-size temptation, Jesus quoted a verse from the Old Testament, Deuteronomy 8:3, which says speaking about God to the Jewish people, "He humbled you, causing you to hunger and then feeding you with manna, which neither you nor your fathers had known, to teach you that man does not live by bread alone but on every word that comes from the mouth of the Lord." While Jesus quoted only a few words of the verse, Satan likely could complete it and knew Jesus was saying his true source of strength didn't come from physical food but from the Words of God. From this story and others in the New Testament, we know that Jesus had an intimate knowledge of the Old Testament and could easily quote it when needed.

JUST A MINUTE

What did Satan hope to accomplish by tempting Jesus? Satan hoped to replay the fall of humanity (Adam and Eve) with the Son of God (see Genesis 3:1–6 and Romans 5:14–15 and 5:18–19). But unlike Adam, Jesus didn't fall prey to Satan's schemes. No doubt Satan hoped to engineer a second great defection and remove Jesus as the viable redeemer for mankind.

When Satan didn't succeed with the first temptation, he tried again: "The devil led him up to a high place and showed him in an instant all of the kingdoms of the world. And he said to him, 'I will give you all their authority and splendor, for it has been given to me, and I can give it to anyone I want to. So if you worship me, it will be yours.' Jesus answered, 'It is written: "Worship the Lord your God and serve him only."'" (Luke 4:5–8)

Satan knew that Jesus would suffer for the sins of the world. It's why Jesus came to the earth. In this second temptation, Satan offered Jesus the ultimate shortcut, essentially saying, "Avoid the cross and all of the suffering and pain because through me you can have your kingdom immediately—only one hitch, worship me."

Jesus knew his purpose on the earth was to bear the sins of humankind; to accept the offer of Satan for the kingdoms of the Earth would only shortcut his work on earth. Once again, Jesus quoted from Deuteronomy (Deuteronomy 6:13) to escape the temptation of Satan.

For the third temptation, Satan tried to follow the pattern of Jesus and quote the Bible. "The devil led him to Jerusalem and had him stand on the highest point of the temple. 'If you are the Son of God,' he said, 'throw yourself down from here. For it is written, "He will command his angels concerning you to guard you carefully; they will lift you up in their hands, so that you will not strike your foot against a stone."' Jesus answered, 'It says, Do not put the Lord your God to the test.'" (Luke 4:9–12)

Satan violated one of the basic principles of biblical interpretation—to let Scripture interpret Scripture. Never set one passage against another passage. Jesus was saying to Satan, "Yes, according to the Bible, the angels will take care of me, but the Bible also says not to put the Lord to the test. I don't have to jump from this building to prove my Heavenly Father's trustworthiness."

Satan was also trying to get Jesus to gain public attention through a spectacle instead of through Jesus' righteous life and message. The key according to Jesus is a righteous life—not some sort of spectacular event. Jesus was saying to Satan that he didn't need to prove God's trustworthiness by jumping off a building and bringing out the angels of God.

At the end of these three temptations, the Gospel of Matthew records, "then the devil left him, and angels came and attended to him." (Matthew 4:11) As though the neighborhood bully had fought with Jesus, now the angels came and brought comfort to the Son of God. It was fitting after his series of battles with Satan.

FIRST FIVE DISCIPLES ARE CALLED

Immediately after Jesus' temptation in the desert, Jesus picked his first five disciples. As a traveling rabbi, it was not unusual to have disciples. Jesus *was* unusual that he didn't select bright young men from the local religious schools. Instead Jesus chose fishermen, political troublemakers, and a tax collector. The first two disciples of Jesus were originally followers of John. When John saw Jesus passing by, "he said, 'Look, the Lamb of God!' When the two disciples heard him say this, they followed Jesus. Turning around, Jesus saw them following him and asked, 'What do you want?' They said, 'Rabbi' (which means "teacher"), 'where are you staying?' 'Come,' he replied, 'and you will see.'" (John 1:36–39)

BIBLICAL FACT

> The new disciples used several names for Jesus: Lamb of God (John 1:36), Rabbi (John 1:38), Messiah (John 1:41), Son of God (John 1:49), and King of Israel (John 1:49). As they got to know Jesus, their appreciation for him increased. While they would learn more about Jesus during the three years of Jesus' public ministry, they would not understand fully until three years later. (Acts 2)

The two men, one of them Andrew who was Peter's brother, followed Jesus. Andrew hurried off and found his brother and told him that they had found the Messiah or the Christ, then Andrew brought Peter to Jesus. The next day, Jesus decided to leave for Galilee and he saw Philip and asked him to follow him. Next Philip found Nathanael and told him to come because they had found the Messiah. The news was quickly spreading but Nathanael learned that Jesus had come from Nazareth and scoffed, "Can anything good come from there?" (John 1:46) Out of curiosity, Nathanael went to see Jesus and Jesus said, "Here is a true Israelite, in whom there is nothing false." (John 1:47)

Stunned at the words from Jesus, Nathanael asked, "How do you know me?" John records their conversation:

Jesus answered, "I saw you while you were still under the tree before Philip called you." Then Nathanael declared, "Rabbi, you are the Son of God; you are the King of Israel." Jesus said, "You believe because I told you that I saw you under the fig tree. You shall see greater things than that." He added, "I tell you the truth, you shall see heaven open, and the angels of God ascending and descending on the Son of Man." (John 1:48–51)

THE FIRST MIRACLE

After Jesus had five of his disciples, they were in Galilee and he attended a wedding in Cana. Jesus' mother was at the wedding and on the third day the wine ran out. As his mother, Mary must have known Jesus could perform miracles. She went to him and said, "They have no more wine." Jesus said to her, "Dear woman, why involve me in this crisis? My time has not come." Mary, knowing Jesus was going to do something about this situation, told the servants, "Do whatever he tells you." Nearby stood six stone water jars, which were the kind the Jewish people used for ceremonial washing. Each of these vessels held 20 to 30 gallons.

Jesus turned to the servants and said, "Fill the jars with water." So they filled the jars to the brim. Then he told them, "Now draw some out and take it to the master of the banquet." The servants brought the glass to the master of the banquet and he tasted the water, which had been turned into wine. He didn't know where it came from but the servants knew they had drawn out water.

CULTURAL FACT

Weddings in Jesus' day were week-long festivals. Banquets were prepared for many guests, and the week would be spent celebrating the new life of the married couple. Often the whole town was invited, and everybody would come—it was considered an insult to refuse an invitation to a wedding. To accommodate many people, careful planning was needed. To run out of wine was more than embarrassing. It broke the strong unwritten laws of hospitality. With his first miracle, Jesus responded to a heartfelt need.

The master of the banquet called the bridegroom aside and said, "Everyone brings out the choice wine first and then the cheaper wine after the guests have had too much to drink, but you have saved the best till now." Then John concludes the story in this Gospel saying, "This, the first of his miraculous signs, Jesus performed in Cana of Galilee. He thus revealed his glory, and his disciples put their faith in him." (John 2:1–11)

THE SERMON ON THE MOUNT AND PUBLIC MINISTRY

The Sermon on the Mount (Matthew 5–7) came several months after Jesus selected his 12 disciples. (Luke 6:12–19) Matthew regarded this sermon as a summary of Jesus' teaching and the entire ministry of Jesus was an illustration of it. Because it contains the heart of Jesus' teaching, many people consider this sermon as the heart of the New Testament, similar to what the Ten Commandments are to the Old Testament.

THE BEATITUDES

Some of the most frequently quoted words of Jesus are found in the Beatitudes. The Beatitudes (Matthew 5:3–12) are composed of three elements:

- A pronouncement of blessing
- A quality of life
- The reason why the recipient should be considered blessed

The pronouncement of blessing is found in the word *blessed,* which introduces each Beatitude. In the Greek, it literally means "Oh, the happiness of _____." (Psalm 1:1) The word was a form of congratulations. The second element of the Beatitudes does not describe different kinds of people but provides a composite picture of the kind of person who wants to enter Christ's kingdom. The third portion of the Beatitudes looks ahead to some aspect of the coming kingdom. Because an individual with the qualities described in these Beatitudes will enter the kingdom, he is to be congratulated. Hear these familiar words:

Blessed are the poor in spirit, for theirs is the kingdom of heaven. Blessed are those who mourn, for they will be comforted. Blessed are the meek, for they will inherit the earth. Blessed are those who hunger and thirst for righteousness, for they will be filled. Blessed are the merciful, for they will be shown mercy. Blessed are the poor in heart, for they will see God. Blessed are the peacemakers, for they will be called the sons of God. Blessed are those who are persecuted because of righteousness, for theirs is the kingdom of heaven. (Matthew 5:3–10)

Jesus used the same literary device as the prophets called an oracle, or a series of divine pronouncements of God's blessing on someone who demonstrates a particular attitude. The rewards from obeying these words of Jesus are more than "happiness" and more significant than "joy." Those faithful who follow the Messiah's admonitions could consider themselves "blessed," as though they are given a heavenly blessing from God himself. This sermon was not an ordinary event.

The message Jesus gave was filled with irony. Under normal circumstances, when someone is blessed, those who are rich throw parties, but not in the kingdom that Jesus describes. Usually those who are oppressed and beaten down remain in this state, but not where Jesus is king. In this special place, the blind see, the deaf hear, and the poor receive good news. And their suffering and pain bring them blessing. Jesus said, "When you are despised, maligned, and even persecuted for the sake of righteousness, then you are blessed." Jesus told the people sitting on the hillside, "Rejoice and be very glad, for great is your reward in heaven." (Matthew 5:12)

PRACTICAL TEACHING

Immediately following these Beatitudes, Jesus gave two illustrations of what it would mean to follow him. With each illustration pointing to the principle that a person's actions should follow their words, Jesus said:

You are the salt of the earth. But if the salt loses its saltiness, how can it be made salty again? It is no longer good for anything, except to be thrown out and trampled by men. You are the light of the world. A city on a hill cannot be hidden. Neither do the people light a lamp and put it under a bowl. Instead they put it on its stand, and it gives light to everyone in the house. In the same way, let your light shine before men, that they may see your good deeds and praise your Father in heaven. (Matthew 5:13–16)

Where salt passively affects its environment, light must be placed so the light radiates out to a room or area. In the same way, Jesus is exhorting his disciples to continually reflect the light of their Heavenly Father.

CULTURAL FACT

Pure salt maintains its flavor. In Israel, some salt was mixed with other ingredients. When it was exposed to the elements, the salt would be "leached out." This leached-out salt was used to coat pathways.

CAME TO FULFILL THE LAW

The crowd around Jesus believed the Messiah would abolish the Laws of God. Jesus made it clear that he was on the earth to fulfill the Law of God. "Do not think that I have come to abolish the Law or the Prophets. I have not come to abolish them but to fulfill them." (Matthew 5:17) To show the contrast between the teachings of the Law and the teachings of Jesus, he continued and established a set of contrasts between the outward demand of the Law and the inner attitude, which God desires. The lessons in the Sermon on the Mount provide practical teaching about how to live and follow Jesus. In his sermon, Jesus taught this contrast:

Law	Spirit
(it has been said)	(but I say)
No Murder	No anger
No Adultery	No lust
No Divorce	Commitment
No Oath-taking	Speak the truth
No Retaliation	Forgiveness
No Hatred of your enemy	Love your enemy

JUST A MINUTE

Jesus cautioned his disciples not to pray repeating the same words over and over like a magic incantation. The repetition doesn't ensure that God will hear the prayer. It's not wrong to come to God many times for the same requests, and Jesus does encourage persistent prayer. In Matthew 6, Jesus condemns the shallow repetition of words that are not offered from a sincere heart.

PRACTICAL TEACHING ON PRAYER

Jesus cautioned his disciples not to pray as the heathen with vain repetitions and many words. The Greeks and the Romans called their gods as many names and titles as possible and often reminded the god of various favors that were owed to them. Jesus taught a model prayer in his Sermon on the Mount that is repeated in church services across the world each week and is known as the Lord's Prayer:

This is how you should pray "Our Father in heaven hallowed be your name, your Kingdom come, your will be done on earth as it is in heaven. Give us today our daily bread. Forgive us our debts, as we also have forgiven our debtors. And lead us not into temptation, but deliver us from the evil one." (Matthew 6:9–13)

As Jesus taught his disciples to pray, he adopted a fairly common Jewish prayer called a Kaddish, which was commonly prayed in the synagogues and included the lines, "Exalted and hallowed be his great name … and may he cause his kingdom to rule." The people used this prayer for the future kingdom.

The Jewish people longed for the ultimate coming of God's reign, when he would rule the earth unchallenged and restore justice and mercy to the entire planet. Then God's name would be shown holy or "hallowed" and the people would no longer profane it or swear oaths or live in a way to dishonor it. To "hallow God's name" was a central principle of Jewish ethics or to live in such a manner among the Gentiles that people will honor God.

POSSESSIONS IN HEAVEN

Also in this important sermon, Jesus told his followers to focus not on earthly possessions but on treasures in heaven: "But store up for yourselves treasures in heaven, where moth and rust do not destroy, and where thieves do not break in and steal. For where your treasure is, there your heart will be also … No one can serve two masters. Either he will hate the one and love the other, or he will be devoted to the one and despise the other. You cannot serve both God and Money." (Matthew 6:19–21, 24)

Treasures refer to the accumulation of wealth. Jesus exhorted the people to focus on "treasures in heaven," or the meritorious benefits of faithfully following God. He knew the ultimate destiny of life is eternal rather than the accumulation of worldly wealth. Jesus understood the consuming nature of money and how man couldn't serve both God and money.

JUST A MINUTE

In Matthew 6:25–34, Jesus tackled worry. In the process, Jesus was not condemning planning. Planning is time well spent, but worrying about tomorrow is time wasted. Sometimes it's difficult to tell the difference. Careful planning is thinking ahead about goals, schedules, and steps and trusting God's guidance. When well done, planning can lessen or eliminate worry. By contrast, worriers are consumed with fear and find it difficult to trust God. They let their plans interfere with their relationship with God. The Scriptures encourage us to be a planner and not a worrier.

After telling the crowd about the danger of possessions, Jesus turned and addressed another danger for those with wealth: worry about their possessions. He told his followers not to worry or be anxious or possess inordinate concern or grief beyond their immediate needs. Even the poor are not to worry about what they will eat or drink:

Therefore I tell you, do not worry about your life, what you will eat or drink; or about your body, what you will wear. Is not life more important than food, and the body more important than clothes? Look at the birds of the air; they do not sow or reap or store away in barns, and yet your heavenly Father feeds them. Are you not much more valuable than they? Who of you by worrying can add a single hour to his life? And why do you worry about clothes?

See how the lilies of the field grow. They do not labor or spin. Yet I tell you that not even Solomon in all his splendor was dressed like one of these. If that is how God clothes the grass of the field, which is here today and tomorrow is thrown into the fire, will he not much more clothe you, O you of little faith? So do not worry, saying, "What shall we eat?" or "What shall we drink?" or "What shall we wear?" For the pagans run after all these things, and your heavenly Father knows that you need them. But seek first his kingdom and his righteousness, and all these things will be given to you as well. Therefore do not worry about tomorrow, for tomorrow will worry about itself. Each day has enough trouble of its own. (Matthew 6:25–34)

In simple language, Jesus tells the people about the dangers of worry and how it can't add a single hour to your life. Instead the key to the spiritual life of faith according to Jesus is to seek first God's kingdom and his righteousness, then everything else will fall into place.

JUDGING OTHERS

After addressing common concerns of possessions and worry, Jesus turns to another sensitive issue in relationships—judging others. It's fairly simple to see the faults in others and be totally blind to our own deficiencies. He exhorted the people saying,

Do not judge, or you, too, will be judged. For in the same way you judge others, you will be judged, and with the measure you use, it will be measured to you. Why do you look at the speck of sawdust in your brother's eye and pay no attention to the plank in your own eye? How can you say to your brother, "Let me take the speck out of your eye," when all the time there is a plank in your own eye? You hypocrite, first take the plank out of your own eye, and then you will see clearly to remove the speck from your brother's eye. (Matthew 7:1–5)

What was Jesus saying to his followers when he told them not to judge? Did he want his disciples to close their eyes to errors and evil? Did he intend that news editors or art critics pull their punches or that managers forgo critical performance reviews of their employees? What about juries in the courts, should they stop judging? Or should people stop any assessments of others because none of us are perfect? No, each of these situations would be misapplications of the teaching of Jesus. He was not commanding blind acceptance, but grace toward others. Since every person is a sinner saved by God's grace, Jesus exhorted people to stop bothering with the failings of others and to begin attending to our own faults. People should not blame others while excusing themselves, according to Jesus.

There is room to assess others but only in the way of Jesus: with empathy and fairness and with a readiness to fully forgive. When people correct others, they should act like a good physician whose purpose is healing and not like an enemy who attacks.

FREQUENT PRAYER

In direct contrast to the outward concerns addressed earlier in the Sermon, Jesus makes a lengthy statement about the importance of perseverance and frequent prayer. Jesus said,

Ask and it will be given to you; seek and you will find; knock and the door will be opened to you. For everyone who asks receives; he who seeks finds; and to him who knocks, the door will be opened. Which of you, if his son asks for bread, will give him a stone? Or if he asks for a fish, will give him a snake? If you, then, though you are evil, know how to give good gifts to your children, how much more will your Father in heaven give good gifts to those who ask him! (Matthew 7:7–11)

Jesus promises the individual everything they need for spiritual success. God's blessings and provisions are available to each of his children.

JUST A MINUTE

Matthew 7:12 in Jesus' Sermon on the Mount is commonly known as the Golden Rule: "So in everything, do to others what you would have them do to you, for this sums up the Law and the Prophets." Many people state this rule negatively: "Don't do to others what you don't want done to you." Because Jesus stated it positively, he made it more significant. It's not very hard to refrain from harming others. It's much more difficult to take the initiative in doing something good for others.

TWO CLEAR CHOICES

At the end of his longest sermon in the Bible, Jesus presents two choices in a series of contrasts:

- Two gates (narrow and wide)
- Two trees (good fruit and bad fruit)

- Two professions
- Two foundations

This method of teaching was a common means for Jewish and Greco-Roman teachers. The best known of these contrasts is the wise and foolish builders:

Therefore everyone who hears these words of mine and puts them into practice is like a wise man who built his house on the rock. The rain came down, the streams rose, and the winds blew and beat against that house; yet it did not fall, because it had its foundation on the rock. But everyone who hears these words of mine and does not put them into practice is like a foolish man who built his house on sand. The rain came down, the streams rose, and the winds blew and beat against that house, and it fell with a great crash. (Matthew 7:24–27)

The key distinction between these two houses was not their external appearance but their foundations. One house was built on sand, and the other was built on rock. It's only through a proper spiritual foundation or relationship with Christ that a person should build their life.

The reaction of the crowd was significant. The Gospel of Matthew says, "When Jesus had finished saying these things, the crowds were amazed at his teaching, because he taught as one who had authority, and not as their teachers of the law." (Matthew 7:28–29)

The teaching of Jesus had impact on the people who heard his Sermon. In the next hour, we'll explore Jesus the great storyteller and his parables.

HOUR'S UP!

It's fascinating to learn about the early life of Jesus Christ. Head knowledge is fine, but the Bible says that it's a book of the heart and applicable to our everyday lives. The following 10 questions will move you beyond the level of knowledge about Jesus to apply this section to your life.

1. John the Baptist drew tremendous crowds with his baptism of repentance and his message. What can you learn for yourself from John's boldness to proclaim the message of God?

2. At first, John the Baptist wanted Jesus to baptize him but then he went ahead and baptized Jesus. Notice how John was obedient to his calling as one who proclaimed the way of the Lord. Is there some area of your life where you are struggling to obey the Lord? How can you learn from John's example of obedience?

3. Immediately after Jesus' baptism, he was tested in the desert. In your life, when you experience great victory are you tested? In these times of testing, how can you learn from the example of Jesus in his temptation?

4. With each temptation from Satan, Jesus turned to the Scriptures. Take some time this week to memorize a few verses to cling to in times of temptation or weakness.

5. The second temptation shows Jesus' commitment to fulfill his purpose in life. Notice Jesus' resolve and commitment to not be thrown off his purpose. What happens when you are thrown off your purpose? How can you learn from the way Jesus handled this temptation?

6. During the third temptation, Satan also quoted Scripture—yet out of context. Because of Jesus' answer, what can we learn about the importance of studying the Bible and knowing the full story as well as memorizing Scripture?

7. Take a few moments and reread the Beatitudes. (Matthew 5:3–12) What stands out to you as something that you need to apply to your life? Possibly becoming a peacemaker or hungering or thirsting after righteousness? Take some time to consider, then pray, asking God to make this Beatitude real in your life.

8. Study the contrast between life under the Law and life under the Spirit. Celebrate the freedom in Christ that you can find through life in the Spirit rather than the Law.

9. Jesus taught about the dangers of possessions and worry. In our culture, it's easy to fall into chasing "earthly treasures" and constant worry. From the lessons in the Sermon on the Mount, what daily strength can you find to help you escape these tensions?

10. At the end of the Sermon on the Mount, Jesus clearly gives four different contrasts. How are you building your life on a foundation of rock rather than sand?

HOUR 16

The Parables of Jesus

CHAPTER SUMMARY

LESSON PLAN:

In this hour, you will learn about …

- Why Jesus taught the crowd in parables.
- The details of several key parables.
- How to interpret or understand the parables of Jesus.

People love a good story. Anyone who speaks in public knows a good story will keep the audience listening intently to the message. Filmmakers know from the opening frame how to keep audiences on the edge of their seats to see the conclusion of the story. Good writers know from the first paragraph how to "grab the reader by their Nikes and not let go." Little children soon learn the power of a story and usually have a favorite book they carry around and grab any adult who will read it to them.

As Jesus Christ knew that telling stories would have a profound affect on his audiences, he told stories or parables. This unusual teaching style completely confused the Sanhedrin, or religious leaders. The Pharisees asked the officers who had been sent to collect Jesus and bring him back to them, "Why haven't you captured him?" "'No one ever spoke the way this man does,' the guards declared. 'You mean he has deceived you also?' the Pharisees retorted." (John 7:46–47)

Even the religious spies were spellbound with the simple storytelling power of Jesus' parables. In fact, these leaders wondered if their spies had also been converted with their question, "He hasn't gotten to you, too, has he?" In this hour, you will learn more about the teaching of Jesus in parables. He taught simple stories yet with authority.

WHAT WAS JESUS' PURPOSE TO TEACH IN PARABLES?

Over the centuries, even those who have not believed Jesus is the Messiah or Christ have spoken and written admirably about Jesus' teaching skill through the parables. These parables are distinct from some of the other teaching of Jesus. They were not metaphors or implied comparisons such as "I am the Vine, and you are the branches." Also, parables were not similes—stories that use "like" or "as" to take a truth and make an exact replica such as "To what can I compare this generation?" (Matthew 11:16) And parables are not intentional exaggeration or hyperbole such as "faith like a mustard seed." (Luke 17:6)

CULTURAL FACT

A mustard seed (Luke 17:6) is small but is alive and growing. Almost invisible at first, it will begin to spread, first under the ground, then above. Like a tiny seed, a small amount of genuine faith in God will take root and grow.

The word *parable* means "to throw alongside" and is a story that delivers a parallel truth. These pithy, fictional stories from Jesus had one purpose: to underscore the focus of the message. The three most important elements of communication are illustration, illustration, and illustration. Jesus used illustration or parable as his most frequent form of teaching.

Although Jesus lived among a storytelling people, his approach to instruction was still unusual. The people remembered his stories although the meaning of the stories was not obvious. While people heard them, they did not necessarily understand them. Few of the people who first heard the parables from Jesus understood them. The disciples in frustration asked Jesus, "Why do you speak to the people in parables?" The disciples didn't understand the stories any better than the crowd.

Jesus gave some insight about why he taught in this fashion, saying:

The knowledge of the secrets of the kingdom of heaven has been given to you, but not to them. Whoever has will be given more, and he will have an abundance. Whoever does not have, even what he has will be taken from him. This is why I speak to them in parables: "Though seeing, they do not see; though hearing, they do not hear or understand. In them is fulfilled the prophecy of Isaiah: 'You will be ever hearing but never understanding; you will be ever seeing but never perceiving. For this people's heart has become calloused; they hardly hear with their ears, and they have closed their eyes.

Otherwise they might see with their eyes, hear with their ears, understand with their hearts and turn, and I would heal them.' But blessed are your eyes because they see, and your ears because they hear." (Matthew 13:11–16)

Jesus' answer reveals a great deal about why he taught in parables. People need to soften their hearts, humble themselves before God, and honestly seek the truth to find it.

The stories of Jesus are like wrapped gifts. The packaging of a gift can either distract or captivate. Yet unless the package is opened, the gift itself remains hidden. Unless a listener understands the core of the parable—the truth and application—the lesson remains hidden. Yet when the listener discovers the application, the lessons prove to be extremely valuable. Millions of people's lives have been transformed over the years through the storytelling or parables of Jesus.

Often Jesus' stories contain multiple applications. The same parable can strike people in different ways. For example, the Parable of the Lost Son (Luke 15:11–32), which is also known as the Prodigal Son, will affect the father quite differently than it would a rebellious son or a jealous older brother. Also the Parable of the Soils (Matthew 13:1–23) can be viewed from at least four distinct vantage points, depending on the person's identification with one of the soils. Some parables are long, such as the story of the Prodigal Son in Luke 15, whereas others are very short, such as Matthew 15:14b: "If a blind man leads a blind man, both will fall into a pit."

When Jesus taught in Jerusalem during his last week before his death, his parables focused on listeners' rejection of him or their acceptance. As he spoke, even the Pharisees and the priests understood that Jesus was speaking about them. (Matthew 21:45) Jesus' parables stung these leaders and they despised his message and him. Yet they were unwilling to give up their pride, seek forgiveness, which they needed, and learn from Jesus. These leaders sensed that if they unwrapped the parables, they would not like what they found, so they refused to learn the truth. Through their actions, they fulfilled the words of Isaiah, who described a people with dull hearts, closed eyes, and hardness of hearing. Ironically, these religious leaders who should have been guiding their people into truth were the most blind to the parables.

EXAMINING SOME KEY PARABLES

During Jesus' three years of teaching and ministry, the four Gospels recorded 40 parables. In the next few minutes, let's examine in detail a few of the key parables, which show different ways Jesus used these illustrations.

THE GOOD SAMARITAN AND THE SILENCED LAWYER

Sometimes parables were used like riddles, to set a trap for the listeners. The parable of the Good Samaritan is one of the best examples of this type of parable. Jesus had been teaching when at a certain point—perhaps an official question and answer session—a lawyer stood and asked a question. The Scriptures describe the lawyer as "testing" Jesus with a question. Here's the passage:

> On one occasion an expert in the law stood up to test Jesus. "Teacher," he asked, "what must I do to inherit eternal life?"
>
> "What is written in the Law?" he [Jesus] replied. "How do you read it?"
>
> He [the lawyer] answered: "Love the Lord your God with all your heart and with all your soul and with all your strength and with all your mind"; and, "Love your neighbor as yourself."
>
> "You have answered correctly," Jesus replied. "Do this and you will live." (Luke 10:25–28)

Can you see the lawyer going through mental gymnastics to see how he can fulfill the Law, which he gave to Jesus? He knew no mortal man on earth could claim to do all of this. Love your God with all your heart, soul, mind, and strength—and also your neighbor? Yet this lawyer continued to stand in front of Jesus. He had the skill of cross-examination so he continued with another question: "But he wanted to justify himself, so he asked Jesus, 'And who is my neighbor?'" (Luke 10:29)

Luke gives insight into this lawyer's motives and heart when he writes the words "to justify himself." Jesus could have responded to the question with another question, "Who is your neighbor? I thought you wanted to inherit eternal life. Have you loved God with all of your heart, soul, strength, and mind? You've got plenty to work on before you try and define the word *neighbor*." Jesus could have reduced this arrogant lawyer with that sort of approach or he could have ignored the question and looked around for another question. Instead, the ever-patient Jesus told a parable:

> In reply Jesus said: "A man was going down from Jerusalem to Jericho, when he fell into the hands of robbers. They stripped him of his clothes, beat him and went away, leaving him half dead. A priest happened to be going down the same road, and when he saw the man, he passed by on the other side. So too, a Levite, when he came to the place and saw him, passed by on the other side. But a Samaritan, as he traveled, came where

the man was; and when he saw him, he took pity on him. He went to him and bandaged his wounds, pouring on oil and wine. Then he put the man on his own donkey, took him to an inn and took care of him. The next day he took out two silver coins and gave them to the innkeeper. 'Look after him,' he said, 'and when I return, I will reimburse you for any extra expense you may have.'

"Which of these three do you think was a neighbor to the man who fell into the hands of robbers?"

The expert in the law replied, "The one who had mercy on him."

Jesus told him, "Go and do likewise." (Luke 10:30–37)

CULTURAL FACT

The road between Jerusalem and Jericho was a 17-mile journey on a road known to harbor many robbers. Thieves would hide in caves along the way and attack their victims.

Jesus knew how to impact this lawyer. Instead of grilling him on the impossibility of loving God with his heart, soul, strength, and mind, Jesus worked on loving the neighbor. As with anyone, the lawyer realized he fell short of obeying this law—much less the entire Law. The lawyer probably wasn't accustomed to such a defeat in the public arena but he had never been cross-examined by Jesus Christ. After this parable, the lawyer probably quietly sat down and decided not to enter into any more questions with Jesus.

THE PARABLE OF THE SOWER

Jesus knew how to reach his audience. The majority of the people in his audience were farmers who raised crops and livestock. Many of his parables are relevant to the farmer and he made an immediate connection with these stories. Jesus spoke:

"Listen! A farmer went out to sow his seed. As he was scattering the seed, some fell along the path, and the birds came and ate it up. Some fell on rocky places, where it did not have much soil. It sprang up quickly, because the soil was shallow. But when the sun came up, the plants were scorched, and they withered because they had no root. Other seed fell among thorns, which grew up and choked the plants, so that they did not bear grain. Still other seed fell on good soil. It came up, grew and produced a crop, multiplying thirty, sixty, or even a hundred times."

Then Jesus said, "He who has ears to hear, let him hear." (Mark 4:3–9)

CULTURAL FACT

Jesus told a story that was easy enough to comprehend. During the planting season, it was common to see men scattering seed by hand over their small fields. They cast the seed over the various kinds of soil Jesus described—smooth pathways running through the fields, rough terrain that hid large rocks just beneath the surface, fields overgrown with weeds, and excellent, rich soil here and there.

According to the story in the Gospels, Jesus didn't say anything else to the crowd. He didn't explain the identity of the sower or what the seed and soils represented. Some of those in the audience must have wondered why Jesus was giving a lesson about planting crops. Other people must have been aware that Jesus was the sower, the Word was the seed, and the people were the different types of soil. Some people scratched their heads, while others were stunned with the power of Jesus' storytelling.

The crowd thinned until only Jesus and the disciples remained. The disciples asked Jesus to explain the parable and he said to them, "The secret of the kingdom of God has been given to you. But to those on the outside everything is said in parables so that, 'they may be ever seeing but never perceiving, and ever hearing but never understanding; otherwise they might turn and be forgiven!'" (Mark 4:11–12)

With his disciples, Jesus reminded them that he told these parables to draw unbelievers to himself. Filled with a heart of love and compassion, Jesus used parables to alert outsiders to the truths about the Kingdom of God. Different listeners received different messages but the prerequisite according to Jesus was to "have ears to hear." The parables were to fill the hearts of the hungry.

In this Gospel, Jesus went on and explained the meaning of the parable of the sower:

Don't you understand this parable? How then will you understand any parable? The farmer sows the word. Some people are like seed along the path, where the word is sown. As soon as they hear it, Satan comes and takes away the word that was sown in them. Others, like seed sown on rocky places, hear the word and at once receive it with joy. But since they have no root, they last only a short time. When trouble or persecution comes because of the word, they quickly fall away. Still others, like seed sown among thorns, hear the word; but the worries of this life, the deceitfulness of wealth and the desires for other things come in and choke the word, making it unfruitful. Others, like seed sown on good soil, hear the word, accept it, and produce a crop—thirty, sixty or even a hundred times what was sown. (Mark 4:13–20)

Jesus hoped to sow in the good soil that would produce a large crop—like in the hearts of his disciples.

THE PARABLE OF THE PRODIGAL SON

As Jesus traveled around and taught, he was often criticized. The teachers of the Law and the Pharisees muttered, "This man welcomes sinners and eats with them." (Luke 15:1) Aware of what the religious leaders thought of him, Jesus told a few parables about lost items and the stories ran in a theme. The shepherd had one hundred sheep, lost one, went out, and found it, rejoicing with his neighbors over the discovery of this lost animal. In one sentence, Jesus tells the reason for the parable of the lost sheep, "I tell you that in the same way there will be more rejoicing in heaven over one sinner who repents than over ninety-nine righteous persons who do not need to repent." (Luke 15:7)

Immediately after the parable of the lost sheep in the Gospel of Luke, Jesus told about a woman who loses a coin and searches for it. To recover the coin, she turns on all the lights and sweeps her home with a broom until she discovers the coin. Then the woman celebrates locating her lost coin. As with the story of the sheep, Jesus used the story of the coin to say, "In the same way, I tell you, there is rejoicing in the presence of the angels of God over one sinner who repents." (Luke 15:10) Then Jesus immediately launched into a third story about a lost son.

Once a man had two sons; the younger son grew restless and wanted to leave home to see the world. This son asked his father whether he could receive his inheritance in advance; the father agreed to divide the property between the two sons.

The younger son headed to a distant country, and spent his money on wild living. After his money was gone, a famine hit the land. He took a job feeding pigs, which was particularly bad for a Jewish person, who was not to touch or eat these animals. (Leviticus 11:7–8) Then he realized the pigs had better food than he was eating. As the son thought about it some more, he knew his father's servants were eating better than he was so he decided to swallow his pride and return home. He determined to go home no longer as a son, but to become one of his father's hired men. On the trip home, he even practiced his speech so his father would take him back.

When the son came close to home, his father looked up and saw him "while he was a long way off." (Luke 15:20) Was this father watching the road and hoping to see his younger son? Filled with compassion, the father ran to meet his son. The son couldn't even begin his practiced speech but his father brought a robe, ring, and sandals to dress his son as a valued member of his family. Then the father planned a feast to celebrate his son's return.

CULTURAL FACT

The robe from the father probably represented the best clothing he had to offer. The ring might have borne the family seal, signifying the son's acceptance back into the family.

An ordinary storyteller would have finished the parable with the son's return, but Jesus was no ordinary storyteller. He continued the story.

The noise of the celebration eventually reached the ears of the older son, who asked what was going on. When the servants told him about the younger son, the older son was angry. After all, he had been working hard in the fields and came home to find music and dancing for his younger brother. He turned his back on the festival and refused to join the celebration.

The father went outside to reason with his older son but the son was disappointed in the celebration—and reasonably so because he had stayed home and worked hard, while his brother squandered the family wealth on prostitutes, before returning home to a celebration. He said to his father, "Look! All these years I've been slaving for you and never disobeyed your orders. Yet you never gave me even a young goat so I could celebrate with my friends." (Luke 15:29) The father gently pointed out that everything in his possession also belonged to the son. Then he told the elder son that he missed the point of the celebration: "But we had to celebrate and be glad, because this brother of yours was dead and is alive again; he was lost and is found." (Luke 15:32)

Jesus knew his audience—especially the experts in the Law and the Pharisees and understood they would relate to the problems of the older brother. It was easy to see how to rejoice over a lost sheep or a lost coin but the celebration changes when a person is involved. These leaders thought the younger son got what he deserved in his slinking back to his father. Instead, Jesus celebrated the return of a lost person. If you are a prodigal, then you tend to grasp for the mercy of God and hold on tight. When you observe a prodigal returning to receive God's forgiveness and mercy, you might not be so quick to understand. Whether someone is a prodigal or a faithful follower, Jesus wanted people to understand the celebration for the lost whenever they return.

THE PARABLE OF THE SHREWD MANAGER

In another parable, Jesus described a shrewd manager. Once a rich man had a manager who was accused of wasting his possessions. He called in the manager and told him that he would no longer be his manager. Suddenly unemployed, the shrewd manager wondered what to do. He thought that he wasn't strong enough to do physical labor and was ashamed to beg so he decided to take some action that would make others like him. He called in the various debtors of his master and downsized their individual debts. One man owed 800 gallons of olive oil and the manager changed it to 400. Another owed 1,000 bushels of wheat and he reduced it to 800. Jesus commended the shrewd manager for his foresight and not his dishonesty. He approved of the manager's way of providing for his future and not his crooked method of achieving his goal. (Luke 16:1–13)

JUST A MINUTE

What right did the steward have to reduce the amount owed to the master? Three explanations are commonly given: (1) The steward simply lowered the price on his own authority, (2) the steward removed the interest charge from the debt, according to the Law (Leviticus 25:36–37), or (3) the steward removed his own commission, sacrificing only his own money and not that of his master. The different rates of reduction reflect the different rates for different commodities. The steward was a shrewd manager because he knew how to manipulate the end result for his master.

As the manager made friends by the manipulative use of his master's goods, Jesus told this story to encourage the honest use of the gifts that God has given every person. Then Jesus concluded this parable with some strong words about the love of money:

I tell you, use worldly wealth to gain friends for yourselves, so that when it is gone, you will be welcomed into eternal dwellings. Whoever can be trusted with very little can also be trusted with much, and whoever is dishonest with very little will also be dishonest with much. So if you have not been trustworthy in handling worldly wealth, who will trust you with true riches? And if you have not been trustworthy with someone else's property, who will give you property of your own? No servant can serve two masters. Either he will hate the one and love the other, or he will be devoted to the one and despise the other. You cannot serve both God and Money. (Luke 16:9–13)

Then notice the reaction of the Pharisees and how Jesus handled these religious leaders: "The Pharisees, who loved money, heard all this and were sneering at Jesus. He said to them, 'You are the ones who justify yourselves in the eyes of men, but God knows your hearts. What is highly valued among men is detestable in God's sight.'" (Luke 16:14–15)

Jesus repeatedly used stories like this parable about the shrewd manager to move his listeners into action and a deeper relationship with God instead of staying in complacency.

THE PARABLE OF THE PHARISEE AND THE TAX COLLECTOR

Sometimes Jesus told parables with clear contrasts to point out the difference between hypocrisy and humility. He told this parable: "Two men went up to the temple to pray, one a Pharisee and the other a tax collector. The Pharisee stood up and prayed about himself: 'God, I thank you that I am not like other men—robbers, evildoers, adulterers—or even like this tax collector. I fast twice a week and give a tenth of all I get.'

"But the tax collector stood at a distance. He would not even look up to heaven, but beat his breast and said, 'God, have mercy on me, a sinner.' I tell you that this man, rather than the other, went home justified before God. For everyone who exalts himself will be humbled, and he who humbles himself will be exalted." (Luke 18:10–14) Jesus had strong words for those who get pleasure from outward acts of kindness, mercy, and even religion.

JUST A MINUTE

The tone of the prayer from the Pharisee reveals his problem. He used the pronoun *I* five times in two verses. The Pharisee's attitude seemed to be that God should be grateful for his commitment. The man obviously looked down on other people and was proud of his fasting and tithing.

INTERPRETING THE PARABLES

Important principles should be used as a guide while reading the stories:

Parables are not allegories. An allegory is usually completely filled with meaning. Every detail in the story means something, which can be traced to the overriding principle of the allegory. Parables usually have one central meaning. If a person tries to oversymbolize them, it can have the effect of tearing them apart. A parable is best understood as a person sees it in simple and entire terms.

The Rule of Three. Remember the stories from childhood like "The Three Pigs" or "Goldilocks and the Three Bears"? Like good storytelling, parables usually follow the Rule of Three. Jesus often used this method when he told his parables. Many parables deliver three important truths.

The Rule of Two. Characters in a parable often follow the Rule of Two. Usually there are two people who experience the tension between sin and righteousness or evil and good. Look for these dual elements in a parable and they will often be the central points.

Key words and phrases. When Jesus taught the parables, he often repeated the same words. For example, he used the phrase "how much more" to move the story from the temporal things into the spiritual reality. Also he uses the phrase, "He who has ears to hear" to call people's attention to important issues of life or death. "I say to you," means that Jesus is speaking with an earnest intensity about something the listener should not miss. Each of these phrases is significant when reading the parables of Jesus.

The kingdom Jesus intended to establish as the Messiah, or Christ, was considerably different than what the Jewish people commonly expected of the Messiah. Many of the parables are about the Kingdom of God, and this concept is grasped with the heart and spirit. Jesus used stories or parables about ordinary, everyday events to illustrate the origin, development, present-day character, and the future of God's Kingdom. His stories conveyed truth in ways which logical explanations could not accomplish. To understand and interpret the parables, it requires a receptive heart rather than a logical mind—which is why the parables in fact obscured Jesus' message from those whose heart was unwilling to listen.

In interpreting the parables, the problem is to know which elements are significant and which ones are merely details included to make the story memorable. Ordinarily a parable is meant to show a single point. Studying the parables provides rich insight into the heart and relationship with God.

Through the parables, Jesus made a direct attack on the religious leaders of the day. Through parables like the Prodigal Son, Jesus blew the cover of the religious leaders. They were neither actively recruiting lost people to their religion nor even pleased when sinners were restored to a relationship with God.

"We've got to get rid of that man," one of the Pharisees must have said to his colleagues. "He's destroying our credibility with the people," another said. "He treats the sinners with more dignity than us," someone else might have added.

The crowd who listened to Jesus tell the story of the Prodigal Son or the Lost Son and the restoration must have glowed with joy and excitement. God was eager to welcome people home from sin and rebellion—being lost. And more than eager—God was going to throw a party in celebration for their return. The news of the parable was almost too good to be true. The power of these stories or parables from Jesus is timeless. No wonder he loved to tell parables.

HOUR'S UP!

When the crowd listened to Jesus, they were captivated with his parables. Yet, these stories are more than tales from Jesus—they have personal application to our everyday lives. In the following 10 questions, consider the application to your life.

1. Jesus used stories to even win over his enemies. Consider the power in stories to change the hearts of people. Jesus used it with the parables. What principles can you gain from the storytelling techniques to help you in your everyday relationships?

2. Understanding the parables has as much to do with the heart relationship as the mind, according to Jesus. (Matthew 13:11–16) Take a few minutes and prepare your heart and ask God to show you insight through the parables.

3. Jesus used the parable about the Good Samaritan to show the lawyer new insight into the expectations of God. What did you learn about who is your neighbor and the importance of not predetermining who will be your neighbor?

4. Samaritans were on the lowest cultural rung in the region where Jesus lived. He used a Samaritan in the parable as a good role model. Consider the lowly who cross your path this week—or maybe they don't cross your path and they should. How can you reach out to these people in some concrete action during the week ahead?

5. The parable of the Sower reveals four different types of soils. What kind of soil do you show through your life? If you are not a good soil, then what steps can you take to open your heart and hear God's Word in a fresh manner, then produce a crop that is a hundred times what was sown?

6. Many of us know a prodigal. Possibly you have strayed or a relative has strayed from the path of following Jesus. If you've been a prodigal, take a few moments and rejoice at how God's grace has been evident in your life. If you know a prodigal, take some concrete action to consistently pray and help this person.

7. When prodigals return from sin, how do you react? Like the older brother in the story of the Prodigal Son? Do you celebrate the changed life or feel bad they have had such fun with sin and been able to have it wiped from their life through the death and resurrection of Jesus Christ? Take a few minutes to evaluate your attitude about those who repent and change their lives. Then determine to throw a party of celebration the next time.

8. Reread the parable of the shrewd manager and the lesson of how you can't serve both God and money. What can you learn about the importance of the lessons of the heart and following God instead of material wealth? Pause and reflect to see how this truth will change some of your decisions during the coming week, month, or year.

9. Some parables clearly contrast the difference between hypocrisy and humility. What insight do you gain from the parable of the Pharisee and the tax collector? It's not our outward actions which count, but the inside message. Pause for a moment and meditate on this truth from the parable. What difference will it make in your life?

10. Through his parables, Jesus attacked the leaders of his day, but also encouraged the common person on the street. Often even in today's world, it's easy to get caught in the trappings of religion (attending church, regular Bible study, and other sorts of "do's and don'ts"). Take a moment to evaluate your motivation for such trappings and see if it's from a heart relationship or some sort of Law in your life. If it's a Law, then ask God to give you joy and a relationship as you continue to follow the disciplines of the spiritual life.

HOUR 17

The Miracles of Jesus

LESSON PLAN:

In this hour, you will learn about …

- How to validate Jesus' miracles.
- Exorcising a demon.
- Raising the dead.
- Feeding the multitudes.
- The healing of physical ailments.

"Step right up," the carnival barkers cry out to the crowd, "It's amazing to see a bearded midget lady." Like metal shavings to a magnet, the crowd is drawn to see the incredible person behind the curtain.

Over the centuries, the miracles of Jesus have been portrayed like some circus act or magic show. Jesus, the Savior of the world, the Christ, was not a freak show for people to see. Jesus performed miracles that have stood the test of time. In this hour, you will explore how to validate the miracles of Jesus, and then look at some of the details related to these miracles.

The New Testament was written in Greek and the original language uses the word *thaumaz,* which is translated as "amazement," more than 40 times. More than any other word, amazement is used to describe the reaction of the people to some action from Jesus. The people didn't have words for the miracle but only awe and amazement.

HOW TO VALIDATE JESUS' MIRACLES

The miracles of Jesus are not something from a circus or something which history faked. Eyewitness accounts are one of the ways to validate the claims about Jesus' miracles. Another means is how the educated people during the days of Jesus validated his miracles.

A Visit from Nicodemus

The people who witnessed the miracles of Jesus were not all naïve, simple-minded, or easily fooled. The Apostle John tells about an educated visitor to Jesus: "Now there was a man of the Pharisees named Nicodemus, a member of the Jewish ruling council. He came to Jesus at night and said, 'Rabbi, we know you are a teacher who has come from God. For no one could perform the miraculous signs you are doing if God were not with him.'" (John 3:1–2)

JUST A MINUTE

Nicodemus was an upper-class Jew and a Pharisee from one of the prominent families of Jerusalem. He came to Jesus alone, at night. During their conversation, Jesus confronted Nicodemus about his need to be "born again," then let him go away to consider his words. (John 3:1–21) The next time Nicodemus appeared in the Gospel, he defended Jesus on a procedural matter. (John 7:45–52) Apparently, Nicodemus never openly identified with Jesus until after the crucifixion, when he helped prepare Jesus' body for burial. (John 19:39)

Nicodemus was a well-taught religious leader. The Jewish people looked to men like Nicodemus as living examples of someone who obeyed God's laws. As Nicodemus had a thorough understanding of the Torah, the Jewish people often turned to him for spiritual discernment and guidance.

During the time of Christ, many people claimed to be the Messiah but then were exposed as imposters. The Pharisees had grown hardened to these claims and were not easily impressed. Now this leader of the Jews was impressed enough with the works of Jesus to describe them as "miracles." Also notice how Nicodemus used the plural to show that some of his colleagues in the Sanhedrin were also convinced about the miracles of Jesus: "We know you are a teacher who has come from God." In the middle of the night, Nicodemus confessed, "My friends and I have been talking about you and we are amazed at what you have done."

A nineteenth-century philosopher, John Locke, said the primary purpose of a miracle in the Bible was to bring credit to the Proposer, or the one who did the miracle. The act was to prove the truthfulness of the actor and to certify that God endorsed this individual and the person was speaking God's truth. Miracles immediately drew the unsuspecting person who witnessed the action into the presence of God.

EYEWITNESS ACCOUNTS

If Jesus had been guilty of fakery, there would have been plenty of evidence. To the contrary, history doesn't record any evidence that the people who were eyewitnesses to his miracles ever doubted their authenticity. No one challenged Jesus' miracles. People viewed extraordinary events from the hand of Jesus and they knew it.

If any eyewitness had a question, it was about the author of the miracle:

Then they brought him a demon-possessed man who was blind and mute, and Jesus healed him, so that he could both talk and see. All the people were astonished and said, "Could this be the Son of David?"

But when the Pharisees heard this, they said, "It is only by Beelzebub, the prince of demons, that this fellow drives out demons."

Jesus knew their thoughts and said to them, "Every kingdom divided against itself will be ruined, and every city or household divided against itself will not stand. If Satan drives out Satan, he is divided against himself. How then can his kingdom stand? And if I drive out demons by Beelzebub, by whom do your people drive them out? So then, they will be your judges. But if I drive out demons by the Spirit of God, then the kingdom of God has come upon you." (Matthew 12:22–28)

The people brought to Jesus a man who couldn't speak or see and also was possessed by a demon. When Jesus healed the man, all the people were astonished (some translations say "amazed"). Some religious leaders were present to witness the healing and they didn't question what they had seen. The man had certainly been healed through the power of Jesus.

This story is actually about two miracles. The first is the healing of a severely disabled man. In a moment, this individual was transformed and awe filled the people who witnessed this life-changing event. Then there was a second miracle, without the Pharisees saying a single word, "Jesus knew their thoughts." Imagine the surprise and how exposed they must have felt when the man from Galilee voiced a concern that was only in their minds.

The Pharisees didn't examine the healed man to see if their eyes were playing tricks on them. These cynics didn't dispute the reality of the miracles around the ministry of Jesus Christ. The man had been transformed in an instant. What these religious leaders *did* question was the author of the miracle. Which deity was responsible?

Understanding their thoughts, Jesus made it clear that only the Spirit of God could have performed this type of miracle. Miracles filled the ministry of Jesus. In the next few minutes, let's examine several of these miracles.

A MAN POSSESSED BY A DEMON

Early in the ministry of Jesus, he and his disciples had crossed a lake in a boat when the waves came up. Jesus was asleep and the disciples woke him and he instantly stilled the water. Terrified, the disciples asked each other, "Who is this? Even the wind and the waves obey him!" (Mark 4:41) Immediately after this miracle of nature, a demon-possessed man came toward Jesus. People had tried to bind him with chains but they had been unsuccessful and the broken chains were on his hands and feet. Nothing had been able to constrain him, as Mark records:

When he saw Jesus from a distance, he ran and fell on his knees in front of him. He shouted at the top of his voice, "What do you want with me, Jesus, Son of the Most High God? Swear to God that you won't torture me!"

For Jesus had said to him, "Come out of this man, you evil spirit!" Then Jesus asked him, "What is your name?"

"My name is Legion," he replied, "for we are many."

And he begged Jesus again and again not to send them out of the area. A large herd of pigs was feeding on the nearby hillside. The demons begged Jesus, "Send us among the pigs; allow us to go into them." He gave them permission, and the evil spirits came out and went into the pigs. The herd, about two thousand in number, rushed down the steep bank into the lake and were drowned. Those tending the pigs ran off and reported this in the town and countryside, and the people went out to see what had happened. When they came to Jesus, they saw the man who had been possessed by the legion of demons sitting there, dressed and in his right mind; and they were afraid. (Mark 5:6–15)

CULTURAL FACT

The demon-possessed man was in the country of Gadarenes, which is on the eastern shore of the Sea of Galilee. The country also is called Gergesenes. The reference *Gergesenes* is used in Matthew 8:28–34, and *Gadarenes* is used in Luke 8:26–27 and Mark 5:1; *Gergesenes* is merely a variant term that refers to the same place. No towns or villages exist along the lake's narrow eastern shore because cliffs several thousand feet high rise up from near the water's edge.

In an instant, this man who no one could contain was transformed, dressed, and in his right mind. The people demanded that Jesus leave the area and the healed man wanted to go with him. Mark continues the story: "Jesus did not let him, but said, 'Go home to your family and tell them how much the Lord has done for you, and how he has had mercy on you.' So the man went away and began to tell in the Decapolis (a federation of 10 cities east of Samaria and Galilee) how much Jesus had done for him. And all the people were amazed." (Mark 5:19–20) The word *amazed* appears again associated with the miracle.

Raising the Dead

On three different occasions during his ministry, Jesus performed the ultimate healing: He raised the dead. Each case was unique and special because of the limited occasions Jesus used this particular power from God.

The Widow's Son

A short story about the compassion of Jesus is in Luke's Gospel. The physician, Luke, must have been fascinated to witness the healing of the widow's son. One day as Jesus and his disciples approached the gate of Nain, a large crowd from the town was with a widow whose only son was carried in a coffin. When Jesus saw the widow, his heart went out to her and he told her, "Don't cry." He reached into the coffin and said, "Young man, I say to you, get up." Immediately the dead boy sat up and began to talk and Jesus gave him back to his mother. And what was the reaction of the large crowd? The Gospel says, "they were all filled with awe and praised God. 'A great prophet has appeared among us,' they said. 'God has come to help his people.' This news about Jesus spread throughout Judea and the surrounding country." (Luke 7:16–17)

CULTURAL FACT

Honoring the dead was important in Jewish tradition. A funeral procession, composed of relatives of the dead person, followed the body, which was wrapped and carried on a kind of stretcher. This procession would make its way through town, and bystanders would be expected to join the procession. In addition, hired mourners would cry aloud and draw attention to the procession. The family's mourning would continue for 30 days.

JAIRUS'S DAUGHTER

One day, Jairus, the main elder in the synagogue, came to Jesus because his 12-year-old daughter was dying. The man fell at Jesus' feet and begged him to come and heal his daughter. Jesus agreed to go to the house. During the journey, someone came from Jairus's house and told him not to bother the teacher because the girl had already died. When Jesus overheard the news, he said to Jairus, "Don't be afraid; just believe, and she will be healed." Jesus affirmed the faith of the synagogue ruler. As the group arrived at the house of Jairus, Jesus did not let anyone go into the room with him except Peter, John, and James, and the child's father and mother.

Meanwhile, all the people were wailing and mourning for the little girl. "Stop wailing," Jesus said. "She is not dead but asleep." Everyone laughed at Jesus, knowing the child was dead. After clearing the room, Jesus took the girl by the hand and said, "My child, get up!" Immediately, her spirit returned, and at once she stood up. Then Jesus told them to give her something to eat. Her parents were astonished (the *amazement* word again), but he ordered them not to tell anyone what had happened. (Luke 8:50–56) The reasons Jesus silenced the parents was unclear because everyone would have known the girl was dead and now alive. Some scholars believe Jesus gave this caution to the parents so raising people from the dead would not become the focus of his healing ministry.

CULTURAL FACT

The synagogue was the local center of worship. Jairus, the synagogue leader, was responsible for administration, building maintenance, and worship supervision. It would have been quite unusual for a respected synagogue leader to fall at the feet of an itinerant preacher and beg him to heal his daughter. Jesus honored this man's humble faith.

LAZARUS

Later, in the final month of Jesus' life, he healed a third man, a friend named Lazarus. Mary, Martha, and Lazarus lived in Bethany. The sisters sent word to Jesus that their brother was ill. Jesus had an unusual response. Instead of leaving immediately to heal Lazarus of his illness, he said, "This sickness will not end in death. No, it is for God's glory so that God's Son may be glorified through it." (John 11:4) Jesus wasn't in a hurry and stayed two more days before traveling toward the village of Bethany.

As they traveled toward Bethany, Jesus told his disciples, "Our friend Lazarus has fallen asleep; but I am going there to wake him up." Not understanding that Jesus meant Lazarus had died, the disciples replied, "Lord, if he sleeps, he will get better." Then Jesus spoke plainly to them and said that Lazarus was dead. "Lazarus is dead, and for your sake I am glad I was not there, so that you may believe. But let us go to him."

When they arrived in Bethany, which was less than two miles from Jerusalem, Lazarus had been dead four days. A large crowd was comforting the two sisters and Jesus asked to see the tomb. When he saw the grief of Mary, Jesus was deeply moved and the shortest verse in the Bible appears: "Jesus wept." (John 11:35) How did the people react to Jesus' tears? One part of the crowd said, "See how much Jesus loved him." But another portion of the people were skeptics and scoffed at Jesus' miracles saying, "Could not he who opened the eyes of the blind man have kept this man from dying?" (John 11:37)

CULTURAL FACT

At the time of Lazarus, tombs were usually carved into the limestone rock of the hillside. A tomb was often large enough for people to walk inside. Several bodies would be placed in one tomb. After burial, a large stone was rolled across the entrance of the tomb.

Jesus asked them to remove the stone from the tomb. Martha objected to the request saying, "Lord, he's been in there four days and by now there is a bad odor from the body." But Jesus insisted they remove the stone. Then he prayed out loud, "Father, I thank you that you have heard me. I knew that you always hear me, but I said this for the benefit of the people standing here, that they may believe that you sent me." Then with a loud voice, Jesus said, "Lazarus, come out." And the dead man walked out of the tomb and Jesus commanded the people to remove his grave clothes so he would be released.

What was the result of this miraculous healing of Lazarus? There were two reactions. One reaction: "Therefore many of the Jews who had come to visit Mary, and had seen what Jesus did, put their faith in him." (John 11:45) The other reaction:

But some of them went to the Pharisees and told them what Jesus had done. Then the chief priests and the Pharisees called a meeting of the Sanhedrin. "What are we accomplishing?" they asked. "Here is this man performing many miraculous signs. If we let him go on like this, everyone will believe in him, and then the Romans will come and take away both our place and our nation." Then one of them, named Caiaphas, who was high priest that year, spoke up, "You know nothing at all! You do not realize that it is better for you that one man die for the people than that the whole nation perish." (John 11:46–50)

The high priest spoke a prophecy about Jesus, one person, who would die for the sins of the nation. And from that time on, the religious leaders plotted to kill Jesus. (John 11:53) The miracle of Lazarus pushed the religious leaders toward the crucifixion of Jesus Christ.

FEEDING THE MULTITUDES

Many people know the miracle of Jesus feeding the multitude. Jesus performed this miracle twice with different groups of people as related in the Gospels.

FEEDING FIVE THOUSAND

The disciples who had been sent out to minister to people then returned to Jesus. They wanted to get away to a quiet place, but many people began to gather. The disciples had been traveling and teaching and had not had a chance to eat. Jesus told them to get away to a quiet place so they could rest. They tried to escape the crowd in a boat but many of the people recognized them and ran ahead on foot and got to the shore ahead of them. When Jesus climbed out of the boat and saw the crowd, the Bible says, he had compassion on them because they were like sheep without a shepherd. He began to teach them many things.

Now it was beginning to be late in the day, and because they were in a remote place, the disciples came to Jesus and said, "This is a remote place and it's already late. Send the people away to the surrounding countryside and villages so they can buy themselves something to eat."

The disciples were shocked at the response of Jesus who said, "You give them something to eat." They responded, "That would take eight months of a man's wages. Should we go and spend that much on bread for the people?"

CULTURAL FACT

The directive of Jesus in Mark 6:37 that says "You give them something to eat" must have startled the disciples. The Latin word *denarii* is the plural of *denarius*, a commonly used silver coin. It was typically paid to a laborer for a day's work. Thomas calculated it would take the wages of 200 days' labor to provide for that multitude.

Even in this remote place, Jesus inquired about their food resources saying, "How many loaves do you have? Go and see." When the disciples checked, they found five loaves of bread and two fish.

Then Jesus directed the disciples to have the people sit down in groups on the green grass. So the crowd sat down in groups of 100s and 50s. Taking the five loaves and the two fish and looking up to heaven, he gave thanks and broke the loaves. Then he gave them to his disciples to set before the people. He also divided the two fish among them all. They all ate and were satisfied, and the disciples picked up 12 basketfuls of broken pieces of bread and fish. The number of the men who had eaten was 5,000. (Mark 6:34–44)

Like God provided manna for the Israelites during their exodus from Egypt, Jesus Christ fed the people with food from heaven and they gathered an abundance after everyone had eaten. Notice Jesus' love of order. He made the people sit down in groups and probably arranged them in circles or semi-circles, which was reminiscent of the Mosaic camp in the desert. Also Jesus commanded that the leftovers be collected. The Jews regarded bread as a gift from God. It was customary to gather all of the scraps at the end of meal-time. The extra food showed the magnitude of Jesus' miracle.

FEEDING SEVEN THOUSAND

A few weeks later, Jesus was teaching another crowd in another remote place. Because the people had nothing to eat, he told his disciples:

"I have compassion for these people; they have already been with me three days and have nothing to eat. If I send them home hungry, they will collapse on the way, because some of them have come a long distance."

His disciples answered, "But where in this remote place can anyone get enough bread to feed them?"

"How many loaves do you have?" Jesus asked. "Seven," they replied. He told the crowd to sit down on the ground. When he had taken the seven loaves and given thanks, he broke them and gave them to his disciples to set before the people, and they did so. They had a few small fish as well; he gave thanks for them also and told the disciples to distribute them. The people ate and were satisfied. Afterward the disciples picked up seven basketfuls of broken pieces that were left over. About four thousand men were present. (Mark 8:2–9)

After feeding 4,000 men, the disciples picked up 7 large baskets of leftovers, or one basket from each original loaf. This was both a memorable witness to the miracle as well as a hint not to waste food. These baskets were much larger than the 12 small personal baskets mentioned in Mark 6:43. It was the type of basket that would later be used to lower Paul over the wall of Damascus. (Acts 9:25)

While these two miracles were amazing for the disciples and the people that Jesus taught, Christ wanted to use these two feedings as additional teaching for the disciples about the Pharisees. Shortly after the second feeding, the Pharisees arrived and asked Jesus for a sign from heaven. He sighed deeply at these leaders and asked, "Why does this generation ask for a miraculous sign? I tell you the truth, no sign will be given to it." (Mark 8:12) Then Jesus got in a boat and crossed over to the other side. In the boat, Jesus cautioned the disciples, "Be careful. Watch out for the yeast of the Pharisees and that of Herod." (Mark 8:15)

The disciples didn't understand the comment about the yeast of the Pharisees and thought that Jesus was asking for some bread. He said to them:

> "Why are you talking about having no bread? Do you still not see or understand? Are your hearts hardened? Do you have eyes but fail to see, and ears but fail to hear? And don't you remember? When I broke the five loaves for the five thousand, how many basketfuls of pieces did you pick up?"
>
> "Twelve," they replied.
>
> "And when I broke the seven loaves for the four thousand, how many basketfuls of pieces did you pick up?"
>
> They answered, "Seven."
>
> He said to them, "Do you still not understand?" (Mark 8:17–21)

In spite of two amazing miracles, the disciples lacked spiritual discernment. Jesus rebuked his disciples so they would recall God's provision and continually trust God for their "daily bread."

PHYSICAL HEALINGS

Throughout the three-year public ministry of Jesus, he performed many physical healings. In the next few sections, let's examine in detail some of these healing miracles.

HEALING A PARALYTIC

Three of the four Gospels record the story of Jesus healing a paralytic, a paralyzed man who couldn't walk. One time Jesus was teaching inside a crowded room and the men couldn't carry their friend into the room so that Jesus could heal him. Instead, they climbed on the roof of the building, removed part of the flat roof, and lowered the man near Jesus. When Jesus saw their faith, he said to the paralytic, "Son, your sins are forgiven." (Matthew 9:2)

CULTURAL FACT

Houses in biblical times were built of stone. They had flat roofs made of mud mixed with straw. Outside stairways led to the roofs. These friends may have carried the paralyzed man up the outside stairs to the roof. Then they could have easily taken apart the mud and straw mixture to make a hole to lower their friend to Jesus.

Knowing that the religious leaders were thinking that Jesus had just blasphemed against God, Jesus confronted the leaders:

"Why are you thinking these things? Which is easier: to say to the paralytic, 'Your sins are forgiven,' or to say, 'Get up, take your mat and walk'? But that you may know that the Son of Man has authority on earth to forgive sins ...." He said to the paralytic, "I tell you, get up, take your mat and go home." He got up, took his mat and walked out in full view of them all. This amazed everyone and they praised God, saying, "We have never seen anything like this!" (Mark 2:1–12)

The reaction of the crowd showed they understood the significance of this miracle.

HEALING THE BLIND

On several different occasions, the Gospel writers mention Jesus healing the blind. One of the most dramatic miracles, which included a confrontation with the religious leaders, was in John 9 about a man born blind. The story answers a fundamental question that many people ask about an illness or blindness: Did the man or his parents sin to cause such an illness?

One day Jesus saw a man blind from birth. His disciples asked him, "Rabbi, who sinned, this man or his parents, that he was born blind?"

"Neither this man nor his parents sinned," said Jesus, "but this happened so that the work of God might be displayed in his life. As long as it is day, we must do the work of him who sent me. Night is coming, when no one can work. While I am in the world, I am the light of the world." Then Jesus spit on the ground, made some mud with the saliva, and put it on the man's eyes. "Go," he told him, "wash in the Pool of Siloam." So the man went and washed, and his blindness was healed. Then the man returned home seeing. (John 9:2–7)

CULTURAL FACT

King Hezekiah built the Pool of Siloam. His workers constructed an underground tunnel from a spring outside the city walls to carry water into the city. Thus, the people could always get water without fear of being attacked. This was particularly important during times of siege. (2 Kings 20:20)

Later when the man could see, his neighbors and people who had formerly seen him begging asked, "Isn't this the same man who used to sit and beg?"

As these people talked about it, some insisted that it was the same man but others said, "No, he only looks like him." Then the man clarified it for them insisting, "I am the man."

The people demanded to know, "How were your eyes opened?"

He responded, "The man they call Jesus made some mud and put it on my eyes. He told me to go to Siloam and wash. So I went and washed, and then I could see."

They inquired, "Where is this man?"

"I don't know," he answered.

They brought the man who had been blind to the Pharisees. Now it turns out it was a Sabbath when Jesus made the mud and opened the man's eyes. So the Pharisees, who were always concerned about keeping God's laws, asked the man how he had received his sight. "He put mud on my eyes," the man replied, "and I washed, and now I see."

Some of the Pharisees claimed Jesus wasn't from God, because he didn't keep the Sabbath, but others asked, "How can a sinner do such miraculous signs?" Their opinions of Jesus were divided. Finally they turned again to the blind man, "What do you have to say about him? It was your eyes he opened."

The man replied, "He is a prophet."

These leaders still didn't believe the man had been blind and received his sight until they sent for the man's parents. "Is this your son?" they asked. "You say he was born blind, so how can he now see?"

"He is our son," the parents answered, "and we know he was born blind. But we don't know how he can see or who opened his eyes. Ask him. He's an adult and can speak for himself." His parents answered in this manner because they were afraid of the Jewish leaders. The leaders had already decided to put anyone out of the synagogue who acknowledged that Jesus was the Christ. So for a second time they summoned the man who had been blind. "Give glory to God," they said. "We know this man, Jesus, is a sinner."

He replied, "I don't know whether he's a sinner or not. All I know is, I was blind but now I see!"

Then they asked him, "What did he do to you? How did he open your eyes?"

He answered, "I have already answered your questions once and you didn't listen. Why do you want to hear it again? Do you want to become his disciples?"

Then they insulted him, saying, "You're this man's disciple! We are disciples of Moses! We know that God spoke to Moses, but we don't even know where Jesus comes from."

The man answered, "Now that's remarkable! You don't know where he comes from, yet he opened my eyes. God doesn't listen to sinners, but to the godly man who does his will. Nobody has ever heard of someone giving sight to a man born blind. If this man weren't from God, he could do nothing."

The leaders replied, "You were sinful from birth; how dare you lecture us!" They then threw him out. After Jesus heard that the Pharisees had thrown him out, he found the man who once was blind and said, "Do you believe in the Son of Man?"

The man replied, "Tell me who he is, sir, so that I may believe in him."

Jesus said, "You've seen him; in fact, I am the one speaking with you."

The man said, "Lord, I believe," and worshipped Jesus.

Jesus said, "For judgment I have come into this world, so that the blind will see and those who see will become blind." (John 9:1–39) The story is a fascinating illustration of how Jesus used his miracles to show his power and also to teach the people and religious leaders.

The Plight of Lepers

In biblical times, one of the most horrible diseases was leprosy. Individuals who contracted leprosy had no means of treatment and the Old Testament law mandated that people with a skin disease be removed from their family and live outside their village. Slowly their limbs deteriorated as the disease ravaged their bodies. Several times Jesus healed lepers but one of the stories in Luke is dramatic and teaches more than about healing:

As Jesus was going into a village, ten men who had leprosy met him. They stood at a distance and called out in a loud voice, "Jesus, Master, have pity on us!"

When he saw them, he said, "Go, show yourselves to the priests." And as they went, they were healed. One of them, when he saw he was healed, returned to Jesus, praising God in a loud voice. This Samaritan threw himself at Jesus' feet and thanked him. Jesus asked, "Weren't all ten cleansed? Where are the other nine? Was no one found to return and give praise to God except this foreigner?" Then Jesus said to the man, "Rise and go; your faith has made you well." (Luke 17:12–19) The man's limbs were miraculously restored but more than the healing of the leper, this story also illustrates the importance of thankfulness.

CULTURAL FACT

People who had leprosy were required to stay away from other people and to announce their presence if they had to come near. Sometimes leprosy went into remission. If a leper thought his leprosy had gone away, he was supposed to present himself to the priest, who could declare him clean. (Leviticus 14)

Healing the Lame

Another type of person that Jesus healed were the lame. Jesus went up on a mountainside near the Sea of Galilee and sat down. Great crowds came to him, bringing the lame, the blind, the crippled, the mute, and many others, and laid them at his feet; and he healed them.

The people were amazed when they saw the mute speaking, the crippled made well, the lame walking, and the blind seeing. And they praised the God of Israel. (Matthew 15:29–31)

Many people were eyewitnesses to the continual miracles Jesus performed during his three years of public ministry. These eyewitness accounts validated the reality of the miracles of Jesus.

HOUR'S UP!

As you read through the miracles of Jesus and learned how they amazed the people who were eyewitnesses, did you catch a glimpse of the awesome power of Jesus? Pause for a moment and reread one of the miracles of Jesus (you choose) and then capture some of the awe and wonder of the miraculous.

1. Some people try to make belief in Jesus seem like something only for the poor and uneducated. Reflect on the education and respect of Nicodemus and how the people of his day had great honor for Nicodemus. Yet in the middle of the night, Nicodemus came and met with Jesus. Turn to John 3 and reflect on Nicodemus and how this leader treated Jesus Christ. What new respect for Jesus can you gain in your daily life?

2. The religious leaders tried to accuse Jesus of working with Satan or Beelzebub, the prince of demons. (Matthew 12) Jesus made a clear distinction between the kingdom of Satan and the kingdom of God. Many people want to believe there is a gray area between these two extremes, but Jesus made it clear that there are only two kingdoms and each person has to choose their particular kingdom. God has granted each of us free will to choose our kingdom. Which kingdom are you a part of? Thank God for the opportunity to live every day as a part of God's kingdom on earth. What difference will the reality of Christ and his miracles make in your life today?

3. Return and reread the story of the demon-possessed man who was filled with Legion and Jesus released from the bondage. (Mark 5:6–20) The life of bondage wasn't something only for the New Testament era but it exists today. Is there anything holding you in bondage (a job, a relationship, money, a possession, or _____). Take a moment and identify what is holding you in bondage, and then pray and ask the Lord Jesus to release you from the bondage. Then listen to the still small voice and follow God's direction about how to escape. Rejoice in the promise of 1 Corinthians 10:13, "No temptation has seized you except what is common to man. And God is faithful; he will not let you be tempted beyond what you can bear. But when you are tempted, he will also provide a way out so that you can stand up under it."

4. Jesus raised the widow's son from the dead and the story shows the compassion of Jesus Christ. After the incident, Jesus' fame grew throughout the region. While Jesus may not have raised someone from the dead that you know, Jesus continues to change lives in radical ways

every day. Is there someone in your church or circle of friends who has been radically changed through an encounter with Jesus Christ? Take a few moments in prayer and celebrate how Jesus continues to change and transform lives—one by one.

5. When Jesus was on the way to Jairus's home, Jairus received the news that he shouldn't bother Jesus because his daughter had died. Notice the response of Jesus, "Don't be afraid; just believe." How often do you begin on a path which you feel that God is guiding, then listen to the nay-sayers and stop and don't move ahead? Recommit yourself to following the words of Jesus for such decisions: "Don't be afraid; just believe."

6. Jesus knew that Lazarus was going to die and predicted it in John 11:4, "so that God's son [Jesus] may be glorified through it." You may never know the "whys" for some of the events of your life. Could one possible reason be so that God would be glorified through your godly response to the trial? Reflect on some of your current or past trials and how these incidents might be an opportunity to grow in your faith and relationship with God and Jesus Christ.

7. Tucked into the story of Jesus and Lazarus is the shortest verse in the Bible. Notice the reaction of the people to the tears and compassion of Jesus. They had two points of view. Sometimes we guard our hearts from feeling compassionate toward others with the words, "I don't want to become too involved." Yet Jesus was compassionate and caring with others. What new insight or courage and commitment can you learn from the response of Jesus Christ?

8. Through the miracle of the 5,000 and the miracle of the 7,000, Jesus showed his power over Creation and the ability to creatively solve problems. What situations or difficulties are you facing in your own life today? Because of the creative power of Jesus in the past, trust God with your current difficulties. Ask for a creative solution to your current need or difficulty.

9. The faith of the paralytic and his friends touched Jesus Christ. He told the paralytic that his sins were forgiven. In faith, the paralytic and his friends went to Jesus for help and Christ healed him. Learn from the faith of the paralytic and his friends so you, too, can trust God increasingly in the everyday and the extraordinary events of your life. As you consider your need for faith, what comes to mind? How can you increase your faith in God? Take some concrete steps of faith to read your Bible more, attend church more regularly, or pray more; then, in faith, ask God to use these actions to increase your faith.

10. Consider the story of the 10 lepers that Jesus healed and how only one of them returned to express his gratitude to Christ for the miracle. A lack of gratitude or thankfulness is rampant in our world. How can you increase your thankfulness and have an attitude of gratitude about the events large and small that happen in your life? Make a point today to be aware of your need for gratitude and consciously increase your thankfulness.

HOUR 18

The Final Days of Jesus' Ministry

CHAPTER SUMMARY

LESSON PLAN:

In this hour, you will learn about …

- Peter's confession.
- The Transfiguration of Jesus.
- The triumphal entry in Jerusalem.
- Why Jesus cleansed the temple.

Over the last couple hours, you've studied some of the highlights of Jesus Christ's three years of public ministry on the earth. From even a brief look at the New Testament, it's clear that Jesus is the central figure. Through studying the Old Testament, readers can see that Jesus is the central figure of this portion of the Bible as well. Moses referred to Jesus as the great prophet to come (Deuteronomy 18); the prophets called Jesus the suffering servant (Isaiah 53); and the line of kings who descended from David pointed to Jesus as the King of the Universe (Psalm 2).

His title, *Christ*, actually corresponds with the Hebrew word *messiah*. Jesus is called Christ more than 550 times in the New Testament, more than any other title or name. In contrast, Jesus is called Lord fewer than 150 times. When Jesus was called Christ, he was being called Jesus the Messiah. The early Church acknowledged Jesus as the long-awaited Christ or Messiah.

When someone studies the teachings of Jesus, they discover how Jesus showed great reluctance to identify himself as the Messiah. Scholars call this "the Messianic secret." In our society, the famous have to hide or they are mobbed in public. As Jesus' fame increased, he frequently avoided the crowds and repeated references to himself as the Messiah. Why?

Jesus' hesitancy or secrecy came from the political culture of the day. The people in Israel were oppressed and under the thumb of Rome. They were looking for a redeemer to be a political leader who could single-handedly overthrow the Romans and restore the Jewish people to leadership among the nations. Jesus knew this political climate and it wasn't the reason that he came to earth. So Jesus was careful not to identify himself with the title of Messiah, which was so widely misunderstood.

When the time arrived for Jesus to teach his disciples that he was the Messiah, Jesus took them away from the crowd to a quiet place. In the hour ahead, we will examine some of the pivotal events in the final days of the life of Jesus. These events are central to understanding the New Testament.

THE IMPORTANCE OF PETER'S CONFESSION

Imagine for a moment traveling with Jesus and his disciples. These men have been together for almost three years and have walked to the extreme northern section of Palestine to the beautiful Caesarea Philippi. This area of the country was a gift to Herod from Augustus Caesar. In honor of Caesar, Herod built a temple. Jesus and his disciples walked around the foot of Mount Hermon, through the Hulah Valley, and into the lush area at its base. They paused at an ancient cultic worship site, which was dedicated to the god Pan, but was also used for emperor worship. Along the walls of the cliff, notches were cut out and held altars to Pan and other gods. A large stream flowed out of a cave at the base of the cliff. For as long as anyone could remember, the cave was used for pagan worship and called the Gates of Hell. This scene provided the backdrop for a private meeting between Jesus and his disciples.

"When Jesus came to the region of Caesarea Philippi, he asked his disciples, 'Who do people say the Son of Man is?'" (Matthew 16:13)

CULTURAL FACT

Caesarea Philippi was located several miles north of the Sea of Galilee in the territory ruled by Philip. The influence of Greek and Roman culture was everywhere. When Philip became ruler, he rebuilt and renamed the city after the emperor (Caesar) and himself. The city was originally called Caesarea, the same name as the capital city of Philip's brother Herod's territory.

Remember, Jesus wasn't talking with the multitude or the religious leaders. He's soliciting an answer to a key question from his closest friends and associates. At his request, they responded:

"They replied, 'Some say John the Baptist; others say Elijah; and still others, Jeremiah or one of the prophets.'" (Matthew 16:14)

A short time earlier, John the Baptist had been taken prisoner and beheaded. When John disappeared, not everyone knew he had been imprisoned and killed. Other people who lived in remote villages didn't know Jesus and John had been active at the same time. These people believed Jesus had raised John the Baptist from the dead. Other people were holding out for the reappearance of Elijah to fulfill the prophecy of the last Old Testament prophet, Malachi. All of the people named in this verse from Matthew were prophets.

While the public opinion said Jesus was a great prophet, Jesus wanted to teach his disciples that he was much more than a prophet. Then Jesus confronted his disciples with the ultimate challenge and a question where they couldn't hide their opinions:

"'But what about you?' he asked. 'Who do you say I am?'

Simon Peter answered, 'You are the Christ, the Son of the living God.'" (Matthew 16:15–16)

JUST A MINUTE

In this brief exchange, three terms for Jesus have been used: Son of Man, Son of God, and Christ. The word *Christ* has messianic implications, and the terms *Son of God* and *Son of Man* have deity and human in them. When the angel Gabriel announced to Mary that she would bear a child conceived by the Holy Spirit, Gabriel declared, "The Holy Spirit will come upon you, and the power of the Most High will overshadow you. So the holy one to be born will be called the Son of God." (Luke 1:35b) See the blending of deity and humanity?

And what about the term Jesus used to open this discussion, "Son of Man"? When Jesus used this term, he was pointing back to the Old Testament prophet Daniel (chapter 7). His disciples would have picked up on the origin of this term as quickly as someone today would know the context of "Little Bo Peep."

In my vision at night, I looked, and there before me was one like a son of man, coming in the clouds of heaven. He approached the Ancient of Days and was led into his presence. He was given authority, glory and sovereign power; all peoples, nations and men of every language worshiped him. His dominion is an everlasting dominion that will not pass away, and his kingdom is one that will never be destroyed. (Daniel 7:13–14)

As Jesus taught, he often called himself the Son of Man and the crowds were astonished. They whispered to one another, "He's claiming to be the one who stands with the Father in heaven and receives all the authority foretold in Daniel." It's no wonder that Jesus threatened the Pharisees and religious leaders. These learned men understood that Jesus was claiming to be God. This title wasn't a title of humility but a claim of absolute authority. When Jesus healed on the Sabbath and was rebuked, how did he respond? "For the Son of Man is Lord of the Sabbath." (Matthew 12:8)

Other times, like with the paralytic, Jesus forgave sins and created an uproar. Can't you hear the religious leaders in the back of the crowd complaining (even in their minds)? With a calm spirit, Jesus told them that he forgave sins so they might know that the Son of Man has authority on earth to forgive sins. (Mark 2:10, Matthew 9:6)

As Jesus gathered his disciples and asked who they said he was, he didn't contradict Peter's answer, "The Christ, the Son of the Living God." Jesus had taught his followers that he was God as much as the Ancient of Days, and in this setting, Peter made his great confession. In response, immediately Jesus blessed Simon Peter saying, "Blessed are you, Simon son of Jonah, for this was not revealed to you by man, but by my Father in heaven." (Matthew 16:17)

THE DISCIPLE PETER IS SINGLED OUT FOR BLESSING

Why did Jesus single out Peter for this blessing? Jesus knew that Peter had not thought of this response on his own but that the information came from God. Until this moment, Jesus had been concealing his full identity. Because of the many miracles and other experiences of the disciples, some people may wonder why they hadn't already known Jesus was God. Before judging these disciples too harshly, understand that Jesus' contemporaries such as John the Baptist were uncertain about Jesus' true identity. It was necessary for a blessing from God to free Peter's mind from the blinders of Jesus' identity. Then Jesus added: "And I tell you that you are Peter, and on this rock I will build my church, and the gates of Hades will not overcome it." (Matthew 16:18)

Jesus referred to the "gates of Hades (or hell)." The words struck the heart of his disciples. Let's recall where this intimate conversation was taking place. Jesus and his disciples were standing at the mouth of a cave that bore the name "the Gates of Hell." They were talking in the key location in the region for pagan worship and Jesus made a powerful political and religious statement. No wonder he had to find a quiet place with only his disciples to talk about such matters. For Jesus to say the "gates of hell" won't prevail against the Church amounted to saying that the political powers and pagans would not prevail against the Church. In fact, Jesus and his followers would prevail against pagan worship and set those imprisoned with unbelief free forever.

THE SPECIAL SIGNIFICANCE FOR ROMAN CATHOLICS

This blessing from Jesus after Peter's confession is especially significant for the Roman Catholic Church. For many centuries, Catholics have used this passage as the basis for their church government. Where is the emphasis in the words of Jesus? What did the "this" mean? "On *this* rock I will build my church"—the man, Peter, or the confession, "You are the Christ, the Son of the living God?" The original Greek words for "Peter" and "rock" have the same root (petra).

To understand some significant portions of the Bible, it would be nice to see a visual picture of Jesus and his disciples. If we had a recording, then we would know from the emphasis in Jesus' voice whether he meant the man or the message. Possibly Jesus pointed to Peter when he spoke or maybe he threw his arms wide open or pointed to himself to show that through his deity, Jesus would be the foundation of the Church. As Jesus spoke to his disciples, he continued saying, "I will give you the keys of the kingdom of heaven; whatever you bind on earth will be bound in heaven, and whatever you loose on earth will be loosed in heaven." (Matthew 16:19)

JUST A MINUTE

Without seeing Jesus' motions or gestures, it's impossible for us to know the exact meaning of Jesus' words. The Roman Catholic Church has always contended that Jesus was referring to the man Peter—or saying, "The Church will be built on you"— and this verse created the foundational case for the papacy. Protestants differ in their opinions whether Jesus was speaking of Peter or of Peter's confession.

If Peter was the first vice-regent of the Church, look at his first official act— he scolded Jesus. "Then Jesus warned his disciples not to tell anyone that he was the Christ. From that time on Jesus began to explain to his disciples that he must go to Jerusalem and suffer many things at the hands of the elders, chief priests and teachers of the law, and that he must be killed and on the third day be raised to life. Peter took him aside and began to rebuke him. 'Never, Lord!' he said. 'This shall never happen to you!'" (Matthew 16:21–22)

If Peter, the first pontiff, had this caution to Jesus, look at the response of Jesus, which hardly was a compliment to the pope: "Jesus turned and said to Peter, 'Get behind me, Satan! You are a stumbling block to me; you do not have in mind the things of God, but the things of men.'" (Matthew 16:23) Jesus took his disciples to a secluded place to talk about these important matters of his deity with only trusted confidants. It wasn't the right time to reveal the "Messianic secret." As Matthew records, "Then Jesus warned his disciples not to tell anyone that he was the Christ." (Matthew 16:20)

Today's culture is so media-driven and publicity conscious. It strikes us as odd for Jesus to say such a thing. The mission of the Church is to proclaim Jesus as the Lord to as many people as possible. Yet why would Jesus tell his disciples and closest followers to keep quiet about his identity? While the purpose of the Church is to proclaim the Good News about Jesus Christ, the timing had to be perfect. It would have been premature to short-circuit Jesus' purpose on earth. If the disciples had proclaimed Jesus the Messiah or Christ, it would have brought about an almost immediate trial and execution. The disciples had the full revelation of the identity of Jesus and the message burned in their hearts, yet they had to wait for the proper timing for this news to be revealed to the world.

The Transfiguration of Jesus

Hundreds of years before Jesus was born, Moses, the great leader of the Jewish people, made a special request to God. Before going to heaven and the after-life, Moses tried to get a peek at something unthinkable—to see the glory of the Lord:

> Then Moses said, "Now show me your glory."
>
> And the Lord said, "I will cause all my goodness to pass in front of you, and I will proclaim my name, the Lord, in your presence. I will have mercy on whom I will have mercy, and I will have compassion on whom I will have compassion. But," he said, "you cannot see my face, for no one may see me and live." Then the Lord said, "There is a place near me where you may stand on a rock. When my glory passes by, I will put you in a cleft in the rock and cover you with my hand until I have passed by. Then I will remove my hand and you will see my back; but my face must not be seen." (Exodus 33:18–23)

Can you feel the anticipation of Moses to see the glory of God in advance of reaching heaven? The Lord rejected Moses' request to directly see his glory, but gave him permission to stand in a crack in the mountainside and see God's back. God wasn't being stingy but the Lord knew that if Moses directly looked at God in his human form, he would instantly die.

"Moses bowed to the ground at once and worshiped." (Exodus 34:8) As God's glory passed through the thin slice of rock, it's little wonder that Moses was completely overwhelmed.

Generations later, the prophet Isaiah also caught a glimpse of God's glory in the temple, and the experience left this upbeat and articulate prophet stunned and filled with the sense of his own unworthiness and depravity. "'Woe to me!' I cried. 'I am ruined! For I am a man of unclean lips, and I live among a people of unclean lips, and my eyes have seen the King, the Lord Almighty.'" (Isaiah 6:5)

One of the key concepts in the Bible is about the glory of God. The word in Hebrew (*kabod*) means literally "worth" or "weight." A common expression says, "His word carries a lot of weight." God's glory or worthiness or holiness carries a lot of weight.

For most of his human experience, Jesus Christ set aside his glory or weight. He didn't "throw his weight around." In the Epistle of Philippians, the Apostle Paul expressed it this way:

[Jesus] being in very nature God, did not consider equality with God something to be grasped, but made himself nothing, taking the very nature of a servant, being made in human likeness. And being found in appearance as a man, he humbled himself and became obedient to death—even death on a cross! Therefore God exalted him to the highest place and gave him the name that is above every name, that at the name of Jesus every knee should bow, in heaven and on earth and under the earth, and every tongue confess that Jesus Christ is Lord, to the glory of God the Father. (Philippians 2:6–11)

CULTURAL FACT

The verses of Philippians 2:5–11 were probably from a hymn sung by the early Christian Church. The passage holds many parallels to the prophecy of the suffering servant in Isaiah 53. As a hymn, it was not meant to be a complete statement about the nature and work of Christ.

Jesus' life on earth is a remarkable example of someone who demonstrated the quality of humility. While Jesus fully possessed the nature of God or the glory, he set it aside during his years on earth. The passage from Paul says that once Jesus finished his task on earth (his death on the cross) and returned to heaven, he reassumed his glorious nature. His life on earth moved from a lowly birth in a cattle stable to the scorn, hatred, and misunderstanding from the religious leaders of his day to the ultimate humiliation during his final week on earth and death on a cross.

From the writers of the four Gospels, occasional glimpses of the glory of Jesus peek through. One of those occasions gives a full glimpse of the glory of Jesus; it's commonly called the Transfiguration.

> After six days Jesus took with him Peter, James and John the brother of James, and led them up a high mountain by themselves. There he was transfigured before them. His face shone like the sun, and his clothes became as white as the light. Just then there appeared before them Moses and Elijah, talking with Jesus. Peter said to Jesus, "Lord, it is good for us to be here. If you wish, I will put up three shelters—one for you, one for Moses and one for Elijah."
>
> While he was still speaking, a bright cloud enveloped them, and a voice from the cloud said, "This is my Son, whom I love; with him I am well pleased. Listen to him!"
>
> When the disciples heard this, they fell face down to the ground, terrified. But Jesus came and touched them. "Get up," he said. "Don't be afraid."
>
> When they looked up, they saw no one except Jesus. As they were coming down the mountain, Jesus instructed them, "Don't tell anyone what you have seen, until the Son of Man has been raised from the dead." (Matthew 17:1–9)

JUST A MINUTE

Peter wanted to build three shrines for these three great men to show how the Hebrew celebration of the Festival of Shelters was fulfilled in the coming of God's Kingdom. Peter had the right idea about Christ, but his timing was wrong. Peter wanted to act, but this was a time for worship and adoration. He wanted to memorialize the moment, but he was supposed to learn and move on.

The disciples had seen the glory of God and lived. They fell to the ground in awe and worship in the presence of the glory and at the sound of God's voice. Then in his compassion and tender love, Jesus reached down and took their hands and raised them to their feet. Like Moses centuries before, Peter, James, and John had seen a flash of God's glory and it scared them to death. Jesus commanded them not to talk about this event but to keep it to themselves.

These three men saw something remarkable and it was beyond what any other human throughout time had seen. God must have sustained and protected them supernaturally or they would not have been able to live through those moments when Jesus was transfigured in front of them. Peter mentioned "the glory" several times in his Epistles to the Church. The Gospel writer John mentioned the glory among his beginning words: "The Word became flesh and made his dwelling among us. We have seen his glory, the glory of the One and Only, who came from the Father, full of grace and truth." (John 1:14)

When Jesus Christ walked the earth, his glory was cloaked in a human form. When this shroud was peeled back, the glory of Jesus left men speechless and stunned and in an overwhelming sense of awe.

THE TRIUMPHAL ENTRY

Jesus and his disciples were together almost three years. He warned his disciples about revealing his glory and true purpose on earth. At first, Jesus avoided Jerusalem and stayed in the outlying areas. He must have been aware of God's timetable for his death. Each year, the Church celebrates Palm Sunday and the account of the Triumphal Entry, the victorious entry of Jesus into Jerusalem. The name Palm Sunday is derived from the palms which the people waved in celebration as Jesus passed on the donkey. Jesus came into the City of David only a few days before his crucifixion and resurrection. For the first time, Jesus used the word "Lord" to refer to himself. This reference marks a change in Jesus and his knowledge about his final days on earth. Note each of the four Gospel accounts include this story.

Matthew recounts the Triumphal Entry in this way:

As they approached Jerusalem and came to Bethphage on the Mount of Olives, Jesus sent two disciples, saying to them, "Go to the village ahead of you, and at once you will find a donkey tied there, with her colt by her. Untie them and bring them to me. If anyone says anything to you, tell him that the Lord needs them, and he will send them right away."

This took place to fulfill what was spoken through the prophet: "Say to the Daughter of Zion, 'See, your king comes to you, gentle and riding on a donkey, on a colt, the foal of a donkey.'" (Matthew 21:1–5)

The disciples went and did as Jesus had instructed them. They brought the donkey and the colt, placed their cloaks on them, and Jesus sat on them. The disciples laid their cloaks on both animals so Jesus could ride on either one. Possibly the mother donkey walked in front, followed by the colt on which Jesus was seated. A very large crowd spread their cloaks on the road, while others cut branches from the trees and spread them on the road. The crowds that went ahead of him and those that followed shouted, "Hosanna to the Son of David!" "Blessed is he who comes in the name of the Lord!" "Hosanna in the highest!" (Matthew 21:6–9)

JUST A MINUTE

Matthew mentioned a donkey and a colt, whereas the other Gospels mention only a colt. This was the same event, but Matthew focused on the prophecy in Zechariah 9:9, where a donkey and a colt are mentioned. He showed how Jesus' actions fulfilled the prophet's words, thus giving another indication that Jesus was, indeed, the Messiah. When Jesus entered Jerusalem on a donkey's colt, he affirmed his messianic royalty as well as humility.

As he rode toward Jerusalem, Jesus Christ knew his time had arrived. He was no longer pressing his disciples to keep the secret about his role as Messiah. When he approached Jerusalem, Jesus was willing to publicly identify with an Old Testament prophecy about the Messiah. In our culture, the symbolism of Jesus riding on a donkey seems strange. As his feet drag on either side of the little animal, it doesn't appear royal enough for the Son of the Most High.

For the Jewish culture, the residents of the City of David were aware that they "rolled out the red carpet" for Jesus Christ. The Messiah riding a donkey's colt fulfilled the prophecy of Zechariah. Like the story about Sir Walter Raleigh throwing his cloak on the roadway before Queen Mary, the people of Jerusalem threw their garments on the roadway for Jesus as a gesture of respect and honor. The people finally shouted, "Hosanna" (a Hebrew expression used as "Praise" but a saying that also meant "Save us now").

Some scholars believe the people were shouting and excited about the arrival of Jesus because they thought Jesus was about to declare that he was the Messiah and overthrow the Roman government. Often the people waved palm branches to celebrate military victories.

As the people were celebrating and Jesus was riding the donkey, suddenly something different happened. Some of the religious leaders who were standing on the fringe of the crowd yelled to Jesus. "Some of the Pharisees in the crowd said to Jesus, 'Teacher, rebuke your disciples!' 'I tell you,' he replied, 'if they keep quiet, the stones will cry out.'" (Luke 19:39–40)

These religious leaders had grown accustomed to Jesus keeping his Messianic secret. At various times, they must have heard him downplay his claim to be the Messiah and Savior of the Jewish people. Although Jesus must have known that many people in the crowd misunderstood the moment, he allowed the celebration to continue. In fact, he warned the Pharisees that if they tried to stop the celebration, even the cobblestones would stand and praise Jesus. The secret was out about the identity of Jesus Christ.

CULTURAL FACT

Luke 19:42 refers to a specific day of prophecy. It was the 173,880th day from the going forth of the decree of Artaxerxes until the Messiah the prince (69 weeks of years is 483 × 360 days or 173,880). God picked out a specific day for the preparation of his son as king to the nation.

These religious leaders seethed with rage. They must have muttered to one another, "Who does Jesus think he is?" Then they increased their plans to execute Jesus before the crowd became increasingly out of their control.

A COMPASSIONATE JESUS

As Jesus came near the City of David, his feelings were more on the surface. He knew the road ahead of him and the cross was clearly in his mind and heart. The Gospel of Luke records the emotional entry of Jesus into Jerusalem:

As he approached Jerusalem and saw the city, he wept over it and said, "If you, even you, had only known on this day what would bring you peace—but now it is hidden from your eyes. The days will come upon you when your enemies will build an embankment against you and encircle you and hem you in on every side. They will dash you to the ground, you and the children within your walls. They will not leave one stone on another, because you did not recognize the time of God's coming to you." (Luke 19:41–44)

Jesus knew that in a short time he would walk the road to Calvary and crucifixion. The crowd that cried out "Hosanna" would soon change its cry to "Crucify him!" He wept with compassion as he thought about the days in the near future.

CLEANSING THE TEMPLE

On this Monday, Jesus entered Jerusalem and went to the temple area. He repeated something that he did at the beginning of his public ministry—he cleared the temple (see John 2:13–22). Luke recounts:

Then he entered the temple area and began driving out those who were selling. "It is written," he said to them, "My house will be a house of prayer [Isaiah 56:7]; but you have made it a den of robbers."

Each day Jesus was in Jerusalem, he was teaching in the temple. But the chief priests, the teachers of the law, and the leaders among the people were trying to kill him. Yet they could not find any way to do it, because all the people hung on his words. (Luke 19:45–48)

Part of the enormous profits from the market stalls inside the temple went to enrich the family of the high priest. Jesus burned with indignation at such a perversion of the people to use God's house. As he did at the beginning of his public ministry, the public cleansing of the temple would only serve to further infuriate the religious leaders in Jerusalem. Jesus knew with each action that his days on the earth grew to only a few that remained.

CULTURAL FACT

Jesus cleansed the temple in anger after seeing that a place of prayer had become an excuse for corrupt commerce. Merchants were selling sacrificial animals in the outer court of the temple at exorbitant prices. Moneychangers were making an excessive profit exchanging currencies for the temple.

HOUR'S UP!

In this hour, you've learned about some of the stories around the last days of Jesus' ministry on earth. How do these stories affect your life today? Take a few moments to consider the following 10 questions and make the material in this hour a personal part of your own spiritual journey.

1. In the final days of Jesus' earthly ministry, he discussed his role as Messiah. The Jewish people were looking for a political redeemer more than a spiritual redeemer. In your life, how central are the spiritual factors in your life? Pause to weigh the importance of your spiritual life compared to some other areas of your life: physical, emotional, political, occupational, and so on. Take a few moments and recommit to increasing the spiritual portion of your life and relationship with Jesus the Messiah.

2. Jesus asked his disciples a key question, "Who do you say the Son of Man is?" or "Who do people say that I am?" Our society calls Jesus a prophet, a good man, and all sorts of other "nice" terms. Who do you say that Jesus is?

3. Jesus claimed absolute authority over mankind as he took his role of Savior, Christ, and Messiah. He had authority over the laws of the Sabbath and the laws of physics (through his healings and other miracles). Does Jesus have absolute authority over all of the aspects of your life? We may give our lives to Jesus but then the next day, we may take back these areas and try to carry them ourselves. What burdens are you carrying which you need to give to Jesus? Spend a few moments in prayer to give Jesus complete authority over every aspect of your life.

4. Why did Jesus warn his disciples not to tell others that he was the Christ? He had a keen sense of timing about his personal destiny and road to the end of his life. Through constant and consistent prayer, Jesus was in touch with his Heavenly Father. What issues are you facing today or this past week? Can you ask God to guide your life and give you a sense of his presence in your everyday life?

5. Moses and others longed to see the glory of God so they could see God while still on earth. Have you ever longed to see God's glory? How through the transfiguration of Jesus did God reveal his glory through Jesus, the Messiah or Christ? As God's glory shines into our lives, it reveals sin and areas of weakness. Take a personal inventory and see if you are moving toward God's glory and increased holiness in your life. If not, ask God to open the way to increase glory and holiness in your everyday life.

6. When Peter, James, and John saw the glory of Jesus Christ, it was a scene they never forgot. It left these men speechless with an overwhelming sense of awe. Think back to the last time an event left you speechless or in awe. What was this event? Consider how to capture this sense of awe in your spiritual relationship.

7. God supernaturally sustained the disciples in the light of his glory. They were protected. Has God's hand protected you from a sudden accident or instant tragedy? Too often we forget these small and major miracles of our life. Take a moment to reflect on these circumstances of your past and use these moments of God's protective hand as a means to celebrate and praise the Creator of the Universe.

8. When Jesus entered Jerusalem on the donkey with the people calling, "Hosanna," he knew he was near the end of his life—despite the celebration. Jesus knew how to take stock of his life course. What is your life course? Is it a fulfilling spiritual one or one that you are simply grinding through? Is God leading you to make a change? If so, take a few minutes and plan how you can change course and follow his will.

9. The crowd that cried, "Hosanna," to Jesus Christ was also counting on him to rescue them from a cultural and political crisis. They wanted to crown him their king; then less than a week later, they were crying, "Crucify him." Talk about a fickle people! The Bible teaches the value of consistency in the spiritual life. Evaluate your spiritual life. Is it consistent or fickle? If fickle, how can you take some steps to give greater consistency?

10. As Jesus cleansed the temple, he knew he was infuriating the religious leaders of his day. The action in the temple only reaffirmed the commitment of these leaders to execute Jesus. Jesus burned with righteous indignation at the sin he saw in his world. Do you ever burn with indignation at some violation of a Biblical principle or truth? Why or why not?

The Death, Resurrection, and Ascension of Jesus

CHAPTER SUMMARY

LESSON PLAN:
In this hour, you will learn about ...

- The importance of Jesus' death on the cross.
- The resurrection of Jesus Christ from the dead.
- The events around Jesus' ascension to heaven.

As you have been teaching yourself about the Bible, have you seen the focus or intensity growing? Some of that intensity will come to a focal point in this particular hour. The events of the Old Testament and the Gospel accounts of the life of Jesus culminate with the events of Jesus' death, resurrection, and ascension into heaven. These key events are the focal point of Christianity and pivotal to understanding the Bible.

For at least the last century, the Western world has executed its criminals under the cover of darkness. Often a newspaper or television report will describe what happened, but there are no pictures or videos of the actual event. During the majority of recorded history, however, executions have been a public spectacle similar to a royal wedding or a sporting event. For centuries, public officials have believed executions should be public for a couple of reasons: The criminal is eliminated, and the general public keeps their own behavior under control after witnessing the execution. With each execution, the public receives a stern warning.

At these public executions, men, women, and even children observed firing squads, hangings, and even beheadings. Imagine the impact of the violent deaths on the common person!

THE SON OF GOD IS NAILED TO A CROSS

When Jesus Christ was crucified, the public execution was meant to handle two objectives for the Jewish leaders and the Roman leaders. First, these leaders wanted to eliminate the troublemaker; second, they wanted to send a message to Jesus' followers and disciples that such behavior would not be tolerated.

CULTURAL FACT

Crucifixion, a practice probably adopted from Persia, was considered by the Romans to be the cruelest form of execution. This punishment was reserved for the worst criminals; Roman citizens were not crucified. The victim usually died after two or three days of agonizing suffering, thirst, exhaustion, and exposure. The victim's arms were nailed to a beam, which was hoisted up and fixed to a post, to which the victim's feet would be nailed. The body weight was supported by a peg on which the victim sat.

During the Roman Empire, tens of thousands of criminals were hung on crosses and crucified. The crucifixion of Jesus Christ was different. The religious and political leaders didn't understand a Holy God had a purpose in allowing his son to die for different reasons than their foolish plans. The Creator of the Universe, namely God himself, not only allowed Jesus to die on the cross but literally commanded Jesus' death for the atonement of the sins of all mankind. While these leaders must have felt a sense of accomplishment for successfully executing Jesus Christ, if God had not foreordained the sacrifice of his son, their plots would have failed.

After the Roman Governor Pilate quizzed Jesus, he believed that the man from Galilee was innocent. However, he had a purpose in allowing Jesus to be treated like an ordinary criminal: Pilate wanted to regain the allegiance of the Jewish leaders.

From then on, Pilate tried to set Jesus free, but the Jews kept shouting, "If you let this man go, you are no friend of Caesar. Anyone who claims to be a king opposes Caesar."

When Pilate heard this, he brought Jesus out and sat down on the judge's seat at a place known as the Stone Pavement (which in Aramaic is Gabbatha). It was the day of Preparation of Passover Week, about the sixth hour. "Here is your king," Pilate said to the Jews. But they shouted, "Take him away! Take him away! Crucify him!"

"Shall I crucify your king?" Pilate asked. "We have no king but Caesar," the chief priests answered. (John 19:12–15)

Against his own conscience, Pilate bowed to the wishes of his subjects in order to ensure their loyalty. As for the Jewish leaders, their motives were clear. The death of Jesus ensured that these religious leaders could preserve their system. That one man should die for the good of everyone was a small matter to them. When Jesus hung on the cross, these leaders stood in front of Jesus. "In the same way the chief priests, the teachers of the law and the elders mocked him. 'He saved others,' they said, 'but he can't save himself! He's the King of Israel! Let him come down now from the cross, and we will believe in him. He trusts in God. Let God rescue him now if he wants him, for he said, "I am the Son of God."'" (Matthew 27:41–43)

For those who were skeptical, Jesus' crucifixion was the confirmation of their feelings of doubt. Possibly these people really wanted to believe but didn't have the strength or the courage. Perhaps their cynical attitude about Jesus had cost them family and friends who had chosen to follow the Savior. Now the venom of their unbelief and alienation came pouring out as Jesus hung on the cross.

"Those who passed by hurled insults at him, shaking their heads and saying, 'You who are going to destroy the temple and build it in three days, save yourself! Come down from the cross, if you are the Son of God!'" (Matthew 27:39–40) Can't you hear those skeptics yelling and making fools of themselves? Even those who were crucified with Jesus also insulted him. (Matthew 27:44)

For the followers of Jesus who stood in the distance from the cross, the crucifixion meant the abrupt end of a dream. The Messiah whom they had followed, believed in, and loved had suddenly been violently removed from them. For the last three years, many of them had been living with, sleeping near, and following Jesus. Now their lives didn't have a purpose. They were flooded with grief and loneliness.

From the sixth hour until the ninth hour darkness came over all the land. At about the ninth hour Jesus cried out in a loud voice, *"Eloi, Eloi, lama sabachthani?"*—which means, "My God, my God, why have you forsaken me?" (Matthew 27:45–46)

The words of Jesus may appear strange. At the moment of his greatest pain and agony on the cross, Jesus shouts poetry? His mind is clear and Jesus is quoting from one of David's psalms (Psalm 22), which has the theme of mourning the pain and affliction of the righteous at the hands of the wicked. From these words, it is clear Jesus, moments before his death, knew that he was about to fulfill Bible prophecy, which had been predicted long ago for the Messiah.

Take a moment and read through a portion of this Psalm:

> My God, my God, why have you forsaken me? Why are you so far from saving me, so far from the words of my groaning? ... All who see me mock me; they hurl insults, shaking their heads:
>
> "He trusts in the Lord; let the Lord rescue him. Let him deliver him, since he delights in him." ... I am poured out like water, and all my bones are out of joint. My heart has turned to wax; it has melted away within me. My strength is dried up like a potsherd, and my tongue sticks to the roof of my mouth; you lay me in the dust of death ... They divide my garments among them and cast lots for my clothing. But you, O Lord, be not far off; O my Strength, come quickly to help me. (Psalm 22:1, 7–8, 14–15, 18–19)

When Jesus cried out to God, he was not simply feeling forsaken, he was forsaken because God had to forsake his only son. He had to bear the sins of the world and satisfy the demands of the justice of God. Jesus bore the full measure of divine wrath.

As Jesus hung on the cross, the guards cast lots for his clothing. (Matthew 27:35) In a matter of a few hours, he fulfilled many prophecies about the Messiah from the Old Testament. Jesus Christ was innocent and knew no sin, yet on the cross the corporate sins of the world were concentrated on him. Jesus voluntarily became the spotless Lamb of God who takes away the sins of the world. As Jesus hung on the cross, he became the most obscene creature in the universe.

CULTURAL FACT

The executioners had the privilege of taking the victim's clothes. In casting lots for Jesus' garments, the soldiers fulfilled the prophecy in Psalm 22:18.

The Apostle Paul described the impact of this moment for mankind in a few verses from his letter to the Galatians:

Christ redeemed us from the curse of the law by becoming a curse for us, for it is written: "Cursed is everyone who is hung on a tree." He redeemed us in order that the blessing given to Abraham might come to the Gentiles through Christ Jesus, so that by faith we might receive the promise of the Spirit. (Galatians 3:13–14)

According to the Apostle Paul, as Jesus hung on the cross, he was cursed. He suffered the pain of our sins, so those who believe in Jesus would not have to bear this pain. As adopted children, anyone who believes in Jesus as Lord and Savior is welcomed to come to God. All of the blessings of a relationship with Jesus Christ and God belong to God's people because in his death, Jesus was cursed.

No one understood the poetry of Jesus on the cross, which was some of his final words:

When some of those standing there heard this, they said, "He's calling Elijah." Immediately one of them ran and got a sponge. He filled it with wine vinegar, put it on a stick, and offered it to Jesus to drink. The rest said, "Now leave him alone. Let's see if Elijah comes to save him." And when Jesus had cried out again in a loud voice, he gave up his spirit. (Matthew 27:47–50)

Darkness hung over the earth at the death of Jesus but in this final moment, it caused another stir:

At that moment the curtain of the temple was torn in two from top to bottom. The earth shook and the rocks split. The tombs broke open and the bodies of many holy people who had died were raised to life. They came out of the tombs, and after Jesus' resurrection they went into the holy city and appeared to many people. When the centurion and those with him who were guarding Jesus saw the earthquake and all that had happened, they were terrified, and exclaimed, "Surely he was the Son of God!" (Matthew 27:51–54)

The large curtain that separated the holy of holies from the inner court in the temple was instantly torn from top to bottom.

CULTURAL FACT

The temple had two veils or curtains: one in front of the holy place, and the other separating the holy place from the Most Holy Place. It was the second of these that was torn, demonstrating that God had opened up access to himself through his son. (Hebrews 6:19) Only God could have torn the veil from top to bottom.

Imagine the surprise when people who were devoted to God and holy in their living returned to life, came out of their tombs, and appeared to many people. In addition, there was an earthquake. Finally the centurion, who had likely watched many men die through crucifixion, saw something unusual in the death of Jesus Christ. He exclaimed, "This man must be the Son of God!"

THE LOCATION OF THE CROSS

Another significant dimension to understanding Jesus' death on the cross is the place where he was executed. For centuries prior to the crucifixion of Jesus, the Jewish people used a ceremony marking the Day of Atonement. Two animals were used to illustrate God's forgiveness for sins. (Leviticus 16:1–34) One animal was a goat, which the priest sacrificed as a burnt offering. The other animal was called a "scapegoat." The priest placed his hands on the goat's head and symbolically put the sins of Israel on the animal. Then the priest turned the scapegoat loose to face the dangers and perils of the barren desert.

Because Jesus was crucified outside the city on the hill called Golgotha or "the skull," he fulfilled both the role of the sin or burnt offering and the scapegoat. Jesus was sent outside the camp and away from the blessing and protection of God. The Messiah was forsaken so those who put their trust and belief in him could be free from the consequences and curse of sin.

CULTURAL FACT

Golgotha is an Aramaic word meaning "place of a skull." The hill might have resembled the bony features of a skull or might have been called this because it was a place of death. The name *Calvary* comes from the Latin word for "skull." This place was very near the city wall. (John 19:20)

The Gospel of Luke describes the final moments that Jesus spent on the cross: "It was now about the sixth hour, and darkness came over the whole land until the ninth hour, for the sun stopped shining. And the curtain of the temple was torn in two. Jesus called out with a loud voice, 'Father, into your hands I commit my spirit.' When he had said this, he breathed his last." (Luke 23:44–46)

As an obedient Son of God, Jesus had completed his assignment on earth. His suffering was complete and for the moment, he was finished. His mission was not fully accomplished.

JESUS RISES FROM THE DEAD

During the time of Jesus, when criminals were executed, their bodies were literally thrown on Jerusalem's smoldering garbage dump known as Gehenna. The body of Jesus wasn't given this sort of humiliating treatment. As the lifeless body of Jesus was removed from the cross, a complete stranger, Joseph of Arimathea offered his own burial tomb:

Now there was a man named Joseph, a member of the Council, a good and upright man, who had not consented to their decision and action. He came from the Judean town of Arimathea and he was waiting for the kingdom of God. Going to Pilate, he asked for Jesus' body. Then he took it down, wrapped it in linen cloth and placed it in a tomb cut in the rock, one in which no one had yet been laid. (Luke 23:50–53)

CULTURAL FACT

Arimathea was about 20 miles northwest of Jerusalem. Mark 15:43 describes Joseph as "a prominent council member, who himself was waiting for the kingdom of God." Luke 23:50 describes him as "a good and just man." But Matthew describes him as rich, a fulfillment of Isaiah 53:9.

Notice this care of Jesus' body immediately following his death on the cross. Joseph carefully prepared Jesus' body for burial. According to Old Testament prophecy, his body was not to "see corruption" (Psalm 16:10) and the Messiah was to be laid in a borrowed tomb (Isaiah 53).

The Gospel of Matthew shows the concern from the Jewish leaders even after Jesus' death:

The next day, the one after Preparation Day, the chief priests and the Pharisees went to Pilate. "Sir," they said, "we remember that while he was still alive that deceiver said, 'After three days I will rise again.' So give the order for the tomb to be made secure until the third day. Otherwise, his disciples may come and steal the body and tell the people that he has been raised from the dead. This last deception will be worse than the first."

"Take a guard," Pilate answered. "Go, make the tomb as secure as you know how." So they went and made the tomb secure by putting a seal on the stone and posting the guard. (Matthew 27:62–66)

Not taking any chances that Jesus might be able to come back from the dead, the officials pressed Pilate to send some guards to the tomb.

JUST A MINUTE

The Pharisees were so afraid of Jesus' predictions about his resurrection that they made sure the tomb was thoroughly sealed and guarded. Because the tomb was hewn out of rock in the side of a hill, there was only one entrance. The tomb was sealed by stringing a cord across the stone that was rolled over the entrance. The cord was sealed at both ends with clay. But the religious leaders took a further caution, asking that guards be placed at the tomb's entrance. With such precautions, the only way the tomb could be empty was for Jesus to rise from the dead.

On the third day after Jesus' death, Matthew writes: "There was a violent earthquake, for an angel of the Lord came down from heaven and, going to the tomb, rolled back the stone and sat on it. His appearance was like lightning, and his clothes were white as snow. The guards were so afraid of him that they shook and became like dead men." (Matthew 28:2–4)

From a violent earthquake, an angel came and rolled the stone from the tomb and the guards shook and ran away. Now that the stone in front of the tomb was rolled away, one of the most important stories in the Bible about the first Easter begins to unfold.

A trio of women returned to the burial place of Jesus on Sunday morning. "On the first day of the week, very early in the morning, the women took the spices they had prepared and went to the tomb. They found the stone rolled away from the tomb." (Luke 24:1–2)

The Gospel of Mark names the three women who came to the tomb on that third day: Mary, the mother of Jesus; Mary Magdalene; and a woman named Salome. Imagine the horrible weight of grief and loss these women must have felt. This man, son to one woman and Savior to all three, had suffered a terrible crucifixion, and because of the late hour had been hastily buried without the proper ceremonial anointing. Jesus had been laid in the tomb of a Gentile stranger. The scene was filled with irony since the Jewish elite scorned no living things more than women and Gentiles, except perhaps swine. These three women were willing to step forward and honor the lifeless body of Jesus with spices.

CULTURAL FACT

The women brought spices to the tomb as a sign of love and respect. The women went home after Jesus' death and kept the Sabbath as the law required, from sundown Friday to sundown Saturday, before gathering up their spices and perfumes and returning to the tomb.

It's small wonder that down through the centuries, the Church that the Messiah had promised would prevail against the "gates of hell" would include the faithfulness, personal sacrifice, and courage of women and Gentiles. These two components are built into the fiber of the Easter story.

What these women learned when they came to the tomb would change the course of human history. Their experience marks one of the greatest events in the entire Bible. The Eternal and Holy God concealed in a lifeless body not only left behind his grave clothes, but Jesus also escaped the limitations of his humanity in that borrowed tomb. The glory of Jesus, which was briefly shown to Peter, James, and John on the Mount of Transfiguration, was about to be revealed to many others.

When the women entered the tomb, they discovered an empty shroud:

> But when they entered, they did not find the body of the Lord Jesus. While they were wondering about this, suddenly two men in clothes that gleamed like lightning stood beside them. In their fright the women bowed down with their faces to the ground, but the men said to them, "Why do you look for the living among the dead? He is not here; he has risen! Remember how he told you, while he was still with you in Galilee: 'The Son of Man must be delivered into the hands of sinful men, be crucified and on the third day be raised again.'"
>
> Then they remembered his words. When they came back from the tomb, they told all these things to the Eleven and to all the others. (Luke 24:3–9)

The disciples of Jesus were struggling to comprehend what the women told them. Their hearts were filled with unbelief and most of them believed the women had gone crazy. "This can't be true," they said to each other. Although it sounded like nonsense, excitable Peter was the first to run to the tomb to see what had happened. John, the beloved disciple, also went with Peter to examine the tomb for himself. The Gospel of Luke records the reaction of Peter: "Bending over, he saw the strips of linen lying by themselves, and he went away, wondering to himself what had happened." (Luke 24:12)

As they walked away, the disciples knew for certain the tomb was empty—but where was Jesus?

MORE THAN A MISSING BODY

The belief in the resurrected Jesus is based on much more than simply a missing body. If the resurrection were based only on the empty tomb, the evidence would be thin and far more likely that grave robbers stole Jesus' body. In fact, the cover-up story from the tomb guards and the Jewish leaders is recorded in the Gospel of Matthew.

While the women were on their way, some of the guards went into the city and reported to the chief priests everything that had happened. When the chief priests had met with the elders and devised a plan, they gave the soldiers a large sum of money, telling them, "You are to say, 'His disciples came during the night and stole him away while we were asleep.' If this report gets to the governor, we will satisfy him and keep you out of trouble." So the soldiers took the money and did as they were instructed. And this story has been widely circulated among the Jews to this very day. (Matthew 28:11–15)

The reliable fact of the resurrection of Jesus Christ is based on the many visits to his people. According to the Gospels, Jesus appeared to the women, to the disciples, to a couple of men traveling on the road to Emmaus, to a group of 500 disciples, and to the Apostle Paul. It is the extraordinary evidence from people who talked with Jesus, ate with Jesus, and touched Jesus that is firm evidence for the truth of the Old Testament prophecies about Jesus Christ.

One of the most fascinating stories about the resurrection of Jesus Christ concerns two men who walked to the town of Emmaus:

Now that same day two of them were going to a village called Emmaus, about seven miles from Jerusalem. They were talking with each other about everything that had happened. As they talked and discussed these things with each other, Jesus himself came up and walked along with them; but they were kept from recognizing him.

He asked them, "What are you discussing together as you walk along?" They stood still, their faces downcast. One of them, named Cleopas, asked him, "Are you only a visitor to Jerusalem and do not know the things that have happened there in these days?" "What things?" he asked. "About Jesus of Nazareth," they replied. "He was a prophet, powerful in word and deed before God and all the people. The chief priests and our rulers handed him over to be sentenced to death, and they crucified him; but we had hoped that he was the one who was going to redeem Israel. And what is more, it is the third day since all this took place. In addition, some of our women amazed us. They went to the tomb early this morning but didn't find his body. They came and told us that they had seen a vision of angels, who said he was alive. Then some of our companions went to the tomb and found it just as the women had said, but him they did not see." (Luke 24:13–24)

These two men had heard the accounts the women had told about angelic conversations and those that Peter and John had told about the empty tomb, yet they had not seen Jesus so they were unconvinced of the reality of the resurrection. "He said to them, 'How foolish you are, and how slow of heart to believe all that the prophets have spoken! Did not the Christ have to suffer these things and then enter his glory?' And beginning with Moses and all the Prophets, he explained to them what was said in all the Scriptures concerning himself." (Luke 24:25–27)

The Gospel of Luke is the only record of this story about the two men walking to Emmaus with Jesus Christ. Wouldn't it have been amazing to have the details of their conversation? Jesus the master storyteller wove together all of the truth from Moses and the Prophets to explain about the death of the Messiah. These two men must have wondered about the identity of this stranger who walked with them.

As they approached the village to which they were going, Jesus acted as if he were going farther. But they urged him strongly, "Stay with us, for it is nearly evening; the day is almost over." So he went in to stay with them. (Luke 24:28–29)

These two unsuspecting men invited the stranger, who was the Creator of the heaven and earth, to join them for the evening. They would likely have been terrified if they knew they were walking with the risen Christ Jesus. "When he was at the table with them, he took bread, gave thanks, broke it and began to give it to them. Then their eyes were opened and they recognized him, and he disappeared from their sight." (Luke 24:30–31)

Prior to the crucifixion and the resurrection, Jesus restricted his earthly body from vanishing in the presence of another person. Nowhere in the Gospel records did Jesus appear and vanish in front of another person—except in this particular story after he had risen from the dead. After the resurrection, Jesus had a glorified body and was capable of appearing and disappearing at will. Like in his days on earth, Jesus continued with his ability to transform the lives of men:

They asked each other, "Were not our hearts burning within us while he talked with us on the road and opened the Scriptures to us?" They got up and returned at once to Jerusalem. There they found the Eleven and those with them, assembled together and saying, "It is true! The Lord has risen and has appeared to Simon." Then the two told what had happened on the way, and how Jesus was recognized by them when he broke the bread. (Luke 24:32–35)

In many churches, the minister and the congregation have a common public conversation. "He is risen," declares the preacher or priest. "He is risen, indeed," responds the congregation. Now the men from Emmaus could echo the words, "He is risen, indeed." The risen Christ appeared numerous times such as:

While they were still talking about this, Jesus himself stood among them and said to them, "Peace be with you." They were startled and frightened, thinking they saw a ghost. He said to them, "Why are you troubled, and why do doubts rise in your minds? Look at my hands and my feet. It is I myself! Touch me and see; a ghost does not have flesh and bones, as you see I have." When he had said this, he showed them his hands and feet. And while they still did not believe it because of joy and amazement, he asked them, "Do you have anything here to eat?" They gave him a piece of broiled fish, and he took it and ate it in their presence. (Luke 24:36–43)

The disciples touched Jesus, examined his hands and feet, and also watched him eat some food. Yes, the Lord Jesus is risen, indeed.

JESUS ASCENDS TO HEAVEN

Jesus taught his disciples many things they didn't understand during the days immediately before his crucifixion and resurrection. His statements didn't make sense when they were spoken but they certainly rang true after his resurrection.

In the upper-room discourse with his disciples right before he went into Jerusalem, then was crucified, Jesus made some important statements about his deity:

Jesus answered [to Thomas], "I am the way and the truth and the life. No one comes to the Father except through me. If you really knew me, you would know my Father as well. From now on, you do know him and have seen him … Don't you believe that I am in the Father, and that the Father is in me? The words I say to you are not just my own. Rather, it is the Father, living in me, who is doing his work … You may ask me for anything in my name, and I will do it. If you love me, you will obey what I command. And I will ask the Father, and he will give you another Counselor to be with you forever—the Spirit of truth. The world cannot accept him, because it neither sees him nor knows him. But you know him, for he lives with you and will be in you. I will not leave you as orphans; I will come to you. Before long, the world will not see me anymore, but you will see me. Because I live, you also will live." (John 14:6–7, 10, 14–19)

Jesus' body was about to ascend into heaven. God the Father was going to restore his son, Jesus, to his glory that had been his since the foundation of the world. John records these words of comfort from Jesus to his disciples. Jesus explained that when he returned to heaven, he would prepare a place of rest for them. Jesus made a covenant with his followers or disciples, that he would return to them some day:

On one occasion, while he was eating with them, he gave them this command: "Do not leave Jerusalem, but wait for the gift my Father promised, which you have heard me speak about. For John baptized with water, but in a few days you will be baptized with the Holy Spirit." So when they met together, they asked him, "Lord, are you at this time going to restore the kingdom to Israel?" He said to them: "It is not for you to know the times or dates the Father has set by his own authority. But you will receive power when the Holy Spirit comes on you; and you will be my witnesses in Jerusalem, and in all Judea and Samaria, and to the ends of the earth." After he said this, he was taken up before their very eyes, and a cloud hid him from their sight. They were looking intently up into the sky as he was going, when suddenly two men dressed in white stood beside them. "Men of Galilee," they said, "why do you stand here looking into the sky? This same Jesus, who has been taken from you into heaven, will come back in the same way you have seen him go into heaven." (Acts 1:4–11)

JUST A MINUTE

After 40 days with his disciples (Acts 1:3), Jesus returned to heaven. The two white-robed men were angels who proclaimed to the disciples that one day Jesus would return in the same way he went—bodily and visibly.

Jesus reassured his disciples that they were bound for heaven. It's one of the greatest assurances for Christians. Heaven is a certainty because Jesus walked the earth; from the eyewitness accounts, Jesus ascended into heaven and now sits at the right hand of God in glory. There is a direct relationship about the Christian's confidence in this reality and the Christian's obedience to the Scriptures. What a man believes about the future always shapes how he lives in the present. The disciples watched Jesus disappear into the clouds.

While Jesus physically left his disciples, he encouraged them with hope and joy for the future. Also Jesus left the Helper, the Comforter, the Holy Spirit, to be with them and to empower them. As the Apostle Paul wrote to the Philippians, "Therefore God exalted him to the highest place and gave him the name that is above every name, that at the name of Jesus every knee should bow, in heaven and on earth and under the earth, and every tongue confess that Jesus Christ is Lord, to the glory of God the Father." (Philippians 2:9–11)

HOUR'S UP!

Death isn't something we like to consider often. Life is fragile but so often we believe that it will happen to other people.

1. Imagine yourself at the foot of the cross of Christ. See him writhing in pain for you and your sins. Jesus was sinless and innocent yet bore your sins on the cross. Take a few minutes to reflect on that sacrifice. How will it change the way you live today?

2. Pilate, the Roman Governor, knew Jesus was innocent; yet to appease the Jewish leaders, he went along with the crucifixion. Are there situations in your daily life (family, work, or neighborhood) where you are not taking a stand for an issue with Christ but instead just going along with the crowd? If not now, prepare to stand for the Bible next time and make that commitment.

3. Doubts, sorrow, loss of a dream, and other feelings were in the disciples; Mary, the mother of Jesus; and others who watched Jesus die from a distance. Are these feelings in your life today? Imagine your feelings as individual burdens that you carry on your back. Now unload those feelings one at a time while standing at the foot of the cross. Christ died for you to have freedom and a life of faithfully following him. Unpack your burdens today through some prayer time.

4. As Jesus hung on the cross, he bore the pain of all humanity. God abandoned Jesus and left him to absorb all of the suffering of humanity through his death. Reflect on the last words of Jesus, "My God, my God, why have you forsaken me?" Have you felt like God has forsaken you? Recommit this area to the Lord in prayer.

5. Think about the different events that occurred the moment Jesus died—the tearing of the curtain in the temple, the darkness that clung to the earth, the earthquake, the holy ones who were dead coming back to life, and the response from the centurion. Does each of these true historical events strengthen your faith in the reality of the sacrifice of Christ? How? Talk with a friend or family member about what it means to you.

6. The Pharisees wanted the Jewish people to believe that grave robbers had stolen Jesus' body. How is the reality of the resurrection based on more than an empty tomb? How does this basis for the resurrection strengthen and affirm your faith?

7. After days of sadness and grief, suddenly three women had good news to share with the disciples. In fact, they had news from an angel. How would you have reacted? With the faith to simply believe, or the necessity like Peter to actually see the empty tomb? Reflect on what it means to have a life of faith as described in Hebrews 11:1: "Now faith is being sure of what we hope for and certain of what we do not see."

8. Turn to the upper-room discourse and focus on John 14. What strength do you gain for your life with the understanding that the Father has provided the Holy Spirit to be with us and live in us? What difference does the Holy Spirit make in your life today?

9. Because Jesus rose from the dead and ascended into heaven, he goes ahead to prepare a place for his disciples. What comfort and strength for today do you gain from his words in John 14:19, "Because I live, you also will live?"

10. When Jesus ascended into heaven, the scene must have been amazing for the disciples. Wouldn't you have stood gawking at the clouds to see if Jesus came back? What inspiration and encouragement and changed plans do you pick up from the words of the angels? "This same Jesus, who has been taken from you into heaven, will come back in the same way you have seen him go into heaven." (Acts 1:11b) How will these words affect your life today?

PART V

The Church Is Born and Letters from the Apostle Paul

HOUR 20

A Church Is Born

CHAPTER SUMMARY

LESSON PLAN:

In this hour, you will learn about …

- The tongues of fire on Pentecost.
- How persecution expanded the church.
- Paul's conversion on the road to Damascus.

Ever waited for the birth of a child? Sometimes it feels like a long nine months until the day of birth arrives and then the celebration begins. Or maybe you've experienced a milestone birthday such as a fortieth or fiftieth birthday where some planning and anticipation is involved. After the Lord Jesus rose into the clouds of heaven, the disciples were told to wait together in Jerusalem until the Counselor or Holy Spirit arrived to help them. What long and anticipating days the disciples must have spent waiting for the moment of birth. During this hour, you will catch some of the anticipation, the trials, and the expansion of the Good News about Jesus to the known world. Let's celebrate the birthday of the Church of Jesus Christ.

THE BIRTH OF THE CHURCH

The birthday of the Church is in the year of our Lord (*Anno Domini*, A.D.) 30, on the fiftieth day after Jesus' resurrection and the tenth day after his ascension into heaven. The event marks the beginning of the Gospel era. This moment or event was groundbreaking and a celebration unlike any that had ever happened or has happened since: the Baptism of the Holy Spirit on the Day of Pentecost:

When the Day of Pentecost came, they were all together in one place. Suddenly a sound like the blowing of a violent wind came from heaven and filled the whole house where they were sitting. They saw what seemed to be tongues of fire that separated and came to rest on each of them. All of them were filled with the Holy Spirit and began to speak in other tongues as the Spirit enabled them.

Now there were staying in Jerusalem God-fearing Jews from every nation under heaven. When they heard this sound, a crowd came together in bewilderment, because each one heard them speaking in his own language. Utterly amazed, they asked: "Are not all these men who are speaking Galileans? Then how is it that each of us hears them in his own native language? Parthians, Medes and Elamites; residents of Mesopotamia, Judea and Cappadocia, Pontus and Asia, Phrygia and Pamphylia, Egypt and the parts of Libya near Cyrene; visitors from Rome (both Jews and converts to Judaism); Cretans and Arabs—we hear them declaring the wonders of God in our own tongues!" Amazed and perplexed, they asked one another, "What does this mean?" (Acts 2:1–12)

CULTURAL FACT

In the first Christian century, Jewish communities were located primarily in the eastern Roman Empire, where Greek was the common language. There were Jewish communities as far west as Italy and as far east as Babylonia. On Pentecost, there were visitors from Mesopotamia and even farther east, from Parthia, Media, and Elam (present-day Iran).

Strangers standing around the temple heard a sudden rushing wind, watched fire, and then experienced the strange "speaking in tongues." It's no wonder they asked, "What's going on here?" If this experience sounds strange to read about, imagine how it felt to the people there when it happened. Peter stood and informed the crowd exactly what was happening. He reminded them of the words of the prophet Joel who predicted that the Holy Spirit would be distributed throughout the nations. Instead of primarily saving the Jewish people, God was calling people from every nation in the world to bend their knee before the Lord and worship him. The event was groundbreaking and like no other in all of history.

Pentecost was also called the Feast of Firstfruits and the Feast of Harvest. It was fitting that this day was selected as the day for the firstfruits of the harvest of the Good News about Jesus, or Gospel, for all the nations.

To understand and make sense of this event, let's go back to some stories in the Old Testament when the Israelites were traveling through the wilderness escaping Egypt and heading for the Promised Land. In Numbers 11, the Jewish people had grown tired of manna and complained about all of the good food they missed in Egypt such as leeks and onions. The people had forgotten their mistreatment as slaves from Pharaoh and the Egyptians. Now they were complaining and longing for the cooking of Egypt. Because of the Israelites' complaints, they rioted and God sent fire, which burned those on the outskirts of their camp. Moses was so furious and frustrated with the people that he begged God to kill him. He said he could no longer stand the responsibility and pressure to lead these rebellious people.

And what is the connection to Pentecost? Read how the Lord resolved Moses' problem:

The Lord said to Moses: "Bring me seventy of Israel's elders who are known to you as leaders and officials among the people. Have them come to the Tent of Meeting, that they may stand there with you. I will come down and speak with you there, and I will take of the Spirit that is on you and put the Spirit on them. They will help you carry the burden of the people so that you will not have to carry it alone." (Numbers 11:16–17)

As the leader of the Jewish people, Moses was the go-between so a Holy God and the people could communicate. This charismatic leader guided the people through a supernatural gift. The people in the Old Testament also had the Holy Spirit because they couldn't have known God without him. During the time of the Old Testament, the Holy Spirit empowered men and women for specific tasks. Judges, kings, prophets, craftsmen, and warriors were "anointed" by God for specific tasks. In the Numbers 11 passage, God dispersed the Holy Spirit and Moses' leadership responsibilities on 70 elders so they could effectively share the workload.

At Pentecost, God's Holy Spirit was spread among his people and empowered them to carry out God's will to the nations of the world. There were three signs of the presence of the Holy Spirit on this remarkable day. These signs provide us with the explicit reality of God's indwelling among his people—then and now. Let's examine these three signs in detail.

THE RUSH OF A MIGHTY WIND

The apostles were sitting, which was the normal position for listening to someone speak rather than standing for prayer. Suddenly a sound like the rush of a mighty wind blew through the area. It was no ordinary wind from some spontaneous cloudburst, but people were hearing the unconstrained movement of a Holy God. The effect of this sound was to catch the people's attention and gather them into one place. The effect of this invisible force was undeniable and left no one untouched. Jesus spoke of the wind saying, "The wind blows wherever it pleases. You hear its sound, but you cannot tell where it comes from or where it is going. So it is with everyone born of the Spirit." (John 3:8)

A Rush of Fire

The second sign of the dramatic entrance of the Holy Spirit was a visual manifestation of God. Fire often indicated the presence of God. Initially God appeared to Moses in a burning bush, which was not consumed. (Exodus 3) When the children of Israel left Egypt, God guided them with a pillar of fire by night (Exodus 13:21–22), and when God came down to Mount Sinai to give the Ten Commandments and Law he descended in fire. (Exodus 19:18) At Pentecost, each person saw tongues of fire resting over the others' heads.

As the prophet Malachi talked about the appearance of God's fire: "But who can endure the day of his coming? Who can stand when he appears? For he will be like a refiner's fire or a launderer's soap. He will sit as a refiner and purifier of silver; he will purify the Levites and refine them like gold and silver. Then the Lord will have men who will bring offerings in righteousness." (Malachi 3:2–3) Fire burns the dross from raw ore for fine metals like gold. God's Holy Spirit came in fire at Pentecost to refine and purify the human spirit.

Speaking in Tongues

The third unusual sign at Pentecost was tongues, as the people were speaking in diverse known languages. This sign underscored the universal outreach of the Church. These witnesses were speaking foreign dialects to the people who had gathered in Jerusalem for the Day of Pentecost from other nations. People who lived outside of Israel traveled to Jerusalem to celebrate the festival. They came from Arabia, Crete, Asia, and even as far away as Rome. Unlike the translator headsets used at the United Nations, these men and women heard the truth of God from the Holy Spirit coming through loud and clear.

JUST A MINUTE

What makes Pentecost distinct and unique is that it happened once. The subsequent episodes of the Holy Spirit beyond this inaugural moment should be understood as an extension of Pentecost through which the entire body of Christ, or the church, is gifted for ministry. The signs were given to affirm the activity of a Holy God and to affirm that even Gentiles received a full measure of the Holy Spirit. In God's economy, there was no longer any distinction between Jews and Gentiles.

After the arrival of the Holy Spirit at Pentecost, Peter preached a sermon and told people the truth about the resurrected Jesus Christ. At the end of his sermon, Peter called for the listeners to repent and be baptized in the name of Jesus for forgiveness of sins and then a believer would receive the gift of the Holy Spirit. (Acts 2:38) Acts 2:41–45 shows the results from the Day of Pentecost, "Those who accepted his [Peter's] message were baptized, and about three thousand were added to their number that day. They devoted themselves to the apostles' teaching and to the fellowship, to the breaking of bread and to prayer. Everyone was filled with awe, and many wonders and miraculous signs were done by the apostles. All the believers were together and had everything in common. Selling their possessions and goods, they gave to anyone as he had need." The winds of change were blowing through the followers of Christ.

CULTURAL FACT

Where were the 3,000 people from Acts 2:41 baptized? Although the location for the baptism isn't mentioned in the text, archaeologists have discovered more than 40 ritual baths in excavations south of the Temple Mount area. They had been used by Jewish worshipers to ritually purify themselves before entering the temple precincts.

PERSECUTION EXPANDS THE CHURCH

In Jesus' final words to his disciples before his ascension, he gave a prophetic overview of the first 30 years of the Church:

"For John baptized with water, but in a few days you will be baptized with the Holy Spirit ... But you will receive power when the Holy Spirit comes on you; and you will be my witnesses in Jerusalem, and in all Judea and Samaria, and to the ends of the earth." (Acts 1:5, 8)

The dramatic events of the Day of Pentecost must have provided a wake-up call to the disciples who heard Jesus talk about the Holy Spirit. They must have commented something like, "We remember Jesus talking about the baptism of the Holy Spirit but we had no idea it would be anything like this." In the same way Jesus predicted the arrival of the Holy Spirit, he also laid out a missionary strategy for spreading the Good News or Gospel message and building the Church. His followers were to begin in their hometown of Jerusalem, then take the message to the ends of the earth. The entire Book of Acts, also known as "The Acts of the Apostles," records how the early church obeyed the command of Jesus. Through the power of the Holy Spirit, the followers of Jesus called people to repentance.

After the religious leaders crucified Jesus, their problems were not over. Instead these problems multiplied, as the disciples called people to repentance and a lifetime of following the teachings of Jesus. The Jewish religious leaders began to monitor the spread of the teachings of Jesus:

They [the high priest and council] called the apostles in and had them flogged. Then they ordered them not to speak in the name of Jesus, and let them go. The apostles left the Sanhedrin, rejoicing because they had been counted worthy of suffering disgrace for the Name. Day after day, in the temple courts and from house to house, they never stopped teaching and proclaiming the good news that Jesus is the Christ. (Acts 5:40–42)

JUST A MINUTE

Gamaliel, who temporarily saved the day for the Apostles (Acts 5:34–40), was the most famous rabbi of his day. It was at the feet of Gamaliel that Saul (later called Paul) had been brought up. (Acts 22:3) Young Saul may have been present at the meeting of the Sanhedrin, since he was a member (Acts 26:10) and not long after this, when the council stoned Stephen, Saul was a participant (Acts 7:58).

THE COURAGE OF STEPHEN

The threats from the Jewish leaders were not working with the disciples. As the religious leaders severely punished the followers of Christ, instead of making the movement stop, they were literally making it grow. Beatings were not slowing down the movement. Jewish leaders would need to take more permanent action against the disciples of Jesus.

The story of Stephen is one of the most remarkable accounts of raw courage in the face of opposition. Stephen first appears when a group of converted Gentiles complained to the 12 apostles that their widows were not receiving enough care:

So the Twelve gathered all the disciples together and said, "It would not be right for us to neglect the ministry of the word of God in order to wait on tables. Brothers, choose seven men from among you who are known to be full of the Spirit and wisdom. We will turn this responsibility over to them and will give our attention to prayer and the ministry of the word." This proposal pleased the whole group. They chose Stephen, a man full of faith and of the Holy Spirit; [and six other men]. (Acts 6:2–5)

JUST A MINUTE

Stephen's particular sphere of labor seems to have been among the Greek Jews. At that time, there were 460 synagogues in Jerusalem, some of which were built by Jews from various countries for their own use.

Because Stephen was a bold witness for Jesus Christ, his life became a target for a group of devout Jews called the Synagogue of Freedmen. These men were displeased with Stephen and his ministry, so they set a trap and got some men to say that Stephen had blasphemed Moses, God, the temple, and the sacred Law. With a band of mercenaries, they seized Stephen and brought him into their presence. "All who were sitting in the Sanhedrin looked intently at Stephen, and they saw that his face was like the face of an angel." (Acts 6:15) Stephen's appearance must have made these religious leaders nervous. "Then the high priest asked him, 'Are these charges true?'" (Acts 7:1)

There is an old saying, "If you don't want the answer, don't ask the question." The high priest shouldn't have asked Stephen this question because ultimately Stephen's answer humiliated and infuriated him. This young disciple of Christ gave one of the greatest sermons recorded in Scripture. Starting with the common ground of the Patriarchs, Stephen told a narrative that pointed out the rebellion of the Jewish people and ultimately their rejection of the Messiah. Near the end of Stephen's message, he took square verbal aim at these religious leaders, "You stiff-necked people, with uncircumcised hearts and ears! You are just like your fathers: You always resist the Holy Spirit!" (Acts 7:51)

These religious leaders didn't take Stephen's oral assault lightly. Instead they covered their ears and dragged Stephen to the edge of the city and prepared to stone him. "While they were stoning him, Stephen prayed, 'Lord Jesus, receive my spirit.' Then he fell on his knees and cried out, 'Lord, do not hold this sin against them.' When he had said this, he fell asleep." (Acts 7:59–60)

Stephen's final words of forgiveness must have stunned his listeners—including one young man, named Saul, who watched the cloaks of the attackers.

FEEDING THE FIRES OF PERSECUTION

The Jewish leaders had established an aggressive plan to eliminate the young church of Jesus Christ. Their plans had the opposite effect. The blood of the martyrs was fueling the spread of the Gospel. "On that day a great persecution broke out against the Church at Jerusalem, and all except the apostles were scattered throughout Judea and Samaria." (Acts 8:1)

One of the great recurring truths in the Bible is that God will use anything to complete his work. He used a godless pharaoh to purify and move out the Israelites. In the days of the young Church, he used religious fanatics to move the Christians out of Jerusalem and to the remote areas of the world. At first the apostles stayed in Jerusalem and the common people went to the surrounding regions to tell others about Jesus. The spread of the Good News was the result of laymen, who were filled with the Holy Spirit and equipped for ministry from the teaching of the apostles.

After these laymen began to leave Jerusalem, some of the apostles also began to leave. Philip, for example, went to Samaria and preached. During Philip's ministry, a man named Simon, who practiced witchcraft and sorcery, was converted. In fact, Simon joined Philip when he witnessed the power of the Holy Spirit working in the hearts of repentant men and women.

While the Holy Spirit continued to spread the good news through the hands and hearts of the laymen, God also directly intervened to spread the Gospel.

At Caesarea there was a man named Cornelius, a centurion in what was known as the Italian Regiment. He and all his family were devout and God-fearing; he gave generously to those in need and prayed to God regularly. One day at about three in the afternoon he had a vision. He distinctly saw an angel of God, who came to him and said, "Cornelius!"

Cornelius stared at him in fear. "What is it, Lord?" he asked. The angel answered, "Your prayers and gifts to the poor have come up as a memorial offering before God. Now send men to Joppa to bring back a man named Simon who is called Peter. He is staying with Simon the tanner, whose house is by the sea." When the angel who spoke to him had gone, Cornelius called two of his servants and a devout soldier who was one of his attendants. He told them everything that had happened and sent them to Joppa. (Acts 10:1–8)

CULTURAL FACT

Cornelius feared God. The words identified him with a category of people. The God-fearers were Gentiles who were interested in Judaism but not necessarily converts or proselytes. They worshipped the same God and observed the same laws the Jews did, but they did not become circumcised. Many of these God-fearers were the first Gentiles to become Christians.

Before the men from Cornelius could reach the apostle Peter, God gave Peter a vision which prepared him to meet these men. In this vision, Peter saw a great sheet filled with a variety of animals that traditionally Jews were forbidden to eat:

Then a voice told him, "Get up, Peter. Kill and eat."

"Surely not, Lord!" Peter replied. "I have never eaten anything impure or unclean."

The voice spoke to him a second time, "Do not call anything impure that God has made clean." This happened three times, and immediately the sheet was taken back to heaven. (Acts 10:13–16)

An angel from God had visited Cornelius, a non-Jew and a foreigner who told him to call on Simon Peter, the disciple of Jesus, but also someone who was a proud exclusive-minded Jew. Simultaneously God gave Peter a vision and prepared him to be willing to widen the scope of God's salvation to include the Gentiles.

After Cornelius arrived and called on Peter, he explained the visitation from an angel of God. Peter was amazed. "Then Peter began to speak: 'I now realize how true it is that God does not show favoritism but accepts men from every nation who fear him and do what is right.'" (Acts 10:34–35)

Peter followed the leading of the Holy Spirit to reach out with the Good News about Jesus to a Roman centurion named Cornelius. The apostle's message of repentance and forgiveness through Christ gave the message to a Gentile who was surrounded by his family and friends:

While Peter was still speaking these words, the Holy Spirit came on all who heard the message. The circumcised believers who had come with Peter were astonished that the gift of the Holy Spirit had been poured out even on the Gentiles. For they heard them speaking in tongues and praising God. Then Peter said, "Can anyone keep these people from being baptized with water? They have received the Holy Spirit just as we have."

So he ordered that they be baptized in the name of Jesus Christ. Then they asked Peter to stay with them for a few days. (Acts 10:44–48)

JUST A MINUTE

This experience of the Holy Spirit falling on people in supernatural ways was extraordinary. God gives his Holy Spirit to every believer—whether they speak in tongues or not. Through this significant story in the book of Acts, God proclaimed his message of salvation for everyone—Jew and Gentile. These visible manifestations were symbols, which underscored the presence and power of the Holy Spirit to reach all nations. Through the persecuted church, the Holy Spirit was reaching out to all peoples to accomplish the will of God.

PAUL'S CONVERSION

The Bible is filled with unpredictable activity from God. There is no logical explanation for a stammering Moses to lead the Israelites out of Egypt or the Lord's selection of the young David to be the greatest king of Israel. There isn't any logic behind the story of a great fish swallowing a rebellious prophet or the birth of God's own son in a cattle stall, yet each of these stories happened in history.

The story of the Apostle Paul, which fills almost a third of the New Testament, fits perfectly into this pattern of sovereign randomness. Remember the young scholar, Saul, who held the cloaks as Stephen was martyred? Who would have guessed this young scholar would be the Lord's selection to bring the Good News to the Gentiles and write letters to the churches, which continue to teach and instruct Christians around the globe. The story defies logic, but the God of the Universe doesn't need our permission to affirm the logic. God is God and acts as he chooses.

The story of Saul begins at the stoning of Stephen but then is picked up again in Acts 9: "Meanwhile, Saul was still breathing out murderous threats against the Lord's disciples. He went to the high priest and asked him for letters to the synagogues in Damascus, so that if he found any there who belonged to the Way, whether men or women, he might take them as prisoners to Jerusalem." (Acts 9:1–2)

CULTURAL FACT

Paul's hometown of Tarsus contains a gate in the city wall known as Cleopatra's Gate, because it is claimed that is where she met Mark Anthony a half-century before the Apostle Paul was born. Little did Saul know that one day as a world traveler he would several times cross the Tarsus Mountains that he could see from Tarsus.

Saul had religious zeal in his attack of Christians. He wanted to rid the world of this heretical sect, which seemed to be undermining Judaism. An educated man, by the time Saul was 21 he had earned the equivalent of two Ph.D.s. He rationally believed that the followers of Jesus Christ could eventually undo rabbinical Judaism. Because of his training and passion, Saul was determined to be active in eliminating these followers of Christ. Yet as he traveled toward Damascus, he was about to have an experience that would transform his life.

"As he [Saul] neared Damascus on his journey, suddenly a light from heaven flashed around him. He fell to the ground and heard a voice say to him, 'Saul, Saul, why do you persecute me?'" (Acts 9:3–4)

As Saul lay in the dusty Damascus road, he must have been overwhelmed. He had seen a great light, which was like the power of a thousand flashbulbs. The light made Paul blind. He wondered, "Whose voice is this? Could it be God? Or worse yet, *Jesus?*" Then Saul heard a voice calling his name twice, "Saul, Saul."

This scholar of the Old Testament recognized the rarity of an event when a name is repeated twice: Moses at the burning bush; Abraham poised with his knife over his only son, Isaac, and about to take his life; and Elisha calling to his mentor, Elijah. The repetition meant the voice knew Saul intimately and it got his instant attention.

CULTURAL FACT

Damascus was located 140 miles northeast of Jerusalem. Rome permitted the Jewish Sanhedrin to control Jewish affairs. At this time, the new church was a Jewish affair. The early believers in Jesus were still attending synagogues. The synagogues in Damascus had to cooperate with anyone who had the authorization Saul possessed. Saul planned to take the followers of Jesus who had escaped to Damascus back to Jerusalem to stand trial before the Sanhedrin and probably face the death sentence.

"'Who are you, Lord?' Saul asked." (Acts 9:5a) Saul asked the question but he knew the answer. He was in the middle of a face-to-face divine encounter.

"'I am Jesus, whom you are persecuting,' he replied." (Acts 9:5b) Jesus didn't say that Saul was persecuting his followers or disciples. He said the attack was on him personally because to attack the followers of Christ is to attack Christ himself.

God had Saul's full attention. "'Now get up and go into the city, and you will be told what you must do.' The men traveling with Saul stood there speechless; they heard the sound but did not see anyone. Saul got up from the ground, but when he opened his eyes he could see nothing. So they led him by the hand into Damascus. For three days he was blind, and did not eat or drink anything." (Acts 9:6–9)

As Saul stood to his feet, he realized he couldn't see and had been blinded from the light. His companions couldn't speak but they helped Saul continue toward Damascus. What an image of these mute men helping their blind and intellectual mentor by the hand into the city. Where would they go?

In Damascus there was a disciple named Ananias. The Lord called to him in a vision, "Ananias!" "Yes, Lord," he answered. The Lord told him, "Go to the house of Judas on Straight Street and ask for a man from Tarsus named Saul, for he is praying. In a vision he has seen a man named Ananias come and place his hands on him to restore his sight." "Lord," Ananias answered, "I have heard many reports about this man and all the harm he has done to your saints in Jerusalem. And he has come here with authority from the chief priests to arrest all who call on your name." (Acts 9:10–14)

Do these objections sound familiar? Ananias had heard about Saul's intent on killing followers of Christ. Like Moses objected to going to Pharaoh and announcing the Lord wanted the Jewish people released, Ananias questioned the wisdom of going to Saul. Maybe it was a bad dream. Surely the Lord didn't want him to have anything to do with Saul.

But the Lord said to Ananias, "Go! This man is my chosen instrument to carry my name before the Gentiles and their kings and before the people of Israel. I will show him how much he must suffer for my name." Then Ananias went to the house and entered it. Placing his hands on Saul, he said, "Brother Saul, the Lord—Jesus, who appeared to you on the road as you were coming here—has sent me so that you may see again and be filled with the Holy Spirit." Immediately, something like scales fell from Saul's eyes, and he could see again. He got up and was baptized, and after taking some food, he regained his strength. Saul spent several days with the disciples in Damascus. (Acts 9:15–19)

The experience on the Damascus road was a defining experience for Saul. Not a person to hide his passions, Saul, who became "Paul," went straight to the temple.

At once he [Paul] began to preach in the synagogues that Jesus is the Son of God. All those who heard him were astonished and asked, "Isn't he the man who raised havoc in Jerusalem among those who call on this name? And hasn't he come here to take them as prisoners to the chief priests?" Yet Saul grew more and more powerful and baffled the Jews living in Damascus by proving that Jesus is the Christ. (Acts 9:20–22)

Imagine the shock to Jews and Christians alike to see the transformation in the life of Paul. Years later, Paul captured some of the reality of this life-change in a letter to his understudy Timothy. Paul wrote:

"I thank Christ Jesus our Lord, who has given me strength, that he considered me faithful, appointing me to his service. Even though I was once a blasphemer and a persecutor and a violent man, I was shown mercy because I acted in ignorance and unbelief. The grace of our Lord was poured out on me abundantly, along with the faith and love that are in Christ Jesus. Here is a trustworthy saying that deserves full acceptance: Christ Jesus came into the world to save sinners—of whom I am the worst." (1 Timothy 1:12–15)

Firsthand, Paul understood his own repentance and God's mercy. It came from his Damascus road experience.

WHY IS PAUL AN APOSTLE?

Throughout the Old Testament, there were constant struggles to distinguish between those who had been truly called by God and the false prophets. This distinction explains why the majority of the prophets spent some time explaining the circumstances of their call to God's service and speaking his words.

Before examining the works of Paul in depth in the subsequent hours, it's good to examine closely why Paul refers to himself as an "apostle."

After the ascension of Jesus Christ, the 12 disciples became known as apostles. There was a fourfold criteria to be an apostle:

- Apostles heard a direct call from Jesus, "Follow me."
- Apostles were eyewitnesses of Jesus during his earthly ministry.
- Apostles were eyewitnesses of the post-resurrected Christ.
- The authenticity of these factors was verified by the other apostles.

Apostles, like prophets, had a clear calling and a personal and physical encounter with Jesus Christ. Because this term isn't clarified specifically in the New Testament, some Christian leaders today use the term "apostle." To use the term, these leaders need to provide the type of proof that Paul was forced to furnish when anyone doubted his apostleship.

Paul had a direct call from Jesus and a direct encounter with Jesus to hear his voice. He was sent back to Jerusalem to visit with the other apostles. At first the other apostles were understandably reluctant to welcome Paul, but eventually Paul convinced them of the authenticity of his apostleship:

When he came to Jerusalem, he tried to join the disciples, but they were all afraid of him, not believing that he really was a disciple. But Barnabas took him and brought him to the apostles. He told them how Saul on his journey had seen the Lord and that the Lord had spoken to him, and how in Damascus he had preached fearlessly in the name of Jesus. So Saul stayed with them and moved about freely in Jerusalem, speaking boldly in the name of the Lord. (Acts 9:26–28)

While the apostles must have been initially apprehensive to welcome this man who had been their archenemy into intimate fellowship, they must have celebrated his changed life. Paul was admitted into the inner circle of apostles and the word spread.

"When the brothers learned of this, they took him down to Caesarea and sent him off to Tarsus. Then the church throughout Judea, Galilee and Samaria enjoyed a time of peace. It was strengthened; and encouraged by the Holy Spirit, it grew in numbers, living in the fear of the Lord." (Acts 9:30–31)

HOUR'S UP!

During this past hour, you've learned about the birth of the church, the expansion, and the conversion of Paul. What relevance do these events have in your life today? Take a few minutes to explore these application questions.

1. The Church calendar celebrates the Day of Pentecost. How do you mark celebrations in your life? Do you have detailed plans or do you simply let them pass? Make plans this year to celebrate Pentecost and the birth of the church.

2. When the people in Jerusalem heard the Gospel of Jesus in their own language, something different had happened. Rarely do we celebrate the opportunity we have to read the Bible in a language we can understand. Literally millions of people are without this opportunity. Pause in gratefulness for the Scriptures in a language you can easily understand.

3. In Numbers 11, God spreads his Spirit on 70 elders besides Moses. Then at Pentecost the Holy Spirit fills believers and empowers them for ministry. How does the Holy Spirit empower your life? If not, ask God to fill your life with his presence and the power of the Holy Spirit.

4. The Spirit came on Pentecost like a rush of mighty wind and changed lives forever. How has God's Holy Spirit entered your life and what changes have resulted?

5. At Pentecost, Peter preached a powerful sermon and many repented, believed in Jesus, and were baptized for the forgiveness of their sins. Can you point to a period of your life or an event where your life was transformed by the Gospel of Jesus Christ? If so, take a moment in prayer to celebrate this event. If not, ask God to forgive you of your sins and believe in the Lord Jesus. It will transform your life.

6. The arrival of the Holy Spirit changed the lives of the believers in Jerusalem in a noticeable manner. They were devoting themselves to the apostles' teaching, fellowship, and prayer. Although we don't have the apostles present physically today, we do have their teaching in the written Bible, and we can fellowship with other followers of Christ and pray. Evaluate your own time in the Scriptures, fellowship, and prayer. Is there an area that needs to be strengthened? If so, make some concrete plans to make changes.

7. Stephen was a man full of faith and the Holy Spirit. It showed in his everyday life and his courage in front of the religious leaders of his day. How can you gain strength and increase your own faith from his example?

8. Persecution and trials for the early Church forced many changes, but also forced them to grow in their faith. Although no one enjoys difficulties or trials, do they bring about growth in your life? Take a moment and consider some of your life trials and whether you've increased your faith in God as a result. If not, learn from the experience so you can have this faith relationship in the trials of the future.

Yes, there will be trials in the future for each of us. It's a question of whether we handle them in the strength of our flesh or in a spiritual sense as we live in faith with God and the power of the Holy Spirit.

9. Cornelius and Peter boldly followed the leading of the Holy Spirit in their everyday lives. Take a moment and reread Acts 10 and write several principles for your life, which you can learn from Cornelius and Peter.

10. The direction of Saul's life was transformed on a dusty road to Damascus. While it doesn't take a vision from Jesus to change your life, how have you experienced changes and growth in your spiritual life? Through reading the Bible, prayer, or spending time with another person who has a deeper relationship with Jesus, we can grow in our faith. Make some plans to grow in your faith this coming week—even a tiny step is better than standing still and doing nothing.

HOUR 21

Paul's Letters to the Churches: Part One

CHAPTER SUMMARY

LESSON PLAN:
In this hour, you will learn about ...

- The nature of Christ's work in the letter to the Romans.
- The various church disorders in the first letter to the Corinthians.
- Paul's vindication of his apostleship in the second letter to the Corinthians.

How recently have you looked in your car owner's manual? In one place, the manual gives all of the information needed to operate your car. Most people haven't read their owner's manual recently. The lack of reading isn't because they've misplaced it. Usually it's kept in the glove box of the car.

Just like your car owner's manual, the Book of Romans is close to an operations manual for our faith. Because the book follows Acts, it's easy to find. Through Romans and 1 and 2 Corinthians, in this hour you will begin to learn how the Apostle Paul wrote under the unrestricted inspiration of the Holy Spirit. The manual of Romans doesn't belong in the dark but in the light of day because of its practical message for everyday life.

As the operations manual for our beliefs, the book of Romans is as near as Paul comes to writing a systematic theology of salvation. Surprisingly, it is relatively brief. The great playwright George Bernard Shaw once wrote a 12-page letter to a friend and at the end of it apologized for writing such a tome. "Forgive me for going on so long," Shaw explained. "I didn't have time to write a shorter letter."

Through the inspiration of the Holy Spirit, Paul took enough time to compress the great themes of the Christian belief system and put them into a single letter to the church at Rome. Throughout the history of the church, God has used Romans to bring revival to more churches than can be numbered. Martin Luther, Charles

Wesley, and Saint Augustine were only a few of those who have been dramatically converted by the truths in Romans. As with any accomplished writer, Paul begins the book and tells the reader the theme of the entire book: "I am not ashamed of the gospel, because it is the power of God for the salvation of everyone who believes: first for the Jew, then for the Gentile. For in the gospel a righteousness from God is revealed, a righteousness that is by faith from first to last, just as it is written: 'The righteous will live by faith.'" (Romans 1:16–17)

JUST A MINUTE

The Good News about Jesus came through the Jewish people. "Salvation is from the Jews" (John 4:22) and also the Messiah, Jesus Christ, was a Jew. The covenants, law, temple worship, revelation of the divine glory, and the Messianic prophecies came to them. These privileges weren't extended because of their superior merit or because of God's partiality toward them. The entrance of the Gospel had to begin at a particular point of history and with a particular people. God selected the Jewish people for this point in history, and now, in turn, this Gospel is carried to the other nations of the world.

THE LIFE OF FAITH

From the opening of his first letter, Paul gives a critical bit of information for living the Christian life: It's impossible to accomplish without faith. Because individuals neither possess nor can achieve a righteousness acceptable to a Holy God, righteousness can only be found as we accept the free gift of God's righteousness in Christ. Once we receive this gift, we do have the ability to live in obedience as we live in God's grace.

The first three chapters of Romans establish that everyone is guilty before God. Because of God's laws and our disobedience, we are exposed as sinners. Jews and Gentiles alike are guilty of sin. Paul emphasized this truth with the reminder: "The law was added so that the trespass might increase." (Romans 5:20a)

And some more bad news for the Christian life: Even if you don't have the law or know about the law of God, the Lord has revealed himself through nature. "For since the creation of the world God's invisible qualities—his eternal power and divine nature—have been clearly seen, being understood from what has been made, so that men are without excuse." (Romans 1:20)

Paul is saying whether man chooses to praise and obey the God of the Universe or not, all of creation will do it anyway. Some skeptics search for a sign of God, but Romans says that signs are posted everywhere. There are no excuses. If anyone ignores God, they face God's judgment and an even more devastating punishment: "Therefore God gave them over in the sinful desires of their hearts to sexual impurity for the degrading of their bodies with one another." (Romans 1:24)

While God's grace is our greatest hope, the removal of this grace represents our greatest hopelessness. The punishment from a holy God to sinful people is to separate them from himself and turn them loose to their own actions. Paul's description of the life without God is as relevant today as it was during the first century. The universal response to God's revelation is disobedience. For us to become holy, it's essential to receive our holiness and righteousness from Jesus Christ.

PAUL ASKS, THEN ANSWERS SOME QUESTIONS

Throughout his writings, Paul teaches in something called *dialecture*. He presumes a question from the reader, then answers it. For example, in chapter 4 Paul assumes that the reader has questions about the patriarchs who lived centuries before the Law was given to Moses and long before Jesus was born in a stable in Bethlehem. Romans 4:1 says, "What then shall we say that Abraham, our forefather, discovered in this matter?"

Paul asks a good question, and then he answers it with a clear and strong response. From the beginning of time, God's grace has been available. And these men received the blessing of that grace by first receiving the gift of faith.

"Abraham believed God, and it was credited to him as righteousness. ... It was not through law that Abraham and his offspring received the promise that he would be heir of the world, but through the righteousness that comes by faith." (Romans 4:3b, 13)

The patriarchs believed God, and then they obeyed. Their works did not save them, but their faith in a holy God provoked them to righteousness. Obedience was a by-product of belief.

Throughout the New Testament, Abraham, the father of the Jewish people, figures prominently into the text. Abraham's faith makes him important to New Testament writers. When God made promises to Abraham that were repeated throughout Israel's history, he had little evidence that God would follow through—certainly less than the New Testament writers. "Abraham believed God, and it was credited to him as righteousness." (Romans 4:3)

GOD MAKES PEACE WITH MANKIND

In Romans 5, Paul presumes these questions from the reader:

- How does Christ take our place?
- From what have we been saved?
- How should we respond to receiving Christ's righteousness?

As before, these are good questions. Here is Paul's answer:

For we know that our old self was crucified with him so that the body of sin might be done away with, that we should no longer be slaves to sin—because anyone who has died has been freed from sin. Now if we died with Christ, we believe that we will also live with him. For we know that since Christ was raised from the dead, he cannot die again; death no longer has mastery over him. The death he died, he died to sin once for all; but the life he lives, he lives to God. In the same way, count yourselves dead to sin but alive to God in Christ Jesus. (Romans 5:6–11)

Because Christ loved us, he willingly took our place and saved us from the wrath of God. Once we understand what we've been liberated from, our response must be a spontaneous celebration, an overflow of gratitude to God for the peace treaty he signed between himself and us with the blood of Jesus Christ.

Romans 6 and 7 remind us that although the "war" is over, the battle continues because surrender is not a simple matter:

As it is, it is no longer I myself who do it, but it is sin living in me. I know that nothing good lives in me, that is, in my sinful nature. For I have the desire to do what is good, but I cannot carry it out. For what I do is not the good I want to do; no, the evil I do not want to do—this I keep on doing. Now if I do what I do not want to do, it is no longer I who do it, but it is sin living in me that does it …. What a wretched man I am! Who will rescue me from this body of death? Thanks be to God—through Jesus Christ our Lord! (Romans 7:18–20, 24–25a)

Sometimes new believers are disillusioned because of the difference between what their faith delivers and what was promised to them. They were told their faith would bring instant prosperity, peace, and happiness. And while they discover these things on the other side of sin, their problems seem to grow.

Because of what we've just seen, this increase in trouble makes perfect sense. The easy-street promises in preconversion made them utterly counterfeit. Reread these verses.

God's punishment for unbelievers is to turn them loose to run without thought through the indulgences of sin. Then, through the gifts of faith and grace, a holy God steps into their lives. Life is no longer lived as an open swamp of lawlessness but within the river boundaries of Jesus Christ's atoning sacrifice. What the unbeliever experienced without apparent consequences is now understood as the reason for the cross. What seemed independent is now being examined through the eyes of a loving Father. What felt like freedom came at the Savior's personal expense.

To live within strict boundaries sounds like a severe life-change to some new believers. The presence of conflict means the close proximity of the Holy Spirit. Our tendency to sin keeps us close to the one who saved us. How does God work through this difficult process of sanctification and take us to triumph or eventual glorification? Romans 8 answers this question with one of the most uplifting and encouraging chapters in the Bible. Paul assures us of God's providential care:

"For those God foreknew he also predestined to be conformed to the likeness of his Son, that he might be the firstborn among many brothers. And those he predestined, he also called; those he called, he also justified; those he justified, he also glorified." (Romans 8:29–30)

Paul also answers a question which many people have, "Can our defiance of God keep him away?"

"No, in all these things we are more than conquerors through him who loved us. For I am convinced that neither death nor life, neither angels nor demons, neither the present nor the future, nor any powers, neither height nor depth, nor anything else in all creation, will be able to separate us from the love of God that is in Christ Jesus our Lord." (Romans 8:38–39)

The love of God is irresistible and unchanging.

In practical terms, Paul in Romans provides some simple descriptions of the Christian life and the results:

The Christian	Result
Presents himself to God (12:1)	Becomes a sacrifice that is living, holy, and pleasing to God (12:1)
Receives transformation by a renewed mind (12:2)	Discovers and displays the will of God (12:2)
Has spiritual gifts according to the grace from God (12:6–8)	Uses spiritual gifts as part of Christ's body (12:6)
Honors civil law (13:1)	Honors God (13:1)
Loves others (13:8)	Fulfills God's Law (13:8)
Pursues peace (14:19)	Serves to edify all (14:19)
Becomes like-minded toward others (15:5)	Glorifies God with others (15:6)

THE PURPOSE OF ROMANS

Romans was written to a vibrant church in the city of Rome. Although the origins of the Roman church are still unknown, new believers who returned from Jerusalem after the outpouring of the Holy Spirit at Pentecost could have established the church. When Paul wrote this letter, he had not personally visited Rome, although for some time he had desired to do so. In the epistle, few clues are included about the Roman believers. Paul admired their faith and prayed regularly for them. It's evident that the church included both Jews and Gentiles.

The Book of Romans includes the most systematic presentation of theology in the Bible. It explains the meaning of the cross for the believer's life. While expounding why Jesus died for all humanity, Paul clarifies the core concepts of the Christian faith: sin and righteousness, faith and works, justification and election. Because the book provides a systematic outline of the essentials of the Christian faith, it is as useful to the mature believer as it is to someone who wants a short introduction to the Christian faith.

LETTERS TO THE CORINTHIANS: BOOK 1

The Apostle Paul was a problem solver. His theological skills were intended for application to a particular situation and problematic individuals. The letters he wrote to the church at Corinth were meant to help them through a grave case of spiritual immaturity. Paul heard some disturbing news about the Corinthian churches. Unlike other churches from which he received letters, Paul had spent 18 months with the Christians in Corinth. Because of a year and a half of teaching, these believers could not claim ignorance and had no excuse for their childish behavior.

CULTURAL FACT

Many scholars agree Paul wrote the letter to the Corinthians while he was ministering in Ephesus during his third missionary journey. In 1 Corinthians 16:8, Paul said that he must remain in Ephesus until Pentecost. This verse, coupled with Acts 20:31, indicates that he wrote it in the last year of his three-year stay in Ephesus, sometime in the spring of A.D. 56. At that time, the Corinthian church would have been about four years old.

The church at Corinth was a seriously troubled group of Christians. Infected with sexual immorality, split by factions that dragged each other into court, and crippled by abuse of the spiritual gifts, this church needed radical spiritual surgery. While true believers, the Corinthians had a great deal of growing up to do. They had to stop following the immoral, selfish, and contentious practices of their pagan neighbors in Corinth. With more than half a million people in Corinth, the city had become known as a center for sexual immorality and idol worship throughout the world. For members of the Corinth church, this pagan influence was apparently unavoidable.

Like a surgeon, Paul diagnosed the problem and aimed his efforts straight at the source: pride and a true lack of love in the church.

The Book of 1 Corinthians was written in reply to two letters. In A.D. 53, Paul left the Corinthian church under the leadership of Aquila and Priscilla to continue his second missionary journey. During his third missionary journey while staying in Ephesus, he received two letters from the Corinthian believers.

One letter was a disturbing report from the household of Chloe. (1 Corinthians 1:11) The report detailed the divisions and immorality in the church. These problems arose because the young Corinthian church failed to protect itself from the decadent culture of the city. These Christians were identifying themselves with a specific leader rather than as followers of Christ.

Brothers, I could not address you as spiritual but as worldly—mere infants in Christ. I gave you milk, not solid food, for you were not yet ready for it. Indeed, you are still not ready. You are still worldly. For since there is jealousy and quarreling among you, are you not worldly? Are you not acting like mere men? For when one says, "I follow Paul," and another, "I follow Apollos," are you not mere men? What, after all, is Apollos? And what is Paul?

Only servants, through whom you came to believe—as the Lord has assigned to each his task. I planted the seed, Apollos watered it, but God made it grow. So neither he who plants nor he who waters is anything, but only God, who makes things grow. The man who plants and the man who waters have one purpose, and each will be rewarded according to his own labor. For we are God's fellow workers; you are God's field, God's building. (1 Corinthians 3:1–9)

The key is to belong to Christ, not to a particular leader.

JUST A MINUTE

Who gets the credit? It's a common question. Paul pointed out the church at Corinth was a joint venture between himself, Apollos, and the Lord. (1 Corinthians 3:5–8) Actually, many others were involved as well, but the point was cooperation and not competition. While Paul was speaking about a startup church, the principles easily apply to today. Who gets the credit is an attitude of selfishness and competition. In contrast, cooperative efforts over time generally result in achievements far greater than any isolated individual.

Also the Corinthians were dragging each other into court. They wanted to settle any differences in court rather than in the church. Paul encourages them to settle their differences in the church and not in public: "I say this to shame you. Is it possible that there is nobody among you wise enough to judge a dispute between believers?" (1 Corinthians 6:5)

In addition, sexual immorality had become a problem in the church. With the context of church discipline, "live and let live" had never been God's idea. One member of the church of Corinth was sleeping with his stepmother. Not wanting to cause a stir, the leadership of the church had simply looked the other way. Paul scolded them for their lack of courage. "Flee from sexual immorality. All other sins a man commits are outside his body, but he who sins sexually sins against his own body. Do you not know that your body is a temple of the Holy Spirit, who is in you, whom you have received from God? You are not your own; you were bought at a price. Therefore honor God with your body." (1 Corinthians 6:18–20)

JUST A MINUTE

Evil can't be remedied through hiding it or covering it up. Paul confronted the church at Corinth about its consistent disobedience to God's expressed will. He challenged it to confront the subtle deterioration it had allowed within its congregation. (1 Corinthians 5:5) Once the perpetrator had repented, it was then to seek his restoration. Even though corrective activity among believers may be severe, confrontation should always be to promote healing rather than expel wrongdoers. Compare Matthew 18:15–22 and 2 Corinthians 10:8. There are no throwaway people in the Kingdom of God.

First Corinthians is also a reply to a second letter that Paul received with a series of questions that Stephanas, Fortunatus, and Archaicus had brought from Corinth. The detailed questions were about marriage and singleness (1 Corinthians 7:1–40) and Christian liberty. (1 Corinthians 8:1–11:1)

STAY SINGLE OR GET MARRIED?

The early Church believed Jesus could return any moment. They lived in expectancy and are role models for the church today. About marriage, Paul taught:

Are you married? Do not seek a divorce. Are you unmarried? Do not look for a wife. But if you do marry, you have not sinned; and if a virgin marries, she has not sinned.

But those who marry will face many troubles in this life, and I want to spare you this. What I mean, brothers, is that the time is short. From now on those who have wives should live as if they had none; those who mourn, as if they did not; those who are happy, as if they were not; those who buy something, as if it were not theirs to keep; those who use the things of the world, as if not engrossed in them.

For this world in its present form is passing away. I would like you to be free from concern. An unmarried man is concerned about the Lord's affairs—how he can please the Lord. But a married man is concerned about the affairs of this world—how he can please his wife—and his interests are divided.

An unmarried woman or virgin is concerned about the Lord's affairs: Her aim is to be devoted to the Lord in both body and spirit. But a married woman is concerned about the affairs of this world—how she can please her husband. I am saying this for your own good, not to restrict you, but that you may live in a right way in undivided devotion to the Lord. (1 Corinthians 7:27–35)

For Paul, it was critical that whether married or single, the Christian be focused with undivided attention on the Lord.

CHRISTIAN LIBERTY TO EAT MEAT

Another problem in the church at Corinth had to do with principles of Christian freedom. In the marketplace, most of the meat that was sold or served at parties had been previously offered to pagan gods. Some Christians felt because those gods weren't real, it didn't matter whether they ate it. Other Christians were horrified at the practice.

Paul established a commonsense rule: "Be careful, however, that the exercise of your freedom does not become a stumbling block to the weak." (1 Corinthians 8:9) Essentially, don't offend people even if you think you know better. Paul determined to do without rather than continue in a practice which might cause a fellow Christian to stumble in their faith. "Therefore, if what I eat causes my brother to fall into sin, I will never eat meat again, so that I will not cause him to fall." (1 Corinthians 8:13)

CULTURAL FACT

Liberty in Greek usually denotes "right," "authority," or even "privilege." In certain contexts like this one in 1 Corinthians 8, it means the freedom to exercise one's right. Specifically Paul was addressing the Corinthians' right to eat meat that might have come from pagan temples. Paul had no problem with those who purchased food that had been left over from these events and was later sold in the marketplace. In his judgment, if they ate it at home, they were not participating in idolatry. They had the liberty—or right—to eat this food in good conscience. The exception was if they would be destroying a weaker believer through their actions. For the sake of these weaker believers, they should abstain.

Although he felt entitled to certain rights and privileges as an apostle, Paul never demanded them. "On the contrary, we put up with anything rather than hinder the gospel of Christ." (1 Corinthians 9:12b) Minor things like food should never interfere with a person's testimony to believers. Later, Paul advises the Christians to accept invitations and dine with unbelievers and "eat whatever is put before you without raising questions of conscience." (1 Corinthians 10:27b)

For Paul, his highest priority was to spread the Gospel of Jesus Christ "Yet when I preach the gospel, I cannot boast, for I am compelled to preach. Woe to me if I do not preach the gospel!" (1 Corinthians 9:6) No matter whom Paul was addressing, he considered himself a servant to the Jew or the

Gentile, the weak or the strong. "I have become all things to all men so that by all possible means I might save some." (1 Corinthians 9:22b) He compared the Christian life to a race and himself to a long-distance runner who was competing with many others for a prize. "Everyone who competes in the games goes into strict training. They do it to get a crown that will not last; but we do it to get a crown that will last forever." (1 Corinthians 9:25)

PROPER USE OF SPIRITUAL GIFTS

At Corinth, people were using their spiritual gifts to impress one another rather than edify one another. Their immaturity was most graphic in this area. Paul explains that the spiritual gifts were intended to unify the believers, not to divide them. Even though there are numerous gifts, there was only one body. Paul compared the church to a human body, which is a single unit even though it's composed of various parts. Jesus, Paul explained, is the head of the body. It's up to the various parts to work together to walk, talk, speak, see, and perform other aspects of the body. The only effective means for the body to function is for each part to perform its own function without being jealous of others or seeking to be self-sufficient.

In the middle of this discussion, Paul delivered the great "love chapter," which is often spoken or sung at weddings. He exhorts the Corinthians that the primary motive for using spiritual gifts was to be one of love for each other, bearing with one another's weaknesses and strengths.

> If I speak in the tongues of men and of angels, but have not love, I am only a resounding gong or a clanging cymbal. If I have the gift of prophecy and can fathom all mysteries and all knowledge, and if I have a faith that can move mountains, but have not love, I am nothing. If I give all I possess to the poor and surrender my body to the flames, but have not love, I gain nothing.
>
> Love is patient, love is kind. It does not envy, it does not boast, it is not proud. It is not rude, it is not self-seeking, it is not easily angered, it keeps no record of wrongs. Love does not delight in evil but rejoices with the truth. It always protects, always trusts, always hopes, always perseveres. Love never fails. (1 Corinthians 13:1–8a)

FEW INTELLIGIBLE WORDS

In the church at Corinth, spiritual gifts were pursued without regard for the common bond of love. Paul says that speaking in tongues is gratifying, but it didn't do the group much good unless someone could interpret what was being said. The Apostle Paul had the gift of speaking in tongues but said, "But in the church I would rather speak five intelligible words to instruct others than ten thousand words in a tongue." (1 Corinthians 14:19) Then he challenged the church to "stop thinking like children. In regard to evil be infants, but in your thinking be adults." (1 Corinthians 14:20)

CULTURAL FACT

The Greek term *glossa* means "tongue" or "language." When the early believers were empowered by the Holy Spirit on the Day of Pentecost, they were given the ability to speak in many different languages, so those people who were visiting from all around the Roman world could heard the Good News in their own language. (Acts 2:2–11) When these languages were spoken in the corporate worship setting, interpretation was needed. Paul required interpretation so others could understand and be edified. (1 Corinthians 14:2–27)

While using the spiritual gifts, order was essential in the church. He instructed: "For God is not a God of disorder but of peace. As in all the congregations of the saints, women should remain silent in the churches. They are not allowed to speak, but must be in submission, as the Law says. If they want to inquire about something, they should ask their own husbands at home; for it is disgraceful for a woman to speak in the church." (1 Corinthians 14:33–35) Many feminists criticize Paul for making these statements. In Paul's defense, many people suggest he was addressing married women in this passage, permitting single women or those with unbelieving husbands to participate. Others feel there were a few particularly disruptive women in Corinth to whom Paul was addressing these particular comments. No matter which viewpoint is accepted, Paul's key emphasis is that order should be established and maintained for group worship.

THE FIRST OF MANY

To close the first letter to Corinth, Paul gives these Christians some holy perspective on their problems and conflicts. He counseled them on the proper use of the spiritual gifts. Now he admonished them on their view of death. And Paul underscored the importance of the resurrection to sound Christian doctrine. He says that without belief in Jesus' resurrection, the Christian faith is futile. (1 Corinthians 15:7) Jesus Christ was only the first person to rise from the dead or the "firstfruits," a term which his readers were familiar. "But Christ has indeed been raised from the dead, the first-fruits of those who have fallen asleep." (1 Corinthians 15:20)

When a person lives with the expectation that if they face death, they will spend eternity in God's presence, should they live with a different outlook than those who don't? Repeatedly Paul had risked his life to tell people about Jesus and train them to live as Christians. If he were not convinced of a literal resurrection from the dead, he might as well eat, drink, and then die without going to so much trouble.

One day, Paul said, his human body (perishable) would be replaced with a spiritual body (imperishable). Even death wouldn't end the life of one who believed in God. "Listen, I tell you a mystery: We will not all sleep, but we will all be changed—in a flash, in the twinkling of an eye, at the last trumpet. For the trumpet will sound, the dead will be raised imperishable, and we will be changed. For the perishable must clothe itself with the imperishable, and the mortal with immortality." (1 Corinthians 15:51–53)

Paul ends the first letter with some stirring words of encouragement: "Therefore, my dear brothers, stand firm. Let nothing move you. Always give yourselves fully to the work of the Lord, because you know that your labor in the Lord is not in vain …. Be on your guard; stand firm in the faith; be men of courage; be strong. Do everything in love." (1 Corinthians 15:58, 16:13–14) And also Paul says that if someone doesn't love the Lord, they have another result: "If anyone does not love the Lord—a curse be on him. Come, O Lord!" (1 Corinthians 16:22)

LETTERS TO THE CORINTHIANS: BOOK 2

The Book of 2 Corinthians is a follow-up letter and probably the most personal of Paul's letters. It was a difficult letter for him to write. In his previous letters, Paul had exhorted the Corinthian church to correct some of the abuses that were in their congregation. However, some false teachers in the church were antagonized from Paul's rebuke and rejected his warnings. As a result, Paul was forced to defend his character and more importantly, his apostolic authority. More than any other book in the Bible, his defense reveals the trials and tribulations and the problems and the pressures of his itinerant ministry. Yet like the rest of Paul's letters, the Second Epistle to the Corinthians points past Paul's tears and sweat to the power behind his actions and words: the Lord Jesus Christ.

CULTURAL FACT

The background of 2 Corinthians has to be pieced together. Paul founded the church and left after 18 months and wrote a letter which is now lost. (1 Corinthians 5:9) Paul talked to some members of Chloe's household about quarrels in the church. (1 Corinthians 1:11) Possibly at this point, Paul sent Timothy on a trip that included Corinth. (1 Corinthians 4:17, 16:10) Then, a committee arrived from Corinth with questions for Paul. (1 Corinthians 7:1, 16:7) After that, Paul wrote the book now called 1 Corinthians. After sending Titus to Corinth with 1 Corinthians, he became deeply concerned about how the Corinthians would respond to his letter. According to early tradition, Paul wrote 2 Corinthians from Philippi.

Paul speaks of the fragile nature of the Christian life that inside contains a great treasure. He reminds his readers …

But we have this treasure in jars of clay to show that this all-surpassing power is from God and not from us. We are hard pressed on every side, but not crushed; perplexed, but not in despair; persecuted, but not abandoned; struck down, but not destroyed. We always carry around in our body the death of Jesus, so that the life of Jesus may also be revealed in our body. (2 Corinthians 4:7–10)

MINISTRY OF RECONCILIATION

Because of the work of Jesus Christ on the cross, Paul reminds the church at Corinth that because of Christ they have become a new creation. "And he has committed to us the message of reconciliation. We are therefore Christ's ambassadors, as though God were making his appeal through us. We implore you on Christ's behalf: Be reconciled to God. God made him who had no sin to be sin for us, so that in him we might become the righteousness of God." (2 Corinthians 5:19–21)

Then Paul points out some of the hardships he has faced on behalf of his work to spread the Good News about Jesus: "troubles, hardships and distresses; in beatings, imprisonments and riots; in hard work, sleepless nights and hunger." (2 Corinthians 6:4b–5) To defend his credibility, Paul speaks of "having nothing, and yet possessing everything." (2 Corinthians 6:10b) He is beginning to defend his credentials because soon he will address those false claims against him.

Also Paul issues a warning to the Corinthian church: "Do not be yoked together with unbelievers. For what do righteousness and wickedness have in common? Or what fellowship can light have with darkness? What harmony is there between Christ and Belial? What does a believer have in common with an unbeliever?" (2 Corinthians 6:14–15)

Imagine two animals that are enemies strapped together in the same yoke. While paired, these animals can't accomplish much productive work. In the same way, Christians who attach too closely with nonbelievers eventually enter a conflict relationship. Frequently this warning is applied to marriages although it is equally as valid in business or any other partnership where different moral standards can lead to disputes. In this reference, Paul might have been referring to the false teachers who were casting doubt on his reputation. If the church yoked themselves to these false teachers, great harm could be done to the ministry and impact the church at Corinth.

PAUL'S INTENSE DEFENSE

The tone of the letter shifts dramatically in chapter 10. The first nine chapters are gentle in approach, probably reflecting Paul's growing appreciation for the Corinthian church. Now Paul turns and addresses his opponents and their criticisms of his ministry.

CULTURAL FACT

The Greek word *leitourgia,* or "service" (2 Corinthians 9:2), indicates "public ministry" or "official duty." The related word *leitourgos* is used frequently in Greek literature to designate a man who preformed some public service. (Romans 13:6) In general, it means a public servant or administrator. Paul used *leitourgia* in connection with the service of those who labored to benefit the church.

Paul feels strongly that his accusers were "false apostles, deceitful workmen, masquerading as apostles of Christ. And no wonder, for Satan himself masquerades as an angel of light. It is not surprising, then, if his servants masquerade as servants of righteousness. Their end will be what their actions deserve." (2 Corinthians 11:13–15)

Then Paul gives his credentials for his teaching and work of the Gospel:

I have worked much harder, been in prison more frequently, been flogged more severely, and been exposed to death again and again. Five times I received from the Jews the forty lashes minus one. Three times I was beaten with rods, once I was stoned, three times I was shipwrecked, I spent a night and a day in the open sea, I have been constantly on the move.

I have been in danger from rivers, in danger from bandits, in danger from my own countrymen, in danger from Gentiles; in danger in the city, in danger in the country, in danger at sea; and in danger from false brothers. I have labored and toiled and have often gone without sleep; I have known hunger and thirst and have often gone without food; I have been cold and naked. Besides everything else, I face daily the pressure of my concern for all the churches. (2 Corinthians 11:23b–28)

Paul concludes this epistle with his reason for writing all the teaching: "This is why I write these things when I am absent, that when I come I may not have to be harsh in my use of authority—the authority the Lord gave me for building you up, not for tearing you down." (2 Corinthians 13:10) Paul wanted to encourage and build up the church at Corinth. Because of the Bible, his words continue to help believers today.

Hour's Up!

The first three books from the Apostle Paul are distinct, yet each contains teaching that has pertinent application to life today. Let's explore the personal application in the following questions.

1. Reread the theme verse of Romans (verses 1:16–17). Consider these verses in your life. Are you ashamed of the Gospel of Jesus Christ? How are you proclaiming the Good News in your sphere of influence? Take a moment to celebrate the life of faith, then begin to have greater courage.

2. In the first chapter of Romans, Paul answers the question about the people who have never heard of God's Law and say they are without excuse. The hopelessness of the world without Jesus Christ motivates us to talk about our faith. Make a commitment to talk about your faith with your family, co-worker, or neighbor this week.

3. In our own strength, Paul tells us that it's impossible to become holy and righteous. Our righteousness and holiness come from a relationship with Jesus Christ. How are you increasing your relationship with Christ through spending time in the Bible and prayer? If so, celebrate but if you have slipped, make a recommitment to spend more time with Christ.

4. From the example of Abraham, we learn that faith provokes obedience and a righteous life. Has your faith grown during the past few weeks or months? If so, how? If not, what steps can you take to increase your faith and trust relationship?

5. Paul reminds us in Romans 6 and 7 that although the war is over when we make a personal commitment to a relationship with Christ, the battle continues against our sin nature. What are you battling? What steps are you taking to turn this area over to Jesus Christ?

6. Study the chart about some of the practical results of following the Christian life. Does something stand out as a quality that you need to have present in your life but don't? Plan a course of action to pray and ask God's Holy Spirit to teach you this quality.

7. The church of Corinth needed radical surgery to get the church back on track. Sometimes God wants to do radical surgery in our lives. Have you had a "radical surgery" experience? Almost everyone has at least one. Take a moment and reflect what God taught you through the experience and how you grew in your faith.

8. The church at Corinth was following a specific leader instead of simply Christ. (1 Corinthians 3) Is it easy sometimes in large (or small) churches to follow the pastor and not Christ? Take a moment to check your own beliefs in this area.

9. Balance is the critical element when it involves exercising our Christian liberty. The Corinthians were out of balance in this area. Paul's highest priority was to preach the Good News and win people to Christ. Is this your highest aim with your Christian freedom? If not, make some attitude adjustments.

10. Reread the love chapter (1 Corinthians 13). Does love permeate your life? If not, ask God to fill your life with love for others through the power of the Holy Spirit. Do something deliberate today to show others in your sphere of contact that you love them.

Paul's Letters to the Churches: Part Two

CHAPTER SUMMARY

LESSON PLAN:

In this hour, you will learn about …

- Paul's letters written in prison to the Ephesians, Philippians, Colossians, and Philemon.
- Paul's mentoring to a younger man through the letters of 1 and 2 Timothy.

The Apostle Paul lived with passion. In his younger years, he persecuted Christians with the infatuation of a zealot, then later defended Jesus Christ with every fiber of his being. When it came to Paul, it was impossible for anyone to be neutral in their opinions. Especially the Jewish leaders who believed Paul was a traitor.

From the accounts recorded in Acts and the summary in 2 Corinthians 11, it's clear that Paul was frequently imprisoned for his faith. Some of these incarcerations were brief, like his overnight stay in the Philippian cell with his colleague Silas. Other times Paul was imprisoned for a longer period, up to two years in Rome under house arrest.

PRISON LETTERS

During these involuntary confinements, Paul wrote four letters: Philippians, Colossians, Ephesians, and the brief note to Philemon. Also in this hour, you'll study the two letters that Paul wrote to the young man he was mentoring, Timothy.

Modern-day prisons are sophisticated, with automatic locks, toilets, and even access to color television sets. That scene is a far cry from the place where Paul wrote his letters to encourage the believers. He wrote with poor light from a dark, vermin-infested, putrid-smelling prison cell. Paul wrote under the inspiration of the Holy Spirit, and he used his poor conditions to affirm his faith and belief in the presence of the Holy Spirit who was his constant companion.

LETTER TO THE PHILIPPIANS

Throughout church history, the letter to the church at Philippi has been called the Epistle of Joy. Sixteen times Paul encourages the Philippian believers to participate in the joy he is experiencing over his salvation. Remember where Paul is writing: in a dark prison cell.

CULTURAL FACT

Philippi is a city of Macedonia (northern Greece) located about 10 miles inland from Neapolis on the Aegean Sea. The original settlement was called Krenides, but in 356 B.C. Philip, King of Macedonia, changed the name when he enlarged the city with many new inhabitants and considerable construction. The first emperor of Rome, Augustus, made Philippi a Roman colony, which gave the city many advantages over most other cities in the Roman Empire. Its citizens had an autonomous government, were immune from tribute, and were treated the same as if they actually lived in Italy.

Certainly we are to weep with those who weep, and it's natural to be sorrowful about our sin and the graphic effects of sinfulness around us. The stance of joy is to be constantly in a Christian's life, according to Paul:

Rejoice in the Lord always. I will say it again: Rejoice! Let your gentleness be evident to all. The Lord is near. Do not be anxious about anything, but in everything, by prayer and petition, with thanksgiving, present your requests to God. And the peace of God, which transcends all understanding, will guard your hearts and your minds in Christ Jesus. (Philippians 4:4–7)

Because Paul was unable to be with the Christians in Philippi at the present time, he reminded them that this was all right. Their salvation and growth as believers were not up to him.

"Therefore, my dear friends, as you have always obeyed—not only in my presence, but now much more in my absence—continue to work out your salvation with fear and trembling, for it is God who works in you to will and to act according to his good purpose." (Philippians 2:12–13)

Paul was saying to his friends in Philippi, "God is working in your lives. Go for the spiritual life with all your passion." Just as faith is a gift as well as God's grace, God's work in our lives begins with his transformation of our desires. Then the Lord grants us his power to implement those re-created desires. The gift of faith, then the gift of grace; the fulfillment of his will through the reformation of our desires, then the empowerment to achieve it. This progression represents God's perfect synergies.

As Paul sat in his prison cell, he wanted to be released—either through his physical release or his death.

> For I know that through your prayers and the help given by the Spirit of Jesus Christ, what has happened to me will turn out for my deliverance. I eagerly expect and hope that I will in no way be ashamed, but will have sufficient courage so that now as always Christ will be exalted in my body, whether by life or by death.

> For to me, to live is Christ and to die is gain. If I am to go on living in the body, this will mean fruitful labor for me. Yet what shall I choose? I do not know! I am torn between the two: I desire to depart and be with Christ, which is better by far; but it is more necessary for you that I remain in the body. Convinced of this, I know that I will remain, and I will continue with all of you for your progress and joy in the faith, so that through my being with you again your joy in Christ Jesus will overflow on account of me. (Philippians 1:19–26)

Paul faced a dilemma. He wasn't sure which he wanted more: to die and live with Christ, which would end his suffering, or to stay on earth and continue the life of faith, supporting, encouraging, and ministering to the people in his life. It's critical to understand that Paul was not contending life is evil. "To live is Christ," sounds like the words from a person who loves life and has significance in his life. But Paul saw eternal life as so much better than life on earth. He could hardly wait.

CULTURAL FACT

"All the saints send you greetings, especially those who belong to Caesar's household." (Philippians 4:22) Most of the early Christians were of the humbler classes. Many of them were slaves. Some of the converts belonged to the emperor's household, whether as slaves or as freedmen, or even as persons of importance.

Also to the church at Philippi, Paul wrote one of the most important comparisons of the deity and the humanity of Christ and our need to follow him. Paul wrote:

Your attitude should be the same as that of Christ Jesus: Who, being in very nature God, did not consider equality with God something to be grasped, but made himself nothing, taking the very nature of a servant, being made in human likeness. And being found in appearance as a man, he humbled himself and became obedient to death—even death on a cross! Therefore God exalted him to the highest place and gave him the name that is above every name, that at the name of Jesus every knee should bow, in heaven and on earth and under the earth, and every tongue confess that Jesus Christ is Lord, to the glory of God the Father. (Philippians 2:5–11)

These verses tackle an ancient question: "When Jesus became human, what did he lose?" In the early Church, some heretics wanted to teach that Jesus lost his deity. In reality, Jesus didn't lose anything in the Incarnation (or coming to earth), he gained his humanity. Jesus emptied himself not of his God nature but of his rights, his prerogatives, and his dignity. These verses are a clarion call for Christians to take a position of humility as they serve the resurrected Jesus Christ. Also these verses remind us that Jesus set aside his glory when he came to earth. Now God the Father has completely restored Jesus to his rightful place in heaven.

Often, suffering brings a new perspective. Although Paul was sitting on the filthy floor of a dark prison cell, his words were from the heart of a man who was looking over the expanse of life as though he were perched on the top of a lofty tower.

> But whatever was to my profit I now consider loss for the sake of Christ. What is more, I consider everything a loss compared to the surpassing greatness of knowing Christ Jesus my Lord, for whose sake I have lost all things. I consider them rubbish, that I may gain Christ and be found in him, not having a righteousness of my own that comes from the law, but that which is through faith in Christ—the righteousness that comes from God and is by faith.

> I want to know Christ and the power of his resurrection and the fellowship of sharing in his sufferings, becoming like him in his death, and so, somehow, to attain to the resurrection from the dead. Not that I have already obtained all this, or have already been made perfect, but I press on to take hold of that for which Christ Jesus took hold of me.

> Brothers, I do not consider myself yet to have taken hold of it. But one thing I do: Forgetting what is behind and straining toward what is ahead, I press on toward the goal to win the prize for which God has called me heavenward in Christ Jesus. (Philippians 3:7–14)

Paul told the Philippian Christians to forget about yesterday, to forget about their past victories and defeats. Instead Christians should focus on pressing forward, regardless of the circumstances. In this short Epistle, Paul gives a course in the value of perspective. For the Apostle Paul, it wasn't enough to run the race that began with a voice and a flash on the road to Damascus— the race had to be finished.

LETTER TO THE COLOSSIANS

Is Jesus Christ the critical connection for life? Writing from prison in Rome, Paul combated false teaching, which had infiltrated the Colossian church. The problem was "syncretism," or the combining of ideas from other philosophies and religions (such as paganism, strains of Judaism, and Greek thought) with Christian truth. The resulting heresy later became known as Gnosticism, which emphasized a special knowledge (*gnosis* in Greek) and denying Christ as God and Savior. To counter this error, Paul wrote the letter to the Colosse church, which stressed Christ's deity—his connection with the Father—and his sacrificial death on the cross for sin. Only by being connected with Christ through faith can anyone have eternal life, and only through a continuing connection with Jesus can anyone have power for living. Christ is God incarnate and the only way to forgiveness and peace with God the Father. Also, Paul emphasized believers' connections with each other as Christ's body on earth.

CULTURAL FACT

Colosse is an ancient city in Phrygia (in modern Turkey) situated about 110 miles inland of Ephesus and about 10 miles up the Lycus Valley from Laodicea. Colosse stood on the most important trade route from Ephesus to the Euphrates and was a place of great importance from early times. But when Laodicea was founded a short distance away, traffic was rerouted through the new city, leaving Colosse to decline in social and commercial importance. In Paul's day, it was only an insignificant market town. The site is now uninhabited.

According to the Gnostics, Jesus could not be the Incarnate God; they claimed he was only spirit, a type of archangel. They imagined a host of deities that functioned as intercessors between mortals and God, and Jesus was simply one among these.

As Paul dealt with this heresy, he had to show that Jesus was superior to all angels. Colossians illuminates Jesus as the cosmic Christ. Not only was Jesus the Redeemer, he was the eternal Word (John 1:1) and the very brightness of the glory of God (Hebrews 1:3). Jesus is the Lord of the Universe, the King over all creation.

He is the image of the invisible God, the firstborn over all creation. For by him all things were created: things in heaven and on earth, visible and invisible, whether thrones or powers or rulers or authorities; all things were created by him and for him. He is before all things, and in him all things hold together. (Colossians 1:15–17)

Jesus didn't make his first appearance in a manger in Bethlehem. He was a full participant in Creation. The universe was made by him, through him, and for him. The Christ of the Bible is grander than we could ever imagine. The Church—the body of Christ—is the continuing work of Jesus Christ in the world, and if we are doing his work, worshiping the cosmic Christ instead of the Christ who was created by consumerism and our materialistic society, we will participate in his victory by means of his suffering. It's a promise from God's Word.

Finally in this letter, Paul turns his attention to the practical consideration from the resurrection of Jesus in our lives. Because our eternal destiny is sure, heaven should fill our thoughts.

Since, then, you have been raised with Christ, set your hearts on things above, where Christ is seated at the right hand of God. Set your minds on things above, not on earthly things. For you died, and your life is now hidden with Christ in God. When Christ, who is your life, appears, then you also will appear with him in glory. (Colossians 3:1–4)

Also Paul exhorts the Colosse church that sexual immorality should not be named among us (Colossians 3:5–8) and truth, love, and peace should mark our lives. (Colossians 3:9–15) Our love for Christ should translate into love for others—friends, fellow believers, spouses, children, parents, slaves, and masters. (Colossians 3:16–4:1) Paul closes this letter with some strong words about prayer and telling others about Jesus:

Devote yourselves to prayer, being watchful and thankful. And pray for us, too, that God may open a door for our message, so that we may proclaim the mystery of Christ, for which I am in chains. Pray that I may proclaim it clearly, as I should. Be wise in the way you act toward outsiders; make the most of every opportunity. Let your conversation be always full of grace, seasoned with salt, so that you may know how to answer everyone. (Colossians 4:2–6)

Paul concludes that in Christ, the Christian has everything needed for salvation and to live the Christian life.

JUST A MINUTE

One of the most prominent Gentile churches Paul established was at Ephesus. The church was established in A.D. 53, during Paul's homeward journey to Jerusalem. A year later, on Paul's third missionary journey, he returned to Ephesus and stayed for three years preaching and teaching with great effectiveness. (Acts 19:1–20) At another time, Paul met with the Ephesian elders and sent Timothy to serve as their leader. (1 Timothy 1:3) A few years later, as a prisoner in Rome, Paul wrote the Epistle to the Ephesians.

LETTER TO THE EPHESIANS

While Paul was a prisoner in Rome, several messengers from various churches visited him, including Tychicus from Ephesus. The Apostle Paul wrote a powerful letter to the church at Ephesus and sent it with Tychicus. Unlike his other letters, Paul doesn't mention any specific individuals even though he knew many people in the city. Some scholars believe the omission was on purpose so the letter could be passed around to other churches.

CULTURAL FACT

Ephesus was a proud, rich, busy port at the end of the caravan route from Asia. From Ephesus, goods were shipped to other Mediterranean ports. This huge city contained a theater that seated about 25,000, a town square that also served as the marketplace of goods and ideas, public baths, a library, and a number of temples. Ephesus was built near the shrine of an old Anatolian fertility goddess and became the center of her cult; this deity was known to the Greeks as Artemis and to the Romans as Diana. (Acts 19:29)

The Epistle to the Ephesians doesn't address a specific problem or counteract a heresy. Instead, it's a recipe for godly living, with two key aspects to the book. First, in the area of theology, Ephesians is as powerful as Paul's writing in Romans. God's design in sending his son Jesus is concisely summarized:

In [Jesus] we have redemption through his blood, the forgiveness of sins, in accordance with the riches of God's grace that he lavished on us with all wisdom and understanding. And he made known to us the mystery of his will according to his good pleasure, which he purposed in Christ, to be put into effect when the times will have reached their fulfillment—to bring all things in heaven and on earth together under one head, even Christ.

In him we were also chosen, having been predestined according to the plan of him who works out everything in conformity with the purpose of his will, in order that we, who were the first to hope in Christ, might be for the praise of his glory. (Ephesians 1:7–12)

The second key aspect of Ephesians is practical. How is faith lived out in a person's life and family and among fellow believers? Paul concludes his letter to the Ephesians with one of the most powerful descriptions of Satan's strategy and our best defense against it. Through his writing, Paul makes theology come to life in an extremely practical manner.

Finally, be strong in the Lord and in his mighty power. Put on the full armor of God so that you can take your stand against the devil's schemes. For our struggle is not against flesh and blood, but against the rulers, against the authorities, against the powers of this dark world and against the spiritual forces of evil in the heavenly realms.

Therefore put on the full armor of God, so that when the day of evil comes, you may be able to stand your ground, and after you have done everything, to stand. Stand firm then, with the belt of truth buckled around your waist, with the breastplate of righteousness in place, and with your feet fitted with the readiness that comes from the gospel of peace.

In addition to all this, take up the shield of faith, with which you can extinguish all the flaming arrows of the evil one. Take the helmet of salvation and the sword of the Spirit, which is the word of God. And pray in the Spirit on all occasions with all kinds of prayers and requests.

With this in mind, be alert and always keep on praying for all the saints. Pray also for me, that whenever I open my mouth, words may be given me so that I will fearlessly make known the mystery of the gospel, for which I am an ambassador in chains. Pray that I may declare it fearlessly, as I should. (Ephesians 6:10–20)

The Apostle Paul knew the schemes of the devil, yet through his willingness to constantly follow Jesus Christ, he was prepared to stand firm against Satan. In his closing words, Paul shows he was not ashamed to ask other believers to pray for courage to be an ambassador for Christ. Even as a prisoner in chains, Paul wanted to faithfully proclaim the Good News about Jesus Christ.

LETTER TO PHILEMON

The short letter of Philemon was written to a believer named Philemon while Paul was in prison. Under Roman law, a slave who ran away from his master could face the death penalty. In spite of this possibility, the Apostle Paul sent Onesimus, a runaway slave and a recent convert to Christianity, back to his owner Philemon to make restitution. The Epistle to Philemon is Paul's plea that Onesimus no longer be viewed as a runaway slave, but rather a "beloved brother." (Philemon 16–17) When Philemon obeyed these requests, it would require forgiveness and restoration—actions that no other slave owner would have to consider in the ancient world.

JUST A MINUTE

The greeting and content of Philemon indicate that Philemon was the intended recipient. Philemon was a slave owner whose home served as the meeting place for a local church. Philemon probably lived in Colosse, a city in the Roman province of Asia Minor. He was converted to Christianity as a result of Paul's ministry, possibly during the Apostle's stay in Ephesus. (Acts 19:26) Apphia was probably his wife, and Archippus may have been his son, possibly serving at this time as the pastor of the church that met in Philemon's home. (Colossians 4:17) The New Testament doesn't reveal what happened to the slave Onesimus. Some have taken him to be the Onesimus who eventually became the bishop of Ephesus, mentioned by Ignatius in the early second century.

The Epistle of Philemon was not written to teach doctrine or refute theological error. However, Paul weaves the concepts of salvation, substitution, and redemption into this short letter. While these ideas speak of Paul's relationship with Onesimus, they remind the Christians of their relationship with Christ. As unbelievers, they were slaves to sin but Christ has redeemed the Christians from the awful fate of death. This letter is an earnest plea for Christian love to confront the cruelty and hatred embodied in the cultural institutions of that day. Paul offers to pay Onesimus's debt. (Philemon 19) The Apostle's love for Onesimus went beyond mere words, and he was willing to give out of his own poverty to guarantee this slave's well-being.

Although brief, this letter from prison is packed with strong, practical reminders of how Christian love is practiced. It's a revealing glimpse into the heart of Paul.

MENTORING: 1 AND 2 TIMOTHY

For teachers, one of the most difficult portions of their job is to let students go, graduate, and then make their own way in the world. You can sense this type of anxiety in Paul's letters to Timothy. He affectionately calls Timothy "a true son" (1 Timothy 1:2) and charges him again and again to remain faithful to what Paul taught him (1 Timothy 1:18; 5:12–16, 21; 6:11–13). The first Epistle ends with Paul's heartfelt cry: "Timothy, guard what has been entrusted to your care." (1 Timothy 6:20) Timothy had accompanied Paul for years (Acts 16:1–3, 17:10, 20:4), assisting him and acting as his liaison to a number of churches. Paul had not only taught Timothy the essentials of the Christian faith, he modeled Christian leadership to him. Now Paul was leaving Timothy in charge of the church at Ephesus. From

Macedonia, Paul wrote to encourage his "son" in the faith. In effect, the first Epistle is Paul's commission to Timothy, his orders from a concerned teacher, the Apostle Paul.

PEOPLE TO KNOW

> Timothy was a native of Lystra. (Acts 16:1) His mother was Jewish and his father was Greek. His mother's name was Eunice, and his grandmother was Lois. (2 Timothy 1:5) He was Paul's convert (1 Timothy 1:2) and joined Paul on his second missionary journey, about A.D. 51. (Acts 16:3)

Other than Jesus instructing his disciples, these two Epistles are the best examples in the New Testament for mentoring—where an older, more experienced teacher passes on his instruction to a younger man. The relationship between Paul and Timothy stands out because of its depth of passion. In the final words of his second Epistle, Paul delivered some of his most passionate expressions of love and encouragement from the Apostle's writings:

You then, my son, be strong in the grace that is in Christ Jesus. And the things you have heard me say in the presence of many witnesses entrust to reliable men who will also be qualified to teach others. Endure hardship with us like a good soldier of Christ Jesus. (2 Timothy 2:1–3)

As mentioned earlier about the Apostle Paul, he was a task theologian. With these two Epistles to Timothy, he is focused on the problem of false doctrine and especially within the confines of the church. In today's church, a great deal of emphasis is placed on relationships and sometimes at the expense of doctrine. This distinction between relationships and doctrine would have been completely foreign to the Apostle Paul. He understood that right doctrine led to healthy relationships. The first line of protection against false doctrine was a right-thinking church. Paul understood that the secret to an effective church fell on the shoulders of the leadership. In his letter to Timothy, Paul addressed the qualifications, requirements, and duties of church leaders. First the bishop or elder:

Here is a trustworthy saying: If anyone sets his heart on being an overseer, he desires a noble task. Now the overseer must be above reproach, the husband of but one wife, temperate, self-controlled, respectable, hospitable, able to teach, not given to drunkenness, not violent but gentle, not quarrelsome, not a lover of money.

He must manage his own family well and see that his children obey him with proper respect. (If anyone does not know how to manage his own family, how can he take care of God's church?) He must not be a recent convert, or he may become conceited and fall under the same judgment as the devil. He must also have a good reputation with outsiders, so that he will not fall into disgrace and into the devil's trap. (1 Timothy 3:1–7)

Many people who read this list of qualifications have decided that anyone holding the office of bishop or elder must be completely deceived or living the life of a hypocrite. Who would ever qualify to be blameless? Some scholars believe this list characterizes idealized traits not for the sake of an exact match but to demonstrate the type of person for this office and the sobriety of it. Because of this list of qualifications, anyone appointed a bishop or elder must fully understand their need for God's grace to adequately fulfill this assignment.

CULTURAL FACT

During the period of Paul, there were no church buildings for worship. These houses of worship were not built until 200 years after the days of Paul. Church buildings didn't come into general use until Constantine put an end to the persecution of Christians. In Paul's day, churches met mostly in the homes of the Christians. Thousands of Christians in and around Ephesus met in small groups in various homes. Each congregation had its own pastoral leadership.

Also Paul spelled out the qualifications of a deacon:

Deacons, likewise, are to be men worthy of respect, sincere, not indulging in much wine, and not pursuing dishonest gain. They must keep hold of the deep truths of the faith with a clear conscience. They must first be tested; and then if there is nothing against them, let them serve as deacons.

In the same way, their wives are to be women worthy of respect, not malicious talkers but temperate and trustworthy in everything. A deacon must be the husband of but one wife and must manage his children and his household well. Those who have served well gain an excellent standing and great assurance in their faith in Christ Jesus. (1 Timothy 3:8–13)

Like the list of qualifications for bishop/elder, this list also has many of the same qualities. The key phrase is "nothing against them" or some translations say, "blameless." These qualities are not simply something for the first-century church. They are relevant for today. The church needs mature, capable, and trained people who have their own families in order to take positions of leadership in God's house. The responsibility for governing the church can't fall on the shoulders of a single individual. To impact a community, the leadership must be portioned out to qualified and committed people.

2 TIMOTHY: PASSING THE BATON OF FAITH

When the Apostle Paul wrote this letter, he must have had a sense that it would be among his last writings. In some ways, this Epistle reads like Paul's last will and testament. He writes "good-bye" to his protégé, a message filled with encouragement, tenderness, affection, and kindhearted warnings.

I thank God, whom I serve, as my forefathers did, with a clear conscience, as night and day I constantly remember you in my prayers. Recalling your tears, I long to see you, so that I may be filled with joy. I have been reminded of your sincere faith. ... For this reason I remind you to fan into flame the gift of God, which is in you through the laying on of my hands. For God did not give us a spirit of timidity, but a spirit of power, of love and of self-discipline. (2 Timothy 1:3–5a, 6–7)

After these words of encouragement, Paul warns Timothy and the others in the leadership to crack down on the corruption that was sweeping the church:

But mark this: There will be terrible times in the last days. People will be lovers of themselves, lovers of money, boastful, proud, abusive, disobedient to their parents, ungrateful, unholy, without love, unforgiving, slanderous, without self-control, brutal, not lovers of the good, treacherous, rash, conceited, lovers of pleasure rather than lovers of God—having a form of godliness but denying its power. Have nothing to do with them. (2 Timothy 3:1–5)

Look at the terrible qualities of these people that Paul was describing like some sort of godless savages, and then recall these were people in the church. The Apostle Paul was exhorting Timothy to have these individuals either change their ways or get out of the church because of their influence. If people were unwilling to change and submit to the power of the Holy Spirit, Paul told Timothy to have them removed from the church.

In today's culture, there are many discussions over how much the early church should appear in contemporary culture. Issues like musical style and formats for worship have been disputed. Paul exhorts Timothy about the critical elements in the church and confidently uses his own example as the model:

You, however, know all about my teaching, my way of life, my purpose, faith, patience, love, endurance, persecutions, sufferings—what kinds of things happened to me in Antioch, Iconium and Lystra, the persecutions I endured. Yet the Lord rescued me from all of them.

In fact, everyone who wants to live a godly life in Christ Jesus will be persecuted, while evil men and impostors will go from bad to worse, deceiving and being deceived. But as for you, continue in what you have learned and have become convinced of, because you know those from whom you learned it, and how from infancy you have known the holy Scriptures, which are able to make you wise for salvation through faith in Christ Jesus. (2 Timothy 3:10–15)

JUST A MINUTE

"Inspiration of God." The Greek word means "God-breathed," from *theos* ("God") and *pneo* ("to breathe"). Although it is difficult to fully re-create the thought of this Greek expression in English, scholars are certain that Paul meant to say that all Scripture was breathed from God. This is the primary meaning. God not only inspired the authors who wrote the words of the Bible, but he also illuminates those who read it with a heart of faith.

Believers, according to Paul, are to preserve everything delivered them in the Bible. The apostolic tradition is to live a life that is rich enough to deserve persecution, and then when persecuted, to bear it without failure. Then Paul delivers to Timothy some of the most pointed words in the Bible about the truth and importance of Scripture:

All Scripture is God-breathed and is useful for teaching, rebuking, correcting and training in righteousness, so that the man of God may be thoroughly equipped for every good work. (2 Timothy 3:16–17)

The issue of the accuracy of the Scriptures has become divisive among believers. Yet the Bible itself in these verses claims to be accurate and inspired by the Holy Spirit. Every word in the Bible can be trusted to help the reader draw the distinction between truth and fiction. If the Bible is faulty and not error-free, what does it say about the character of God? If a Christian begins to doubt the accuracy of the Bible, then where does the slippery slope end? Paul warns Timothy to avoid this philosophical step.

Finally Paul tells Timothy good-bye and summarizes his life and calling:

I have fought the good fight, I have finished the race, I have kept the faith. Now there is in store for me the crown of righteousness, which the Lord, the righteous Judge, will award to me on that day—and not only to me, but also to all who have longed for his appearing. (2 Timothy 4:7–8)

The early church history recounts shortly after Paul wrote these words to Timothy, the sword of Nero fell on Paul's neck. Because he passed the baton to his student, this powerful apostle had run the race and fallen exhausted into the arms of Jesus Christ. Now Timothy and other leaders after him carry on this tradition of godly leadership in the church.

Hour's Up!

The Apostle Paul spent the last years of his life capturing his accumulated wisdom into a series of Epistles that he wrote in prison. During this hour, you've examined the key points in these letters. Yet how do they apply to your life? Let's see how Paul's teaching applies to everyday life:

1. Paul lived with passion about his faith and his relationship to Christ. Take a moment and consider your faith relationship. Is it passionate and ever-growing or stagnant? What steps can you take to turn up the passion about your spiritual life? (Increased prayer, Bible reading, more time in a local church, listening to Bible instruction tapes, meeting one on one with an older Christian, and so on.) Take an active step to become passionate about your faith.

2. Sixteen times in the Epistle to the Philippians, Paul exhorts the believers to rejoice or participate in the joy that he is experiencing. How much joy fills your life? Meditate on Paul's situation in a dark prison then contrasted with his joy. The emotion didn't spring from his conditions but from a relationship. Focus today on joy and the decision to rejoice in every situation. How will your day be different because of this choice?

3. Without a doubt, even in chains, Paul knew that God was working in his life. (Philippians 2:12–13) Consider your life. How is God working in your daily life? Become more aware of God's intervention in your daily life and talk about it with a family member or a friend.

4. In his life, Paul struck a balance between longing for heaven and being conscious of the good he was doing while on earth. How balanced is your life in this area? Some people are too heavenly minded to be earthly good or are always focused on the eternal, whereas others don't think about heaven at all. Make some effort today to be balanced in your consideration of heaven, yet willing to tell others about Christ.

5. Paul was neither focused on the past or the future, but celebrated the present and his desire to press on toward the goal to which God had called him. Are you stuck in the past or constantly dreaming about the future? How can you focus on what's in front of you and not be caught in this emotional trap?

6. Turn to Paul's prayer for the Colossians (4:2–6). Take the verses and read them aloud, personalizing them for your life. "Lord, I pray that I may proclaim the Gospel and proclaim it clearly. I ask you to help me be wise in the way I act toward outsiders and make the most of every opportunity."

7. Reread Paul's words about the armor of God in Ephesians 6:10–20. Make a mental picture of yourself and put on each of the different pieces of armor to protect your life against the schemes of the devil. Make a note card or something to remind you throughout the day how the Lord of the Universe is protecting and guarding your life.

8. The little Epistle of Philemon gives us a reminder of our need to forgive and love others and restore our relationship with others. It's not an easy step but one that we can do not in our own power but in the power of Christ in our lives. Are you struggling with a personal relationship? How can you take action to follow the example of Philemon to forgive and restore it?

9. As he sat in prison, Paul knew well what it was to "endure hardship like a good soldier of Jesus Christ." (2 Timothy 2:3) How are you enduring hardship and faithfully growing in your relationship with Christ?

10. With strong words, Paul wrote Timothy about the accuracy and truth of the Bible. (2 Timothy 3:16–17) Where do you stand in your belief in the accuracy of the Bible? If you take some of it and not all of it, which parts? Do you see the danger of only taking parts of it? Pause in prayer and celebrate with God the preservation of the Bible and how we have the Scriptures for teaching, rebuking, correcting, and training in righteousness.

HOUR 23

Hebrews and the General Epistles

CHAPTER SUMMARY

LESSON PLAN:
In this hour, you'll learn about ...

- Christ the mediator of a new covenant in the letter to the Hebrews.

- Practical instruction in the Christian life in the letter from James.

- Encouragement to the persecuted church and a prediction about church heresy in the letters from the Apostle Peter.

Over the last two hours, we've studied the letters of the Apostle Paul. In this hour, we're moving into some of the letters from Paul's associates. Some of the content of these Epistles will be familiar but they also contain some new ideas and perspectives.

Hebrews is a goldmine of instruction and brings together the themes from the entire Bible—unlike any other book in Scripture. The Old Testament and New Testament are integrated into a singular message. The literary style, form, and structure are unlike any other book. The author of the book remains a mystery. Scholars speculate it might have been Paul, Barnabas, Apollos, Luke, Philip, or even Priscilla. Without a major archaeological discovery, no one will ever know exactly who wrote this book.

This Epistle emphasizes the supremacy of Jesus Christ over all things. The writer paints a portrait of Christ as exalted, glorified, and lifted up as "better than" any other figure in history. Here's how the writer describes this supremacy of Christ:

In the past God spoke to our forefathers through the prophets at many times and in various ways, but in these last days he has spoken to us by his Son, whom he appointed heir of all things, and through whom he made the universe. The Son is the radiance of God's glory and the exact representation of his being, sustaining all things by his powerful word. After he had provided purification for sins, he sat down at the right hand of the Majesty in heaven. So he became as much superior to the angels as the name he has inherited is superior to theirs. (Hebrews 1:1–4)

JUST A MINUTE

In the King James Version, the Book of Hebrews is called "The Epistle of Paul to the Hebrews." Later Bible translations simply call it "The Epistle to the Hebrews," because the oldest manuscripts, discovered since the King James translation, do not name the author. The Eastern church accepted from the beginning that the Apostle Paul wrote this letter. Not until the fourth century did the Western church accept it as the work of Paul. The church fathers were not unanimous in their opinion. Eusebius and Origen considered Paul the author, Tertullian called it the Epistle of Barnabas, and Clement of Alexandria thought that Paul wrote it in Hebrew and that Luke translated it into Greek (it is written in excellent Greek). Later, Martin Luther guessed it was Apollos, an opinion for which there is no ancient evidence but some possible indirect support. Other possible authors include Priscilla and Aquila, as well as Clement of Rome, one of the early church fathers. Regardless who was the author, as a literary work, Hebrews is superb: orderly and logical.

God has spoken from Genesis to Revelation "in various ways." The writer calls Jesus "the radiance of God's glory." Throughout Scripture, God has carefully revealed his glory; not because he's stingy, but because if God revealed his glory humankind could not bear the awesome intensity. In these verses, God's son is called the radiance of God's holiness. His perfection is beyond our comprehension. The author of Hebrews wanted his readers to understand the magnitude of the person of Christ.

THE OLD COVENANT VS. THE NEW COVENANT

The author of Hebrews was writing to discouraged Jewish Christians who had survived extinction under Roman persecution. In the early portion of the book, he contrasts the old covenant with the new covenant and makes it clear the Old Testament is good but the New Testament is better. The old covenant foreshadowed the full expression of God's redemptive will but it should not be seen as a failure. The old law was fulfilled and therefore replaced, through the birth, life, death, and resurrection of Jesus Christ.

Jesus is shown to be "better than" Moses, who mediated the old covenant:

> ... just as Moses was faithful in all God's house. Jesus has been found worthy of greater honor than Moses, just as the builder of a house has greater honor than the house itself. For every house is built by someone, but God is the builder of everything. Moses was faithful as a servant in all God's house, testifying to what would be said in the future.

> But Christ is faithful as a son over God's house. And we are his house, if we hold on to our courage and the hope of which we boast. (Hebrews 3:2b–6)

Notice how the writer of this Epistle didn't mince any words. It must have been difficult information for any Jew to hear. Moses was the servant of the house but God was the builder and Jesus Christ was the head. The tone of these words is similar to the conversation that Moses had with God at the burning bush in the Midian desert. As Moses was reluctant to go and speak with Pharaoh, God said, "Who made your mouth?" Or God's fiery response to the complaints of Job, "Where were you when I laid the foundations of the earth?" While the Jewish forefathers or patriarchs were significant, Jesus Christ was better. No more discussion.

Jesus was also better than the priesthood. The readers of this book must have asked, "How can anyone be better than the high priest?" Each year on the Day of Atonement, the high priest sacrificed as the people's representative, yet this sacrifice was temporary and had to be repeated. Jesus Christ was better because his atonement was permanent. The animal sacrifices in the Old Testament were symbolic and important because of what they signified and not on their own merit. The sacrificial death of Jesus confirmed his superiority. Jesus is a perfect High Priest who offered the superior sacrifice once for all.

JUST A MINUTE

The Levitical priests offered sacrifices year in and year out. Christ died once for all. Their sacrifices were unavailing. Jesus' sacrifice removed sin forever. *Eternal* is one of the favorite words in this letter: eternal salvation (Hebrews 5:9), eternal judgment (Hebrews 6:2), eternal redemption (Hebrews 9:12), eternal Spirit (Hebrews 9:14), eternal inheritance (Hebrews 9:15), eternal covenant (Hebrews 13:20).

PRIEST OF MELCHIZEDEK

The Jewish people who were reading this Epistle for the first time likely paused and asked a technical question, "All of the priests are to come from the tribe of Levi. How could Jesus be a priest even though he didn't come from Levi?"

The people knew Jesus was born into the tribe of the kings, Judah, and was a descendant of David. He wasn't from the priestly tribe of Levi. Using the same technique that the Apostle Paul used in his letters, the writer of Hebrews raises an important question, then answers it. He introduces the reader to the ancient character of Melchizedek, an ancestor of Abraham. While this explanation may seem odd, it made a convincing argument with the Jewish reader.

The writer called Jesus "a high priest forever, in the order of Melchizedek." (Hebrews 5:10, 6:20) Abraham paid tribute to Melchizedek who served as his priest. (Genesis 14) Before the Law was established through Moses, Melchizedek was a priest for God. Under the Law, the priests had to come from the tribe of Levi but Melchizedek predated the tribes. While Jesus Christ wasn't from the tribe of Levi (he was from Judah), he nevertheless fulfilled the role of high priest, "Unlike the other high priests, he does not need to offer sacrifices day after day, first for his own sins, and then for the sins of the people. He sacrificed for their sins once for all when he offered himself." (Hebrews 7:27)

Through Jesus Christ, God was establishing a new covenant with his people:

But the ministry Jesus has received is as superior to theirs as the covenant of which he is mediator is superior to the old one, and it is founded on better promises. For if there had been nothing wrong with that first covenant, no place would have been sought for another.

But God found fault with the people and said: "The time is coming, declares the Lord, when I will make a new covenant with the house of Israel and with the house of Judah. It will not be like the covenant I made with their forefathers when I took them by the hand to lead them out of Egypt, because they did not remain faithful to my covenant, and I turned away from them, declares the Lord.

This is the covenant I will make with the house of Israel after that time, declares the Lord. I will put my laws in their minds and write them on their hearts. I will be their God, and they will be my people. No longer will a man teach his neighbor, or a man his brother, saying, 'Know the Lord,' because they will all know me, from the least of them to the greatest. For I will forgive their wickedness and will remember their sins no more."

By calling this covenant "new," he has made the first one obsolete; and what is obsolete and aging will soon disappear. (Hebrews 8:6–13)

JUST A MINUTE

Christ brought humanity to a new covenant. The first covenant, which centered on the Ten Commandments and tabernacle services, had served its purpose. (Hebrews 9:1–5) Its laws had been inscribed on stone tablets (Hebrews 9:4), whereas Christ's laws would be written on the believers' hearts (Hebrews 8:10). *Better* is another favorite word for this Epistle: better hope (Hebrews 7:19); better covenant (Hebrews 8:6 KJV; NIV, superior); better promises (Hebrews 8:6); better possessions in heaven (Hebrews 10:34); better country—heaven, not Canaan (Hebrews 11:16); better resurrection—never to die again (Hebrews 11:35).

Under the old covenant, only the high priest could enter the Most Holy Place, and then only once a year after making a blood sacrifice for his own sins and then the sins of the people. The writer of Hebrews doesn't downplay the importance of the Law. Instead, he says the Law was "only a shadow of the good things that are coming." (Hebrews 10:1) While the priest offered animal sacrifices as an annual reminder of sins (Hebrews 10:3), "it is impossible for the blood of bulls and goats to take away sins." (Hebrews 10:4) Because of the blood of Jesus Christ, his sacrifice was "once for all" (Hebrews 9:12, 26) and he was a superior high priest.

For Christians, the difference between the old covenant and the new covenant involves accessibility to God. If the sins of believers no longer separate them from a holy God, the relationship between God and the people can become much stronger. The author of Hebrews gives a number of challenges for Christians:

Let us draw near to God with a sincere heart in full assurance of faith, having our hearts sprinkled to cleanse us from a guilty conscience and having our bodies washed with pure water. Let us hold unswervingly to the hope we profess, for he who promised is faithful. And let us consider how we may spur one another on toward love and good deeds. Let us not give up meeting together, as some are in the habit of doing, but let us encourage one another— and all the more as you see the Day approaching. (Hebrews 10:22–25)

The writer challenges Christians to draw near to God, hold fast to faith, consider how to encourage others, and finally to consistently meet together. Then the writer turns and warns that this method of forgiveness for sins is the only option. God continues as the judge: "For we know him who said, 'It is mine to avenge; I will repay,' and again, 'The Lord will judge his people.' It is a dreadful thing to fall into the hands of the living God." (Hebrews 10:30–31) The words are quite sobering. If God judged people from the Old Testament times with limited knowledge of God, how much more will the Lord judge those who have so much information about salvation? The writer was comfortable admonishing his readers in the New Testament days; they had much greater access to information concerning sin and redemption than did their ancestors. You can imagine all the more how strong his words would be for today's world.

THE HALL OF FAITH

In one of the final chapters of this Epistle, the writer provides a tour of the Hall of Faith.

"Now faith is being sure of what we hope for and certain of what we do not see. This is what the ancients were commended for. By faith we understand that the universe was formed at God's command, so that what is seen was not made out of what was visible." (Hebrews 11:1–3)

Faith is defined as tangible substance in place of invisible hope or evidence instead of "things not seen." Just in case the readers believed their faith in Jesus Christ meant the faithful lives of the people in the Old Testament were inconsequential, the writer takes the reader on a walk down the corridor of time, past the portraits of the saints. The faith of the Patriarchs was followed by their obedience. Centuries before the arrival of Jesus Christ, their faith in the Lord God was counted to them as righteousness.

Hebrews 11 mentions a number of Old Testament men and women whose faith is legendary, and who are worthy of recognition as heroes of faith. Here are some of these people:

Abel's faith	He offered the first sacrifice for sin made by faith and not works. (v. 4; Genesis 4:1–15)
Enoch's faith	He walked with God, pleased him, and was taken away by him. (vv. 5–6; Genesis 5:22, 24)
Noah's faith	He kept on building the Ark when nobody thought there would be any use for it. (v. 7; Genesis 6:14–22)
Joshua's faith	He made the walls of Jericho fall. (v. 30; Joshua 6:20)
Rahab's faith	She cast her lot with Israel. (v. 31; Joshua 2:9, 6:23)
Jeremiah's faith	He was tortured for his faith. (vv. 32, 35; Jeremiah 20:2)
Elijah's faith	He raised the dead. (vv. 32, 35; 1 Kings 17:17–24)
Elisha's faith	He raised the dead. (vv. 32, 35; 2 Kings 4:8–37)
Isaiah's faith	He was sawed in two for his faith, according to tradition. (vv. 32, 37)

Like entering a polished hallway of history, the writer walks us past the faithful saints who have gone before: Abel, Enoch, Noah, Abraham, Sarah, Isaac, Jacob, Joseph, Moses, Joshua, Rahab, Gideon, Barak, Samson, Jephthah, David, and Samuel. As you near the end of the hallway with portraits, the second-to-last picture is a group portrait. While none of the faces are recognized, the tour guide stuns us with his description of the picture:

Others were tortured and refused to be released, so that they might gain a better resurrection. Some faced jeers and flogging, while still others were chained and put in prison. They were stoned; they were sawed in two; they were put to death by the sword. They went about in sheepskins and goatskins, destitute, persecuted and mistreated—the world was not worthy of them. (Hebrews 11:35b–38a)

No one in this large portrait is named, and yet the author of Hebrews says these saints were spiritual giants. Persecuted, rejected, and forgotten, the enemies of God would not have been worthy to even host these precious heroes of the faith, much less persecute them.

WITNESSES SURROUND US

The final picture in the Hallway of Faith is not a portrait but a mirror to the faith of the reader:

Therefore, since we are surrounded by such a great cloud of witnesses, let us throw off everything that hinders and the sin that so easily entangles, and let us run with perseverance the race marked out for us. Let us fix our eyes on Jesus, the author and perfecter of our faith, who for the joy set before him endured the cross, scorning its shame, and sat down at the right hand of the throne of God. Consider him who endured such opposition from sinful men, so that you will not grow weary and lose heart. (Hebrews 12:1–3)

As Christians look in the mirror, their hearts are filled with a sense of wonder and gratitude. Because of God's mercy in sending Jesus Christ, believers can receive the gift of faith and God's grace.

The writer of Hebrews describes a group of believers who lived in the past and are now cheering the Christians ahead. Their encouraging voices sound above the things that distract and intrude in the life of obedience and following Jesus. Their example of faith gives believers the courage to "throw off everything that hinders" our obedience. The example of their contrition gives believers the strength to confess sin, which has overpowered their lives.

Finally the writer warns that no one knows what is ahead or the course of life's race. Ultimately the task of the Christian is to "fix their eyes on Jesus."

No discipline [the life of obedience to God and the Scriptures] seems pleasant at the time, but painful. Later on, however, it produces a harvest of righteousness and peace for those who have been trained by it. Therefore, strengthen your feeble arms and weak knees. "Make level paths for your feet," so that the lame may not be disabled, but rather healed. Make every effort to live in peace with all men and to be holy; without holiness no one will see the Lord. (Hebrews 12:11–14)

JAMES: A PRACTICAL BOOK

"How-to" books are some of the most popular nonfiction books. They give helpful pointers and illustrations about a particular subject. The Epistle of James is the "how-to" book of the Christian life. It is one of the most practical books in the New Testament because it offers instruction and exhortation to Christians who are experiencing problems. While there is no unifying theme, James addresses practical and ethical concerns.

PEOPLE TO KNOW

James, the half-brother of Jesus, was an unusually good man, and his countrymen called him James the Just. Tradition says he spent so much time on his knees in prayer that they became hard and callused like a camel's knees. He is thought to have been married. (1 Corinthians 9:5) He was influential among the Jews and in the church. James was a very strict Jew himself, yet also the author of the tolerant letter to the Gentile Christians in Acts 15:13–29. He endorsed Paul's work among the Gentiles, but his work was mainly concerned with Jews. His life work was to win Jews to Christ.

While the Epistle is clear that a Jew named James wrote the book, it's unclear which James. Four men are named James in the New Testament: (1) James, the son of Zebedee and brother of John (Matthew 4:21), a disciple and apostle of Christ; (2) James, the son of Alphaeus (Matthew 10:3), called "the less" or "the Younger," also one of the apostles; (3) James, the father of an apostle named Judas (Luke 6:16); and (4) James, the half-brother of Jesus, traditionally called "the Just" (Matthew 13:55). He became the leader of the Jerusalem church (Acts 15:3, Galatians 2:9) and seems to be the most probable author of this Epistle. What makes the book special is that if it was written by James the Just, the son of Mary and Joseph, it was written by a man who knew the Savior in a very intimate way as only a brother would know him. If he was the author, it is noteworthy that he did not mention his relation to Jesus in this letter. Instead his sole claim to authority was his spiritual servanthood to the Lord Jesus Christ. (James 1:1)

JUST A MINUTE

Although scholars don't universally agree, the evidence is strong that the Book of James is one of the oldest books in the New Testament. Because the letter contains no specific reference to time or events that would indicate a particular date, one must consider the Jewish tone of the letter and the letter's accurate reflection of the general situation found in the early apostolic church. Many scholars assign a date somewhere between A.D. 44 and 62. The first date is the time when James became the leader of the Jerusalem church, taking Peter's place after he was released from prison in the year Herod Agrippa I died. (Acts 12:5–23) The second date is the date given by Josephus, the first-century Jewish historian, for the martyrdom of James. In the end, an early date of around A.D. 46 seems reasonable for this letter.

Because this Epistle is specifically addressed to Jewish Christians who are being punished for following Jesus, James begins the letter with one of the most authoritative perspectives on suffering in the Bible:

Consider it pure joy, my brothers, whenever you face trials of many kinds, because you know that the testing of your faith develops perseverance. Perseverance must finish its work so that you may be mature and complete, not lacking anything. (James 1:2–4)

In the eyes of the world, suffering is to be avoided because it is a meaningless interruption and a huge waste of time and energy. Yet in God's economy, suffering is critical to spiritual growth. Because maturity and completion are desirable characteristics for every Christian, suffering is not to be sidestepped but welcomed. In fact, James calls suffering a gift.

Every good and perfect gift is from above, coming down from the Father of the heavenly lights, who does not change like shifting shadows. (James 1:17)

Every person enjoys receiving "good" gifts, which are wrapped in colorful paper and tied with special ribbons. But James tells the reader that the "perfect" gifts (the ones wrapped in suffering, growth, and completeness) are just as precious.

As a Jew, James was well acquainted with the writings of King Solomon. The writings of Solomon are filled with wisdom and warnings to follow wisdom. James asks the question, "But what if I'm only wise enough to know I need more wisdom?"

If any of you lacks wisdom, he should ask God, who gives generously to all without finding fault, and it will be given to him. But when he asks, he must believe and not doubt, because he who doubts is like a wave of the sea, blown and tossed by the wind. That man should not think he will receive anything from the Lord; he is a double-minded man, unstable in all he does. (James 1:5–8)

James challenges the motives of the Christians. He essentially says, "So you want wisdom? Then ask God for it, and really want wisdom. Otherwise don't waste your time or God's."

FAITH OR WORKS?

For centuries, Biblical scholars have debated the supposed conflict between the theologies of James and Paul. James writes about works, and Paul writes about faith. This dichotomy is false. James never contends that doing good deeds will save a man from his sin. However, he does communicate that faith will always reveal itself in a life of good works.

But someone will say, "You have faith; I have deeds." Show me your faith without deeds, and I will show you my faith by what I do. You believe that there is one God. Good! Even the demons believe that—and shudder. You foolish man, do you want evidence that faith without deeds is useless? Was not our ancestor Abraham considered righteous for what he did when he offered his son Isaac on the altar?

You see that his faith and his actions were working together, and his faith was made complete by what he did. And the scripture was fulfilled that says, "Abraham believed God, and it was credited to him as righteousness," and he was called God's friend. You see that a person is justified by what he does and not by faith alone. (James 2:18–24)

Is James contradicting these statements from Paul?

We who are Jews by birth and not "Gentile sinners" know that a man is not justified by observing the law, but by faith in Jesus Christ. So we, too, have put our faith in Christ Jesus that we may be justified by faith in Christ and not by observing the law, because by observing the law no one will be justified. (Galatians 2:15–16)

For it is by grace you have been saved, through faith—and this not from yourselves, it is the gift of God. (Ephesians 2:8)

When James uses the word *justify* it indicates vindication before God and before men. In other words, man is vindicated for his improper behavior in front of others through his good works and not by his faith only. And man is vindicated for his sin in the final judgment by the demonstration of his faith in good works.

In "faith" Paul is talking about the source of our righteousness, but in "works" James is talking about the demonstration of our faith. Consider the two distinct audiences of both men. Paul was writing to Gentiles who were bound in legalism and James was writing to Jewish Christians who believed that through Jesus Christ they had been released from the Law to live without boundaries. Paul's audience needed the freedom of grace and James's audience needed the limitations of obedience. While these two men's messages were different, their thinking was compatible.

CULTURAL FACT

According to the Jewish historian Josephus, and Hegesippus, a Christian historian of the second century, whose narrative Eusebius (another church father) accepts, James died a martyr for Jesus, his brother and his Lord. Shortly before the Roman army destroyed Jerusalem (A.D. 70), Jews were embracing Christianity in large numbers. Ananias, the high priests, the scribes, and the Pharisees assembled the Sanhedrin around the year A.D. 62 and commanded James, "the brother of Jesus who was called Christ," to proclaim from one of the galleries of the temple that Jesus was not the Messiah. Instead, James cried out that Jesus was the Son of God and the Judge of the World. Then his enraged enemies hurled him on the ground and stoned him until a charitable bystander ended his sufferings with a club, while James was on his knees praying, "Father, forgive them, they know not what they do."

BRIDLE THE TONGUE

As the half-brother of Jesus, it's easy to believe James was present when Jesus gave his Sermon on the Mount. (Matthew 5–7) He would have been familiar with Jesus' admonition about spoken words, "Simply let your 'Yes' be 'Yes,' and your 'No,' 'No'; anything beyond this comes from the evil one." (Matthew 5:37) In his Epistle, James repeated Jesus' warning almost word for word. (James 5:12) In addition, James had some important words about the power of speech:

We all stumble in many ways. If anyone is never at fault in what he says, he is a perfect man, able to keep his whole body in check. When we put bits into the mouths of horses to make them obey us, we can turn the whole animal. Or take ships as an example. Although they are so large and are driven by strong winds, they are steered by a very small rudder wherever the pilot wants to go.

Likewise the tongue is a small part of the body, but it makes great boasts. Consider what a great forest is set on fire by a small spark. The tongue also is a fire, a world of evil among the parts of the body. It corrupts the whole person, sets the whole course of his life on fire, and is itself set on fire by hell. All kinds of animals, birds, reptiles and creatures of the sea are being tamed and have been tamed by man, but no man can tame the tongue. It is a restless evil, full of deadly poison. (James 3:2–8)

Some may believe that James is exaggerating with his comparisons about the tongue. The words are not overstated because careless words can destroy a priceless relationship. Also James makes it clear that our speech comes from inside. Polluted words will discharge from a bad heart, and uncontaminated words will flow from a clean heart.

Out of the same mouth come praise and cursing. My brothers, this should not be. Can both fresh water and salt water flow from the same spring? My brothers, can a fig tree bear olives, or a grapevine bear figs? Neither can a salt spring produce fresh water. (James 3:10–12)

In the final words of this epistle, James encourages the believers to have compassion and pray for one another:

Is any one of you in trouble? He should pray. Is anyone happy? Let him sing songs of praise. Is any one of you sick? He should call the elders of the church to pray over him and anoint him with oil in the name of the Lord. And the prayer offered in faith will make the sick person well; the Lord will raise him up. If he has sinned, he will be forgiven.

Therefore confess your sins to each other and pray for each other so that you may be healed. The prayer of a righteous man is powerful and effective. (James 5:13–16)

These final thoughts are filled with empathy and kindness. As the younger brother of Jesus, James had learned well.

PEOPLE TO KNOW

From Jesus' words in John 21:18, the Apostle Peter must have died a martyr's death. Some church historians think there is not sufficient evidence that Peter was ever in Rome. Most of them, however, agree that it is probable that in or about the last year of his life, Peter did go to Rome, either by the order of Nero or of his own accord, to help steady the Christians under Nero's persecutions. There is a tradition that says Peter, giving in to the urgings of friends to save himself, was fleeing Rome when, in the night on the Appian Way, he met Jesus in a vision and said, "Where are you going, Lord?" Jesus answered, "I am going to Rome to be crucified again." Peter, utterly ashamed and humiliated, returned to the city and was crucified upside down at his own request, feeling unworthy to be crucified as his Lord had been. This story of Peter's crucifixion is only a tradition, and it's unknown how much historical fact it contains.

1 AND 2 PETER: LETTERS OF ENCOURAGEMENT

Like the early sections of James's Epistle, the letters from Peter are filled with encouragement to Christians who are hurting. Peter knew believers who were being tortured for their faith. He used the root word for "suffering" 16 times in these two short books. The Christians of Asia Minor who received this letter from Peter discovered that a life lived for God is often a life of many difficulties. Peter writes to reassure them:

Dear friends, do not be surprised at the painful trial you are suffering, as though something strange were happening to you. But rejoice that you participate in the sufferings of Christ, so that you may be overjoyed when his glory is revealed. (1 Peter 4:12–13)

Suffering is not God's great error; it's at the core of his plan for every believer. During the past few decades, some strange teaching has crept into the church that is radically different than these words from Peter. Churches and some televangelists have used words like *prosperity*, *health*, and *wealth gospel*. In essence this teaching says that God wills nothing but blessing and happiness for his people. If you are experiencing anything other than these high points of life, then you must be living in sin and unbelief.

A proper understanding of the Scripture will counter this false teaching from today's church. Church history will verify that godly living is the repeated account of suffering. The Scriptures are clear that believers are like refugees in a foreign land and serving God faithfully in the midst of struggle and pain. Such suffering isn't a burden but the privilege of the Christian life. God is in the midst of the natural pain. The true health and wealth is waiting for every Christian in heaven. Believers can rejoice in the hope of heaven now, even though they take possession at a later day. As Peter wrote:

Praise be to the God and Father of our Lord Jesus Christ! In his great mercy he has given us new birth into a living hope through the resurrection of Jesus Christ from the dead, and into an inheritance that can never perish, spoil or fade—kept in heaven for you, who through faith are shielded by God's power until the coming of the salvation that is ready to be revealed in the last time. (1 Peter 1:3–5)

God's blessings from a life of faith are worth more than anything from prosperity.

Peter's second letter to the churches addresses the heresy and division among the churches. He reminds his readers of the abundant gifts of God that would sustain them:

Grace and peace be yours in abundance through the knowledge of God and of Jesus our Lord. His divine power has given us everything we need for life and godliness through our knowledge of him who called us by his own glory and goodness. Through these he has given us his very great and precious promises, so that through them you may participate in the divine nature and escape the corruption in the world caused by evil desires. For this very reason, make every effort to add to your faith goodness; and to goodness, knowledge. (2 Peter 1:2–5)

To become a Christlike disciple isn't a one-time event, but a lifelong process.

HOUR'S UP!

In this hour, we've examined some of the practical teaching about the Christian life in Hebrews, James, and 1 and 2 Peter. Let's take a few minutes to consider how this teaching applies to your life.

1. Through Jesus, God has carefully revealed his glory and allowed us a means of escape from the Law to a new covenant of grace. Consider the new covenant and what difference Jesus Christ is making in your everyday life. Take a few moments in prayer to celebrate this difference because of the new covenant and how it's written on your heart.

2. The Book of Hebrews tells us that Jesus is the mediator between God and man. Define a mediator and his role in a dispute or unresolved situation. How is Jesus your mediator as you approach a Holy God? Are you availing yourself of this spiritual resource?

3. Hebrews 10:22–25 gives a number of challenges for every believer. Name these challenges, then take a moment to evaluate your own life and how you are meeting these challenges.

4. Hebrews 11 gives a Hall of Faith—men and women who serve as examples of a life of faith. Take a moment and look through the list in this chapter. Whom do you identify with? At different points in your life, you will identify with different people. For example, if you are struggling at work, possibly you identify with Daniel in the lion's den. How can you step out in faith and increase your trust like these men and women?

5. Whether we like it or not, the life of faith often involves suffering and sacrifice. How do you draw the strength and encouragement that Jesus will walk through the difficulties of life with you?

6. How do you fix your eyes daily on Jesus, "the author and perfecter of our faith"? Create several reminders of Jesus today (maybe it's a rubberband on your wrist or finger and every time you see it, you think of Jesus).

7. James tells us that trials develop perseverance and maturity. How has James 1:2–4 been true in your life? Have you ever considered suffering a "gift"?

8. Proverbs and James examine the topic of wisdom. James says that wisdom comes from God, who gives generously. Have you asked God recently for wisdom? Pause for a moment and ask God to fill your day with his truth and wisdom.

9. Think about the small size of your tongue and the immense damage it can do. Have you been the recipient of a careless word? How did it make you feel? Consider the power to heal and to hurt with your tongue, then ask God to guide your words day in and day out.

10. The Book of 2 Peter discusses the life of faith and its value more than prosperity. How are you achieving this balance in your own life between living by faith and trusting God and experiencing God's divine gifts in your life? Make a small list of these blessings, then thank God for his provision.

Hour 24

Letters from the Apostle John

CHAPTER SUMMARY

LESSON PLAN:

In this hour, you will learn about …

- The three Epistles from John.
- 1 John teaches the key ingredient is love.
- In 2 John, the Apostle answers false teaching.
- In 3 John, the Apostle responds to internal church struggles.
- The mystery of the final book of the Bible—Revelation.

In this final hour, it's time to examine the writings of John, who even in his Gospel was identified in the third person as "the disciple whom Jesus loved." John wrote three brief Epistles that bear his name, then wrote the final book of the New Testament, the Book of Revelation.

Of all the books in the entire Bible, the Book of Revelation is by far the most difficult to understand. If a roomful of Biblical prophecy scholars gathered, probably no two people would agree on every aspect of Revelation. Because the language is symbolic, it leads to a variety of interpretations. Revelation contains a blessing to the reader: "Blessed is the one who reads the words of this prophecy, and blessed are those who hear it and take to heart what is written in it, because the time is near." (Revelation 1:3) So … what are you waiting for? Let's begin with the Epistles from John.

1 JOHN: TEACHING THE GODLY TO LIVE IN LOVE

The arrogance of human nature is to believe that you know more about a particular topic than others. The Apostle John in the first Epistle addresses the problem of false teachers who are making lofty claims about their knowledge about the deity and nature of Christ. John counters their false claims by reminding the readers of the eyewitness accounts of the apostles, including himself. John's words are filled with the exactness of an insider's experience.

That which was from the beginning, which we have heard, which we have seen with our eyes, which we have looked at and our hands have touched— this we proclaim concerning the Word of life. The life appeared; we have seen it and testify to it, and we proclaim to you the eternal life, which was with the Father and has appeared to us. We proclaim to you what we have seen and heard, so that you also may have fellowship with us. And our fellowship is with the Father and with his Son, Jesus Christ. (1 John 1:1–3)

PEOPLE TO KNOW

According to a very ancient tradition, John made Jerusalem his headquarters. There he cared for Jesus' mother, Mary, until her death, and after the destruction of Jerusalem, he moved to Ephesus, which by the end of the apostolic generation had become the geographic center of the Christian church. Here John lived to a very old age, and here he wrote his Gospel and his three letters. Among his pupils were Polycarp, Papias, and Ignatius, who became bishops of Smyrna, Hierapolis, and Antioch, respectively. They are among the earliest of the so-called church fathers.

The importance of the discussion in the last hour about the difference between works and faith is highlighted again in a tender and diplomatic fashion from the Apostle John in his first Epistle:

My dear children, I write this to you so that you will not sin. But if anybody does sin, we have one who speaks to the Father in our defense—Jesus Christ, the Righteous One. He is the atoning sacrifice for our sins, and not only for ours but also for the sins of the whole world. (1 John 2:1–2)

John challenges his readers to "not sin"—the righteousness of works. But then he makes the accommodation that if anyone does sin, the gift of faith and God's grace through Jesus, the advocate, is available. Immediately in the next verses, John delivers perhaps the most concise summary of faith versus works in all of Scripture:

We know that we have come to know him if we obey his commands. The man who says, "I know him," but does not do what he commands is a liar, and the truth is not in him. But if anyone obeys his word, God's love is truly made complete in him. This is how we know we are in him: Whoever claims to live in him must walk as Jesus did. (1 John 2:3–6)

According to this passage, through action or works, the godly person is constrained by God's love to live in obedience to the Lord's will. He is not compelled by obligation or threatened by reproof; the believer is strangely drawn to obedience and righteousness because of the Savior's sacrificial affection. Because of the example of Jesus Christ and his life, the Christian is drawn to love others.

Like the other Epistle writers, John encourages his audience to stand firm when they meet persecution, pain, or loneliness.

Do not be surprised, my brothers, if the world hates you. We know that we have passed from death to life, because we love our brothers. Anyone who does not love remains in death. Anyone who hates his brother is a murderer, and you know that no murderer has eternal life in him. This is how we know what love is: Jesus Christ laid down his life for us. And we ought to lay down our lives for our brothers. (1 John 3:13–16)

Actions speak much louder than all of the promises or pronouncements. God's love according to John is expressed through self-sacrifice. He urges his readers to love other believers more than themselves and to be willing to give their lives for others, even as Christ gave his life.

BIBLICAL FACT

Cerinthus, a false teacher in the days of the Apostle John, denied the Incarnation of Christ by teaching that the divine Christ descended on the human Jesus at his baptism and then departed before his crucifixion. (1 John 2:22) John teaches that Jesus did not merely enter into an already existing human being, but he came as a human being. The Greek tense of the verb "has come" and the meaning of the noun "flesh" indicate that not only did Jesus come as a human being, he was still a human being even as John wrote. God the Son is forever fully God and fully man. He is immortal and has received a resurrected human body of flesh that does not age or die. A denial of Jesus' full and true humanity proves that a teacher is not of God.

John challenges Christians to be discerning about whether a teacher is truly from God and filled with the Holy Spirit.

Dear friends, do not believe every spirit, but test the spirits to see whether they are from God, because many false prophets have gone out into the world. This is how you can recognize the Spirit of God: Every spirit that acknowledges that Jesus Christ has come in the flesh is from God, but every spirit that does not acknowledge Jesus is not from God. (1 John 4:1–3a)

One of the false teachings that were creeping into the early church was the denial of the humanity of Jesus. With these words, John lays to rest this concern saying, "Jesus Christ has come in the flesh."

2 JOHN: REFUTING FALSE TEACHINGS

The early church had its hands full with false teachers. Each group brought its own version of the truth. Second John is a testimony to the fact that no question consumed more attention than "Who is Jesus?" The false teachers who prompted John to write this letter were promoting a heresy called Docetism, which taught that Christ didn't actually come in the flesh. In other words, Christ did not have a body but only *seemed* to have a body and to suffer and die on the cross. Yet these teachers claimed to be Christians and to be teaching the truths of Jesus' life and death.

John wouldn't have anything to do with this sort of false teaching. He urged the believers to cling to the truth: Jesus Christ came in the flesh. The word "truth" appears five times in the first four verses. John wanted believers to guard against falsehood, and the best way to do that would be to arm themselves with the truth.

The early church made it a practice to support traveling teachers and ministers with hospitality and financial gifts. In each church, Christians would house these missionaries and provide for their needs. Because false teachers also relied on this hospitality, John urged his readers to show discernment and not support traveling teachers "who do not acknowledge Jesus Christ as coming in the flesh, have gone out into the world. Any such person is the deceiver and the antichrist." (2 John v. 7)

JUST A MINUTE

John possibly wrote this letter to a single person, a woman. If so, the Epistle marks the only book in the New Testament addressed to a woman. The phrase "elect lady" makes sense as a title for a well-known and respected woman. The reference to her children walking in the truth also makes sense when taken literally. The greeting from her sister's children in verse 13 would fit this interpretation.

John includes some strong warnings in this Epistle, "Watch out that you do not lose what you have worked for, but that you may be rewarded fully. Anyone who runs ahead and does not continue in the teaching of Christ does not have God; whoever continues in the teaching has both the Father and the Son. If anyone comes to you and does not bring this teaching, do not take him into your house or welcome him. Anyone who welcomes him shares in his wicked work." (2 John vv. 8–11)

John says that if a Christian is seduced by a false teacher, then it's one way they can lose their reward of eternal life at judgment. Every believer has the potential of a full reward or a complete loss of reward. (1 Corinthians 3:15) The determining factor is our faithfulness to Christ.

This Epistle is one short chapter because John plans to visit the audience and speak more in depth, face to face. "I have much to write to you, but I do not want to use paper and ink. Instead, I hope to visit you and talk with you face to face, so that our joy may be complete." (2 John v. 12)

The key verse in this second Epistle is: "And now, dear lady, I am not writing you a new command but one we have had from the beginning. I ask that we love one another. And this is love: that we walk in obedience to his commands. As you have heard from the beginning, his command is that you walk in love." (2 John vv. 5–6)

The Apostle John makes a strong case for walking in love and obeying the commands of Jesus in this short Epistle.

3 JOHN: RESPONSE TO INTERNAL CHURCH STRUGGLES

Struggles with forces outside the church can be harmful enough, but when the struggle is inside the church, it can be devastating. Third John was written in response to one of these struggles within the church. It's a personal letter but allows us to have an inside glimpse into the early church.

CULTURAL FACT

Traveling missionaries during the early church neither asked for nor accepted anything from nonbelievers because they didn't want anyone questioning their motives for preaching. God's true preachers do not preach to make money but to express their love for God. It is the church's responsibility to care for Christian workers; this should never be left to nonbelievers.

John writes to Gaius, who had a habit of hospitality and a reputation for friendship and generosity, especially to traveling teachers and missionaries. To affirm and thank Gaius for his Christian lifestyle, and to encourage him in his faith, John wrote this personal note. The letter centers around three men: Gaius, the one who follows Christ and loves others (3 John 1:1–8); Diotrephes, the self-proclaimed church leader who doesn't reflect God's values (1:9–11); and Demetrius, who also follows the truth (1:12). John encourages Gaius to practice hospitality and continue walking in the truth to do what is right.

The key verse for this Epistle relates to hospitality and faithfulness in the Christian life: "Dear friend, you are faithful in what you are doing for the brothers, even though they are strangers to you." (3 John 1:5)

The words are good reminders for every Christian to continue in faithfulness and hospitality to others.

THE BOOK OF REVELATION

The first-century church faced outside persecutions against Christians but also internal problems. They struggled with spiritual warfare, suffering, heretical doctrine and practice, and spiritual apathy. Christ had promised to return—but when? And how? And what would he do about the problems facing the church when he did return?

In the face of these circumstances, the original readers of Revelation needed to be encouraged and exhorted. On the one hand, Revelation was intended to be a promise of divine protection from God's judgment on the world. On the other hand, those who read the book were to take it to heart and obey. In recording Revelation, the Apostle John wanted to reassure his readers that Jesus Christ controls the course and climax of history. Revelation is the confident prediction of the new world and also the description of the end of the present world.

JUST A MINUTE

The Book of Revelation is apocalyptic (meaning "uncovered," "unveiled," or "revealed") in style. This style of ancient literature usually featured spectacular and mysterious imagery, and such literature was written under the name of an ancient hero. John was well acquainted with Jewish apocalyptic works, but his book is different in several ways: (1) He uses his own name rather than the name of an ancient hero, (2) he denounces evil and exhorts people to high Christian standards, and (3) he offers hope rather than gloom. John was not a psychic attempting to predict the future; he was a prophet of God describing what God had shown him.

JOHN'S EXILE

Like the Apostle Paul, John had been arrested for his bold teaching and courageous beliefs concerning Jesus Christ. Finally the Roman authorities had enough and banished the apostle to the tiny volcanic island called Patmos, located in the Aegean Sea. On this island, John was imprisoned and lived out the rest of his life. While the Bible doesn't give any details of his physical surroundings, John's neighbors were political prisoners and convicted criminals.

I, John, your brother and companion in the suffering and kingdom and patient endurance that are ours in Jesus, was on the island of Patmos because of the word of God and the testimony of Jesus. (Revelation 1:9)

The Book of Revelation contains some of the most mysterious and glorious language concerning the last days. The writing uses a form called apocalyptic writing, which is a special subdivision of a theology called *eschatology*, a theology focused on the final consummation of God's work in the world.

JUST A MINUTE

There are six blessed assurances in Revelation:

- Blessed is the one who reads the words of this prophecy, and blessed are those who hear it and take to heart what is written in it. (Revelation 1:3)
- Blessed are the dead who die in the Lord from now on. (Revelation 14:13)
- Blessed is he who stays awake [for the Lord's coming]. (Revelation 16:15)
- Blessed are those who are invited to the wedding supper of the Lamb. (Revelation 19:9)
- Blessed is he who keeps the words of the prophecy in this book. (Revelation 22:7)
- Blessed are those who wash their robes that they might have a right to the tree of life. (Revelation 22:14)

FOUR MAIN INTERPRETATIONS OF REVELATION

There are many different interpretations to the Book of Revelation. The four most common are usually called the *idealist*, *preterist*, *historical*, and *futurist* interpretations. Each one has many variations and each has its difficulties. No matter which viewpoint one accepts, the details in Revelation require some straining to fit.

IDEALIST

People who take this viewpoint see Revelation as a highly symbolic book. Not designed to give the reader a specific chronology of future events, John's writing describes the kinds of occurrences that have happened throughout church history. Revelation teaches a fundamental message of the triumph of God over Satan through seven different visions. The people who hold this viewpoint are either amillennialists or postmillennialists.

PRETERIST

The preterist interpretation regards the book as referring to its own day: Christianity's struggle with the Roman Empire. It assumes that everything was fulfilled during the period it was written and that the story was told with imagery and symbolism to hide its meaning from the late-first-century pagans. For example, the destruction of the city of Jerusalem, which took place in A.D. 70, was John's primary end-times focus.

HISTORICAL

Those who take the historical view see the first five chapters of Revelation as addressed to the early church. After chapter six, the book is a description of the whole of church history. This viewpoint is called historical premillennialism.

FUTURIST

Futurists read the book of Revelation as a blueprint for a series of events that will precede the imminent return of Jesus Christ. According to this view, readers are waiting for the fulfillment of the prophesied events of this book from Revelation chapter 6 onward. From this perspective, dispensationalism was developed.

JUST A MINUTE

Throughout the Bible, the number seven is significant. The Scriptures begin in Genesis with seven days of Creation; it ends with a book built on sevens that tells the ultimate destiny of that creation. The Sabbath was the seventh day. The Levitical system in the Old Testament was built on a cycle of sevens. Jericho fell after seven priests with seven trumpets marched around its walls for seven days and blew their trumpets seven times on the seventh day. Seven is a favorite number of God's. There are seven days in a week, seven colors in a rainbow.

Symbolically, seven is thought to stand for completeness, fullness, totality, a whole—both positive and negative. On the other hand, the beast of Revelation 13 has seven heads, which definitely doesn't represent holiness.

DATE OF WRITING REVELATION

The actual date of John's writing is also an area where scholars disagree.

> The revelation of Jesus Christ was given to him by God to show his servants what must soon take place. He made it known by sending his angel to his servant John, who testifies to everything he saw—that is, the word of God and the testimony of Jesus Christ. (Revelation 1:1–2)

Some Biblical scholars say Revelation was written at the close of the first century, A.D. 95 to 106, which is decades after Jerusalem had been destroyed. But John's words make it clear that what he was predicting was about to happen soon or shortly. The judgment that falls on Jerusalem is the most significant event that happened around this time period. In Chapter 11, John makes reference to an angel telling him to measure the Temple in the present tense, something that could not have been done if the Temple had already been ruined. As a result, many sources say John wrote Revelation at some time just before A.D. 70, the year Jerusalem fell.

CULTURAL FACT

"Lamb" is Revelation's favorite name for Christ: The Lamb took the sealed book and opened it (Revelation 5:6–7, 6:1); the living creatures and elders worship the Lamb (Revelation 5:8,14); 100,000,000 angels worship the Lamb (Revelation 5:11–13); the great day of the Lamb's wrath is come (Revelation 6:16–17); multitudes from all nations worship the Lamb (Revelation 7:9–10); their robes are washed in the blood of the Lamb (Revelation 7:14); the Lamb leads them to fountains of living waters (Revelation 7:17); they overcome Satan by the blood of the Lamb (Revelation 12:11); the 144,000 follow the Lamb (Revelation 14:1,4); the Lamb is the Lord of Lords and King of Kings (Revelation 17:14).

CONNECTING THE OLD AND NEW COVENANTS

Reminding the reader of the accounts from the Old Testament, John is permitted the opportunity to peek behind the veil, into the inner workings of heaven.

> At once I was in the Spirit, and there before me was a throne in heaven with someone sitting on it. And the one who sat there had the appearance of jasper and carnelian. A rainbow, resembling an emerald, encircled the throne. Surrounding the throne were twenty-four other thrones, and seated on them were twenty-four elders. They were dressed in white and had crowns of gold on their heads. From the throne came flashes of lightning, rumblings and peals of thunder.

Before the throne, seven lamps were blazing. These are the seven spirits of God. Also before the throne there was what looked like a sea of glass, clear as crystal. In the center, around the throne, were four living creatures, and they were covered with eyes, in front and in back. The first living creature was like a lion, the second was like an ox, the third had a face like a man, the fourth was like a flying eagle. Each of the four living creatures had six wings and was covered with eyes all around, even under his wings.

Day and night they never stop saying: "Holy, holy, holy is the Lord God Almighty, who was, and is, and is to come." Whenever the living creatures give glory, honor and thanks to him who sits on the throne and who lives for ever and ever, the twenty-four elders fall down before him who sits on the throne, and worship him who lives for ever and ever. They lay their crowns before the throne and say: "You are worthy, our Lord and God, to receive glory and honor and power, for you created all things, and by your will they were created and have their being." (Revelation 4:2–11)

JUST A MINUTE

Four times in the Book of Revelation John says he was "in the Spirit" (Revelation 1:10, 4:2, 17:3, and 21:10). This expression means that the Holy Spirit was giving him a vision—showing him situations and events he could not have seen with mere human eyesight. All true prophecy comes from God through the Holy Spirit. (2 Peter 1:20–21)

Don't these images remind us of some other scenes in the Old Testament—such as Ezekiel's vision of the wheel or Isaiah's account of his visit to the Lord's Temple? John writes a vivid rendering of God's throne room. We can hear the voices, smell the burning lamps, see the flashes of the lightning. The reader can feel the rhythm of the bowing elders and their songs of praise. These images give a glimpse of the way that Revelation is to be read and experienced.

The scene continues in a way that ties together the Old and New Testaments.

Then I saw in the right hand of him who sat on the throne a scroll with writing on both sides and sealed with seven seals. And I saw a mighty angel proclaiming in a loud voice, "Who is worthy to break the seals and open the scroll?" But no one in heaven or on earth or under the earth could open the scroll or even look inside it. I wept and wept because no one was found who was worthy to open the scroll or look inside. (Revelation 5:1–4)

Originally the Bible was written on scrolls. The common writings used both sides of the scroll, but the biblical record was written on only one side. The sealed scroll in John's vision was written on both sides—exactly like the two-sided scroll in Ezekiel 2:10. Possibly one side of the scroll contained God's blessings and the other side his covenant cursings.

CULTURAL FACT

> In John's day, books were written on scrolls—pieces of papyrus or vellum up to 30 feet long, rolled up, and sealed with clay or wax. The scroll that John sees contains the full account of what God has in store for the world. The seven seals indicate the importance of its contents. The seals are located throughout the scroll so that as each one is broken, more of the scroll can be read to reveal another phase of God's plan for the end of the world. Only Christ is worthy to break the seals and open the scroll. (Revelation 5:3–5)

Imagine the drama in this scene and the building tension as God's representative calls out, "Who is worthy to break the seals and open the scroll?" Everyone looks around the room to see who will answer this question and who can open the scroll to reveal its secrets. The beasts aren't worthy and the elders aren't worthy. Who can open this scroll?

Then one of the elders said to me, "Do not weep! See, the Lion of the tribe of Judah, the Root of David, has triumphed. He is able to open the scroll and its seven seals." Then I saw a Lamb, looking as if it had been slain, standing in the center of the throne, encircled by the four living creatures and the elders. He had seven horns and seven eyes, which are the seven spirits of God sent out into all the earth. He came and took the scroll from the right hand of him who sat on the throne. (Revelation 5:5–7)

Like the sword stuck in the stone in the legends of King Arthur, the scroll remained unopened; like the bow of Ulysses that remained unstrung, the scroll waited for the Lamb. The audience reading Revelation is plunged into despair, with no hope of resolution. Then the hero arrives to fulfill his destiny.

CHRIST IN REVELATION

The audience is waiting expectantly for someone to open the scroll. Jesus Christ steps forward to take the scroll and breaks its seals. Finally, salvation comes to God's people and they are overwhelmed with gratitude and joy. Then in the tradition of Moses, Deborah, and Mary, the people raise their voices in song:

Then I looked and heard the voice of many angels, numbering thousands upon thousands, and ten thousand times ten thousand. They encircled the throne and the living creatures and the elders. In a loud voice they sang: "Worthy is the Lamb, who was slain, to receive power and wealth and wisdom and strength and honor and glory and praise!" Then I heard every creature in heaven and on earth and under the earth and on the sea, and all that is in them, singing: "To him who sits on the throne and to the Lamb be praise and honor and glory and power, for ever and ever!" The four living creatures said, "Amen," and the elders fell down and worshiped. (Revelation 5:11–14)

Jesus Christ, the Lamb of God, had accomplished his mission and was worthy to receive their worship. It's no surprise that John is ready to lavish unbridled praise on Jesus. As a disciple, he knew the Savior. In his first Epistle, John heard, saw, and literally touched God's Son. As one of Jesus' closest friends, John was present at the Mount of Transfiguration and experienced an unforgettable moment. Finally as John begins to write this Book of Revelation, he gives an almost breathtaking portrait of the Messiah:

> I turned around to see the voice that was speaking to me. And when I turned I saw seven golden lampstands, and among the lampstands was someone "like a son of man," dressed in a robe reaching down to his feet and with a golden sash around his chest. His head and hair were white like wool, as white as snow, and his eyes were like blazing fire. His feet were like bronze glowing in a furnace, and his voice was like the sound of rushing waters.

> In his right hand he held seven stars, and out of his mouth came a sharp double-edged sword. His face was like the sun shining in all its brilliance. When I saw him, I fell at his feet as though dead. Then he placed his right hand on me and said: "Do not be afraid. I am the First and the Last. I am the Living One; I was dead, and behold I am alive for ever and ever!" (Revelation 1:12–18a)

This portrait is a far cry from the baby in the stable, whom the religious elite ridiculed and tried in a kangaroo court, then executed like a common criminal. This Jesus sounds like the person the Apostle Paul called the "highly exalted" savior ... the Lamb who is worthy.

It's unimportant the interpretative grid used to understand Revelation. The underlying message of Revelation hears the thunderous cry that Jesus Christ, the Lamb of God, is victorious.

THE GLORY OF THE LORD

Almost every day, life on this earth seems consuming. John in Revelation shows the reader that life on earth is temporary. He paints a new picture of the eternal and the destiny of those who follow Jesus Christ:

Then I saw a new heaven and a new earth, for the first heaven and the first earth had passed away, and there was no longer any sea. I saw the Holy City, the new Jerusalem, coming down out of heaven from God, prepared as a bride beautifully dressed for her husband. And I heard a loud voice from the throne saying, "Now the dwelling of God is with men, and he will live with them. They will be his people, and God himself will be with them and be their God. He will wipe every tear from their eyes. There will be no more death or mourning or crying or pain, for the old order of things has passed away." (Revelation 21:1–4)

CULTURAL FACT

The Greek term for "New Jerusalem" denotes "the brand-new Jerusalem." The New Jerusalem that comes out of heaven is plainly distinct from the earthly Jerusalem, the former capital of Israel. This is the city Abraham looked for, the city that has foundations, whose builder and maker is God. (Hebrews 11:10) This is the city that exists even now in heaven, for Paul calls it the Jerusalem that is above. (Galatians 4:26)

In the next world, there will be "no more sea." In Jewish culture, the sea was unknown. The Jewish parents told their children stories of sea monsters along with the Exodus story where the sea destroyed the Egyptian army. This reference to no sea is a promise of safety.

These verses also promise the final relief from suffering. Everyone on the earth lives with a death sentence in that eventually they will die. For those who trust Jesus Christ, death will be a moment, but eternity will be living in the presence of God where he wipes every tear and makes everything new.

THE REBUILDING OF THE CITY

John was told to carefully write this next part of the vision so the reader would be encouraged from these words of hope:

One of the seven angels who had the seven bowls full of the seven last plagues came and said to me, "Come, I will show you the bride, the wife of the Lamb." And he carried me away in the Spirit to a mountain great and high, and showed me the Holy City, Jerusalem, coming down out of heaven from God. It shone with the glory of God. (Revelation 21:9–11a)

Throughout history the city of Jerusalem was built, destroyed, and then rebuilt many times. Each time it was restored and the people promised that it would never be destroyed again—yet sooner or later, its enemies would demolish the city again. John describes a Holy City, the New Jerusalem, which will be built of indestructible materials.

John's brilliant images are only shadows of the true nature of heaven. "I did not see a temple in the city, because the Lord God Almighty and the Lamb are its temple." (Revelation 21:22)

The Jewish reader would panic at the thought of no temple. In spite of all its glory, the temple was only a symbol and according to John, it would be replaced with the permanent presence of a Holy God.

The city does not need the sun or the moon to shine on it, for the glory of God gives it light, and the Lamb is its lamp. (Revelation 21:23)

In the light of God's radiance, no moon or sun are necessary. Instead the people in heaven live in the glory of God. Through the pages of this book and the Bible itself, readers have been shown various images of God's glory: Moses tasting God's glory, the prophet Isaiah catching a brief glimpse in the temple. Jacob and Ezekiel were visited by the glory of God while they slept. The shepherds in the field who heard the angels talk about the birth of Jesus tasted a tiny glimpse of God's glory. Three disciples basked in the glory of God for an instant when Jesus was transfigured on the mountain. On the road to Damascus, Saul was struck in the glory's brilliance. Yet in heaven, the believers will be awash in God's glory to drink of it and soak in it.

Then the angel showed me the river of the water of life, as clear as crystal, flowing from the throne of God and of the Lamb. (Revelation 22:1)

In the heavenly city, a river flows under the throne of God to nourish the New Jerusalem. The very essence of a sovereign God sustains those in the city of God. This power of God is true know but not fully known. In heaven, God's power and presence will be constantly clear.

The Spirit and the bride say, "Come!" And let him who hears say, "Come!" Whoever is thirsty, let him come; and whoever wishes, let him take the free gift of the water of life. (Revelation 22:17)

John's vision is clear: God has spoken, and those who believe in Jesus Christ can live today with the hope of the glory of God.

Hour's Up!

Through three personal letters and the vivid imagery in the Book of Revelation, the Apostle John taught some key principles about the spiritual life. More than an academic exercise, these 10 questions will help you explore how John's letters and Revelation apply to your everyday life.

1. In 1 John, the false teachers claimed to know more than others about the deity and nature of Christ. It's easy to feel self-important with a little knowledge. How do you prevent this feeling from entering your own relationships?

2. Jesus Christ has sacrificed for our sins and the sins of the whole world according to 1 John 2. Reflect on this gift from God and pause in gratitude and thanksgiving for God's gift of Jesus.

3. Because of Christ's sacrificial love, how has obedience and righteousness become a part of your daily spiritual relationship?

4. 1 John 3 encourages us not to be surprised if the world hates us. How have you encountered spiritual opposition in your everyday life? What measures do you take to stand against this opposition?

5. John also teaches Christians to become discerning about whether teaching or a teacher is from God and filled with the Holy Spirit. How can you become more sensitive to this guideline and how will this sensitivity determine your choices in everyday life?

6. If a false teacher seduces a Christian, what are some of the ramifications according to John? According to John, faithfulness to Christ is the determining factor. How can you increase your daily faithfulness to Christ and dependence on him?

7. Hospitality plays an important part according to 3 John. In our society, this virtue is almost a lost art. How can you increase your kindness and hospitality to others? Plan some practical steps today.

8. The Book of Revelation provides glimpses of God's glory. As your awareness increases of God's presence and glory in your life, what changes do you notice? How will you be different because of that awareness of God in your life?

9. Contrast the Jesus in the Gospels and the Jesus whom John describes in Revelation 1:12–18a. Celebrate in prayer how Jesus has been victorious over death and is the Lamb of God.

10. Often in this busy, hurried world, it's difficult to meditate on heaven and the eternal city. Reread some of the verses John writes about the Holy City and then throughout the day pause for a few moments and think about God's glory and your future eternal life in the Heavenly City.

APPENDIX A
The Books of the Bible

THE OLD TESTAMENT

LAW

Genesis
Exodus
Leviticus
Numbers
Deuteronomy

HISTORIES

Joshua
Judges
Ruth
1 Samuel
2 Samuel
1 Kings
2 Kings
1 Chronicles
2 Chronicles
Ezra
Nehemiah

WRITINGS

Esther
Job
Psalms
Proverbs
Ecclesiastes
Song of Solomon

PROPHETS

Isaiah	Jonah
Jeremiah	Micah
Lamentations	Habakkuk
Ezekiel	Nahum
Daniel	Zephaniah
Hosea	Haggai
Joel	Zechariah
Amos	Malachi
Obadiah	

THE NEW TESTAMENT

GOSPELS

Matthew
Mark
Luke
John

HISTORY

Acts

EPISTLES

Romans	Titus
1 Corinthians	Philemon
2 Corinthians	Hebrews
Galatians	James
Ephesians	1 Peter
Philippians	2 Peter
Colossians	1 John
1 Thessalonians	2 John
2 Thessalonians	3 John
1 Timothy	Jude
2 Timothy	

APOCALYPSE

Revelation

APPENDIX B
Last Days

When will Jesus return? Even Jesus said that he didn't know the day or the hour—yet he encouraged his disciples to live every day as though he were returning tomorrow. Near the end of his life on earth, Jesus told them:

No one knows about that day or hour, not even the angels in heaven, nor the Son, but only the Father. As it was in the days of Noah, so it will be at the coming of the Son of Man. For in the days before the flood, people were eating and drinking, marrying and giving in marriage, up to the day Noah entered the ark; and they knew nothing about what would happen until the flood came and took them all away. That is how it will be at the coming of the Son of Man. Two men will be in the field; one will be taken and the other left. Two women will be grinding with a hand mill; one will be taken and the other left. "Therefore keep watch, because you do not know on what day your Lord will come." (Matthew 24:36–42)

With the phenomenal success of the *Left Behind* fiction series by Tim LaHaye and Jerry B. Jenkins (Tyndale House Publishers), which have sold more than 50 million copies, many people have a keen interest in what the Bible says about these last days. The *Left Behind* series approaches the Bible from one point of view: dispensational premillennial.

On one aspect, the scholars agree: There is no agreement about when Christ will return or which viewpoint is "correct." Among some churches, people joke about a new last days viewpoint: panmillennialist. This person believes that "it will all pan out in the end." It's probably the safest view-point if you want to have complete confidence in one of these views because the Scriptures are not clear and each viewpoint has proponents who shape Scriptures to "prove" their case.

Here are the four common viewpoints and what they mean:

- **Amillennialists** are people who see Revelation 20 as a description of the spiritual reign of Christ with the saints throughout the entire pres-ent age, which is characterized by the growth of good and evil. The present "millennial" age will be followed by the second coming of Christ, the general resurrection, the Last Judgment, and the new heaven and the new earth.

- **Postmillennialists,** like amillennialists, teach that the thousand years of Revelation 20 occurs prior to the Second Coming. Some postmil-lennialists teach that the millennial age is the entire period of time between Christ's first and second advents, while others teach that it is the last 1,000 years of the present age. According to postmillennial-ism, in the present age the Holy Spirit will draw unprecedented multi-tudes to Christ through the faithful preaching of the gospel. Among the multitudes who will be converted are the ethnic Israelites who have thus far rejected the Messiah. At the end of the present age, Christ will return, there will be a general resurrection of the just and the unjust, and the final judgment will take place.

- **Premillennialists** teach that at the end of the present age there will be the Great Tribulation, followed by the second coming of Christ. At Christ's coming, the Antichrist will be judged, the righteous will be resurrected, Satan will be bound, and Christ will establish his reign on earth, which will last for a thousand years and be a time of unprece-dented blessing for the church. At the end of the Millennium (1,000 years), Satan will be released and will instigate a rebellion, which will be quickly crushed. The unrighteous will at this point be raised for judgment, after which the eternal state will begin.

- **Dispensational Premillennialists** believe the present church age will end with the rapture of the church, which, along with the appearance of the Antichrist, will indicate the beginning of the seven-year Great Tribulation on earth. The Tribulation will end with the Battle of Armageddon, in the midst of which Christ will return to destroy his enemies. The nations will then be gathered for judgment. Those who supported Israel will enter into Christ's millennial kingdom, and the rest will be cast into hell to await the Last Judgment. Christ will sit on the throne of David and rule the world from Jerusalem. Israel will be given the place of honor among the nations again. The temple will be rebuilt and the temple sacrifices will be reinstituted as memorial sacrifices. At the end of the Millennium, Satan will be released and lead unbelievers in rebellion against Christ and the New Jerusalem. Fire from heaven will crush the rebellion and Satan will be cast into the lake of fire. The wicked will be brought before the Great White Throne, judged, and cast into the lake of fire, and at this point the eternal state will commence.

APPENDIX C
Basic Bible Study Tools

If you want to have more tools to study the Bible, whether you begin searching online or look in the Bible reference section of a Christian bookstore, the choices can be overwhelming because of the sheer number and variety. It's especially the case if you aren't sure which books you will need. Most of these choices fall into a few categories:

- Tools that give you an overview of the Bible and help you read the Bible with understanding: a Bible handbook and a study Bible.

- Tools that help you find verses and passages in the Bible: a concordance and a topical Bible.

- Tools that help you understand things in the Bible: a Bible dictionary and a commentary.

Here's some additional explanation about each of these tools:

- A Bible handbook is a companion to Bible reading. It is arranged in the order of the books of the Bible and provides background before you read through a Bible book, explanation and illustrations as you read, and topical and historical notes to expand your understanding.

- A study Bible is the foundation of any Bible reference library. It is the complete Bible with notes and other helpful materials added, such as maps, introductions to each book of the Bible, and cross-references to other Scriptures.

- A concordance lists common words found in the Bible and shows the places where they occur. For example, under the entry *faith* you would find the locations in the Bible where the word *faith* is used. A concordance enables you to do word studies as well as locate verses you vaguely remember.

- A topical Bible is a guide to different subjects or topics addressed in the Bible. Under *faith*, it will list not only the most important verses where the word *faith* is found, but also verses that talk about faith without using the word—for example Genesis 15:6, "Abraham believed the Lord."

- A Bible dictionary gives more detailed information about people, places, words, and events in the Bible. You could use it to learn more about what the Bible says about kings, for example, or about Paul or Midian or parables.

- A commentary is a single or multivolume work that explains the meaning of Bible passages.

APPENDIX D
Read Through the Bible

The Bible looks like a challenging book to read from cover to cover. Because the chapters in the Bible are short, however, if you have half an hour each day, you can easily read through the Bible in one year. If you miss a day, you will have to do double-duty the next day to catch up.

This one-year program includes some readings from the Old Testament for the mornings and readings from the New Testament in the evenings. The point of the reading is to have basic understanding—not to research or study the passage. The regular habit of reading the Scriptures will build something important into your spiritual life and become a habit that might be difficult to stop.

ONE-YEAR PROGRAM

Date	Morning	Evening
Jan. 1	Gen 1–2	Mat 1:1–11
Jan. 2	Gen 3–5	Mat 1:12–2:12
Jan. 3	Gen 6–8	Mat 2:13–3:17
Jan. 4	Gen 9:1–11:9	Mat 4
Jan. 5	Gen 11:10–13:18	Mat 5:1–16
Jan. 6	Gen 14:1–17:8	Mat 5:17–37
Jan. 7	Gen 17:9–19:11	Mat 5:38–6:15
Jan. 8	Gen 19:12–21:34	Mat 6:16–7:12
Jan. 9	Gen 22:1–24:27	Mat 7:13–8:13
Jan. 10	Gen 24:28–25:34	Mat 8:14–22
Jan. 11	Gen 26–27	Mat 8:23–9:8
Jan. 12	Gen 28:1–30:13	Mat 9:9–31
Jan. 13	Gen 30:14–31:42	Mat 9:32–10:15
Jan. 14	Gen 31:43–33:20	Mat 10:16–42
Jan. 15	Gen 34:1–36:19	Mat 11:1–6
Jan. 16	Gen 36:20–38:11	Mat 11:7–30
Jan. 17	Gen 38:12–40:23	Mat 12:1–21
Jan. 18	Gen 41:1–42:17	Mat 12:22–50
Jan. 19	Gen 42:18–43:34	Mat 13:1–9
Jan. 20	Gen 44:1–46:27	Mat 13:10–35
Jan. 21	Gen 46:28–48:22	Mat 13:36–58
Jan. 22	Gen 49–50; Exo 1:1–14	Mat 14:1–21
Jan. 23	Exo 1:15–4:9	Mat 14:22–15:20
Jan. 24	Exo 4:10–6:13	Mat 15:21–31
Jan. 25	Exo 6:14–9:12	Mat 15:32–16:12
Jan. 26	Exo 9:13–11:10	Mat 16:13–17:13
Jan. 27	Exo 12–13	Mat 17:14–18:14
Jan. 28	Exo 14–15	Mat 18:15–35
Jan. 29	Exo 16–18	Mat 19:1–12
Jan. 30	Exo 19:1–21:21	Mat 19:13–20:16
Jan. 31	Exo 21:22–24:8	Mat 20:17–21:11

Date	Morning	Evening
Feb. 1	Exo 24:9–26:25	Mat 21:12–32
Feb. 2	Exo 26:26–28:43	Mat 21:33–22:14
Feb. 3	Exo 29:1–30:10	Mat 22:15–33
Feb. 4	Exo 30:11–32:24	Mat 22:34–23:12
Feb. 5	Exo 32:25–34:35	Mat 23:13–39
Feb. 6	Exo 35:1–36:7	Mat 24:1–31
Feb. 7	Exo 36:8–38:8	Mat 24:32–44
Feb. 8	Exo 38:9–39:43	Mat 24:45–25:13
Feb. 9	Exo 40; Lev 1–3	Mat 25:14–46
Feb. 10	Lev 4:1–6:13	Mat 26:1–25
Feb. 11	Lev 6:14–8:21	Mat 26:26–46
Feb. 12	Lev 8:22–11:8	Mat 26:47–56
Feb. 13	Lev 11:9–13:17	Mat 26:57–75
Feb. 14	Lev 13:18–14:20	Mat 27:1–26
Feb. 15	Lev 14:21–15:33	Mat 27:27–66
Feb. 16	Lev 16:1–18:18	Mat 28
Feb. 17	Lev 18:19–20:27	Mark 1:1–11
Feb. 18	Lev 21:1–23:8	Mark 1:12–45
Feb. 19	Lev 23:9–25:12	Mark 2
Feb. 20	Lev 25:13–26:26	Mark 3:1–19
Feb. 21	Lev 26:27–27:34; Num 1:1–31	Mark 3:20–4:9
Feb. 22	Num 1:32–3:10	Mark 4:10–20
Feb. 23	Num 3:11–4:28	Mark 4:21–41
Feb. 24	Num 4:29–5:31	Mark 5:1–20
Feb. 25	Num 6:1–7:47	Mark 5:21–43
Feb. 26	Num 7:48–9:14	Mark 6:1–13
Feb. 27	Num 9:15–11:23	Mark 6:14–44
Feb. 28	Num 11:24–13:33	Mark 6:45–7:13
Mar. 1	Num 14:1–15:21	Mark 7:14–37
Mar. 2	Num 15:22–16:40	Mark 8:1–21
Mar. 3	Num 16:41–19:10	Mark 8:22–38
Mar. 4	Num 19:11–22:14	Mark 9:1–29
Mar. 5	Num 22:15–23:30	Mark 9:30–50

Date	Morning	Evening
Mar. 6	Num 24:1–26:22	Mark 10:1–22
Mar. 7	Num 26:23–27:23	Mark 10:23–45
Mar. 8	Num 28–29	Mark 10:46–52
Mar. 9	Num 30–31	Mark 11:1–18
Mar. 10	Num 32:1–33:49	Mark 11:19–12:12
Mar. 11	Num 33:50–35:34	Mark 12:13–34
Mar. 12	Num 36; Deu 1:1–2:15	Mark 12:35–13:13
Mar. 13	Deu 2:16–4:24	Mark 13:14–23
Mar. 14	Deu 4:25–6:15	Mark 13:24–14:11
Mar. 15	Deu 6:16–8:20	Mark 14:12–42
Mar. 16	Deu 9:1–11:12	Mark 14:43–65
Mar. 17	Deu 11:13–13:18	Mark 14:66–72
Mar. 18	Deu 14:1–16:8	Mark 15:1–32
Mar. 19	Deu 16:9–19:10	Mark 15:33–16:8
Mar. 20	Deu 19:11–22:11	Mark 16:9–20; Luke 1:1–17
Mar. 21	Deu 22:12–24:22	Luke 1:18–38
Mar. 22	Deu 25–27	Luke 1:39–55
Mar. 23	Deu 28	Luke 1:56–80
Mar. 24	Deu 29–30	Luke 2:1–20
Mar. 25	Deu 31–32	Luke 2:21–52
Mar. 26	Deu 33–34; Josh 1	Luke 3:1–22
Mar. 27	Josh 2–4	Luke 3:23–38
Mar. 28	Josh 5–7	Luke 4:1–30
Mar. 29	Josh 8:1–10:11	Luke 4:31–5:11
Mar. 30	Josh 10:12–12:6	Luke 5:12–39
Mar. 31	Josh 12:7–15:12	Luke 6:1–26
Apr. 1	Josh 15:13–17:6	Luke 6:27–38
Apr. 2	Josh 17:7–19:23	Luke 6:39–7:10
Apr. 3	Josh 19:24–21:33	Luke 7:11–35
Apr. 4	Josh 21:34–24:13	Luke 7:36–8:15
Apr. 5	Josh 24:14–33; Judg 1:1–2:10	Luke 8:16–25
Apr. 6	Judg 2:11–4:24	Luke 8:26–56
Apr. 7	Judg 5:1–6:32	Luke 9:1–27
Apr. 8	Judg 6:33–8:21	Luke 9:28–62

Date	Morning	Evening
Apr. 9	Judg 8:22–9:57	Luke 10:1–24
Apr. 10	Judg 10–12	Luke 10:25–37
Apr. 11	Judg 13:1–15:8	Luke 10:38–11:13
Apr. 12	Judg 15:9–18:10	Luke 11:14–41
Apr. 13	Judg 18:11–20:11	Luke 11:42–12:12
Apr. 14	Judg 20:12–21:25; Ruth 1:1–14	Luke 12:13–34
Apr. 15	Ruth 1:15–4:12	Luke 12:35–48
Apr. 16	Ruth 4:13–22; 1 Sam 1:1–2:21	Luke 12:49–13:9
Apr. 17	1 Sam 2:22–5:12	Luke 13:10–35
Apr. 18	1 Sam 6–8	Luke 14:1–24
Apr. 19	1 Sam 9–10	Luke 14:25–15:10
Apr. 20	1 Sam 11:1–13:7	Luke 15:11–19
Apr. 21	1 Sam 13:8–14:52	Luke 15:20–16:13
Apr. 22	1 Sam 15:1–17:11	Luke 16:14–17:10
Apr. 23	1 Sam 17:12–18:19	Luke 17:11–37
Apr. 24	1 Sam 18:20–20:34	Luke 18:1–14
Apr. 25	1 Sam 20:35–23:29	Luke 18:15–43
Apr. 26	1 Sam 24:1–25:31	Luke 19:1–27
Apr. 27	1 Sam 25:32–28:25	Luke 19:28–48
Apr. 28	1 Sam 29–31; 2 Sam 1	Luke 20:1–18
Apr. 29	2 Sam 2:1–3:21	Luke 20:19–26
Apr. 30	2 Sam 3:22–6:11	Luke 20:27–47
May 1	2 Sam 6:12–9:13	Luke 21:1–19
May 2	2 Sam 10–12	Luke 21:20–38
May 3	2 Sam 13–14	Luke 22:1–23
May 4	2 Sam 15:1–17:14	Luke 22:24–34
May 5	2 Sam 17:15–19:30	Luke 22:35–62
May 6	2 Sam 19:31–22:10	Luke 22:63–23:12
May 7	2 Sam 22:11–23:17	Luke 23:13–38
May 8	2 Sam 23:18–24:25	Luke 23:39–56
May 9	1 Ki 1:1–2:9	Luke 24:1–23
May 10	1 Ki 2:10–3:15	Luke 24:24–53
May 11	1 Ki 3:16–6:22	John 1:1–18
May 12	1 Ki 6:23–8:11	John 1:19–42

Date	Morning	Evening
May 13	1 Ki 8:12–9:9	John 1:43–51
May 14	1 Ki 9:10–11:13	John 2
May 15	1 Ki 11:14–12:33	John 3:1–21
May 16	1 Ki 13:1–15:15	John 3:22–4:12
May 17	1 Ki 15:16–17:24	John 4:13–38
May 18	1 Ki 18–19	John 4:39–54
May 19	1 Ki 20–21	John 5:1–29
May 20	1 Ki 22; 2 Ki 1:1–2:14	John 5:30–6:14
May 21	2 Ki 2:15–4:44	John 6:15–40
May 22	2 Ki 5–7	John 6:41–59
May 23	2 Ki 8–9	John 6:60–71
May 24	2 Ki 10:1–12:8	John 7:1–24
May 25	2 Ki 12:9–14:29	John 7:25–53
May 26	2 Ki 15:1–17:18	John 8:1–20
May 27	2 Ki 17:19–18:37	John 8:21–30
May 28	2 Ki 19:1–21:9	John 8:31–59
May 29	2 Ki 21:10–23:37	John 9:1–23
May 30	2 Ki 24–25; 1 Chr 1:1–16	John 9:24–41
May 31	1 Chr 1:17–2:55	John 10:1–30
June 1	1 Chr 3:1–5:10	John 10:31–42
June 2	1 Chr 5:11–6:70	John 11:1–29
June 3	1 Chr 6:71–8:40	John 11:30–57
June 4	1 Chr 9:1–11:21	John 12:1–26
June 5	1 Chr 11:22–13:14	John 12:27–50
June 6	1 Chr 14:1–16:36	John 13:1–11
June 7	1 Chr 16:37–19:19	John 13:12–30
June 8	1 Chr 20:1–23:11	John 13:31–14:11
June 9	1 Chr 23:12–25:31	John 14:12–31
June 10	1 Chr 26–27	John 15
June 11	1 Chr 28–29; 2 Chr 1	John 16:1–11
June 12	2 Chr 2–4	John 16:12–33
June 13	2 Chr 5:1–7:10	John 17
June 14	2 Chr 7:11–9:21	John 18:1–24
June 15	2 Chr 9:22–12:16	John 18:25–40

Date	Morning	Evening
June 16	2 Chr 13–16	John 19:1–30
June 17	2 Chr 17–19	John 19:31–20:10
June 18	2 Chr 20–22	John 20:11–31
June 19	2 Chr 23–25	John 21
June 20	2 Chr 26:1–29:11	Acts 1:1–11
June 21	2 Chr 29:12–31:21	Acts 1:12–2:13
June 22	2 Chr 32–34	Acts 2:14–36
June 23	2 Chr 35–36	Acts 2:37–3:10
June 24	Ezra 1:1–4:16	Acts 3:11–4:12
June 25	Ezra 4:17–7:28	Acts 4:13–22
June 26	Ezra 8:1–10:24	Acts 4:23–5:11
June 27	Ezra 10:25–44; Neh 1–3	Acts 5:12–32
June 28	Neh 4–6	Acts 5:33–6:15
June 29	Neh 7–8	Acts 7:1–29
June 30	Neh 9:1–11:9	Acts 7:30–43
July 1	Neh 11:10–12:47	Acts 7:44–60
July 2	Neh 13; Est 1:1–9	Acts 8:1–24
July 3	Est 1:10–5:14	Acts 8:25–9:9
July 4	Est 6–9	Acts 9:10–22
July 5	Est 10; Job 1–3	Acts 9:23–43
July 6	Job 4–6	Acts 10:1–22
July 7	Job 7:1–9:24	Acts 10:23–48
July 8	Job 9:25–12:12	Acts 11
July 9	Job 12:13–15:16	Acts 12:1–10
July 10	Job 15:17–18:21	Acts 12:11–13:12
July 11	Job 19:1–21:16	Acts 13:13–31
July 12	Job 21:17–24:12	Acts 13:32–52
July 13	Job 24:13–28:11	Acts 14:1–18
July 14	Job 28:12–31:12	Acts 14:19–28
July 15	Job 31:13–33:22	Acts 15:1–21
July 16	Job 33:23–36:16	Acts 15:22–41
July 17	Job 36:17–38:41	Acts 16:1–18
July 18	Job 39:1–41:23	Acts 16:19–40

Date	Morning	Evening
July 19	Job 41:24–42:17; Psa 1–2	Acts 17:1–9
July 20	Psa 3–5	Acts 17:10–34
July 21	Psa 6:1–8:2	Acts 18
July 22	Psa 8:3–10:4	Acts 19:1–20
July 23	Psa 10:5–14:7	Acts 19:21–28
July 24	Psa 15–17	Acts 19:29–20:12
July 25	Psa 18:1–36	Acts 20:13–38
July 26	Psa 18:37–20:9	Acts 21:1–26
July 27	Psa 21:1–22:24	Acts 21:27–22:11
July 28	Psa 22:25–25:11	Acts 22:12–21
July 29	Psa 25:12–27:6	Acts 22:22–23:10
July 30	Psa 27:7–30:5	Acts 23:11–35
July 31	Psa 30:6–31:24	Acts 24
Aug. 1	Psa 32:1–34:7	Acts 25
Aug. 2	Psa 34:8–35:28	Acts 26:1–14
Aug. 3	Psa 36:1–37:22	Acts 26:15–27:8
Aug. 4	Psa 37:23–38:22	Acts 27:9–36
Aug. 5	Psa 39:1–41:3	Acts 27:37–28:10
Aug. 6	Psa 41:4–44:3	Acts 28:11–31
Aug. 7	Psa 44:4–45:12	Rom 1:1–15
Aug. 8	Psa 45:13–47:9	Rom 1:16–2:16
Aug. 9	Psa 48:1–50:6	Rom 2:17–3:18
Aug. 10	Psa 50:7–51:19	Rom 3:19–4:15
Aug. 11	Psa 52–54	Rom 4:16–25
Aug. 12	Psa 55–56	Rom 5
Aug. 13	Psa 57:1–59:8	Rom 6
Aug. 14	Psa 59:9–62:8	Rom 7:1–13
Aug. 15	Psa 62:9–65:8	Rom 7:14–8:11
Aug. 16	Psa 65:9–68:4	Rom 8:12–25
Aug. 17	Psa 68:5–27	Rom 8:26–9:13
Aug. 18	Psa 68:28–69:28	Rom 9:14–10:15
Aug. 19	Psa 69:29–71:24	Rom 10:16–11:10
Aug. 20	Psa 72:1–73:20	Rom 11:11–36

Date	Morning	Evening
Aug. 21	Psa 73:21–75:5	Rom 12:1–8
Aug. 22	Psa 75:6–77:15	Rom 12:9–13:14
Aug. 23	Psa 77:16–78:39	Rom 14
Aug. 24	Psa 78:40–79:7	Rom 15
Aug. 25	Psa 79:8–81:16	Rom 16
Aug. 26	Psa 82–84	1 Cor 1:1–17
Aug. 27	Psa 85:1–88:9	1 Cor 1:18–2:16
Aug. 28	Psa 88:10–89:37	1 Cor 3
Aug. 29	Psa 89:38–91:4	1 Cor 4
Aug. 30	Psa 91:5–93:5	1 Cor 5
Aug. 31	Psa 94–95	1 Cor 6
Sept. 1	Psa 96–98	1 Cor 7:1–24
Sept. 2	Psa 99:1–102:7	1 Cor 7:25–8:13
Sept. 3	Psa 102:8–103:14	1 Cor 9
Sept. 4	Psa 103:15–104:23	1 Cor 10:1–13
Sept. 5	Psa 104:24–105:36	1 Cor 10:14–11:16
Sept. 6	Psa 105:37–106:33	1 Cor 11:17–12:11
Sept. 7	Psa 106:34–107:22	1 Cor 12:12–31
Sept. 8	Psa 107:23–109:5	1 Cor 13:1–14:12
Sept. 9	Psa 109:6–111:6	1 Cor 14:13–25
Sept. 10	Psa 111:7–114:8	1 Cor 14:26–15:11
Sept. 11	Psa 115–117	1 Cor 15:12–34
Sept. 12	Psa 118:1–119:16	1 Cor 15:35–58
Sept. 13	Psa 119:17–56	1 Cor 16:1–9
Sept. 14	Psa 119:57–104	1 Cor 16:10–24; 2 Cor 1:1–11
Sept. 15	Psa 119:105–152	2 Cor 1:12–2:17
Sept. 16	Psa 119:153–122:5	2 Cor 3–4
Sept. 17	Psa 122:6–127:5	2 Cor 5
Sept. 18	Psa 128:1–132:9	2 Cor 6:1–13
Sept. 19	Psa 132:10–135:14	2 Cor 6:14–7:16
Sept. 20	Psa 135:15–137:3	2 Cor 8
Sept. 21	Psa 137:4–139:18	2 Cor 9–10
Sept. 22	Psa 139:19–141:10	2 Cor 11

Date	Morning	Evening
Sept. 23	Psa 142:1–145:7	2 Cor 12:1–10
Sept. 24	Psa 145:8–147:11	2 Cor 12:11–13:14
Sept. 25	Psa 147:12–150:6	Gal 1
Sept. 26	Prov 1:1–3:26	Gal 2
Sept. 27	Prov 3:27–5:23	Gal 3
Sept. 28	Prov 6–7	Gal 4:1–11
Sept. 29	Prov 8:1–10:11	Gal 4:12–31
Sept. 30	Prov 10:12–12:10	Gal 5
Oct. 1	Prov 12:11–14:13	Gal 6
Oct. 2	Prov 14:14–16:15	Eph 1:1–14
Oct. 3	Prov 16:16–19:15	Eph 1:15–2:10
Oct. 4	Prov 19:16–22:16	Eph 2:11–3:13
Oct. 5	Prov 22:17–24:22	Eph 3:14–4:16
Oct. 6	Prov 24:23–27:10	Eph 4:17–5:14
Oct. 7	Prov 27:11–30:9	Eph 5:15–33
Oct. 8	Prov 30:10–31:31; Eccl 1	Eph 6
Oct. 9	Eccl 2:1–5:9	Phil 1
Oct. 10	Eccl 5:10–8:17	Phil 2:1–18
Oct. 11	Eccl 9–12	Phil 2:19–3:13
Oct. 12	Song 1–6	Phil 3:14–21
Oct. 13	Song 7–8; Isa 1:1–2:11	Phil 4
Oct. 14	Isa 2:12–5:30	Col 1:1–23
Oct. 15	Isa 6–8	Col 1:24–2:15
Oct. 16	Isa 9–11	Col 2:16–3:11
Oct. 17	Isa 12–15	Col 3:12–25
Oct. 18	Isa 16–20	Col 4
Oct. 19	Isa 21:1–24:6	1 Th 1:1–2:12
Oct. 20	Isa 24:7–27:13	1 Th 2:13–3:13
Oct. 21	Isa 28:1–30:17	1 Th 4
Oct. 22	Isa 30:18–33:24	1 Th 5
Oct. 23	Isa 34:1–37:29	2 Th 1–2
Oct. 24	Isa 37:30–40:20	2 Th 3; 1 Tim 1:1–11
Oct. 25	Isa 40:21–43:13	1 Tim 1:12–2:15

Date	Morning	Evening
Oct. 26	Isa 43:14–46:13	1 Tim 3
Oct. 27	Isa 47–50	1 Tim 4:1–5:16
Oct. 28	Isa 51–54	1 Tim 5:17–6:10
Oct. 29	Isa 55–58	1 Tim 6:11–21; 2 Tim 1
Oct. 30	Isa 59–62	2 Tim 2
Oct. 31	Isa 63:1–66:6	2 Tim 3
Nov. 1	Isa 66:7–24; Jer 1:1–2:25	2 Tim 4
Nov. 2	Jer 2:26–4:31	Titus 1–2
Nov. 3	Jer 5:1–7:15	Titus 3; Phile 1:1–7
Nov. 4	Jer 7:16–9:26	Phile 1:8–25
Nov. 5	Jer 10–12	Heb 1
Nov. 6	Jer 13–15	Heb 2
Nov. 7	Jer 16:1–18:12	Heb 3
Nov. 8	Jer 18:13–22:9	Heb 4–5
Nov. 9	Jer 22:10–24:10	Heb 6:1–12
Nov. 10	Jer 25:1–27:11	Heb 6:13–7:10
Nov. 11	Jer 27:12–30:11	Heb 7:11–8:13
Nov. 12	Jer 30:12–32:15	Heb 9
Nov. 13	Jer 32:16–34:11	Heb 10:1–31
Nov. 14	Jer 34:12–36:32	Heb 10:32–39
Nov. 15	Jer 37–39	Heb 11:1–31
Nov. 16	Jer 40–42	Heb 11:32–12:13
Nov. 17	Jer 43:1–46:12	Heb 12:14–13:6
Nov. 18	Jer 46:13–48:47	Heb 13:7–25
Nov. 19	Jer 49:1–50:32	James 1:1–11
Nov. 20	Jer 50:33–51:53	James 1:12–2:13
Nov. 21	Jer 51:54–52:34; Lam 1	James 2:14–3:12
Nov. 22	Lam 2–3	James 3:13–4:10
Nov. 23	Lam 4–5; Ezek 1	James 4:11–5:11
Nov. 24	Ezek 2–6	James 5:12–20
Nov. 25	Ezek 7:1–10:8	1 Pet 1
Nov. 26	Ezek 10:9–13:7	1 Pet 2
Nov. 27	Ezek 13:8–16:29	1 Pet 3

Date	Morning	Evening
Nov. 28	Ezek 16:30–18:13	1 Pet 4:1–11
Nov. 29	Ezek 18:14–20:49	1 Pet 4:12–5:14
Nov. 30	Ezek 21–22	2 Pet 1
Dec. 1	Ezek 23–24	2 Pet 2
Dec. 2	Ezek 25:1–27:25	2 Pet 3
Dec. 3	Ezek 27:26–30:12	1 John 1
Dec. 4	Ezek 30:13–32:23	1 John 2:1–17
Dec. 5	Ezek 32:24–34:24	1 John 2:18–3:12
Dec. 6	Ezek 34:25–37:10	1 John 3:13–4:6
Dec. 7	Ezek 37:11–39:29	1 John 4:7–5:12
Dec. 8	Ezek 40–41	1 John 5:13–21
Dec. 9	Ezek 42:1–44:14	2 John; 3 John
Dec. 10	Ezek 44:15–47:12	Jude
Dec. 11	Ezek 47:13–48:35; Dan 1	Rev 1
Dec. 12	Dan 2:1–3:12	Rev 2
Dec. 13	Dan 3:13–4:37	Rev 3:1–13
Dec. 14	Dan 5–6	Rev 3:14–4:11
Dec. 15	Dan 7–9	Rev 5:1–6:8
Dec. 16	Dan 10–12	Rev 6:9–7:8
Dec. 17	Hosea 1–4	Rev 7:9–17
Dec. 18	Hosea 5–9	Rev 8:1–9:11
Dec. 19	Hosea 10–14; Joel 1:1–12	Rev 9:12–10:11
Dec. 20	Joel 1:13–3:21; Amos 1	Rev 11
Dec. 21	Amos 2–6	Rev 12:1–13:10
Dec. 22	Amos 7–9; Oba 1:1–9	Rev 13:11–18
Dec. 23	Oba 1:10–21; Jonah; Micah 1	Rev 14
Dec. 24	Micah 2:1–7:8	Rev 15:1–16:9
Dec. 25	Micah 7:9–20; Nahum; Hab 1	Rev 16:10–17:8
Dec. 26	Hab 2–3; Zep 1	Rev 17:9–18:13
Dec. 27	Zep 2–3; Hag	Rev 18:14–24
Dec. 28	Zec 1–5	Rev 19
Dec. 29	Zec 6–9	Rev 20:1–21:8
Dec. 30	Zec 10–14	Rev 21:9–27
Dec. 31	Mal	Rev 22

Index